D1600962

KOREA: A HISTORY

KOREA
A History

by Bong-youn Choy

최봉윤

FORMER PROFESSOR OF POLITICAL SCIENCE
SEOUL NATIONAL UNIVERSITY, AND
FORMER VISITING PROFESSOR SEATTLE PACIFIC COLLEGE

foreword by Younghill Kang

Charles E. Tuttle Company
RUTLAND/VERMONT : TOKYO/JAPAN

Representatives

FOR CONTINENTAL EUROPE
Boxerbooks, Inc., Zurich

FOR THE BRITISH ISLES
Prentice-Hall International, Inc., London

FOR AUSTRALASIA
Paul Flesch & Co., Pty. Ltd., Melbourne

FOR CANADA
M. G. Hurtig Ltd., Edmonton

Published by the Charles E. Tuttle Company, Inc.
of Rutland, Vermont & Tokyo, Japan
with editorial offices at
Suido 1-chome, 2-6, Bunkyo-ku, Tokyo

Library of Congress Catalog Card No: 73-147180
International Standard Book No: 0-8048-0249-1

First printing, 1971

PRINTED IN JAPAN

Dedicated to
Mrs. Henriette Lehman

TABLE OF CONTENTS

PART II. THE NEW KOREA

PART III. KOREA'S FUTURE

TABLES

MAPS

FOREWORD

Korea has deeply penetrated the American consciousness, in ebb and flow of emotional tides: embarassment, anxiety, tension, frustration, fear, anger, and finally uneasy oblivion.

From June 25, 1950, to July 27, 1953, in the 1129 days of the Korean War, the United States suffered 145,000 battle casualties, with 33,000 killed or missing (as reported by the U.S. Department of Defense). In a so-called police action, in support it was said of self-determination and democratic processes, the United States alone spent twenty billion dollars upon an internal war in a small remote country of the Asian mainland, whose background and motivations were very little known. By June 1955 the United States had spent one and a half billion dollars more in reconstruction, and each year since has sent generous sums in support of South Korean governments. No responsible Korean will deny corruption and mismanagement in the use of such economic assistance.

For the U.S. the Korean War resulted in as many American battle casualties as the American Revolutionary War, the War of 1812, the Mexican War, and the Spanish-American War all combined. The Korean War lies in the past, along with the Joseph McCarthy era. But the number of Americans who want more research done before sending American men to foreign battlefields without prior approval from Congress has increased.

In Asia the question is even more violent and agonizing. If Americans have been shaken by the twentieth century and its problems, imagine what it has been like for the inhabitants of Korea and southeastern Asia, to be shocked awake by detonations of the A-bomb, the H-bomb, from their close-knit genealogical dreams lasting thousands of years.

WHAT SHALL WE DO TO BE SAVED? WHERE IS SALVATION?

they ask. But the ancient dreams of prayer and ecstasy and union with the eternal seem to have been lost in the fray. Who believes now that the shamans of southeastern Asia can raise up any dream spirit like Aladdin with his lamp to lend supernatural comfort and aid? Terror is sleepless. Such is the twentieth century shock, that Asia seems not able to sleep again and will require much reassurance in order to dream wise dreams now.

The antiquities of this branch of mankind can hardly be exaggerated. Perhaps twenty thousand years ago, perhaps fifty thousand, the people moved at a slow pace from a birth point in central Asia, gradually populating Manchuria and the Korean peninsula. Such wandering belongs to prehistory, a period of legend and artifact. The history of Korea as verified by documents goes back about two thousand years. My friend Bong-youn Choy begins his book at this point.

His is a social, economic, and political history, with an eye to geographic, psychological, and anthropological data, that which connects and that which cuts off. In this scientific spirit he treats the ruling classes, the agrarian economic system, centralized feudalism, land reform, the social structure, Korea under Japan, the Korean Independence Movement, the Student Movement, the Student Uprising, Syngman Rhee as an ousted dictator, the present condition of Korea, and the future of Korea. Facts are well marshalled, the reading is not dull. And obviously it is more a political history than a psychological dream-world.

Mr. Choy, like many other Korean refugees, has chosen to live in the U.S. During the Rhee regime immediately following the Korean War he had a tough time. Syngman Rhee took a passionate interest in all Koreans in America even if they were naturalized citizens; they must be Rhee men and not anti-Rhee men or suffer the consequences. He did his best to discredit all anti-Rhee men and even to have them deported. If deported, execution awaited. Knowledgeable American friends helped many Koreans during this period. A Korean student of journalism at a Southern university was allowed to continue his studies under a permanent visa; he has since become naturalized and is doing well. Another young Korean writer was forced to flee the long arm of Syngman Rhee by going to Europe, only returning when Rhee was no longer a threat to Koreans in America. Before the Student Uprising, when Rhee was forced to flee the country, it was simply not permitted to say that the Rhee elections were rigged, free speech was brutally suppressed, and the incompetent Rhee regime was maintained by strong-arm tactics. In those days, "not a communist, no, but an anti-Rhee man" was a damning indictment even in America. A popular Korean woman novelist at that time was invited by the U.S. State Department to travel and study in this country. By threats of reprisal when she got back, Rhee was able to break her contract for translation of her book, which has not yet been published in translation. Toward the end the frustrations of the Rhee regime in America became agonizing. A member of the Korean legation, a one-time foreign minister, flew south to remand a speaker already announced in papers of a certain university-town, and was not successful. When a speaker was invited from New Haven, an anti-Rhee Korean, to deliver a paper on "Oriental Influences on Western Art" at a certain student banquet in New York, rather than reject this speaker as ordered by Rhee adherents, the party divided: some stayed with the banquet, some went to hear the speaker downtown.

The rule of Syngman Rhee lasted in Korea only twelve years. But it was long enough to ruin the careers of many Koreans in America for life. With many intellectuals it became a time of odd jobs and private tutoring. The most prodemocratic Koreans were profoundly anti-Rhee. The Student Uprising against Rhee was touched off by the finding of a student's body in the bay, butchered by the Rhee police. The police fired into the mob. There were nine hundred casualties. But Syngman Rhee was finally forced to flee the country, and the shadow of a native fascism in South Korea was alleviated. To most Koreans the Rhee years seem an irony of the Korean War, fought in support of democratic processes and self-determination.

Younghill Kang
THE GRASS ROOF
HUNTINGTON, NEW YORK

PREFACE

Many books have been written about Korea, both in the native language and in foreign languages. Each has approached the subject from a different angle, and each has its merits and shortcomings. In this book I have attempted to present Korean political history from the socioeconomic standpoint, covering the old and the new Korea—from the Three Kingdoms period (57 B.C.) to the present two governments. The last two chapters deal with the unification problem and with the future prospects of the Korean people.

I do not expect all readers to agree with the views set forth in this introductory study. I will feel my efforts rewarded if it merely serves to stimulate further interest in Korea.

In English-speaking countries Korean studies in general, and history in particular, have been handicapped by a lack of sources in English. The two main works on Korean history, *The History of Korea* by Homer B. Hulbert and *A History of the Korean People* by James S. Gale were written more than a half century ago. Prof. Shannon McCune, author of *Korea's Heritage: A Regional and Social Geography*, has stated that, as a temporary measure, English translations of modern Korean history works "would be a real service to Korean studies." Original research, on the other hand, is difficult, because mastery of Korean, Chinese, and Japanese is required.

It is perhaps best to note here that the Japanese and Korean names in the text are written with the family name before the personal name, as they are in their native countries.

I wish to express my sincere gratitude for proofreading and valuable suggestions to Mrs. Evelyn B. McCune, Korean born, member of a distinguished family of American missionaries and scholars, whom I have known for more than thirty years. My thanks also go to my publisher.

To Mrs. Henriette Lehman I owe an immeasurable debt for her genuine personal interest and for her kindness of many years, without which I would never have been able to write this book. I dedicate it to her. My thanks also go to Mr. Max Knight of the University of California Press, who glued my broken English together and painstakingly went over the manuscript many times, advising and making valuable suggestions. My wife, author of *The Art of Oriental Cooking*, and my four children have been patient while I concentrated on this study.

B.Y.C.

BERKELEY, CALIFORNIA

PART I

THE OLD KOREA

CHAPTER 1

THE THREE KINGDOMS

57 B.C.–A.D. 668

Recorded Korean history begins with the Three Kingdoms period. This period derives its name from the three kingdoms of Koguryo, Paekche, and Silla, which, according to tradition, were founded about a half century before the time of Christ. They each occupied a section of the peninsula: Koguryo was in the northwestern section, which included the greater part of Manchuria; Paekche in the southwestern section; and Silla in the southeastern section.

The Koguryo people are said to stem from a tribe of hunting nomads known as the Buye, and originally lived in the northwestern part of Manchuria, somewhere along the Songhwa River. In the second century B.C. they moved to the central section of the Yalu River, in the mountainous area between Manchuria and northern Korea. Here the tribe, which was composed of five clans, defended itself against intruders and was able to maintain its independence even when the peninsula fell under the control of the Han dynasty of China.[1]

According to tradition, the chief of the tribe, Chu Mong, became the first king of Koguryo in 37 B.C., thereby establishing the Koguryo kingdom. The new kingdom, with Tonggoo as its capital, expanded rapidly and soon conquered the east-coast area, including Hamkyong-do and Kangwoon-do. During the third and fourth centuries of the Christian Era, it extended its jurisdiction over the greater part of Manchuria and the southern half of the peninsula. In 427, when King Chang Shoo moved the capital from Tonggoo to Pyongyang, Koguryo was the most powerful kingdom in Korea and Manchuria.

In A.D. 327 Buddhism was introduced into the kingdom along with Confucianism and other features of Chinese civilization, such as astronomy and medicine. The aristocratic ruling class, the court of the Koguryo kingdom, adopted Buddhism as the state religion and the state political ideology, and many temples were erected with government funds.

From the beginning of the seventh century the kingdom of Koguryo was the target of military attacks from China. The Sui dynasty launched three expeditionary campaigns from 612 to 614, but all were repelled by Koguryo under the military leadership of Ulji Moonduk. In 657 the T'ang dynasty began a series of military campaigns against the Koguryo kingdom that lasted fifty years.

Also during this period, the three kingdoms engaged in wars against each other that eventually resulted in the unification of the peninsula. In the final movement toward unification, Silla first sided with the T'ang army and conquered Paekche. Then the allied Silla-T'ang armies overthrew the Koguryo kingdom, which had been greatly weakened by destruction of its agricultural economy in fifty years of war and by internal political struggles for the throne.[2] Korea was thus united for the first time in 668.

The history of the kingdoms of Paekche and Silla begins with a tribe called Han that lived in the central southern half of the peninsula in the first century B.C. The Han tribe was dominated until the fourth century after Christ by the Han dynasty of China (the two names have the same pronunciation but are written with different characters); yet it developed an autonomous political system and an indigenous culture, particularly in the southeastern part of the country. In contrast to the nomadic Koguryo people, the Han tribe, from the first century after Christ, engaged in farming, which included cultivating rice, planting grains, and raising silk worms, pigs, and cows. Farming and kitchen utensils made of iron were probably used, and some of them sent to China for trade or tribute.

At the time of the decline of the Han dynasty of China, at the beginning of the third century after Christ, the Han tribe revolted against the Chinese administration and set up three communal states: Mahan in the southwestern part of the peninsula, Chinhan in the southeastern, and Bunhan Kyongsang-namdo in the extreme southern area. Chinese control over the coast of the central western part of the peninsula, however, continued in some degree until the beginning of the fourth century.

Before we discuss the history of Paekche, it might be well to say a few

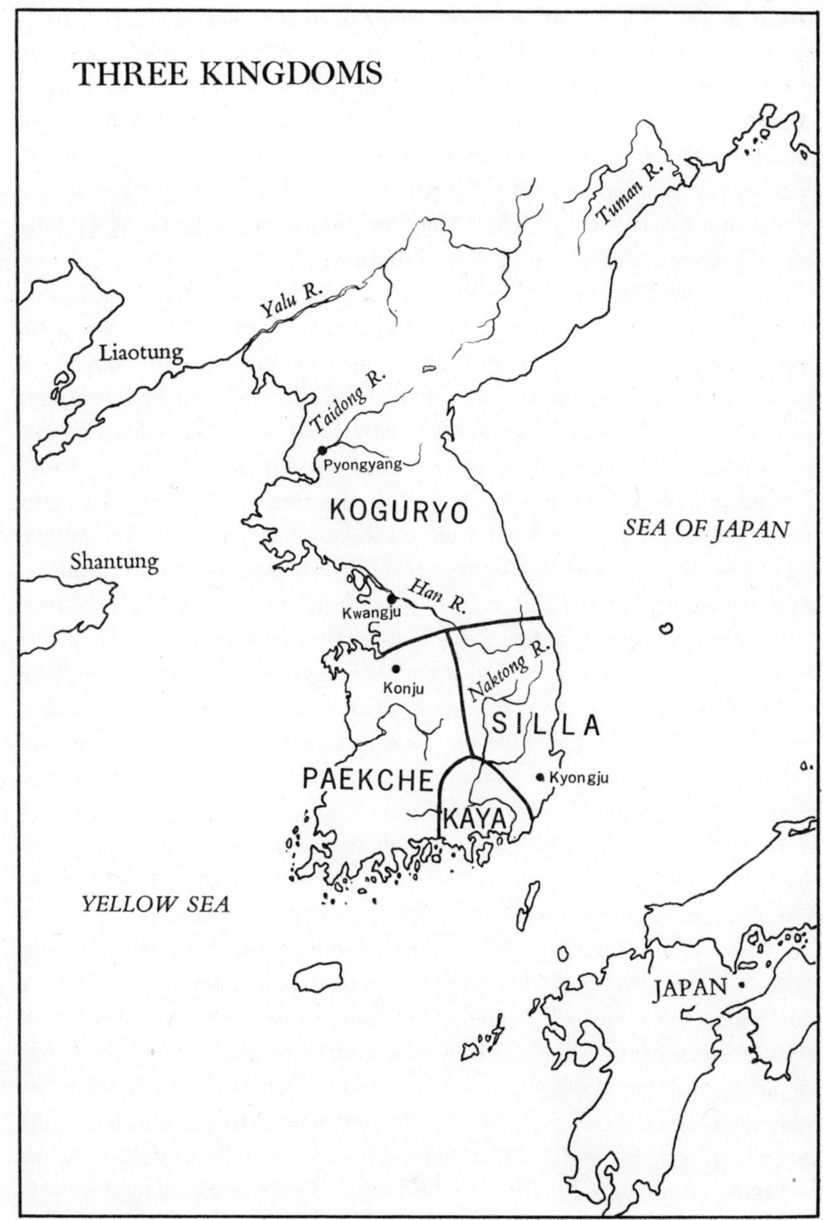
THREE KINGDOMS
Tuman R.
Yalu R.
Liaotung
Taidong R.
Pyongyang
KOGURYO
SEA OF JAPAN
Shantung
Han R.
Kwangju
Naktong R.
Konju
SILLA
PAEKCHE
Kyongju
KAYA
YELLOW SEA
JAPAN

words about Chinese influence on colonial areas in the southern part of Korea. The Han dynasty of China left its mark on that part by creating a class society based on Confucianism, which stressed filial piety, absolute obedience in relations between ruler and subject and between inferior and superior social classes, the custom of weak countries paying tribute to strong ones, heavy taxation in kind to be paid to the ruling class, and agricultural production by slave labor. These Han institutions were taken over by Silla, later by Koryo, and finally by the Yi dynasty.

The traditional story of the origin of Paekche is recorded in *Samguk-chi*, a history of the three kingdoms. The Paekche clan originally resided in the central part of Korea, the Kyonggi and Kangwoon provinces of today. Onjo (a son of Chu Mong, the founder of the northern Koguryo kingdom) and his younger brother moved south because they had lost to their oldest brother in a fight for succession to the throne. In A.D. 350 Onjo, who was to become the first king of Paekche, established a small communal city-state in Kwangju, near Seoul. This city-state was the nucleus and capital of the Paekche kingdom until constant attacks from Koguryo forced the capital to be moved further south, to Kongju in 474 and to Chungchong in 538.

Paekche came under attack from both north and south. From the north the Koguryo kingdom launched three military campaigns against Paekche in the course of 125 years and usurped much of its land. With the establishment of the Kingdom of Silla on the southeastern coast of the peninsula, Paekche was attacked from the south also, and in an attempt to strengthen itself it made an alliance with Japan.

But Paekche never became strong, militarily, economically, or culturally, although it possessed agricultural land, a warm climate, and a large population. One reason for its weakness was the fact that the ruling elements were composed of political refugees from the northern kingdom; in its entire existence Paekche never had its own native rulers. Consequently, the southern Han people felt themselves to be under foreign rule. Another reason for its weakness was that the people of Han, especially those who lived on the southwest coast, had been ruled by the Han dynasty of China for longer than any other section of the country and lacked experience in self-government. And, also, a large segment of the population had been made politically incompetent by having been worked as slaves in the fields and generally exploited for centuries by the ruling classes of local and central government. In short, the brief existence of the Paekche kingdom may be attributed to long alien rule, to the lack of an autonomous native government, and to the practice of slavery.

The Paekche kingdom came to an end when soldiers of T'ang and Silla occupied the capital city. Its territory was annexed to the Silla kingdom, and the T'ang army stayed for eight years.

Silla was formed about the middle of the fourth century after Christ and was the newest of the three kingdoms. It was founded in the village of Kyongju and gradually extended its jurisdiction over the southeast coast. Silla's political, military, and economic affairs were controlled by a rigid aristocracy, and it showed the most interesting development of indigenous institutions. The latter was partly due to Silla's geographical isolation from rival and hostile communities; particularly, the Taipaek mountains acted as a protective wall against Koguryo. It was partly due to the fact that the climate and soil were suitable for the development of an agrarian economy that made the kingdom more or less self-supporting. But perhaps the greatest reason was that of the three kingdoms Silla had been the least influenced by early Chinese administration and culture, though it eventually did, along with other reforms patterned after Chinese models, adopt Buddhism as the state religion and the Chinese title of *wang* (king) to designate the ruler of Silla.

The traditional story of the origin of Silla tells of six communal chiefs calling a conference in the village of Kyongju, which later became the capital city of Silla and for centuries was considered its cultural and intellectual center. Tradition says that such conferences were customarily held either at a riverside or on a hilltop, and that each clan sent its chief as a representative. The first order of business was to elect one chief as head of all the clans and then to decide upon important affairs that concerned the community, such as declaring war and making peace. At the first conference Huk Kesei was elected head chief of the six clans, thereby becoming the first ruler of Silla. The chiefs also elected the commanding military chief, who, besides performing his military functions, also exercised judicial power over the community.

In 660 Silla joined forces with T'ang and overthrew the Kingdom of

Paekche. Then these two forces attacked Koguryo and subdued it in 668. In this way Silla and T'ang unified the peninsula. After the withdrawal of the T'ang forces nearly a decade later, Silla became the sole ruler of Korea and remained so for nearly three centuries, until 935.

THE RULERS

Koguryo. The Koguryo aristocracy, which was composed of five clans,[3] practiced a primitive democratic procedure in selecting their chief. The members of each clan selected their own clan chief, and at the clan-chiefs' conference the five elected clan chiefs selected one head chief as the ruler of the whole community. It is not clear how long this practice was continued.

At the beginning of the third century after Christ, the aristocracy was divided into three groups: the royal family of the Ge-no clan, who had the privilege of kingship by birth; the nobles, who had the privilege of being allowed to marry members of the royal family; and the warriors, who defended the state from enemy invasion. These three groups composed the ruling class of the Koguryo kingdom.

Political power was shared more or less evenly by the three groups: the king was the head of state, the nobles were the heads of the administration, and the warriors had military power. The three groups divided land and slaves among themselves according to rank. The slaves were considered the most valuable property, because they produced food, weapons, and other necessary items for the ruling classes. For this reason the main objective of territorial expansion was the capture of slaves.

In the latter half of the Koguryo kingdom, the warrior class was the most powerful. The number of warriors had increased because of the constant wars against neighboring tribal states. They won almost every war with their neighbors—against the Manchus, the Chinese, Silla, and Paekche. The Koguryo warrior class produced a few brilliant military men, like Ulji Moonduk and Yunke Somoon. During the first part of the fourth century, Pyongyang became the new capital of the kingdom. Koguryo was then the most powerful and aggressive kingdom in the peninsula. The warriors at that time totaled ten thousand out of a population of one million. Most of them owned large estates and slaves, but they did not coalesce into a rigid military class like the samurai in Japan. No hereditary warriors existed. Some warriors, like Yunke Somoon, became de facto rulers, powerful enough to place different persons on the throne.

Paekche. The ruling class of Paekche was composed entirely of northerners and did not command the loyalty of the native Han people. As mentioned before, Onjo, who was from the Buye tribe and the third son of the first king of the Koguryo kingdom, moved south to establish Paekche and become himself the king. His descendants continued to succeed to the throne until the end of the kingdom in the seventh century, and his relatives became the court nobles and occupied all high government positions.

The royal family and the court nobles lived in castles known as *tan-ee*,[4] built by forced Han labor. The *tan-ee* of both the nobility and the local rulers were completely segregated from the residences of the commoners. Until the administrative reorganization in the sixth century, the *tan-ee* were also used as military headquarters and as tax-collecting offices. The main concern of the court nobles was to collect taxes from the natives, not to govern. The nobles employed some influential natives as retainers in the local administration, authorizing them to impose and collect taxes from the peasants. The retainers collected taxes twice, once for the nobles and once for themselves. Thus the Han people had to serve two masters, the native local rulers and the nobles of the Buye tribe.

During the sixth century the court nobles reorganized the administration to meet the threats of Koguryo and Silla. The capital city was divided into five sections for defense purposes: upper, middle, low, front, and back. Each section had its own military head appointed by the king and was defended by five hundred soldiers. The local territory was divided into five subdivisions called *bang*. Each *bang* had its military commander, who was appointed by the king and commanded from five to seven hundred soldiers. During the militaristic administration some native Han people, especially the warrior clans, had an opportunity to advance their social status by rendering services to the king, but none of them became a court noble in the central administration. Under the militaristic administration the natives had to pay heavy taxes, and every able-bodied male was subject to be drafted. Severe exploitation of the people by the ruling class was characteristic of the Paekche kingdom.

Silla. As mentioned before, the six clans living in the vicinity of Kyongju called a conference to select one leader for the whole community. The leader was elected by unanimous agreement of the six clan chiefs (any resolution passed by this conference required unanimity). This practice came to an end in the fourth century upon the formation of a strong kingdom; the chiefs' convention system was superseded by the King's Council. The council had the authority to make decisions on important issues, such as succession to the throne, declaration of war, and conclusion of peace treaties.

When Silla extended its authority over other sections of the peninsula, many new communal chiefs came under its control, but they were excluded from the ruling class. Gradually the six original clans were divided into five different classes according to the "kinship division" system.[5] The first kinship division was called Sungkol, and only three clans, Park, Suk, and Kim, were given the privilege of belonging to this division. The king was selected from one of these three clans. Marriages were allowed between the members of the first kinship group. At the beginning of the fifth century the Kim family wielded enough power to establish hereditary succession to the throne.

The second kinship group, called Jinkol, was composed of persons who had some blood relationship to the royal family. This group was excluded from the King's Council and had no voice in state affairs. Most of them became heads of the administration.

The third group was called Duknan; the fourth, Sadupum; and the fifth, Odupum. These groups had no voice in the policy-making decisions of state affairs either; they were given less important administrative positions in the central and local governments. All members of these classes were granted land and slaves by the king.

A significant development in the Silla kingdom was the early rise of a military group from the first two ruling classes. This group was known as Hwarang.[6] It started during the third century after Christ; at that time it was a social and religious group, organized by the youths of royal and noble families and engaged in festival ceremonies and pilgrimages. These youths had a code of honor based on Buddhist doctrines, and they performed ancestor and nature worship as conducted by native shamans, and observed the Confucian ethics of filial piety, devotion, and faithfulness.

In the sixth century the Hwarang code began to change from social and religious concerns to political and military programs. The religious and festival ceremonies were replaced by prayers for victory in wars with the neighboring kingdoms; and pride in being a soldier, bravery, and loyalty to the Silla kingdom became the new code of honor. They became well-trained soldiers. Three outstanding warriors among them were Sata Ham, who became a famous general and subjugated the Kaya tribal kingdom; Kim You-shin, who became a hero for bringing about unification of the country; and Kwan Chang, who subdued the Paekche kingdom. One of the decisive factors in Silla's victory over the Koguryo and Paekche kingdoms in the unification war of 668 was that Silla had the military skill of the Hwarang.

After unification the members of the Hwarang were rewarded with lands and slaves. Some of them became retainers of the king in the central government, and many were sent to the country as local officials. Like the Koguryo warrior class, the Hwarang never became a rigid military class but they maintained their power throughout the existence of the Silla kingdom.

THE MASSES

Two sharply differentiated social classes composed the three kingdoms: the rulers and the masses. The privileged minority was nonproductive but owned the means of production—the land, the handicraft industries, and the slaves. The peasants and slaves—the productive forces in the society—owned none of the means of production.

The land of the three kingdoms belonged exclusively to the kings; they could dispose of it any way they chose. The court nobles, retainers, and government officials received land from the king as grants, but since private property rights were not recognized, the "granted" land still belonged to the king in theory. Under this economic system no independent peasant class could develop; peasants were merely tenants on the lands of the king, without rights or privileges. They were called commoners (*sumin*).

Many factors were responsible for the slave system in Korean history, but during the Three Kingdoms period, war was the main factor. During the wars between Koguryo and China, many Chinese soldiers were captured. They were treated as community property by king and nobles, who employed them both in the state-owned handicraft industry and in agriculture. The three kingdoms engaged in a series of wars among themselves to capture more slaves. Koguryo captured sixteen thousand persons from Paekche and eight thousand from Silla; Paekche captured five thousand from both Silla and Koguryo; and Silla captured six thousand from both Paekche and Koguryo during the three centuries of wars among these kingdoms.[7]

The legalization of slaves was another factor in the rise of the slave system. Any person who killed a horse or cow without permission was subject to become a slave; theft, adultery, and private and public debt were also punished by enslavement. Once a person became a slave, his status could not be changed; his offspring were also slaves.

The slaves were divided into five occupational groups.[8] The first group was that of handicraft workers. Most skilled slaves were assigned work in the state-owned handicraft industries, which usually were situated in the capital and sometimes in the royal palaces. They produced silk fabrics, pottery, and other articles for the members of the royal family. The second group was that of metals workers. They produced luxurious decorative articles made of gold, silver, or copper. The third group was that of architects. They designed pagodas, stone buildings, and Buddhist temples. The fourth was that of personal servants. This group, called *nobi,* consisted of entertainers (singers and dancers) and those engaged in general housework for government officials. The last group was that of agricultural slaves. Agriculture, the economic foundation of the kingdoms, was dependent entirely on human labor, so a large percentage of all slaves engaged in farming.

THE AGRARIAN ECONOMIC SYSTEM

The general characteristics of the primitive agrarian economy of the three kingdoms were similar. The land belonged to the king, who gave away land to his retainers and to the members of the royal family. The commoners and slaves were the forces of production, but no landlord class existed; hence no economic and social relations between landlords and tenants developed. Instead, a primitive type of collective farming under the supervision of public officials was common. The main problem in this economy was a shortage of manpower. The total population of the three kingdoms is estimated to have been two million. Of this number fewer than one million were actively working, subtracting the young, old, and disabled. The number of aristocrats, including the members of the royal family and the warriors, is estimated at sixty thousand. To solve the manpower problem the rulers squeezed more work from the slaves they had and waged war against weak neighboring states to capture more.

The land system[9] of the three kingdoms can be classified into the following four categories:

Kwan-don, the land of the king and the royal family. It was worked by public slaves under the supervision of government officials. All produce was used for the king and his family. Some *kwan-don* were used for hunting and playgrounds for the royal family.

Sa-don, the land granted by the king to the nobles and warriors. This land was not considered the private property of the receivers; they had only the right to use it as long as the king considered them loyal. Public slaves as well as private slaves of the nobles and warriors cultivated the land.

Sikyup-don, the land of the local clan chiefs. The king granted land to the local chiefs as rewards for their war services. Within the kingdom there were many local clans which did not pledge loyalty to the king. When the country was invaded by a neighboring state, the king often granted autonomy to the clan chiefs as reward for military services. In this case, the territory of the clan chief became *sikyup-don,* and the chief could dispose of the land to his own subordinates without interference from the king. The *sikyup-don* land led to the development of feudalism, as will be discussed later.

Chonrak-kongyou-chi, the village common. This type of land consisted of large tracts of mountain and forest lands and pasture which were cultivated by collective labor only. Under this system everyone in the village engaged in farming under the supervision of the local clan chief, and the grain was shared equally by the members of that community. Under this primitive type of collective farming the legal owner of the land was still the king.

CHAPTER 2

SILLA UNIFIES THE PENINSULA

668–935

In the middle of the seventh century constant invasions of Koguryo (six times within fifty years, including one major war with China in 613) caused a gradual deterioration of the agrarian economy and of the poverty-stricken people's will to fight. A further disintegrating factor was the division of the ruling classes into two factions, which were split over the controversy about succession to the throne.

At this time the ambitious Kingdom of Silla made an alliance with the distant T'ang dynasty of China. Their combined armies invaded the southwestern part of the peninsula and conquered the Paekche kingdom in 660; later they invaded Koguryo territory simultaneously from both north and south. Finally in 668 the capital city, Pyongyang, fell to the invaders. Thus the Koguryo kingdom came to an end.

The T'ang army occupied most of the territories of the two conquered kingdoms and established a military administration, which lasted eight years after Silla had supposedly unified the country in 668. Silla's rulers were anxious to get rid of the T'ang military occupation. They adopted a policy of rewarding with land and title those loyal to Silla rather than to the T'ang regime.

In 670 Silla forces invaded the southwestern section of the peninsula with the aid of former Paekche ruling groups and ousted the T'ang military regime. Soon they launched an expedition against the northern part also, but failed to defeat the T'ang army there. About this time, a new powerful kingdom, Balhai-wang-guk,[1] came into existence in northern China and began to challenge the supremacy of the T'ang dynasty. Exploiting the weakness of T'ang, Silla prepared still another military attack on the Chinese army.

This time the T'ang rulers withdrew their army from the northern Korean peninsula, in 676.

Silla now extended its jurisdiction over the northeast and northwest, including the Taidong River area, and became the sole ruler of the Korean peninsula. Many local aristocrats, members of the former royal families, and nobles joined the Silla ruling class and were rewarded with lands and titles for their services during the unification struggle.

The unification of the peninsula by Silla is historically significant for three reasons: first, two tribes, the northern Koguryo-zok and the southern Han-zok, were welded into one nationality, that known as the Korean nationality today; second, a kingdom was installed that lasted until the Japanese annexation; and last, a unified national history, language, and culture began to develop.[2]

Characteristics of the Ruling Class. Silla's ruling class, composed of the Kim, Park, and Suk clans, continued with little change to wield power after unification. As before, the Kim clan was privileged in the succession to the throne. Kim Chun-chu became king of unified Silla, and Gen. Kim You-shin became a national hero for his military exploits in the unification struggle. The members of the Park and Suk clans were next in rank. The local rulers, the members of the former Paekche and Koguryo royal families, and the chiefs of the tribes became territorial lords with local autonomy. Thus the traditional Silla ruling class concentrated political power in its hands for the following two and a half centuries.

In order to understand the characteristics of the Silla ruling class, it is necessary to trace some of the political and socioeconomic developments which took place before the unification. Beginning in A.D. 502 the peasants began to employ the cow for cultivation of the land and thus increased production. This was a giant step forward from the primitive agrarian economy that had used only human labor. During that time the title of king in reference to the ruler was adopted, and uniforms for public officials were introduced to distinguish the rulers and the ruled. Buddhism became a state religion, and the government ordered the building of temples by peasants and slaves. Time was counted from the beginning of the founding of Silla, 536 being the first year.

In politics, kinship was still the predominant factor, and clan membership determined who succeeded to the throne and who held high positions in the central government. In local administration, however, the tribal chiefs were the rulers, and their kinship system dominated local politics. In view of this fact, the king was not an absolute ruler. A power-sharing system between the central and local rulers maintained the kingdom as a political entity.

A classical example of this system was the relationship between the Kumkwan-Kaya tribal chief and the Silla king.[3] The chief surrendered his formal authority to the king and in return received title and land. The chief's granddaughter was married to a prince and later became an empress; and one of the chief's grandsons, Gen. Kim You-shin, became a member of the royal family by marriage. The chief himself remained as the actual ruler over the territory of Kumkwan-Kaya. Other tribal chiefs voluntarily surrendered their authority to the king following more or less the pattern of the Kumkwan-Kaya chief; they also became members of the ruling classes of the central government while remaining de facto rulers in their own territories.

The Ideological Foundation. In the seventh century Buddhism became the political ideology of the ruling classes and influenced the way of life of the intellectuals. The Mahayana branch of Buddhism was popular in Silla, because it preached the doctrine of "blessing and happiness" for the ruling classes and "protection of state." Neither the doctrine of salvation nor the four noble truths and eight noble paths nor the idea of nirvana were introduced at this period. Many outstanding scholars, such as Woon Yo, Sung Jun, and their students, were sent to China and India by the government to study Buddhism. The capital city of Silla, Kyongju, became the center of Buddhist intellectual activity and the model of Buddhist culture in the peninsula.

Many temples, monastaries, and pagodas of great size and splendor were erected throughout the country by slaves under government supervision. Among them were the Bulguksa, Whangnongsa-goojungtap, Bongsongsa-sungdun and Bongduksa-dongjong temples. Some of them still remain as monuments of this period.

A special government administrative office was established to build temples. Great amounts of land and large numbers of slaves were bestowed on the temples by the king; the priests became the virtual owners of these, and consequently their influence in politics increased. The political philosophy, art, architecture, and sculpture of Silla were by and large the product of Buddhism.

Slaves and Commoners. The mass of the people consisted of slaves and commoners whose status was determined by birth. Although slaves were originally considered community property, this concept gradually changed until the idea of private ownership became dominant, and the ruling classes came to own great numbers of slaves. With the collapse of the Silla kingdom these slaves became serfs in the Asiatic type of feudalism that developed in the succeeding Koryo kingdom, as will be described later.

The productive activities of the slaves covered almost all economic fields: they worked on the farms, in the handicraft industry, and on public construction projects. There were specially trained slave groups like the palace slaves (*gungnobi*), who worked for the royal families, and the public slaves (*kwannobi*), who worked at the residences of government officials. A third group worked in Buddhist temples and were called *sanobi*.

The commoners were the peasants. They did not own land until the central government completed the land reform in the middle of the eighth century. Peasants cultivated the government lands and paid excessive taxes in kind to the government. Most of them lived in poverty and had no opportunity to advance their social and economic status; many of them became slaves because they contracted debts or committed crimes.

The public and government services became the monopoly of the local and central aristocratic ruling classes. The civil service examination system benefited exclusively the members of the aristocratic families because preparation for the examinations took years of schooling.

The Centralization of Power. After unification the need for reorganization became pressing, for territory and population had trebled. A plan for reorganization of the administration was adopted which took as a model the administration of the T'ang dynasty of China. This project was completed during the reign of King Kyungduk (742–65).

The reorganization consisted of the centralization of political power and the reorganization of the military.[4] Thirteen administrative departments were created: the General National Administration, three military administrations, the Department of Ceremony, the Department of Impeachment, the Department of Construction, the Department of Shipping, the Department of External Affairs, the Department of Civil Service, the Department of the Court, the Capital City Improvement Administration, and the Administration for the Improvement of the Seven Great Temples.

The territory of Silla was divided into nine provinces. Each province was subdivided into four administrative units: *gun, hyun, hyang,* and *bukok,* the last being the local unit. Administrative positions, both central and local, high and low, were reserved for the members of the ruling classes. The king appointed the heads of departments from his own family in accordance with kinship relations; that is, the closest relative became the highest government official and distant relatives became less important officials. The local government positions were divided among the members of the local aristocracy.

Government officials were paid for their services with fixed amounts of land. They were not the owners of the land, but they had the right to collect taxes in kind from the peasants who cultivated this "granted" land. As described later, the land-compensation system developed into a system of autonomous local political units and laid the foundations for later feudalism. The central government also began to grant land to the peasants, with the right of cultivation but not the right to sell, and collected taxes in kind from them. Thus the peasants became tenants of the government.

Military reorganization was based on the principle that all subjects were soldiers and every able-bodied male obligated to serve in the army. As mentioned already, Silla adopted the standing-army system at an early date, with the Hwarang or warrior group playing an important role.

The military reorganization consisted in the establishment of four units: *dung, sae, kung,* and *byun.* The *dung* unit, corresponding to an army division, was installed in every major city, including the capital; about forty-five *dung* existed throughout the country. *Sae* was a special army unit, composed of prisoners of war and Chinese and Japanese who had become naturalized subjects. There were five units of this kind, and they were placed in remote areas. *Kung,* the bow unit, was the skilled unit in the army. Silla had two bow units. *Byun* was the coast-guard unit; there were three such units.

In the capital city, the sentinel division, composed of three thousand well-trained soldiers, was installed for the protection of the palace, the nobles, and the government officials.

In the reorganization plans, *bukok,* the local administrative unit, had special significance because most peasants lived in *bukok.* The word *bukok* consists of two Chinese characters; the Chinese used them to express slavery.

According to Prof. Pack Nam-woon, *bukok* was the name of the village where slaves lived; later most of them became serfs in the feudal society. The official adoption by the Silla ruling class of *bukok* as the local administrative unit was "the sanction of slavery status for the peasants."[5]

Land Reform (687–757). After unification the concept that all land belonged to the king gradually changed, and limited recognition of the ownership of private land came into being. Every adult peasant was entitled to receive a fixed amount of land from the government with the right of cultivation. He could use the land for his own benefit without interference from the government until he reached the age of sixty; then he had to return the land to the government for redistribution to other peasants. In addition, private ownership and the right to inherit land were tacitly and unconditionally granted by the government to the ruling classes. Hence, when the king "granted" land, it was transformed into the private land of royal families, nobles, aristocrats, and priests. In this way the aristocrats gradually became great landlords.[6]

There were two reasons for the land reform measures. First, after the formation of the standing army, the central government faced a shortage of food supplies and needed a rapid increase of agricultural production. Limited recognition of the peasants' right to land ownership was an incentive for more production. Second, the reorganized administration system (centralization of power) did not work effectively because local aristocrats hesitated to support the king. Tacit recognition of private land ownership and the right of inheritance was the price the government paid for the support of local rulers.

According to the *Samguk-saki,* the traditional history of the three kingdoms, the land reform started in 687 and was completed in 757.[7] The reform created five types of land.

Sikyup-che, an autonomous district. The history of this goes back to A.D. 532 (before unification) when the Silla king granted autonomy to the tribal chief of Kumkwan-guk as reward for his voluntary submission to the authority of the king. After unification the king continued this method as a means of obtaining the support of local chiefs. The chief of an autonomous district was given the right to govern his tribesmen freely as long as he pledged his loyalty to the king in time of war. Thus the chiefs were able to maintain economic independence from the Silla king and eventually become powerful landlords.

Rokyup-che, land of the officials. As pointed out before, government officials were entitled to collect taxes in kind from the government-granted land. They had no right to dispose of the land. However, many high government officials were able to establish themselves as landlords.

Dondon-che, land for the soldiers. The beginning of the *dondon-che* goes back to the period of the T'ang occupation of the peninsula. The military authorities of T'ang practiced a farming system for soldiers to ensure self-support in the occupied territories. The Silla king retained the *dondon-che* in the former Koguryo and Paekche territories, and the local warriors as well as the military commanders made the soldiers farm their own land.

Sawoon-don, the land of Buddhist temples. The king granted vast amounts of land to Buddhist temples. In addition, members of the royal families and nobles donated lands and slaves to temples to purchase for themselves blessings and happiness. The land of Buddhist temples was exempted from government taxation. By the end of the Silla kingdom priests had become rich landlords.

Jung-don, land for the peasants. One of the significant features of the land reform was the distribution of land to the peasants. This was the first time the landless peasants were entitled to cultivate land for their own benefit. They were allowed to do this until they reached the age of sixty. The age limitation was perhaps imposed because after sixty the peasants were considered not strong enough to farm the land. There is no information as to what happened to the old peasants after they lost their land; evidently thereafter their livelihood depended on the support of their adult sons.

The land reform had important political, socioeconomic consequences. Contrary to what the central government expected, the authority of the king declined because he was no longer the legal owner of the land, and he depended on the good faith of the local rulers in matters of tax collection and defense. The gradual decentralization of power and the reappearance of the warrior states were the political consequences of the land reform. At the same time, a new system emerged: the tacit and partial recognition of private land ownership by the central government created feudal landlords and serf tenants. Thus feudalism came into being at the end of the Silla period.

The State-owned Handicraft Industry and Commerce. The handicraft industry was well developed under state ownership and operated by slaves. The capital city, Kyongju, became the center of this industry as well as of commerce. Domestic and foreign trade were also under the control of the central government. China was the principal outlet for external trade, and trading with China was conducted in the form of the annual tributary mission. There was also some minor trading with Japan.

Three kinds of handicraft industries existed:[8] the most highly skilled slaves engaged in the production of silk and other fabrics for the members of the royal family, nobles, and high government officials; the textile industry produced less valuable fabrics from hemp and cotton for minor government officials and their families; and the metal industry produced gold, silver, and copper-made articles or simple weapons and horse saddles. The gold and silver ornaments of royal families that have come to light in some of the recent discoveries in Kyongju tombs show excellent taste and high skill.

The government installed three public markets in the capital to dispose of government surplus goods and to supervise business activities among the people. Under the supervision of the government, only licensed persons were permitted to do business in the public markets.

The Fall of Silla. There are four reasons for the collapse of the Silla kingdom. First, the transformation of land from state ownership to private ownership ruined the national treasury. From the end of the ninth century local officials became landlords and refused to collect taxes for the central government. Instead they collected from the peasants for their own benefit and imposed high rents on their tenants. The king sent his tax collectors to the country, but these were usually bribed by the local landlords and frequently did not return to the capital. Thus at the beginning of the tenth century the national warehouses were empty and the central government faced financial ruin. Many local landlords established their own private armies and challenged the authority of the central government. The local priests also formed private armies and even manufactured weapons for the protection of Buddhist property.

Second, the poverty-stricken peasantry revolted against both central and local rulers, but the ruling classes suppressed them. In 806 the combined forces of slaves and peasants threatened the central government in a mass rebellion and invaded the capital city. This revolt was also put down by force, but this time the king publicly admitted his misgovernings, acknowledged the existence of the rebellious movement, and abdicated.[9]

Third, the economic and military disintegration and social unrest led to the reappearance in Silla of the warrior states; at the end of the ninth century two rival warrior states came into being. The Fu-paekche kingdom was installed in the southwestern section, and the Fu-koguryo kingdom in the northeast. The three rival states waged a series of wars for fifty years, but none of them was strong enough to completely subdue the others.

Fourth, in 918 Wang Kon came into power in the Fu-koguryo kingdom and formulated new policies. He approached the rebellious peasants and slaves with a conciliatory and compromising attitude. He made political deals with the landlords and the Silla ruling circles, and in 935 formed the new kingdom of Koryo.

CHAPTER 3

THE KORYO KINGDOM

935–1392

CENTRALIZED FEUDALISM

The rise of the Koryo kingdom in the tenth century had two significant consequences: the transformation of a slave society into a feudal society and the formation of a centralized political administration under the newly emerged aristocracy.

At the end of the ninth century the slaves and peasants rebelled against the ruling classes; their struggle for economic and social betterment continued during the warriors' civil-war period, which lasted more than a half century. The revolts by the discontented slaves and peasants intensified the power struggles among the sectional warriors and weakened the authority of the Silla kingdom, contributing to its final downfall. However, the slaves and peasants fought for a lost cause. As soon as the new rulers under Wang Kon had seized political power, they reduced the majority of the population to serfdom. The period of centralized feudalism in Korea had begun.

The formation of the capital-centered administration[1] took more than a half century, because the long civil war among the warriors ended without a clear-cut military victory for any group. The Wang Kon group finally came into power through compromise and by buying off opponents with high position, land, and serfs. The former king of Silla was given the whole Kyongju territory and serfs to cultivate the land. Wang Kon allowed his daughter to marry the former king, Kim Don. The territory of Yangju was given to Park Young-kuy (a retainer of Fu-peakche), who then pledged his loyalty to the new king. Wang Kon himself became king of Koryo. It was during this period that the name Korea came to be applied to the country by Western nations. Songdo (Kaesung) became the new capital.

The capital-centered administration rested on centralization of politics, economics, and military strength. For more than a hundred years the new capital city was being remodeled by the building of new palaces, castles, offices, temples, and roads. More than 340 thousand compulsory laborers were employed. The beauty and magnificence of the capital city was admired even by the envoy of the Sung dynasty of China. All government offices and buildings were concentrated in the capital, and the king appointed all high officials from his retainers. The capital city was heavily guarded, and the kingdom was divided into military subdivisions to defend the capital from enemy attack. The capital symbolized the authority of the king and was the center of the activities of the ruling classes.

Local administration was subordinated to the central government. The country was subdivided into provinces, counties, districts, towns, villages, and places. The central government appointed officials above the county level; officials below that level were under the control of the local aristocracy. As a result of this system officials of the central government had no contact with the people; they did not rule directly. To correct this situation, the central government created two offices: one was the office of local administrator (*hyangsa*), which was filled through an election by the local residents. The main responsibilities of the local administrator were collecting taxes and recruiting compulsory laborers for the central government. He also acted as mediator in disputes among the people. Officially he did not belong to the central administrative bureaucratic classes—he was a servant charged to do its work. Yet he was in a position to know of economic conditions and political stirrings among the peasants, so his influence in the local administration could not be overlooked by the central government.

The other official was the *sashimkwan* (inspector). One was appointed to each district by the central government to supervise and restrict the activities of the *hyangsa*. Thus the locally elected *hyangsa* was always under the eye of the central government. Furthermore, to insure the *hyangsa's* loyalty to the central government, one of his sons was required to live in the capital as a hostage (*gooin*).

THE CHARACTERISTICS OF FEUDALISM

The feudal society that began with the Koryo period[2] continued without substantial changes until the end of the Yi dynasty in the first part of the twentieth century, that is, until the annexation of Korea by the Japanese in

1910. Annexation meant no more, however, than replacement of the ruling class of the old feudal system by the Japanese, with the native ruling class, the feudal lords, remaining as subordinates and collaborators of the Japanese colonial administrators for more than three decades.

The beginning of the Koryo period had three characteristics. First, the economic foundation of feudalism was land. Products of the land made possible a primitive self-sufficient economy for the feudalistic rulers, including local and central administrators. Economic activities were limited to the exchange of goods among feudal domains. The territorial chiefs, feudal lords, were able to maintain economic independence. The main economic activities carried out by the central government in each local area were the collection of taxes in kind and its transportation by compulsory laborers, slaves, and peasants.

Second, the bulk of the agricultural labor force of the feudal lords consisted of slaves and landless peasants allocated by the king. They had no right to leave or to move from one place of farming to another without permission from their masters.

Third, agricultural methods were still primitive. The peasants cultivated the land collectively as laborers under the command of the local magnates; this system, in which no tenant-landlord relationship existed, was commonly called the "collective serfdom" system.

After the formation of the Koryo kingdom, the ruling classes pressed for greater production and more farming land. They attempted to achieve these objectives by centralizing economic authority in the hands of the king and concentrating the productive forces in the hands of the local magnates. The result was a highly centralized feudalism.

Korean historians hold various views on Korean feudalism. One school of thought, representing the "conceptional" historians,[3] argues that no feudalism existed in Korea, because the essential features of feudalism, as in western Europe, are decentralization of political power, economics, and cultural life. In Europe, landed property belonged to the feudal lords, who were the actual territorial rulers, and the peasants lived under their rule.

In Korea, however, the land was always the property of the state, and the magnates were only given the right to collect taxes or sometimes to collect rent from the peasants who cultivated the state lands. Thus, this school contends, the local magnates never became feudal lords in a real sense. Furthermore, there occurred no disintegration of political and economic authority after the unification of the peninsula under Silla, except for the brief period of military dictatorship under the Choi clan (1196–1257).

However, it would seem that there is no merit in denying the existence of feudalism merely because the term will not fit a definition of feudalism fashioned for western European conditions. Feudalism developed differently in different periods in non-European countries, especially in China, Japan, India, and the Middle East.[4] Feudalism existed in Europe in a decentralized form, and in a broader sense it also existed in China during the T'ang period and in Japan during the Tokugawa period, but in a centralized form.

The decisive element in the definition of feudalism is not the superstructure, but the presence of servile and dependent tenants under lords or local magnates together with a rigid hierarchy which allows little social mobility. Both the Koryo and Yi kingdoms were characterized by the economic and social elements of feudalism—dependent tenants and hierarchy, thriving in a highly centralized superstructure.

Another view is expressed by the "modern school" of thought, representing socioeconomic considerations. The central argument runs as follows. After the unification of the country in the seventh century A.D., the western type of feudalism had not developed in Korea, but the native society contained all essential elements of feudalism as a matter of long established custom. This social system remained in existence until the end of the Yi dynasty.

The historian Lee In-yong advanced three reasons why the western European or Japanese type of feudalism did not develop in Korea: (1) Geography necessitated a centralized political structure—the territorial integrity of Korea was threatened by the Mongolians and Manchus from the north, by the Chinese from the southwest, and by the Japanese from the southeast. Therefore, the ruling classes, to protect the country from the invasion of outsiders, did not decentralize power. (2) The unique character of the land system—all lands belonged to the king—hampered the development of the concept of private property, so that social and economic relations between tenants and landlords did not develop as in most feudalistic societies in other countries, until Japanese capitalism penetrated Korea in the latter part of the nineteenth century. (3) Civilian supremacy over the military made impossible the appearance of militaristic feudalism as in Japan.

Lee concludes that in politics the civilian bureaucrats had always been stronger than the military bureaucrats. Civilian bureaucrats practiced *kywijok sahai-juii* (aristocratic socialism), whereby, in theory, the land belonged to the king but, in reality, it was the common property of the ruling classes, including central and local aristocrats. The slaves and peasants cultivated the land for the ruling masters. For this reason the system can be characterized as slave feudalism.[5]

LAND REFORM

In 976 the ruling class of the Koryo kingdom introduced a new land system[6] based on landed property centered in the capital. The new land system facilitated the setting up of a centralized administration by which the aristocrats in the capital could maintain their power over local aristocratic rivals. Land became the economic foundation of political power.

The land reform provided for three categories: the private property system of the aristocrats; the centralized property system; and the individual small-landholder system, which later developed into the independent-peasant system.

A. The private property system. Three types of private landed property existed from the time of the Silla kingdom in the seventh century: land of the local autonomous chief, land of the meritorious retainer, and land bestowed by the king. All three types remained in the Koryo kingdom but were now made inheritable.

B. The centralized property system. This system concentrated property in the hands of the central aristocracy. The following two reform measures were adopted:

1. *Kwadon-che.* This was land allocated to incumbent high government officials in the central government. The lowest aristocrats, usually former warriors, received about eighteen acres. Neither the right to sell nor to bequeath the land was recognized under this plan but the right to collect taxes (sometimes called rent) was given to the so-called landlords. The public slaves and the landless peasants farmed for the masters. All land had to be returned to the state when the original recipient died.

This meant that in principle the land belonged to the state (king) as public property; hence some historians called this practice aristocratic socialism.

2. *Konghai-donshi.* Land of this category belonged to the executive body (*konghai*) of the government. Income from the land was considered national revenue and was used for national expenditures. Two types of *konghai-donshi* existed: the central *konghai-donshi,* which furnished the central government revenues that were used for government buildings, royal palaces, and other public buildings; and the local *konghai-donshi,* which provided for the general expenses of the local administration, including the salaries of the local government employees. The local *konghai-donshi* was subdivided into six local budgetary divisions to meet the general expenditures of the local administrative units.

C. The individual small-landholder system. Under this system the commoners (peasants) had an opportunity to become small landowners. There were five different ways to distribute land among the commoners: (1) *Gun-don* (soldiers' land). Every able-bodied male was required to take the national examination. Those who passed the test were entitled to receive a certain amount of the land at the age of twenty, and they had the right to cultivate the land for their own use until they reached the age of sixty. These peasant-soldiers were obligated to farm in peacetime and fight in wartime. *Gun-don* land was exempt from taxation because it represented the salary for military service. (2) *Youngyup-don* (permanent working land). This was an extension of the *gun-don* system. If the soldier had a son, the land was given to the son when the father reached retirement age. (3) *Kubon-don* (literally, "mouth-share land"). If the soldier reached retirement age without having a son, he was entitled to continue farming the land until the age of seventy; if he lived still longer, the land was given to him as private property. (4) *Waiyuk-don* (land for government service). Civilian government employees were entitled to a certain amount of land in place of an annual compensation. They had the right to collect rent from land so allocated; when government service was terminated the land was supposed to be returned to the state. However, as in the case of the *gun-don* land, the central government gradually recognized private property rights in order to insure support, including the right to bequeath the land. (5) *Toohwa-don* (land for naturalized subjects). Many aliens, mostly Chinese and Japanese, became subjects of the Koryo kingdom. Because of the labor shortage in the northeastern provinces, the central government allocated lands to naturalized subjects to encourage immigration to Koryo; later the government also conceded rights of private property to them.

THE SOCIAL STRUCTURE

The feudal society of Koryo was composed of two segments: a small minority of the privileged ruling class[7] and the vast underprivileged classes.[8] The ruling class included five groups: *wangzok* (the royal family), *munkwan* (civil bureaucrats), *mookwan* (central military bureaucrats), *tohogun* (local military bureaucrats), and the priesthood. The underprivileged consisted of the handicraft workers and merchants, the low professional class (*chunmin*), the serfs, and the slaves.

The Royal Family. The king was the supreme landlord. In theory at least, he was the sole owner of the land in the country and entitled to dispose of it at will without restriction. The members of the royal family included the king, the queen, princes, and princesses. During the Koryo period, which lasted 460 years, there were thirty-two kings.

The private royal lands were scattered throughout the country in 360 specific places, despite the fact that legally the king and his family owned all land anyway. The public slaves (sometimes called palace slaves) farmed these lands under the supervision of officials appointed by the central government.

Munkwan, the Civil Bureaucrats. This group was composed of the ministers of the king, retainers, court nobles, and other bureaucrats. The first three were appointees of the king; the others were called merit-system bureaucrats because they took the state civil service examination to become government officials. State civil service examinations were held only 253 times during four and a half centuries and only about sixty-five hundred persons passed the tests; that is, only a little more than twenty-five were recruited by the merit system each time. The high-ranking civil aristocrats, the king's personal appointees, numbered about five hundred—less than sixteen in the reign of one king—but they wielded the power until the military group took over.

Mookwan, the Military Bureaucrats. In the beginning the military bureaucrats accepted the idea of civilian supremacy in politics and occupied the second rank in prestige and power. The long tradition of civilian supremacy was broken, however, when Chung Jong-bu, the commanding general of the Sentinel Corps in the capital, seized power by a coup d'etat in A.D. 1170. For about one hundred years thereafter, the military group ruled the country in the name of the king, who was reduced to the status of a puppet of the military bureaucrats. However, because of lack of experience in politics and because of rivalry among the military factions, a stable military regime like the Tokugawa shogunate in Japan was never established, and power shifted nine times from one clan to another. The Choi clan became the strongest and ruled more than six decades.

The principles of the military bureaucracy were characterized by the *kashin* (generalissimo) system of absolute centralization of power under a generalissimo, redistribution of lands and serfs among the military vassals, and protection of the vassal's land.

The military bureaucracy was divided into a central and a local sector. The central administration was called the *kashin* system; the local administration was called the *tohogun* (that is, local military bureaucrats) system. The *kashin* replaced the Council of State, the civilian administration headed by the king. The *kashin* clique was composed of retainers and soldiers of the generalissimo, the de facto ruler in the kingdom. The size and organization of the *kashin* administration varied, because each generalissimo set up his own type of administration.

Tohogun, the Local Military Bureaucrats. To understand the gradual appearance of the *tohogun,* it is necessary to go back to the land reform measures of 976. As pointed out, the newly emerged ruling class headed by the Wang Kon clan distributed land to peasant soldiers in pay for military service. Later, under the retirement system, most of the peasant soldiers became landowners.

This group was ready to fight against any encroachments on their lands by the central government. The local small landlords joined this group and formed a united front against the central aristocrats, who tried to expand their landed interests into local areas. When the military seized power from the civilian bureaucrats, the local landlords and the independent peasants took the side of the former, and their properties were well protected. This was the beginning of local forces based on landed interests under the leadership of former peasant soldiers; some of the leaders advanced their social status to that of local military bureaucrats, *tohogun*.

The national conscription system also contributed to the appearance of the local aristocrats. In 1041 the king granted as a special privilege to the high-ranking aristocrats the exemption of the first-born son from military service. At the same time, the central government issued a directive stating that the commoners, which meant the peasant soldiers, should be barred from wearing long swords. This order was regarded by the local military aristocrats as disarming of the peasant soldiers, and some defied the order. The exemption from military service of privileged clans also caused the indignation of underprivileged social groups toward the central aristocrats. These two events made it possible for local forces, the underprivileged social groups, and the military groups to unite and challenge the supremacy of the civilian authority of the central government.

The priesthood. As mentioned before, the ruling class of the Koryo kingdom accepted Buddhism as the state religion and state political ideology. Mahayana Buddhism had been popular among the aristocrats because it promised a happy life for the ruling class and Buddha's protection for the kings. The king granted land and slaves to temples. Members of the royal family and aristocrats also contributed lands and slaves to Buddhist temples in order to obtain happiness and blessings from Buddha.

Thus the priests gradually emerged as powerful landlords and their influence on politics grew significantly. The government could not intervene in the affairs of Buddhist temples. The priests usurped authority by organizing the so-called temple armies under the pretext of protecting Buddhist property. They also established textile and wine industries by using slave labor, and manufactured weapons for the temple soldiers. The morality and intellectual leadership of the priests began to deteriorate when their life became luxurious and their power increased. Buddhism declined when the Koryo kingdom came to an end in the last years of the fourteenth century.

During the Koryo period a census registration system was adopted to make a clear distinction in official records between the ruling class and the ruled. Two registration records existed; one for the *yangban* class and one for the *sangmin* class; to the former belonged the civilian and military bureaucrats, to the latter the commoners, that is, the peasants, serfs, and slaves. Census registration was required every year for the commoners and every three years for the aristocrats. The government census bureau made two copies of each record for the aristocrats, one for the official files and the other for the aristocrats themselves as a certification of their social status. The commoners received no official certification of their status.

There were three reasons for taking an annual census of the commoners. First, conscription for military service; every male commoner was drafted at the age of twenty and retired from active service at the age of sixty. Second, conscription of labor for public works; the draft age for public works was sixteen; a commoner could be called at any time until he reached sixty. Third, the government wanted to know the number of productive workers in agriculture, and also in handicraft industries, fishery, business, and the other occupations.

The caste system and the many subdivisions of the ruled class were complicated and will not be presented here. Besides, the terminology used in describing them has been a controversial subject among Korean historians. The term "serf" (*nogno*), for example, was not used by government officials in reference to the actual cultivator of feudal land. Instead, such terms as *donmin* (people of the land), *sangmin* or *soomin* (commoners), *nongmin* (peasants), and *changmin* or *changho* (people cultivating the land of a manor) were used. Therefore some historians, for purely semantic reasons, insist that no serfs existed in Korea because the word was not used during the Koryo or Yi kingdoms.

According to the government documents of the Koryo kingdom, the word "peasant" (*nongmin*) referred to twelve different classes engaged in farming—from slave to independent peasant.

The Handicraft Workers and Merchants. In principle, all handicraft industries were under the control of the central government; the allocation of manpower, raw materials, and tools of production also were supervised by the government. The importance of the handicraft industry in the economy was second to that of agriculture; hence the social status of the industrial slave workers was below that of the peasants.

The weapons, minerals, textiles, pottery, and musical instrument industries were located in the capital. The manufacture of brushes, ink, paper, and kitchen utensils was concentrated in regional areas. At the end of the Koryo period a few private industries were allowed in the country, but they were small, employing at the most five workers. The best trained and skilled workers were in industries in the capital, especially in the palace handicraft industries that produced beautiful and luxurious articles for the royal families and aristocrats.

No regular compensation or wage system existed for these workers; they worked from dawn till dusk seven days a week under the eyes of government-appointed supervisors. Anyone who worked more than three hundred days a year received extra rice as compensation for his industry.

Three types of merchants existed—storekeepers, government merchants, and peddlers. The first group included government employees without official title who worked in government stores and shops. Some of them were former slaves who now worked as salesmen in the capital and local markets. Former slaves who did janitorial service in the stores were also included in this group. The second group were government-appointed officials, such as supervisors, inspectors, and store managers, as well as officials of the "tributary mission" to be described later. The third group were the "private merchants" who carried a bundle of merchandise on their backs: the *bojim-jangsa,* or pack-peddlers. The *bojim-jangsa* traded mostly in the countryside.

There is in adequate source material on the origin of the private merchant class, but it would seem that one segment of the "free" village peasants developed into peddlers when they lost their small land holdings to the local aristocrats. This group, however, never had a chance to advance their social status. In fact, the social status of the merchants was lower than that of the peasants and artisans.

All business activity was under the control of the government. The government established three types of markets in the geographical divisions of the country. The capital city market was established in a fixed section of the capital. Only government merchants, officials, and general employees were allowed to live in this sector. The market existed exclusively for the government officials and their families. A special market for the members of the royal family and the nobles was known as *bangshi*. This market was also open to foreign tributary missions, especially the Chinese mission sent by the Chinese emperor as a sign of courtesy. Special market days were observed on which the famous silk fabrics and handicraft products, such as gold and silver ornaments, were displayed.

The provincial market was one in which supervisors, inspectors, and general managers were central government appointees; local people were employed as storekeepers, salesmen, and servants. These markets were established in every provincial capital. They stocked such items as rice, textiles, and kitchen utensils. These were government surplus goods which came from the central warehouse in the national capital. The public marketing days were fixed, usually one every five days.

The sidewalk market was a public market but was also under the supervision of the government. The sidewalk market was not allowed in the capital. It was usually established in the poorer sections of the provincial capitals. Barter was common practice, although metal coins were introduced in the twelfth century. No valuable or luxury articles could be seen in this market. The most common merchandise were foodstuffs, such as vegetables, fruits, and rice cookies, and domestic products, especially textiles. The merchants displayed their goods on the sidewalk or carried them around from one street to another. Women generally carried goods on their heads, the men on their backs.

The government monopoly type of business establishment came into being for political rather than economic reasons. The wine shops and the system of inns were under the direct management of the central government. In 983 wine shops were established in politically important urban areas throughout the country to serve as centers for business deals between national and local merchants, and to provide assembly halls for official banquets and entertainment for aristocrats. About one hundred years later, government wine shops were established in every local administrative unit as well as in every communication and transportation center. Government officials used the wine shops as public meeting places to explain official policies to the local people. For example, in 1104 the government sent out representatives of the king to the local areas to explain and encourage the use of coin money for trade in place of barter.

There were two types of inns: one mainly for the peddlers, the other for foreign merchants. In the remote rural areas, inns were built by the central government in order to provide places where pack-peddlers could get free room and board. The expenses were met by the produce of government-granted lands.

In the capital a guest inn was established for foreign merchants. Later all important cities, especially the coast cities, had from one to three guest inns. All foreign merchant missions were treated as state guests; usually they were not just businessmen but also representatives of foreign states, such as the envoys of the Chinese emperor, who sometimes delivered political messages to the king. When a Chinese mission was scheduled to visit, the whole capital was busy with special preparations, such as the planning of welcome banquets, street cleanings, and, if necessary, the construction of new inns. For example, in 1055 more than three hundred merchants from the Sung dynasty visited the capital city, Songdo, and beforehand three new guest inns were especially constructed in order to provide accommodations for them.

The Low Professional Class: Chunmin. The *chunmin* class embraced six professional occupations. A member of this group could never change his status, and his offspring had to follow his father's occupation. The six occupations were as follows: ferrymen, who were engaged in sea transportation, including river crossings by ferryboat, for community and government; government station workers, who worked in the government-established "station," the transportation and communication center in strategic towns and villages throughout the country, carried official directives and orders to the heads of the towns and villages, and at the same time transmitted the tributes and grains collected as taxes from the peasants to the government; village servants, who repaired roads and bridges; general skilled laborers, who weighed grains and other commodities in the public markets, took care of the official scales and other devices of measurement, worked as public butchers, or engaged in handicrafts such as making baskets, boxes, and suitcases from willow branches; and the entertainers and the musicians, who sang, danced, and played musical instruments at festivals and ceremonies.

Members of these six groups were looked upon as outcasts despite their skill and usefulness. If the butchers had refused to kill cows, pigs, and chickens, the aristocrats would have had no meat because no other group of the people could do the butchers' job. Or if the basket-makers had given up their profession, families would have been without many domestic utensils. The outcast status of certain professions goes back to the influences of Buddhism and Confucianism, especially the precept of "do not kill animals and do not eat meat." Acceptance of the Confucian social scale placed the scholar and gentry class on top and the artisans and merchants at the bottom, which hampered the development of technology, industry, and commerce.

The Serfs. Wang Kon, the founder of the Koryo kingdom, attempted to release the slaves when he came to power, but was stopped by slave owners. About thirty years later King Kwangjong issued a slave-release order on the grounds that "keeping slaves is no longer profitable for the slave owners." At that time the private and public slaves had tried to resist the cruel and excessive exploitation of their masters; many of them ran away and others refused to work. Bloody fights took place between masters and slaves. This meant that a large segment of the national productive force came in conflict with the owners of the means of production, and as a result a decline of production in agriculture and handicraft industry became inevitable. Realizing the political and economic consequences of this situation, the ruling class released some of the slaves, but this brought little relief to the slaves; for most of them became the nucleus of a new social class, the serfs.

Five different groups of people gradually changed their social status to that of serfs: First, there were serfs who were formerly slaves. As a result of the slave-release order most public (government) slaves became serfs of the royal family and of the civilian and military bureaucrats. Those who cultivated the lands of the royal family were called *changmin* (people of the manorial land); those who farmed the civilian bureaucrats' lands were known as *pyonmin* ("the bunch"). The *changmin* and *pyonmin* worked the lands of the government officials; they had to pay tribute and rent to their masters and taxes to the government; and they were also forced to do other work for their masters without pay during the winter or whenever the master demanded. Under such an exploitative system, the economic conditions of the *changmin* and *pyonmin* were no better than before.

When the military bureaucrats came into power, the burden of the serfs became heavier than ever, because each military chief built his own private army supported by his own income.

During the military regime, production and the general living conditions of the people reached their lowest level. Fearing violence by the people, Choi Chung-hyun modified his land policy and ordered the "return of the confiscated lands to the original owners." However, the order was merely a political gesture, a means of retaining power. For more than six decades the productive classes as a whole remained serfs.

From the first part of the fourteenth century, the time of the collapse of the Koryo kingdom, the centralized land system disintegrated and private land ownership developed. Most of the government-owned lands, such as *yok-don* (station land) and *hak-don* (school land), were released to the public and fifty-six powerful local aristocrats became large landholders by taking advantage of the land-release set. Many small bloody wars between aristocratic families for the acquisition of land and serfs were waged throughout the country for more than a decade. The people who cultivated the land of the private landlords (not government officials) were called *donmin* (people of the land); they lived under the absolute rule of their masters. Most *donmin* were former slaves who had worked on government lands.

Second, there were serfs who were formerly peasant soldiers. Most persons who were engaged in farming in *gun-don* (soldiers land) and *kubun-don* (mouth-share land) were forced to become serfs. When the general disarmament policy became effective, most peasant soldiers lost their land to the powerful local aristocrats and gradually became serfs of the private landlords.

The composition of the third group was complex, because it consisted of people from many underprivileged social groups; they had been slaves, commoners, and even members of aristocratic families, and were known collectively as the *paekchung* group. (This group should not be confused with the butcher Paekchung during the Yi period, described later.) Those who belonged to this social group usually worked in the military and transportation centers of the central government.

The fourth group consisted of serfs of Japanese and Chinese origin who had become naturalized subjects. They lived in the northern section of the peninsula and cultivated land known as *toohwa-don,* which was granted to them by the government during the land reform. Many of them lost their land to local aristocrats when the right of private land ownership was recognized, and became serfs of the local landlords in the middle of the fourteenth century.

Finally, there were serfs who had formerly been handicraft industrial workers. Some of the government-owned handicraft industries were decentralized, and local private ownership of industries was allowed. Many handicraft industrial workers were slaves captured in wars between rival tribes. As soon as the decentralization became effective, some workers were released from the government industries and transferred to the land of aristocrats, where they were forced to farm as serfs. When the central government adopted the policy of *nongbon-juii* (physiocracy) in the eleventh century, most textile industrial workers were released in order to participate in agricultural production.

To sum up, the serfs of the Koryo period were composed of slaves, peasant soldiers, *paekchung,* naturalized subjects, and workers of the handicraft industry. The central government issued so-called slave-release orders on the ground that keeping slaves was no longer profitable because of their rebellious attitude toward their masters. The released slaves became serfs when the centralized land system disintegrated and private land ownership was established. The number of serfs increased when the government released the handicraft workers from government-owned industries.

When the military came into power, replacing the civilian bureaucracy, the general living conditions of the people, especially of the peasants, became worse, and many were reduced to serfdom.

The Slaves. Despite the so-called slave-release order, the slave system continued to exist. The significant change in the slave system during the Koryo period was that the slaves were no longer considered the main productive forces when the serf system came into being. Slaves were no longer kept primarily for economic reasons but for the personal convenience of the aristocrats.

The slave system was continued because on many occasions the slaves fought for the interests of their master's clan. During the military regime many slaves became private soldiers of the military bureaucrats, and some of them even advanced in status and became bodyguards of their masters. Slaves were also kept for trading purposes; private slaves were traded between aristocrats like commodities. During the Sonjong rule (995–1005) the price for slaves was fixed by the government at the equivalent of about one hundred pounds of rice. The male slave was cheaper than the female because the latter could become a concubine of the master and produce more slaves for him.

Four types of slaves existed during the Koryo period. (a) Palace slaves, who worked in the royal palaces. The most skilled male slaves worked in the palace handicraft industries and produced ornaments for the royal family. (b) Government slaves, who worked in the transportation stations and warehouses and did cleaning, repairing, etc. The number of government slaves was estimated at more than a half million even after the slave-release act became effective. (c) Family slaves. They were the private slaves of the aristocrats. (d) Temple slaves. The temples had slaves since the Silla period, and their number steadily increased during the Koryo kingdom because many aristocrats contributed slaves. The temple slaves engaged in farming of the temple lands and also worked in the temple handicraft and textile industries.

The total number of private slaves was more than a quarter million during the Koryo period. The slave-act of 987 did not greatly affect the private slave owners because many loopholes were left. One of them was the conditional-release clause: under this provision a slave who desired to free himself from the master had to agree to work harder than previously for a specific period. During this period (no length of time was fixed by the act) if the slave failed to fulfill his duties as judged by the master, he would not be released. Another loophole was that if the slave expressed resentment toward his former master after his release he had to return to slave status again.

SUMMARY OF THE KORYO PERIOD

The economic foundation of the Koryo kingdom was agriculture; the primitive handicraft industry and commerce held a subordinate position.

Buddhism was accepted as the state religion as well as the state political ideology. There were two social classes: the ruling aristocrats and the ruled subordinate social groups. The political apparatus was a centralized feudal system.

The Koryo kingdom lasted about four and a half centuries (935–1392). The entire Koryo period, however, can be divided into three stages from the standpoint of political events: the initial stage of the formation of a centralized feudal society, which lasted from King Wang Kon to King Mukjong, about ninety years; the prosperous period of centralized feudalism from King Jyunjong to King Uijong, about one hundred years; and the period of the Mongolian invasions—the decline of the Koryo kingdom—from King Choongnol to King Kongyang, one hundred years. In 1392 General Yi made himself king and established the Yi dynasty. Thus the Koryo kingdom came to an end.

CHAPTER 4

THE YI DYNASTY (1392–1910) CENTRALIZED FEUDAL SOCIETY

THE REAPPEARANCE OF CENTRALIZED FEUDALISM

In order to understand the significance of the establishment of the Yi dynasty it is necessary to recall conditions at the end of the Koryo kingdom. The state landed property system had changed to a private landed property system, and the local magnates had become landlords. Because of excessive exploitation by the ruling class, the masses were rebellious and social unrest was widespread. The Mongolian invasions and domination of the Koryo kingdom ruined the country economically and reduced it to tributary status.

The Ming dynasty rose in China and its challenge to the ruling Yuan dynasty created two rival political factions in the Koryo ruling class, one independent and one pro-Ming. Eventually the pro-Ming clique, headed by General Yi Sung-gai, seized power in 1392 and eliminated all opposition, including the Koryo royal family. When Yi ascended the throne in 1392, he sought from the Ming emperor authorization of his right to rule the Korean peninsula; the Ming emperor complied, confirming Yi as ruler of the new dynasty and suggested for the country the new name of "Chosun," which had been the name of the peninsula when under the rule of Kiza in 1122 B.C. Yi Sung-gai accepted the name. He also substituted Confucianism for Buddhism as the creed of the new regime. The government was reorganized following the Ming model.

The state land system became again the economic foundation of the country, and a new land reform was introduced. As described later in detail, the land reform abolished the private land system as well as the landed property of the Buddhist temples, which had developed during the last part of the Koryo dynasty. Public ownership of lands that were worked in the interest of the new ruling class was restored; the new rulers became powerful landlords under the guise of public ownership of the land, and the overwhelming majority of the masses remained serfs. Thus the essential features of centralized feudalism were reestablished—namely, centralization of power under an absolute monarch, monopolization of the national economy, and aristocratic dominance of land, handicraft industry, and commerce; and also, there continued the rigid social distinction between the privileged few and the underprivileged many.

The Yi dynasty had been in power 518 years, from 1392 to 1910, when it succumbed to the Japanese. The dynasty produced twenty-seven kings. Yi Sung-gai, the founder of the dynasty, moved the capital from Songdo to Hanyang, or Seoul, as it is known today.

During its five centuries of rule the Yi dynasty passed through a brilliant period of cultural achievement and technical and military progress. Perhaps the most noticeable achievements were the Korean phonetic alphabet (consisting of ten vowels and fourteen consonants), the development of movable metal type for printing (half a century before Gutenberg printed the Bible), the use of astronomical instruments, compasses, cannons, and shells, and the invention of the ironclad "turtle ship." Most of these achievements took place in the first two hundred years of the new dynasty, from the fourteenth to the sixteenth century. In 1592 the dynasty suffered from the first big-scale Japanese invasion, under Toyotomi Hideyoshi, and in 1636 from the Manchu invasion. Thereafter Korea entered self-imposed isolation for the next two and a half centuries, during which time it was known as the hermit kingdom. However, the Yi dynasty maintained contact with the Ching dynasty during that period. During the isolation period factionalism (*tang-zang*) developed.

Attempts by the French in 1866 and the Americans in 1871 to open the doors of the hermit kingdom failed, but the isolation policy was broken when Korea was forced to conclude a commercial treaty with Japan in 1876. The treaty with Japan was followed by treaties with the United States in 1882, and within the next five years with Russia, France, and England.

For the four decades after the Yi dynasty had opened her door to foreign powers, Korea was a political battleground for the colonial states of the Far East. In the meantime, the age-old social, economic, and political feudal system disintegrated. Military and political revolts against the feudal regime took place in 1882 and 1884. Ten years later, a large-scale peasant revolt occurred under the leadership of a scholarly society known as Tonghak-dan.

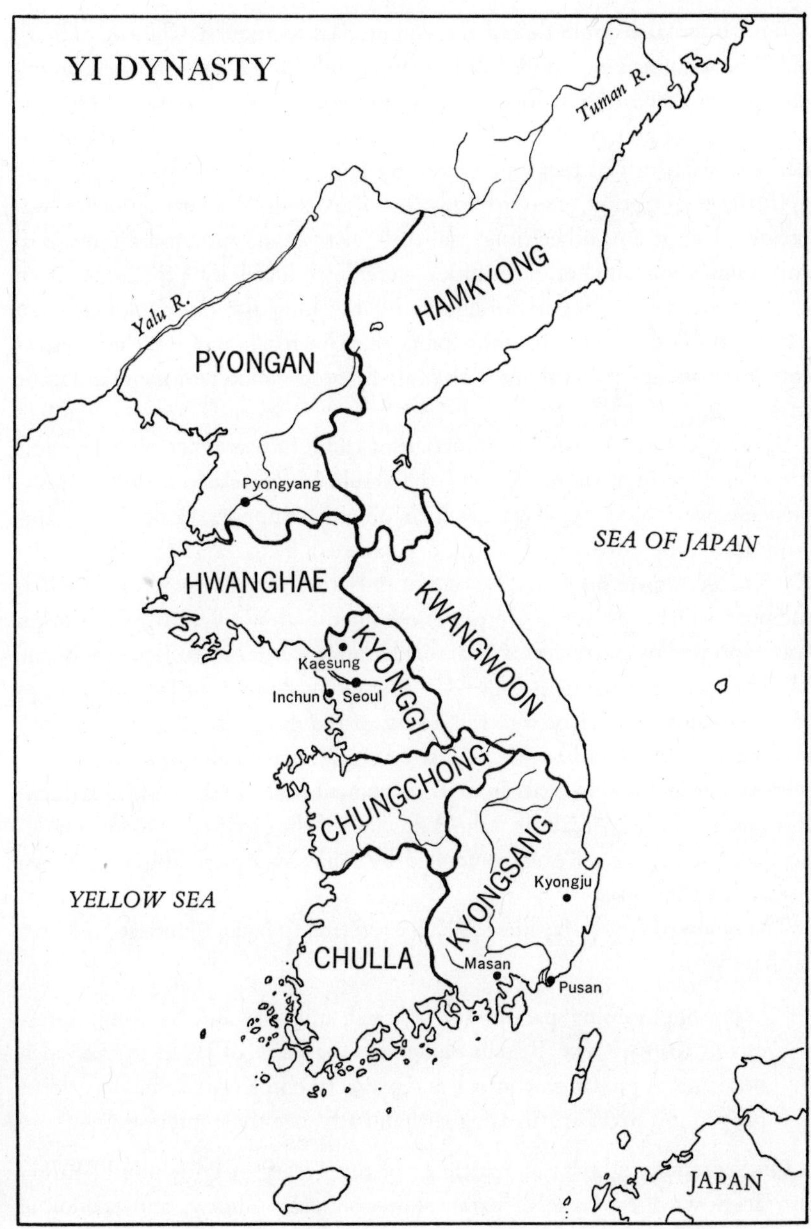
YI DYNASTY
Tuman R.
Yalu R.
HAMKYONG
PYONGAN
Pyongyang
SEA OF JAPAN
HWANGHAE
KWANGWOON
KYONGGI
Kaesung
Inchun
Seoul
CHUNGCHONG
KYONGSANG
Kyongju
YELLOW SEA
CHULLA
Masan
Pusan
JAPAN

This internal trouble caused the ruling class to request Chinese military aid. The Chinese sent troops to the capital, and this gave the Japanese an excuse to send their own troops to Seoul. In the ensuing short war of 1894 the Japanese were able to eliminate Chinese influence in Korea. The "independence" of Korea was then guaranteed by both China and Japan.

In the next period, 1895 to 1910, the impact of Western influence was greater than at any other time; railroads were built, and modern means of communication and public utilities were introduced by private Western companies; concessions to foreigners by the king for the exploitation of natural resources were common practice. The foreign powers established extraterritoriality rights along with most-favored-nation treatment and trade concessions.

Among the rivals, Russian imperialism came into conflict with Japanese imperial expansion in Korea, and the result of this clash was the Russo-Japanese war (1904–05). Japan, which obtained support from the Anglo-American bloc through the Anglo-Japanese alliance and the Roosevelt-Katsura secret pact on Korea,[1] won not only the war but established itself as the predominant power in Korea. The United States government's position was expressed by Secretary of War William Howard Taft to Japanese Prime Minister Count Katsura as follows: "The establishment by Japanese troops of a suzerainty over Korea to the extent of requiring that Korea enter into no foreign treaties without the consent of Japan was the logical result of the present war and would contribute to permanent peace in the East." President Roosevelt held that "realistic politics demanded the sacrifice of Korean independence, and that a Korea controlled by Japan was preferable to a Korea controlled by Russia."[2]

The renewed Anglo-Japanese Alliance referred to Japan's interests in Korea in these words:

> Japan possessing paramount political, military, and economic interests in Korea, Great Britain recognizes the right of Japan to take such measures of guidance, control, and protection in Korea as she may deem proper and necessary to safeguard and advance these interests.[3]

On September 5, 1905 in Article 11 of the Treaty of Portsmouth, Russia also acknowledged Japan's "paramount political, military, and economic interests" in Korea. With this international sanction the Japanese government forced the ministers of the king to sign the Japanese protective treaty on November 17, 1905. Finally, on August 29, 1910, Japan proclaimed the annexation of Korea. The Yi dynasty ceased to exist and Korea thereafter was under Japanese colonial rule for thirty-five years.

THE NEW CREED OF THE YI DYNASTY: CONFUCIANISM

When the Koryo kingdom collapsed, Buddhism was no longer acceptable to the new ruler as the governing religion of the new regime. Confucianism became the creed of the Yi dynasty. The rapid change from Buddhism to Confucianism was based on two factors, one internal and one external. As mentioned already, at the end of the Koryo kingdom the Buddhist priests controlled a great segment of the national economy, wielded power at the court, and became the de facto rulers in the local areas. When Yi Sung-gai and his retainers seized power, the Buddhists opposed the centralization of power as well as the land reform based on public ownership. But centralization of power and land reform were vital in order for the new ruling class to maintain its position; hence they confiscated the property of the Buddhist temples and disarmed the so-called Buddhist army which had been formed under the pretext of protecting Buddhist property.

The Essence of the Confucian Political Philosophy. Confucian political thought could be comprehensively summed up in the eight steps to becoming a "true man or gentleman."[4] These are: investigate nature, extend the boundary of knowledge, make your purpose sincere, regulate the mind, cultivate personal virtue, rule the family, govern the state, and pacify the world.

Confucius postulated five virtues and five fundamental relationships as ethical principles.[5] The five virtues are benevolent love, righteousness, proper conduct, wisdom, and faithfulness. Among these, conduct (or ceremony) is the most important and is the cardinal tenet of Confucianism. Proper worship of Heaven, nature, and ancestors were the most important ceremonies. The ruler, son of Heaven, was the highest priest, and one of his duties was to perform the ceremony for the worship of Heaven on behalf of his subjects.

The five principles in human relationships are the relationships between father and son, sovereign and subject, husband and wife, old and young, and friend and friend. To keep proper relationships between these pairs, Confucius laid down five articles of morality: intimacy, righteousness, distinction, obedience, and faithfulness. When everybody observes these principles, a harmonious and peaceful social order will prevail.

He also taught the doctrine of inequality, saying, "As soon as there was heaven and earth, there was the distinction of above and below (superior and inferior); when the first wise king arose, the country he occupied had the division of classes. The ancient kings established the rules of proper conduct and divided the people into nobles and commoners, so that everybody would be under someone's control."[6] According to the Confucian view, inequality and distinction between superior and inferior were the natural order or "innate in nature for the good of society." Therefore, everyone and everything should be under someone's control. Responsibility and benevolence descend from above, from heaven and the emperor; and obedience, loyalty, and respect ascend from below, from the common people.

In the book *High Learning* Confucius said: "Give me morality and nothing else is necessary; without virtue there would be no government, no ruler, and no society. He who is virtuous will be sure to receive the appointment of Heaven."[7] Government, according to Confucian theory, was not an institution based on law, but on morals. Therefore, to govern means "to rectify" the subjects according to the rule of proper conduct. In Confucian society the ultimate goal of the individual was to become a sage, a virtuous man; and government by moral example was the highest form of government. The goal of good government was to introduce moral realism in which the peace and happiness of the people would prevail. This was the utopian society of the Confucian state system.

The Political Consequences of Confucian-Authoritarian Politics. The doctrine of inequality was an authoritarian element in Confucian thought. Confucius considered abolition of inequality as a return to a state of barbarism and chaos, in which men's desires have no limit; therefore, an orderly and happy society was possible only as long as everybody had a fixed station and a master to serve. Hence, he taught that everyone and everything should be under someone's control.

The five virtues and five fundamental ethical principles in human relationships were the explicit expression of an authoritarian feudalism. Responsibility and authority should be in the hands of the superior virtuous man, whereas filial devotion and unconditional obedience should be the duty of the inferior. Therefore, the concepts of individual rights, freedom, and equality were alien to Confucian thought. The Confucian doctrine of inequality justified the social structure of the Yi dynasty, under which the population was divided into two classes, the rulers and the ruled.

The ruler, son of Heaven, was the apex of the Confucian state pyramid; he could do no wrong, because he was chosen by Heaven for his "surpassing virtue." In theory, the benevolent ruler's duty was to look after the welfare of each subject from childhood to old age; all men were his children. The rules of proper conduct, benevolent love, and filial devotion were applicable to the relations of sovereign and subject. But in practice the ruler was often an authoritarian: despotism was common in both China and Korea.

The Confucian concept of the ruler was, therefore, the most forceful and convenient political ideology for Yi Sung-gai and his followers to set up an absolute monarchy. The concept of paternalistic government allowed no room for the voice of the people. Government of the ruler, by the ruler, and for the ruler was good government.

The concept of government by virtuous men gave the Confucian gentry an opportunity in setting up a Confucian bureaucratic regime in Korea. The business of politics was monopolized by the Confucian hierarchy, because government positions depended on civil service examinations, determined by the knowledge of Confucian classics, a knowledge reserved for those whose resources allowed them time for years of study.

During the Yi dynasty, the Confucian scholars became the landed aristocracy; they each wore a long gown and a special hat, and let their finger nails grow long as a sign that they did not engage in manual labor. They considered manual labor inferior and made a sharp distinction between it and mental labor. They cultivated extreme conservatism and hindered progress. They emphasized "formalism," such as the correct ceremony of marriage, funeral service, and ancestor worship; they preached "asceticism," which proposed purity of scholarship based on the idea of fidelity and avoidance of material gain.[8]

Confucianism and its idea of inferior and superior nations also determined the relationship between Korea and China for more than five centuries.[9] The theory of Confucian international relations was based on *li,* the rule of proper conduct, and not on international law as in the Western states. According to Confucius, just as *li* governed individual, family, and social relations in China, so international relations were an extension of the same principle. Inequality among nations, as among individuals, was the natural order of the world on the ground that equality in relations between two nations would produce disorder or war. Inequality among nations meant that China was superior because she was the land of the sages and virtue, and under the rule of *li.* Chinese rulers viewed all non-Chinese as uncivilized people who needed the guidance of the virtuous Chinese; accordingly, they treated the neighboring small states as tributary kingdoms. The rulers of the Ming dynasty began to dominate the neighboring kingdoms through the penetration of Confucianism and Chinese culture, rather than by using military power as the Mongols had done.

The relationship between the Ming dynasty and the Yi dynasty was that of one between a superior and an inferior. In theory, the relation between two countries was to be that of an elder and younger brother; but in practice, Korea under the Yi dynasty was a tributary state to China.

Yi Sung-gai and his ministers acknowledged the superiority of China, asking the Ming emperor's authorization of Yi Sung-gai's right to rule Korea and requesting a name for the new kingdom.

Yi built a special hall for the official reception and entertainment of the Chinese mission. Kings of the Yi dynasty also sent an annual tributary mission to China and a special envoy at the time of the death of the Ming emperor and the ascension to the throne of his successor.

The Yi dynasty continued to pay tribute to China until the end of the nineteenth century in order to retain political power. When the peasant revolt took place in 1894 the Korean king asked military assistance from China; the Peking government responded at once and announced that "the Middle Kingdom was merely following the traditional practice of protecting its tributary states." This official note was resented by Japan, which then sent troops to Korea under the pretext of protecting her legation, consulates, and business interests. These actions resulted in the Sino-Japanese war of 1894–95. When the war ended with Japan's victory, Korea's longstanding tributary relationship with China was ended.

Because of the tributary status to China which lasted for centuries, the Yi dynasty had no opportunity to develop an independent foreign policy; instead, it developed what is known as the *sadae-sasang,* the policy of reliance upon a big power as a safeguard of independence. The Yi rulers believed that China, as a big-brother nation, could protect Korea from any threat by non-Chinese states. After the Sino-Japanese war the ruling classes split into many factions, pro-Japanese, pro-Russian, pro-American, and pro-Chinese, and each group made efforts to obtain foreign support to preserve national independence. The result was the end of the Korean state itself.

THE ECONOMIC SYSTEM

The Land System and Its Nature.[10] The development of the land system during the Yi dynasty can be divided into four periods: the period of reestablishment of state ownership, or centralization, which was known as *kwadon-che* (1392–1600); the period of confusion as a result of the Japanese and Manchu invasions (1600–1767); the period of the beginning of the private land system (1767–1876); and the period of introduction of the new system of private land (1876–1910). Of the five hundred years of Yi rule, however, most land reform took place during the first century.

The first reforms were introduced as measures that would effect a situation substantially the same as that of the early period of the Koryo kingdom—centralization of the lands in the hands of the high government officials. All Kyonggi province was given to retainers as granted land; lands of the central government existed in all other provinces; and during the same era army lands also came into being. The revenues from those lands covered the expenditures of the central government and the armed forces.

Rokkwadon-che was also introduced. Under this system each local government official, military and civilian, received, in accordance with his rank, a certain amount of land with the right to collect taxes. The land was classified by soil quality into first- second- and third-class land; and the rate of taxation was determined by the percentage of the crops.

In 1898, during the fourth period, the Office of Land Surveying was established and made a survey of the public lands. In 1901, the Office of Land

Contract was installed and issued a land certification by which private landed property was legally guaranteed. This was the beginning of official recognition of private property in general (a modern concept) and of land in particular (Western capitalism).

During the Yi dynasty, as during the Koryo kingdom, the land theoretically belonged to the state, but in practice the king distributed it to his retainers as rewards for services. Under the systems of *kwa-don* and *rokkwa-don* the members of the new royal family and retainers became powerful landlords; the Confucian gentry replaced the Buddhist priesthood as landlords; and most government officials became landlords under the system of government-granted land in place of wages. Thus landed property once again became the economic foundation of the ruling class. At the same time, the economic and social status of the ruling and ruled classes was fixed by the Confucian code of absolute obedience.

As during the Koryo period, the *nongbon-juii* principle—priority of agriculture—was the main governmental economic policy. More production was encouraged. But improved farming methods were not introduced; hence no increased agricultural production resulted.

The land system of the Yi dynasty can be classified into seven different categories.[11]

1. *Sa-don.* The system of private land in the Yi dynasty is not to be understood in the modern sense, because the modern concept of private property was not introduced until the end of the nineteenth century. "Private land" meant merely land that the individual was allowed to use, not land that he could sell. Most private land was land granted by the king.

Four different kinds of private land existed: Kyonggi province was designated as *kwa-don,* from which government officials received land from the king. The highest group, including the members of the royal family and the *yangban* class, received one hundred fifty *gul;* the lowest received ten *gul* (a *gul* was a little more than one acre). *Kongshin-don* was land for retainers who took the side of Yi Sung-gai during the struggle for power. These retainers were divided further into groups. *Sapai-don* was land which the new dynasty designated for use (collection of taxes) by the former royal family, who became powerful landlords at the end of the Koryo period. Finally, *zik-don* was land granted to low-ranking government employees as a substitute for an annual salary. During the first two decades of the Yi dynasty, Kyonggi province was large enough for all claimants under the *kwa-don* system, but the rapid increase of government employees made it necessary to adopt a new land system. Under the *zik-don* system every government employee was entitled to the cultivation of land as compensation for his service.

2. *Konghai-don* was land whose revenue covered the expenses of the government, with exception of salary for employees.

No single national budgetary system, however, existed under one national treasury. Instead, each governmental department had its own sources of income, and this came from government land. Thus the *konghai-don* was subdivided into three divisions: palace land, for the maintenance of the royal family and the palace in the capital; land of the central government for the maintenance of the government buildings and miscellaneous expenses; and land of the local government, for expenses of the local administration.

Each department chief had freedom in dealing with the collection and expenditure of taxes. Most officials imposed excessive taxes on the peasant tenants who cultivated government land. Thus the officials emerged as de facto landlords, used public property for their own interest, and acted as rulers of the local people in defiance of the central government.

3. *Zei-don,* worship land. When Yi Sung-gai succeeded to the throne he bestowed a certain amount of land to the members of the royal family. The revenues from this land were used for the maintenance of the tombs of the founders of the Koryo dynasty and for worship ceremonies for the souls of the former kings. This ancestor worship of the former rulers was the result of Confucian influences. Yi Sung-gai used the ancestor-worship policy to pacify the aristocrats, still loyal to the Koryo dynasty.

4. *Zok-don,* king-cultivated land. Since the Koryo period the king supposedly demonstrated to the people how to cultivate the land according to physiocratic tenets of agriculture. The revenues from this land were used for the ceremonial worship of Heaven in the national shrine, performed by the king himself in thanksgiving for good crops.

Later some of the best *zok-don* lands became the private property of the royal family.

5. *Hak-don,* school land. During the Yi dynasty two school systems came

into being, public and private. Learning institutes became centers of Confucian learning because the civil service examination was based on the Confucian classics. The government granted land to the public schools to cover the expenses of teachers' salaries, buildings, and libraries.

The public school system consisted of the Sungkyun-kwan, the highest learning institute, situated in the capital with land of four hundred *gul;* second-ranking institutes, situated in each province, with ten *gul;* city and town institutes with seven *gul;* and county and district institutes with five *gul.* Usually the landless peasants cultivated the school lands as tenants of the teacher-landlords.

6. *Soowon-don,* private-school land. Some private schools received government financial aid in the form of land called *soowon-don.* The financial resources of the private schools depended on the contributions from the Confucian landed aristocrats, the *yangban.*

Following Confucian principles, many landed aristocrats donated land to private schools; thus *soowon* gradually became a powerful political institute of the ruling class.

An ascetic and formalistic doctrine practiced by the Chu Za sect became the principal study of Confucian students in the private schools. Kang Jiwoon, in his book *Recent Korean Political History,* said: "The doctrine of Chu Za, one of the Confucian sects, became a code of the political system of the absolute and bureaucratic Yi dynasty. The doctrine also was the basic principle of the daily life of the people. During the Silla and Koryo periods, Buddhist priests participated in politics but only on a minor scale. However, the Confucian scholars became a ruling class in the Yi Dynasty, and wielded real power."[12]

The institutes of the *soowon-don* became centers of the ruling class. They were supposed to be sacred learning institutions; instead, they became nests of academic cliques and political factions; and they were also used as bases for rascals who exploited the commoners in the country. This practice lasted three hundred years, subverting the *soowon* system. Most Confucian intellectuals were the products of this system. Cliques caused bloody factional fights and national disunity for generations.

The vast *soowon-don* were under the management of the Confucian landed aristocrats; slaves and landless peasants cultivated the lands. The relationship of the aristocrats and the cultivators was that of landlords and tenants, in conformity with the Confucian doctrine of inequality.

When the central authority disintegrated after the Japanese and Manchu invasions, *soowon* aristocrats became the local rulers, collected taxes from the peasants, and reduced many commoners who could not pay their debts to slaves.

7. *Nongjang-che,* the manorial system. The aristocrats increased their land bestowed by the king through confiscation of land from Buddhist temples and rebellious leaders, through purchase, and through reclamation of waste land. The manors thus created existed throughout the country but primarily in the southern part. They were protected by the central government to prevent the rise of local power.

The owners of *nongjang-don* were central bureaucrats who had become absentee landlords, most of them living in the capital. They appointed lower government agents as supervisors of the land. The supervisors became direct masters over the slave cultivators of the land. Thus the slave groups were under the direct rule of neither the local feudal lords nor the central landlords.

The Tax System. No systematic, unified national tax system existed during the Yi dynasty. The rules and types of taxation changed depending on who was in power. Only two facts remained: land and peasantry were the bases of taxation; the purpose of taxation was to meet the needs of the rulers, not of the people.

The tax system can be divided into two periods: the period from 1392 to 1592, just before the Japanese invasion, and the period from 1593 to the end of the nineteenth century, when the monetary system was introduced.

During the first two hundred years of the Yi regime, three kinds of taxes existed: the land tax, the head tax, and the tributary tax. The land tax constituted a rent because in theory the land was publicly owned; the tax consisted of a share of the crops. The head of each government department exercised independent authority according to its need to impose and to collect taxes. The amount and rate of taxes therefore were different from one department to another. It is said that the general rate of land tax was about 70 percent of the total crop. The head tax was imposed on every member of the family aged sixteen to sixty. The tributary tax was assessed to the districts or sections where the peasant lived, on the ground that the local product, rice for example, was necessary for the government and, presumably, the military. The total of the three types of taxes amounted to well over 80 percent of the total harvest of the peasant.

The tax system was revised when the Japanese invaded Korea in 1592. Originating as a war tax, it was continued for the next three hundred years. Five different types of taxes were collected from the people under this system.[13]

The Handicraft Industry. Under the doctrine of *nongbon-juii* (physiocracy), agriculture was the basic economic wealth. The handicraft industry held a subordinate position in economics in terms of total output and the number of laborers employed. A large segment of the industry was under the control of the central government, and most of it was established in or near the capital. The supply of raw materials and the volume of production were controlled by the Department of Industry.

Even in the private sector of handicraft industry the output was regulated by the government, and overproduction was punishable. The status of the industrial worker was lower than that of the peasant. About one-half of all industrial workers were employed in the government-owned establishments in the capital and the provinces.[14] More than thirty types of industries were in operation.

The government-controlled industries produced consumer goods and luxury articles for the ruling class, not for the general public. The most important handicraft industries in the capital were silk spinning, metal working, and pottery. The silk-spinning industry produced beautiful clothing materials for the royal family and high government officials; the metal-working industry manufactured general kitchen utensils, decorative ornaments, and jewelry. The pottery workers were famous for their high technical skill, especially in decoration. In addition to these industries, armament factories operated in the capital under the supervision of military officials of the government.

The privately controlled industries flourished mostly in the rural communities. Most of them were family centered and the principal consumers were the members of the village or town. Simple agricultural tools like hoes, sickles, hatchets, and saws were manufactured by the village blacksmith. Kitchen utensils and home furniture were made by special artisans. Almost every family made its own clothing materials—woven hemp, cotton, and silk.

The family-centered, primitive type of "self-sustaining" rural industry had not improved since unification of the country in the seventh century. According to the *Hanguk-chi*, "Korea still was the country of family economy, and the idea of division of labor was entirely lacking. All essential articles for daily living were made by the members of the family. The housewife, daughters, and female servants did the spinning, dyeing, and sewing; the male members engaged in farming, carpentry, stone masonry, and gathering firewood. All this activity was assigned by the head of the family, that is, the oldest male, usually the grandfather or father. The family also made wine and simple furniture, and agricultural tools for family consumption."[15]

Industry stagnated because of government policy. The Yi regime pressed most of the trained laborers who produced the beautiful pottery into domestic service for the wealthy. It was the official policy to keep technical skills secret and controlled by the government in order to prevent the techniques from spreading to the general public. Hence nobody was easily able to learn the methods of making Koryo pottery. In later days, neither the government nor the people were able to preserve the techniques of Koryo pottery. Korea never recovered the originality of the Koryo pottery baking technique.

The technique of making blue bricks was also lost. By government order blue-brick roofs were used only for the palace and certain temples; the general public was not allowed to use them. Therefore only a few skilled laborers knew the technique, and they were strictly watched by the government. The secret of the technique was not passed on to posterity.

The government collected heavy taxes from persons who invented new techniques. A Buddhist priest learned how to manufacture writing paper, but soon was forced to stop making it because of excessive taxes. A farmer in South Chulla province learned how to raise mandarin oranges, but he had to destroy his mandarin trees when government taxes became too oppressive.

In addition to government restrictions, the traditional rigid social setting hampered progress. Many gifted potential technicians were barred from active participation in industry.

Business. During the Yi dynasty commerce and business[16] were almost entirely government controlled. "Free enterprise" in the modern sense did not exist, but some small-scale private trade flourished, such as that of peddlers, fabric and leather merchants, and small products of foreign trade. Even many of these served merely as brokers between government officials and the public.

In the traditional Confucian social hierarchy, merchants occupied the lowest position; their profession was considered disgraceful because merchants sought profits, which was contradictory to Confucian ethics.

The land-owning Confucian aristocrats could purchase lucrative government positions. After the late part of the eighteenth century, government officials began to accumulate wealth. During the autumn they bought grain cheaply from the peasants and stored it in public warehouses until the spring when the price of grain went up. Business establishments and activities centered in the urban area, especially in the capital; most market commodities consisted of consumer goods, including food and clothing for the royal family and government officials.

The merchants were either *zasang* ("sitdown merchants"), *haengsang* (peddlers), or *kaik-ju* (specialized private shopkeepers under government supervision).

The government established shops in the national and provincial capitals and appointed employees, called *zasang*. They did business in a store and did not travel from one place to another. In the beginning there were about forty stores in the national capital on Chongno Street, but this number dropped to six at the end of the Yi dynasty. Each store carried one specialty item under the supervision of the government. For example, one carried woven fabrics such as silk, cotton and hemp; another marine products or kitchen utensils. The manager of a store usually assembled the tributary merchandise for China under government instruction. The *zasang* organized a society vaguely corresponding to a guild of medieval Europe; but it was a semi-governmental organ for advancing the ruler's interests. Many *zasang* later became moneylenders.

Haengsang (peddlers) were the traveling merchants.[17] They carried small articles such as thread, needles, dyestuff, and simple woven fabrics wrapped in a bundle on their backs, or they used the coolie-rack burden-carrier employed for centuries by the peasants. Their main articles were kitchen utensils, porcelain, and earthenware dishes. The history of the *haengsang* is almost as old as Korean history; it goes back to the period of the Three Kingdoms. The peddlers were the strongest private business group in the country. As a means of protecting their interests they organized a business association, electing a national chairman and provincial and district officials. If a member violated the rules of the association, the officials had the authority to expel him. The membership of the association is estimated to have been one million at its peak.

On many occasions the peddlers, as individuals or as a group, participated in wars. During the Manchu invasion in the seventeenth century, more than five hundred peddlers volunteered to transport food and weapons to the front lines. And when in 1811 the Hong Kyong-nai revolt occurred in the northern provinces, the king mobilized one thousand strong peddlers as an auxiliary to the regular armed forces; they successfully defended the government front against the rebels. When the French expeditionary fleet attempted to land on the island of Kanghwa in 1866 under the pretext of protecting her Catholic missions, the king sent a thousand peddlers to the island along with the regular army; they prevented the French from landing.

In 1882 the government provided protection, relief, and supervision but also control and taxation of the members of the peddlers' association, which soon was integrated into the Department of Commerce. After integration its political activities became reactionary; for example, when the 1894 peasant revolt occurred, thousands of peddlers took the side of the government and helped suppress the rebels; and in the same year when the liberal Independence Club, led by the American educated Dr. Shu Chai-pil, held a mass protest meeting in the capital against official corruption, the government mobilized the peddlers, who forcibly dissolved the meeting.

The business of the peddlers included the delivery of merchandise to the peasant families, who otherwise would have had to go to distant markets. Thus the peddlers became well acquainted with the peasants' needs. The peddlers made good profits and accumulated cash, which was a precondition for their later role as moneylenders. When the government adopted a monetary system in the middle of the nineteenth century, many peddlers became moneylenders for the needy peasants, who had to pay taxes with borrowed money or with the money they earned by selling rice. Since most of the capital accumulated by peddlers was used for lending rather than as investment for building up commerce or industry, no native independent business class arose during the Yi dynasty.

Kaik-ju were the private merchants who traded in general woven materials, animal skins, leather, and writing paper. They had small shops in the capital and other cities. The shops were open to the public, but management and trading were government supervised. *Yo-kak* was the name for the marine and dry goods merchants; they traded in salt, fish, seaweeds, rice, beans, millet, tobacco, and fruits for the general public. Some of them engaged privately in foreign trade, but the number was very limited because the government controlled foreign trade. *Gook-wan* were the brokers between sellers and buyers. They acted particularly as go-betweens on behalf of the other two groups. Some of the more successful merchants of these groups also became moneylenders.

Lending. Two types of lending establishments existed during the Yi dynasty, one government controlled and the other private. The working capital of the lenders was grain or currency. The lenders collected from 20 to 50 percent interest, usually from the peasants; and they were not interested in capital investment of their profits for the improvement of agricultural production or for modernization of industry. A great part of the surplus capital was used to bribe officials and to buy government positions. H. B. Hulbert, former educator and long a resident in Korea, writes: "Public offices were bought and sold like any other goods. There was a regular schedule of the price of offices, ranging from fifty thousand won for a provincial governorship to five hundred won for a small magistrate's position."[18] In another place he stated: "The power of money began to make itself felt, and the size of the purse came to figure more prominently in the question of eligibility of office."[19]

The government got into the lending business by establishing grain warehouses. The *Hanguk-chi* reported that the first grain storehouse was established at the end of the sixteenth century.[20] After the withdrawal of the Japanese army from the peninsula in 1592, the Korean government began to accumulate grain as a military food supply; one grain store was established in each local administrative unit, the *hyang*. The local government officials were in charge of the grain stores. To prevent loss of the grains by rotting during indefinite storage, the government loaned one-half of the grains to the peasants, charging 10 percent annual interest; the local officials were then given the right to collect the loaned grain from the peasants in autumn.

In 1789 the government established the Office of Public Loan; the legal interest rates were 10 percent for a monthly loan, 50 percent for an annual loan, and 100 percent for loans more than one year. The penalties for nonpayment of a loan at the fixed time were very severe; the debtor himself and his family including relatives were subject to punishment; sometimes they were made public slaves.[21]

Many local officials took advantage of the grain loan system. During the nineteenth century more than 80 percent of the grain in local warehouses was used for loans to peasants, and less than 20 percent went for military and relief purposes at times of flood or drought. As the grain loan percentage increased, the local officials had a chance to get rich, because they could put the surplus profits of the loans in their pockets after payment of the official percentage to the central government.

To correct this malpractice, the government reorganized the local warehouse system. An autonomous district governing body was formed for the management of the warehouse, and the local officials were removed from the management. Construction of new grain warehouses and maintenance fees for both old and new warehouses were the concern of the district; and the collected grain was to be used exclusively for public relief during calamities as well as for loans to needy peasants during spring.

However, the new plan did not work out for the benefit of the peasants in the end. The autonomous body was composed of local aristocrats, the peasants being barred from management of the warehouse. And worse, the peasants were required to contribute "voluntary" labor for the new warehouse construction. The rate of interest for loans remained as before. The local officials, although barred from management of the warehouses, were in charge of collecting taxes. Most of them collected taxes two or three times. The tax collectors usually stored "their" rice in the local warehouse until next spring, and loaned rice to the needy peasants at high interests until autumn.

Three types of persons engaged in the private lending business: the peddlers, the landlords, and the Japanese. The first group was discussed earlier. The second group, the landlords, purchased all available surplus grain in the autumn and stored it in their private warehouses together with their share crops or rent in kind, which were collected from the tenants. The tenants' food supplies usually lasted for five or six months after the harvest; after that they had to borrow money or grain from their landlords until the next crop. In spring the price of grain went up from 30 to 50 percent above that in autumn, and the interest rate of loaned money went up accordingly.

The Japanese lending business—money loans and pawnage—began after the commercial treaty between Korea and Japan in 1876. The capital city was the main center of the Japanese lending business. As one Japanese reported, Japanese pawnshops lined Seoul Street "like flies in the month of May."[22] Many Japanese also established pawnshops in the harbors and cities throughout the country. To compete with the native moneylenders, the Japanese, at the beginning at least, charged lower interest rates and also offered easy long-term repayment on their loans; they accepted real estate and personal articles (jewelry) as collateral for cash loans. From the late part of the nineteenth century many small native landholders (independent peasants) began to mortgage their lands and houses to pay their debts. Most of them borrowed money from Japanese moneylenders. As a result native moneylenders were forced out of business. Japanese moneylenders gradually became landlords, because many peasants could not repay their loans and were forced to give up their land and became tenants.

THE SOCIAL STRUCTURE

During the Yi dynasty two social groups existed: members of the royal family and Confucian *yangban* on one hand, and the vast underprivileged masses of peasants, handicraft laborers, and slaves on the other. Under Confucian ethical principles, each person's social status was fixed by his occupation; the scholar was on the top, followed by farmer, artisan, and merchant.

In the course of the dynasty's five-hundred-year rule, the line of demarcation between the ruler and ruled became even more sharply drawn. When Yi Sung-gai came to power in 1392, he had to depend heavily on the Confucian literati for the administration of the new regime, because they were the only group with the necessary know-how in politics. After Yi became king he confiscated all lands of the opposition leaders and the Buddhist temples and redistributed them to the literati. This political favoritism led to a concentration of land in the hands of the newly privileged class, and the literati thus joined the group of powerful landlords.

Confucianism, as a state creed, blocked progress, preserved the established social order, and perpetuated the literati's position of power. The concentration of power and wealth in the hands of a small privileged clique fostered the development of an authoritarian regime, because the clique's interests ran counter to those of the underprivileged masses. As a result the Yi dynasty ruled without the support of the masses.

The ruling group consisted of the royal family and the Confucian aristocrats (*yangban*); the latter were divided into the *munkwan* (civilian) and the *mookwan* (military). The social status of the *munkwan* was higher than that of the *mookwan* because of the Confucian traditional concept of the civilian supremacy over the military, and because of the lack of administrative experience of the military men.

The title of *yangban* was bestowed by the king and could be inherited. Civilian and military retainers who helped in establishing the Yi dynasty entered the *yangban* class; later the title also was given to those who passed the state civil service examination. When the Yi dynasty declined the same title was often sold to landlords.

The central *yangban* held the most important government positions in the central government. They established their family residences in the capital. The local *yangban* had their legal residence in the local urban areas and were not allowed to establish their homes in the capital. The illegitimate offspring of a class member and their concubines were excluded from the *yangban* class and not entitled to hold high public office or to inherit fortune or title from their fathers. Most *jungin* (the illegitimate children of the *yangban*) were employed as technical officials such as government interpreters, auditors, and inspectors, which were regarded as lower-ranking positions. As described later, some *jungin* participated in the peasant rebellion against the ruling class. Some of them, like Song Byong-jun, became traitors by advancing the idea of Japanese annexation of Korea at the beginning of the twentieth century.

For public identification the *yangban* wore different garments, hats, and shoes. Their residential sections were segregated from those of the commoners. In the capital the southern and northern section of the city were reserved for them, and in the provincial cities the inner sections of the castles were usually their residences. Intermarriage betweeen the *yangban* and commoners was prohibited.

FACTIONALISM

The ruling class was characterized by factionalism based on southern versus northern provincialism, on fights over the division of landed property, and on the split between traditional Confucianism and the "progressive" Chu Za doctrine.

Yi Sung-gai was a northerner by birth. When he became the first king of the dynasty, he appointed many southerners to important central government positions, but he excluded northerners from such positions. The king regarded the northerners as troublemakers and rebels and eliminated them from the central *yangban*. This practice more or less continued during the whole period of the Yi dynasty. This meant that the southern *yangban* became the core of the ruling class for more than five hundred years. Provincialism in politics did not recede until the Japanese took over Korea; it then became subordinated to Korean nationalism.

The conflict of landed interests among the *yangban* was another basis of factionalism.[23] Under the first and second land reform the central *yangban* emerged as powerful landlords. At the beginning of the sixteenth century, however, no further lands were available for those who passed the civil service examinations. In addition, the families of the central *yangban* doubled in size in a century, mainly because most of them had concubines and a number of illegitimate children who depended on the father's income. Furthermore, the class as a whole became more extravagant and needed more land.

They were divided between the latecomer "have-nots" and the older propertied *yangban*. Factional disputes broke out between the two groups. The winners of the struggle took all property of the losers, and most of the losers were exterminated.

The third basis of factional disputes was the differences between Confucianism and the Chu Za doctrine. A minority of the *yangban* families of the central government claimed they were the orthodox believers of Confucianism, and accused the other faction of heresy. The Chu Za adherents emphasized the idea of "purity" in politics and economics on the one hand and of the attainment of knowledge through reason on the other. This school was represented by the younger and more progressive elements of the local *yangban* families. No fundamentally different political ideologies divided these two groups, however, because both believed in Confucianism and were loyal to the king.

The history of factional dispute has two stages:[24] the period of Sahwa (Confucianism versus Chu Za) from 1498 to 1560; and the period of Tangzang (dispute among the parties) from 1568 to the end of the nineteenth century.

During the sixty-two years of the first stage, four disputes took place. One characteristic of the period was that the king played an important part in it. Usually the group siding with the king won in the fight. Each dispute was named after the calendar year; for example, the first one was called Muoo Sahwa because it happened in the year of Muoo.

The Muoo Sahwa of 1498. Two political factions competed with each other at the court of autocratic King Yonsan-gun: one was headed by Yu Za-kwang, representing the orthodox Confucian group; the other by Kim Jong-zik, representing the Chu Za group, which was then in power. Two incidents became immediate causes for conflict. One was brought about by Kim Jong-zik's criticism of King Seijong, Yonsan-gun's grandfather, for having succeeded to the throne by a coup d'etat. The other incident resulted from an accusation by Kim Il-son, a follower of the Kim Jong-zik faction, of immoral conduct by the magnate of Chulla province, a member of the other faction. The king condemned Kim Jong-zik as a traitor and persecuted his followers. More than one hundred prominent scholars who believed in the

Chu Za doctrine were executed and their properties redistributed to the old guard.

The Kapza Sahwa of 1504. Factional dispute continued between the old guard and the progressive wing even after the large-scale persecution of the latter. Yonsan-gun was still the king, and this time the old guard spread a story accusing the progressive leaders of having participated in a plot to kill the king's mother. Yonsan-gun used the opportunity to execute or exile opposition leaders and their families.

The Kimmyo Sahwa of 1519. After King Yonsan-gun's death, Jung-jong succeeded to the throne and attempted to end the factional disputes. He appointed Cho Kwang-zo, a scholar of the Chu Za school and a leader of the progressive group, as prime minister. Cho formulated three new policies:[25] first, adoption of a new civil service system by which to select all local government officials, including the governors of the provinces, heads of the counties, and chiefs of districts; second, abolishment of the title of Chungnan-Kongshin that had been gained by services at the time of Jung-jong's succession to the throne, and confiscation of the land of the Chungnan-Kongshin; and last, establishment of Chu Za institutes in each local district in the country.

The old guard organized itself into a party to contest the power of the progressive group. This was the first time that factional dispute was waged by more or less organized party forces. The old guard engaged in a propaganda campaign against the progressive group, accusing the progressive group of planning to depose King Jung-jong and make Cho Kwang-zo the king. King Jung-jong ordered the execution of Cho Kwang-zo and the banishment of progressive leaders to remote islands. The old guard returned to power.

The Ulsa Sahwa of 1545. The Ulsa Sahwa was a bid for power by the relatives of the king's mother.[26] The old guard was in power but divided into two factions, the Nam-sim faction and the Kim faction. The first wife of Jung-jong did not produce a male heir, but his second and third wife each bore a male child. When Jung-jong died, In-jong, the son of the second wife, succeeded to the throne but died after only eight months, in 1544. Thereupon, Myong-jong, the son of Jung-jong's third wife, became king. Jung-jong's second and third wives each had a brother; Yun Im was the brother of the second wife and Yun Woon-hyung was the brother of the third. Both were ambitious politicians and each formed his own political group; Yun Im's group was known as the Dai-yun faction and Yun Woon-hyung's group as the So-yun faction. The old-guard Nam-sim faction joined the So-yun group, and the Kim faction joined the Dai-yun group.

When In-jong (the son of Jung-jong's second wife) succeeded to the throne, the Dai-yun group had an opportunity to exert power by influencing the young king's mother.

The sudden death of In-jong and the succession of Myong-jong (son of Jung-jong's third wife) led to a new dispute between the Dai-yun and the So-yun groups. As in the case of In-jong's reign, the new king, Myong-jong, was still a young boy, unable to rule the country and dependent on his mother. This meant that the So-yun group headed by Yun Woon-hyung, could challenge the supremacy of the Dai-yun in power. More than one hundred Dai-yun leaders were executed or exiled, and the old guard once again returned to power.

The second stage of factional war between the parties took place during the Tang-zang period. A brief historical background of the Tang-zang might be necessary to describe this phase, which lasted more than three hundred years.

The influence of Yun Woon-hyung, head of the So-yun faction, over palace affairs ended when his sister (mother of King Myong-jong) died in 1568. Sim Ui-kyun, who was the brother-in-law of Myong-jong, became a spokesman of the old guard, representing the So-yun faction as well as the traditional Confucian scholars.

The progressive group also found a new leader, Kim Hyo-woon, a nationally known writer who was appointed minister of state. He enjoyed the support of the young and progressive elements of the *yangban* groups. Kim quarreled with Sim, the opposition leader, and factional war broke out once again. The *yangban,* central and local, conservative and progressive, were divided into two groups, siding with Kim or Sim. Kim's faction was called Tong-in men of the East, because he lived in the eastern section of the capital; Sim's faction was known as Sei-in men of the West, because his residence was in the western section. This division was the beginning of the Tong-in and Sei-in party war.

Both party leaders realized that the conventional political tactics which their predecessors had employed—personal accusations and plots—were no longer effective; they organized "political parties" of like-minded individuals. In the past, even when the members of one faction had won a power contest, they could not hold it long because they had no organized body; both Kim and Sim believed that a party victory would bring political stability as well as economic security.

The Era of the Tong-in (1575–1623). In 1568 hostility between the two opposition leaders moved from inside the court to large-scale party campaigns outside the court. In 1575 King Son-zo asked Yi Yul-gok, a scholar respected by both party leaders, to arbitrate between Tong-in and Sei-in. Yi Yul-gok attempted to solve the problems by removing both Kim Hyo-woon and Sim Ui-kyun from the central government. Kim was sent to Kyonghung as the head of the district in the northwestern section of the peninsula, an area remote from the capital. Sim was appointed mayor of Kaesong, about fifty miles from the capital. Kim's appointment was condemned by the Tong-in party as constituting exile from the capital, for he could not get in touch with his followers who resided in Seoul. Sim's appointment was considered political favoritism because he was sent only twenty miles from his followers. As a result of this criticism, Yi sent Kim to Kangwoon province and Sim to Chulla province.

Yi Yul-gok's arbitration failed because Kim's Tong-in party became stronger than the Sei-in party and was ready to take over political power from their opponents without compromise. Furthermore, the sudden death of Yi in 1584 brought the end of the king's arbitration policy; the era of the Tong-in faction began.[27]

The Tong-in came to power by a coup d'etat and expelled all Sei-in leaders from the central government. The Tong-in administration gradually became reactionary.

After the death of Kim Hyo-woon, two individuals, Woo Wong-don and Yi Hwal, fought for leadership of the party. Woo's supporters were called Nam-in because they lived in the southern section of the capital; Yi's followers were known as Buk-in, because their residences were in the northern section. Yi submitted to the king written accusations against the Nam-in leaders; the king dismissed Woo and his followers and replaced them with Yi's men. Yi's faction stayed in power until succession to the throne became the subject of a controversy among party leaders.

King Son-zo had three sons; he wished his second son to succeed to the throne because he believed that the first son was not qualified. The king's decision was supported by Chung In-hong, one of the leaders of the inner-factional groups of Yi's party, the Buk-in faction. A few years later, as a result of another controversy, the king expelled Chung In-hong, and the New Yong-kyong clique came into power. These events caused the fall of the Tong-in party.

The Coalition of the Sei-Nam Factions (1623–80). King Son-zo died in 1609 and his second son, Kwanghai-gun, became king.[28] He ousted all members of the New Yong-kyong clique from the court and called Chung In-hong in for the formation of a new administration.

The general public condemned the Buk-in faction in power on the ground that their influence was responsible for certain cruel punishments of the king. The Sei-in, who had been out of power for more than thirty years, proposed uniting with the Nam-in group (which also had been ousted by the Buk-in group) to overthrow King Kwanghai-gun and the Buk-in.

The Era of Sei-in (1680–1864). The Nam-in party lost power as the result of an abortive plot to assassinate King Suk-jong. The king learned of the plot through the Sei-in and executed the two principal plotters; he also ordered banishment of most Nam-in party leaders. The Nam-in party never recovered its strength.

King Suk-jong had no son by his first wife. A boy was born by his second wife (a concubine), but this child, according to Confucian ethics, was considered illegitimate. The king wanted to make this son the crown prince, and a group within the Sei-in party known as the So-ron sided with the king; another group within the party called No-ron opposed the king. Thus the party was split into two factions. Cabinets changed continually from one faction to another during the Suk-jong period.

Political stability was more or less achieved when Yung-zo, a well-read and able ruler, became king in 1724. He endeavored to stamp out factionalism by purging extremists from the government. He pronounced the principle of balance of power as the basis for the formation of a new government. This principle was implemented by the establishment of a coalition government composed of the moderate leaders of both factions in the Sei-in party.

The balance of power policy, however, came to an early end in 1728 when the ousted extremists, headed by the So-ron group of the Sei-in party, attempted to seize power by armed revolt. The king managed to put down the rebellion and expelled all members of the So-ron group from the government. The No-ron group of the Sei-in party became the government party until 1864.

Daewon-gun (1864–74). In 1864 Daewon-gun became regent because the crown prince was a minor. The regent soon set himself up as a dictator and ruled for ten years. He expelled the No-ron group, which had been in power for more than a century, eliminated traditional political interference by the female line of the royal family in palace affairs (such as succession to the throne and royal marriages), and adopted isolationism as his foreign policy by closing the door to foreign countries, excluding trade even with China and Japan.

As internal political reforms,[29] he introduced equal opportunity to individuals of all political groups—So-ron, No-ron, Nam-in, and Buk-in—taking all men of talent into government service. He abolished the central-government school-financing system by encouraging private and local self-supporting schools. He also transferred the administrative authority to a new executive cabinet and reorganized the land and tax systems.

Daewon-gun was determined to stamp out factional warfare between the aristocrats and the royal family. He concentrated power in his hands as the regent and cleaned up all factional influences in the government. He then announced his policy of "equal opportunity," hoping in this way to eliminate the danger of a one-party political monopoly.

Adoption of a self-supporting school system in place of the governmental financed system was a long-range policy to remedy factionalism. The Confucian learning institutions produced Confucian scholars who played an important role in making policy as well as in palace affairs, especially in matters of throne succession and royal marriages and divorces. Any disagreement on these issues among the scholars intensified factional strife between the different political groups because any issue could be considered from the point of view of how it agreed with Confucian teachings or ethics. Daewon-gun thought that government-financed Confucian institutions had served as sources of factionalism, and that decentralization of the educational system would reduce the influence of the scholars on national policy and palace affairs. Elimination of the scholars' influences on national politics would eventually reduce factionalism among the aristocrats.

Daewon-gun established an executive cabinet which was controlled by himself; he chose the government officials and directed national policies. No individual or political group could challenge his power. According to his readjustment of the land and tax system, the lands which had been granted to the Confucian institutions by the government were now transferred to the local and private institutions; and in the meantime the government imposed taxes on the properties of the *yangban*.

Daewon-gun's new programs, however, did not succeed, because his main concern was to exterminate factionalism rather than to introduce a new two-party system based on different policies and ideologies. His principle of equal opportunity in politics was workable so long as no one group was strong enough to overthrow all other groups. The decentralization of the Confucian institutions did not, of course, introduce a new political ideology, because the same Confucian classics were taught by the same teachers in the private and local institutions. By the establishment of the executive council, Daewon-gun himself acted as a generalissimo, appointing the members of the cabinet from among his henchmen.

The new land and tax system did not release the commoners from the heavy burden of taxes. On the contrary, Daewon-gun imposed more taxes. He also demanded compulsory labor service from the peasants to reconstruct the Kyongbok palace, which had been destroyed during the Japanese invasion in 1592.

The rise of new factions caused Daewon-gun's sudden downfall in 1874; a coalition between the Min family (the queen's family) and the No-ron clique under the leadership of the queen forced Daewon-gun to resign; this was the end of a strong one-man rule.

THE CONCEPT OF RELIANCE UPON A BIG POWER (SADAE-SASANG)

During the period of the Silla and Yi dynasties, Korea's foreign policy was based on the concept of reliance on a big power (the principle of *sadae-sasang*) as a safeguard of independence. This policy was adopted on the assumption that the big power would then not interfere in Korea's domestic affairs. Korea acknowledged China as superior in land, wisdom, and culture. China treated Korea as a "civilized tributary state," and until the end of the nineteenth century based the relationship on the Confucian principle of *li*—proper conduct between superior and inferior.

From the beginning of the Yi dynasty, the policy of reliance meant, more specifically, a pro-Ming or a pro-Ching policy. It became the practice for each new ruler of the Yi dynasty to seek investiture of his authority by the emperor of China. The old name of Chosun was revived by a Ming emperor as the official name for Korea.

During the fourteenth century, on urging from the Ming emperor the Korean court had Confucianism substituted for Buddhism as the new state ideology and established a state-supported Confucian learning institute in the new capital of Seoul. The central and local administrations were reorganized on the Ming dynasty model, and the Ming criminal code was introduced. The relationship between the Yi dynsty and the Ming dynasty was looked upon as one of father and son according to Confucian ethics; later, during the Ching dynasty, the relationship was significantly changed to that of older and younger brother.

The official Chinese view on the status of Korea was expressed by the Chinese envoy, who said that "because our Imperial Master has confidence in the devotion and allegiance of the Eastern Kingdom (Chosun) we regard you as different from all other states."[30] The official attitude of Korea toward China was expressed by King Yi Sung-gai, who stated, "Our little kingdom may well serve as fence and wall and still do grace to the wide and limitless favor of the Emperor."[31]

The fact that the Korean king annually sent a good-will tributary envoy to the Chinese emperor illustrated the nature of the relations between two countries. During the earlier period of the Yi dynasty, custom called for one annual presentation of all the tribute due for the year, but after the first part of the eighteenth century tributary missions took place three or four times a year, counting the missions of special envoys on occasions such as that of the emperors' birthdays, the beginning of the new year, and the accession to the throne of new rulers. The number of persons participating in a mission, the articles of tribute, the ceremonies for presentation, and the routes of the mission were fixed by the Chinese government. The mission was to be composed of not more than one hundred persons and was to be headed either by the king himself or his special envoy. The mission had to come by way of the city of Feng-wang and then to Mukden through Shanhaikwan.[32] The tribute had to be composed of one hundred *picul* of rice, two hundred *picul* of white silk, one hundred *picul* of red silk, one hundred *picul* of blue silk, three hundred *picul* of seal skins, five thousand rolls of paper, and ten swords. Only twenty persons of the hundred were permitted to enter the Chinese capital; the rest waited at coastal ports. During the presentation ceremony the Chinese emperor might, or might not, ask the envoys to seat themselves in the audience. A dinner was usually given by the emperor before the mission left the capital, and on this occasion the emperor bestowed personal gifts on the Chosun king which sometimes exceeded in value those of the tribute. The mission also received the imperial calendar for the coming year.

The tributary missions were allowed to bring merchandise other than the tribute for trade, and they were given permission to sell their merchandise to the public within a fixed time, which was usually three to five days. The mission members were also allowed to purchase Chinese goods from government officials.

The Chinese emperor, in turn, annually sent a mission to Korea. This "pay back mission" was given a royal reception, and the king welcomed the mission in person. A special building was erected for its reception, and a state banquet was given. Usually the Chinese mission brought merchandise worth more than the tribute of the Korean mission, both in value and quantity. Thus from the Chinese point of view the tributary system served as a symbol of political prestige of the emperor and as a sign of economic aid to the vassal state. This system encouraged the native ruling class to remain in the Chinese sphere of influence. From the Korean point of view, the tributary mission was an official act of the Yi dynasty acknowledging the superiority of China in the Confucian family of nations.

Split of the Sadae-sasang: Pro-Chinese and Pro-Japanese (1876–1894). In 1876, under Japanese pressure, the self-imposed national isolation was broken, and Korea concluded a commercial treaty with Japan. In the following ten years Korea also concluded treaties with Western powers, including the United States, Great Britain, Germany, France, and Russia. The Chinese government consented to these treaties. At the same time, native Confucian conservatism was challenged by progressive political forces influenced by Western ideologies. Young and progressive leaders, inspired by the rapid rise of Japan after the Meiji Restoration in 1868, organized a new party, known as the Reform party. The history of this party goes back to 1881, when a group of young people went to Japan to study the rapid modernization there. They were impressed by the modernization of the Japanese military in terms of organization, training, and production of weapons. Upon their return from Japan, they recommended to the king, among many other things, a military reorganization program on the Japanese model. The king invited a Japanese military official, Horimoto, who was then a military attache to the Japanese Embassy in Seoul, to act as instructor at the Korean Military Academy. He was assigned to train one hundred Korean officials from *yangban* families.

Under the military reorganization program more than one thousand soldiers were discharged without being given a reason. The discharge aroused anti-Japanese feelings among the veterans and the pro-Chinese clique. They accused the progressives of plotting to gain political power. In 1882 the veterans led an armed revolt. More than ten government officials were assassinated by the rebels; the Japanese consulate building was burned to the ground, and the Japanese military instructor was killed by the rebels. Japan was forced to withdraw her consular staff from Seoul.

A few months later, Japan sent troops to the port of Inchun under General Takahashi; it also sent a new envoy to Seoul, who lodged a strong protest and demanded an indemnity for the consulate from the Korean government. Under Japanese pressure a new commercial treaty was signed, by which the Japanese government was given extraterritorial rights, the right to establish businesses in the newly opened Korean ports, and 650 thousand won of cash payment for reconstruction of the Japanese consulate. The Korean government also agreed to send "the king's personal apology mission" to the Japanese emperor.[33]

The mission was composed of five progressive leaders. After they discharged their duty, they remained in Japan and began to organize the Reform party as an opposition party to the conservative party, which was in power. This new political movement was supported by the Japanese government and funds were advanced by the Yokohama Specie Bank.[34] The newly appointed Japanese minister in Seoul, Takezoe, was given authority to supervise and aid the Reform party.

In 1884 an opportunity for a political coup d'etat by the Reform party presented itself when some of the Chinese troops in Seoul returned to the mainland because of the war with France over Tong-king. This meant that China would not be in a position to aid the conservatives in a political crisis. The Japanese minister in Seoul, after an audience with the king, stated that "the Japanese government would be happy to see Korea assert her real independence according to international law";[35] he also talked of the injustice of present Chinese policies that treated Korea as a vassal state.

On December 4, 1884, a Japanese-inspired coup d'etat occurred which took advantage of the ceremony opening the Bureau of the Post Office in Seoul. Park Young-ho, former head of the king's apology mission to the Japanese emperor, directed the coup; as soon as the ceremony was over the Reform party members rushed to the royal palace, seized the king, and pressured him into asking the Japanese minister to protect him. The minister surrounded the palace with troops; the rebels issued orders in the king's name, and summoned the members of the conservative clique. When the six cabinet ministers arrived they were executed. A new cabinet was formed by the leaders of the Reform party; three ministers were former members of the king's apology mission.

The cabinet issued a fifteen-point program,[36] which can be summed up into the following categories: (a) Rejection of the traditional *sadae-sasang* policy and restoration of national independence. "Traditional *sadae-sasang*" meant the tributary relation to China. The cabinet members were determined to break this and to establish a sovereign independent state like Japan. (b)

Abolition of the feudalistic social structure and practice of the principles of inequality. This meant abolition of the feudalistic political ideology (Confucian creed of the state), of social settings, and of class relations between individuals. Instead, they advocated human equality before the law and equal opportunity for all in access to government position according to individual ability. (c) Liquidation of the feudalistic economic system and adoption of the capitalistic economic system. This meant cessation of government control of the economy in land, industry, and trade; they proposed a new tax system and a competitive free enterprise economy like that of the Western states. (d) Reorganization of the central administration, the executive. They proposed a strong executive based on executive supremacy over the legislative and judicial branches. Only six departments were to be established. They demanded that the departments of finance and interior be given authority in dealing with domestic reform and reorganization. (e) Reorganization of the military and police forces.

The reform program represented the revolutionary principles of the Western-oriented middle class. The native progressive elements, with an upper-class background, adopted the middle-class liberal program to overthrow the Confucian feudalism of political, economic, and social institutions. The leaders of the Reform party were inspired and impressed by the success of the Meiji Restoration movement of Japan, and their political coup d'etat took place without the support of either the middle class or the masses, as in the case of the Meiji Restoration; the changes of the Reform party constituted a revolt from the top rather than from the bottom. Therefore it cannot be called a social revolution any more than can the Meiji Restoration. The so-called Reform party movement was a Japanese-inspired and directed conspiracy mainly for the overthrow of the pro-Chinese Korean government.

The pro-Japanese cabinet lasted only three days because the quick action of the queen freed the king from the hands of the Japanese; at the request of the queen (later assassinated by the Japanese), Yuan Shi-kai, then a Chinese resident in Korea, mobilized the Chinese army in Seoul, expelled the Japanese guard, and set the king free. The Japanese minister did not want to get directly involved in the coup d'etat, and some of the Japanese leaders feared that involvement might arouse world opinion against Japan. Therefore, the Tokyo government refused to render the promised financial aid to the

Reform party government in Seoul. Finally, native conservative political power backed by the able Yuan Shi-kai was still stronger than the Reform party in economic resources and political support from the *yangban*.

The king dissolved the Reform party cabinet and declared the members traitors. Most of them escaped to Japan. Takezoe was recalled by Tokyo.

Sadae-sasang under Imperialism: Japan versus Russia. After the failure of the Japanese-inspired coup d'etat of 1884, the conservative pro-Chinese faction returned to power. Queen Min, who had played an important part in the victory of the conservatives during the crisis, became the most influential figure in domestic politics; Yuan Shi-kai became a spokesman on external affairs on behalf of the Korean king. However, the conservative regime was opposed by a new intellectual force, coming from Christian missionary groups and influenced by Western liberalism, and also by the newly arising peasant movement.

In 1894 a large-scale peasant revolt against the conservative regime and foreign intervention occurred in southern Korea and gained considerable support from the middle and lower social groups; the conservative government was threatened by the militant attacks of the rebels. At the request of the king, Chinese troops from the mainland arrived in Korea; but the Japanese government also sent troops, without a request from the Korean king, again under the pretext of protecting the Japanese consulate and property. The Japanese government was determined to act decisively to end Chinese supremacy over Korea. Japanese soldiers took over the duty of guarding the palace, and the Japanese envoy presented "reform measures" to the Korean government. This Japanese action became the immediate cause of the Sino-Japanese war, which after only a few months ended with the victory of Japan. The Shimonoseki Treaty, signed by China and Japan on April 17, 1895, guaranteed the so-called independence of Korea by Japan, and Korea's tributary relationship with China was formally brought to an end.

The Japanese government now embarked on a new plan to exert its influence on the Korean court. Under the direction of the Japanese minister in Seoul, a cabinet headed by Daewon-gun was formed that included pro-Japanese members, although "neutrals" were in the majority. The Japanese move was based on three considerations. First, Daewon-gun had a reputation as an anti-foreign isolationist; the Japanese thought that his cabinet would impress both Koreans and foreigners as a nationalistic and completely independent government. Second, as a result of the Sino-Japanese war and internal revolt, social conditions in Korea were chaotic, so that a strong man like Daewon-gun was expected to be able to restore law and order. Third, Daewon-gun was considered a member of the anti-Min faction (the queen's family), so it appeared that Daewon-gun would eventually ask for Japanese support to stay in power.

The Japanese reform measures included, among other things, the formation of a Chamber of Affairs for the State Militant as an advisory body to the Daewon-gun cabinet. The authority and jurisdiction of the Chamber of Affairs covered military reorganization, financial and educational reform, and industrial and commercial development. At the request of the Japanese minister in Seoul, Kim Hong-jip was appointed head. The minister then insisted that he be consulted on all recommendations and proposals of the Chamber of Affairs before they were submitted to the cabinet. Thus the Daewon-gun cabinet was to be under the control of the Chamber of Affairs for the State Militant, which, in return, was to be supervised by the Japanese minister. Nevertheless, the Daewon-gun cabinet paid no attention to the recommendations of the Chamber of Affairs and was able to impede the Japanese reform program.

As a result, the Japanese government sent a new minister, Count Inoue, one of its ablest bureaucratic statesmen, to Seoul with new instructions. He presented a new reform program to the Korean king, composed of twenty recommendations.[37] He held many unsuccessful conferences with Daewon-gun to persuade him to accept the Japanese recommendations but finally decided to oust Daewon-gun from the Korean government.

The Japanese minister denounced Daewon-gun as a "conspirator" who had plotted to destroy the Japanese armed forces in Korea in the midst of the Sino-Japanese war. The Japanese legation in Seoul disclosed secret documents. According to the Japanese, one of the documents, signed by Daewon-gun, urged the Chinese government to send more military aid to Korea to destroy the Japanese forces and the pro-Japanese political organizations. Finally, the Daewon-gun cabinet resigned under the pressure of the Japanese minister. Then Inoue forced the Korean king to accept his Fourteen Clauses of the

Great Charter.[38] Its main points were: confirmation that all authority was lodged in the king; abandonment of the concept of dependence on China—instead, cultivation of a spirit of national independence; revision of the financial, legal, military, and educational system; regulation of the royal succession and the administration of the royal household; invitation of foreign advisers for each government department; and establishment of a cabinet system following the Japanese model.

At the request of the Japanese minister, the Korean king took the oath of Korea's independence from China at the shrine of the ancestral temple; the Fourteen Clauses of the Great Charter were made public as the reform measures for the coming year. At the request of Inoue, the king also pardoned all political prisoners who took part in the 1884 coup d'etat, and a new cabinet on the Japanese model was organized by the exiled pro-Japanese Koreans. Kim Hong-jip headed the new cabinet as prime minister; Park Young-ho, head of the pro-Japanese clique and a long-time resident of Tokyo, became minister of the interior, who controlled the police; Shu Kwang-bum, exiled in the United States after the 1884 coup, was appointed minister of justice; and Shin Ki-sun, another United States exile, was appointed minister of public works. This cabinet was known as the Inoue-directed coalition government.

The new Japanese political strategy was shrewd and produced some results. On the surface, Japan insisted on full Korean independence from China, which put the pro-Japanese Koreans into a better position to attack the pro-Chinese conservatives who still favored a continuation of tributary relations with China. Inoue's program of twenty recommendations contained comprehensive reform measures for the modernization of Korea. Thus the conservatives in power could not oppose the recommendations.

The political objectives of the Japanese government were twofold: to stamp out Chinese influence in Korea and to introduce the Japanese political system by supporting pro-Japanese Koreans. Inoue's recommendations aimed at these objectives. His first recommendation, for example, which later became Article 1 of the Great Charter, provided that "the king is the source of all powers." This meant that if the Japanese could control the Korean king, then they could dictate the Korean cabinet to execute their programs in the name of the king. This technique was used by the Japanese after the Meiji

Restoration in Japan. Furthermore, the new Korean cabinet was asked to invite Japanese advisers, who were to become the de facto rulers of each department; the national administration was reorganized on the principle of centralization of power; the minister of the interior, as in Japan, was given authority to control the public. The Japanese-imposed reforms were nothing but a means to serve the interests of the Japanese.

The Inoue-directed Korean cabinet, however, lasted only one year. Two events caused its downfall. The first was that the Japanese government recalled Inoue and replaced him by General Viscount Miura Goro, a believer in direct action, as minister in Seoul. During the period of exchange of ministers the anti-Japanese political group, headed by the queen and the Min family, blocked the reform program with the indirect support and encouragement of the Russian legation in Seoul. Thus the new Japanese minister found himself surrounded by a hostile Korean cabinet. At this point, pro-Japanese Koreans advised the Japanese minister to restore Daewon-gun to power as a counterweight to the queen's faction. According to the record of the Japanese court which investigated subsequent events, the Korean War Department and the Japanese legation conspired to put Daewon-gun in power and to murder the queen.

On October 8, 1895, Daewon-gun was escorted to the royal palace by a Japanese-trained Korean detachment and Japanese guards. The chief of the Korean palace guard was shot dead and the palace was surrounded. The queen was murdered by the Japanese guards. Later, the new Japanese minister, Miura, appeared at the palace and forced the Korean king to appoint a list of Koreans to the new cabinet.

The Japanese triumph, however, was met with great resentment, not only from the Korean people, but also from the various diplomatic representatives in Seoul, England, the United States, France, Germany, and Russia. The Japanese government was forced to recall Miura and the legation staff.

The second event was the diplomatic setback suffered by Japan after the Sino-Japanese war. Japan, although victorious, was forced to give up possession of the Liaotung Peninsula, because of the strong opposition of Russia, France, and Germany against Japanese jurisdiction in this vital territory. This damaged the prestige of the Japanese ruling class both at home and abroad. The Japanese diplomatic defeat became a decisive factor in the replacement of Japanese influence in Korea in favor of that of the Russians. As soon as the news of the Japanese retreat from the Liaotung Peninsula became known in the Korean capital, the pro-Japanese Korean cabinet began to lose ground to the pro-Russian group.

RUSSIAN INFLUENCE ON THE KOREAN COURT

About a year before the dramatic events that led to the murder of the queen, aggressive Russian policy began in Korea. The queen, after the outbreak of the Sino-Japanese war in 1894, turned to Russia for help against the pro-Japanese factions in Korea; no help was to be expected from China, busy with the war. The queen declared that since the Russian government had concluded a treaty with Korea pledging to protect the royal family, Korea must rely on Russia.[39]

Thus the Russian legation in Seoul was able to influence the faction of the queen, then known as "loyalists." As early as November 1894, the loyalists planned to rescue the king from the palace, which was guarded by the Japanese, and take him to the Russian legation. This plan was finally carried out on February 11, 1896, under Alexis de Speyer, the Russian minister in Seoul. The Korean king and the crown prince, despite a heavy guard, succeeded in escaping from the palace and were given asylum in the Russian legation. From the legation the king issued a proclamation branding the pro-Japanese cabinet members traitors and annulling most of the Japanese-imposed reform laws. Then a new cabinet was formed by Koreans who took political refuge in the Russian and American legations. The sole governing power was returned to the king, the old Council of State was reestablished, and the Japanese-sponsored cabinet was abolished. Many pro-Japanese cabinet members were killed by mobs in the street. Thus the entire basis of Japanese influence built up since the Korean-Japanese commercial treaty of 1876 was destroyed—at least temporarily.

Korean affairs from 1896 to 1898 were conducted under the influence of Russian policy, so that the period can be characterized as "the era of Russian sponsorship."[40] During the first few months at least, Russian policy was less militant and less interventionist in the internal affairs of Korea than that of the Japanese. The king, for example, was allowed to choose his ministers without interference from the Russian legation, and he had the crown prince returned without Russian protest to a new palace constructed near the American legation. Upon Russian advice the king dropped the name of Chosun as the official name of Korea in favor of the name Daehan; the king was now called the emperor of Daehan. This Russian move flattered the Korean king and the members of the reestablished Council of State, because the king was given the same official title as the Japanese and Chinese emperors, and Daehan means Great Korea, comparable to Dainippon, Great Japan.

Russia appeared as the new protector of Korean independence. The Korean emperor's representative negotiated a new agreement with the Russian government; Russia wanted not only to control Korean finances and armed forces but also to conduct all Korean state affairs through Russian advisers. While the Korean king was in the Russian legation, economic concessions were made to Russian companies granting them a twenty-year lumber monopoly in the Musan district on the Tuman River and mining rights in Hamkyong province; Russian officials were employed as instructors to the Korean army, and the palace guard was under Russian supervision.

Toward the end of 1897 Russia started a more aggressive policy, knowing her influence was strong in Korea. The Russian minister, Weber, who succeeded de Speyer, informed the Korean emperor that he must accept Russian advice on all matters.[41] The Russian government agreed to grant loans, established a Russian-Korean bank, and sent more military instructors and financial advisers to the Korean government. On the other hand, the Russian representative in Korea demanded a concession on Deer Island, a small island in the harbor of the southern port of Pusan, for a Russian coaling station, and also made demands of land for Russian settlements in the important port areas along the coast. Many members of the Council of State, especially the foreign minister, opposed such concessions, which resulted in wholesale cabinet changes under Russian pressure. Still the majority of remaining council members disapproved of the Russian demands. Three times the entire Council of State submitted its resignation to the emperor. A compromise agreement was reached between the Korean foreign office and the Russian legation, but was rejected by the Russian government. Now the Russian government delivered an ultimatum to the Korean emperor, saying that if military and financial advisers were not considered necessary by the Korean government, the Russian government would withdraw aid, and the Korean government would have to maintain its independence without Russian help.[42]

When the Russian statement was made known to the public, anti-Russian feelings developed among the members of many Korean organizations, including pro-Japanese and pro-American groups. Under the sponsorship of the Independence Club, headed by Shu Chai-pil (Philip Jaisohn by his American name), who had studied in the United States, anti-Russian mass meetings were held in many cities. The general public demanded that the government should accept the Russian threat of withdrawal of aid and should express appreciation for Russia's past aid to Korea. Thus Russia's aggressive policy lost ground in Korea; she retreated from the peninsula temporarily in 1898. Six years later Russia tried a military comeback but was defeated by the Japanese.

AN ERA OF PRO-JAPANESE QUISLINGS (1904–10)

When a state faces a national crisis because of the threat of foreign invasion, two groups usually emerge: an anti-foreign nationalistic group, and a subversive group collaborating with the enemy—quislings or traitors. Korea was no exception. There were three quislings and one subversive political organization when Korea fell under the sway of the Japanese empire.

Yi Wan-yong had long been a political opportunist. During and after the Sino-Japanese war he belonged to the liberal political group, the Independence Club, which advocated independence without foreign intervention. When the Russian empire appeared to be becoming stronger than China and Japan after the Sino-Japanese war, he joined the pro-Russian group, headed by the queen and the Min family, and played an important role in persuading the king to take asylum in the Russian legation in 1896. Just before the Russo-Japanese war he joined the pro-Japanese group and was appointed minister of education in the newly formed pro-Japanese cabinet. The Japanese government favored him. He was the first cabinet member to approve the protectorate treaty of 1905, and he agreed to abdication of the anti-Japanese Korean emperor in favor of the fourteen-year-old crown prince in 1907. He favored annexation of Korea by Japan, and signed the treaty of annexation in 1910 as prime minister. He was rewarded by the Japanese with a gift of money and the title of marquis.

Song Pyong-jun was a Japanized Korean. As a young man he was sent to Japan by the Min family to assassinate the pro-Japanese leader Kim Ok-kyun, who had escaped to Japan after the 1884 coup d'etat. However, Song gave up his mission after talking with Kim. At the suggestion of Kim he studied Japanese history and politics for several years. During the Russo-Japanese war he worked as personal interpreter to General Otani and returned to Korea under the assumed name of Noda Haijiro. Song organized a subversive political group, the Iljin-hai (Ishin-kai in Japanese), as described later. After the annexation he too was rewarded by the Japanese government, with money and the title of viscount.

Yi Yong-ku identified himself as spokesman of the Japanese government representing the Iljin-hai, and defended Japanese policy in Korea. He started out as a revolutionist against the regime and foreign intervention. He was sentenced to death, but was able to escape to China. A few years later he returned to Korea and organized the Progressive Society. When he noticed that the Japanese were winning the war against Russia, he joined the Iljin-hai by merging his own political group with it; he was subsequently elected president of the Iljin-hai. Henceforth he became the main propagandist on behalf of the Japanese government, urging the Korean people to cooperate with the Japanese. He was rewarded with money and with the title of viscount.

No reliable materials are available on the origins of the subversive Iljin-hai, or who instructed Song Pyong-jun to organize it. But it is generally believed that the group was started as the result of discussions between the pro-Japanese Korean group in Japan headed by Kim Ok-kyun and nationalistic, militaristic Japanese leaders like Bogetsu Ryotaro, Gamitani Taku, Toyama Mitsuro, and Uchida Ryohei. There is evidence that the Black Dragon Society, an ultranationalist terrorist organization, headed by Toyama, rendered assistance to the Iljin-hai by sending money and propagandists; the Iljin-hai's activities were supervised by the Japanese military commanding general in Korea; its public statements were drafted with the advice and approval of the general.

The president of the Iljin-hai,[43] Yi Yong-ku, issued in 1905 the first public statement which favored a Japanese protectorate over Korea. The statement expressed the explicit faith of the *sadae-sasang* policy. The existing regime was old and corrupt; there was no hope for the old regime to survive after the Russo-Japanese war. According to the pro-Japanese Koreans, Japan was the inevitable new "protector" of Korea, and they paved the way for a new master by urging the Korean people to accept Japanese rule. As described later, the Korean people not only rejected this policy but went into action against both the subversive organization and Japanese imperialism.

Aware of the violent public resentment against any new move by the Japanese, a secret meeting was held between the quislings and Marquis Ito, the special representative of the Japanese emperor. They agreed to conclude the protectorate treaty on November 17, 1905. The Korean emperor and the majority of the ministers, including Prime Minister Han Kyu-sul and Foreign Minister Park Chai-sun, at first refused to sign the treaty, but when Japanese soldiers were placed around the palace with machine guns and the prime minister was dragged out of the conference hall by Japanese guards, the remaining ministers signed, but under protest. Only three ministers—the minister of education, the minister of agriculture and industry, and the minister of the army—signed the treaty voluntarily. This treaty, after being kept secret for five days, was made public on November 23. Public demonstrations protested against it, and several high officials, including Min Yong-whan, former minister of the army, committed suicide in protest.

The Korean emperor sent the following secret message to Mr. Hulbert, his one-time adviser: "I declare that the so-called treaty of protectorate recently concluded between Korea and Japan was extorted at the point of the sword and under duress and therefore is null and void."[44] The emperor asked for help from the United States government under the Korean-American Treaty, but President Theodore Roosevelt ignored the appeal. The emperor was unaware of the existence of the Roosevelt-Katsura Secret Pact on Korea, signed on July 29, 1905—nearly four months before the protectorate treaty—by which the United States government had already recognized that "the establishment by Japanese troops of a suzerainty over Korea . . . was the logical result of the present war and would directly contribute to permanent peace in the East."[45]

Japan now became the virtual ruler of Korea, and Marquis Ito assumed the post of first resident-general at Seoul in February 1906. The Japanese resident-general became the dictator in Korea; he organized a new Korean cabinet headed by Yi Wan-yong as prime minister, and each department was under the control of a Japanese civilian adviser.

But as far as the Japanese government was concerned, two obstacles had to be removed to bring about complete domination of Korea: the emperor and the Korean army. To overcome these obstacles, the quislings and the Japanese used "the incident of the Korean emperor's secret mission" to the Second International Peace Conference. The emperor had sent three plenipotentiary delegates to the Hague Peace Conference in 1907 to protest Japanese dominance and to proclaim that Korea was entitled as an independent state to have direct diplomatic relations with foreign states.

Resident-General Ito charged that the Korean emperor's action was a violation of the treaty,[46] according to which "Korea's foreign affairs will hereafter be handled through the government of Japan." Ito instructed the puppet cabinet to propose that the emperor abdicate in favor of the fourteen-year-old crown prince. Thus the emperor was compelled to abdicate. He even issued the following statement: "In abdicating my throne I acted in obedience to the dictate of my conviction; my action was not the result of any outside advice or pressure."[47]

A new agreement was now reached between Korea and Japan, according to which (a) all laws would be subject to approval of the resident-general, (b) judicial and administrative affairs would be separated, (c) the resident-general would exercise appointment and dismissal authority over Korean officials, and (d) without the advance concurrence of the resident-general the Korean government would not employ foreigners.[48]

The final step was the preparation for a treaty of annexation. On April 10, 1909, Prime Minister Katsura, Foreign Minister Komura, and Resident-General Ito in Seoul held a secret conference and agreed that only annexation would solve the Korean question. This decision was approved by the Japanese Cabinet and obtained the emperor's sanction, but it was kept in secrecy until a proper opportunity should arise.

The Korean quislings now embarked on a propaganda campaign for annexation: a secret staff meeting of the Iljin-hai was held at the residence of Minister Yi Yong-ku. When Ito was assassinated by a Korean, Ahn Jung-kun, at Harbin in October 1909, the Iljin-hai members decided to send an apology mission to Japan. Song Pyong-jun went to Japan as the head of the mission, and got in touch with Uchida Ryohei, who kept close relations with the Katsura cabinet. Song also had an opportunity to become acquainted with General Terauchi, war minister since 1902 and successor to Ito as governor-general of Korea. In accordance with Uchida's advice, the Song Pyong-jun–Yi Yong-ku clique submitted a petition for "Korean-Japanese amalgamation" to the Japanese government, stating that the Korean people favored Japanese rule.

About this time the Iljin-hai split into two factions, the Song faction and the Yi Wan-yong faction. The former ("radical") group, favored immediate annexation of Korea by Japan; the latter ("conservative") group advocated a gradual annexation. The conservative group, which then was in power in the cabinet, was concerned about the relations between Song Pyong-jun and General Terauchi, the newly arrived governor-general, because they heard about the possibility of the formation of a Song cabinet by Terauchi. Yi Wan-yong sent his private secretary, Yi In-sik, to the governor-general's office, where he had a talk with the bureau chief of foreign affairs, Gomatsu Roku. Gomatsu told Yi In-sik that no plan for the formation of a new cabinet existed. In the meantime, Gomatsu got the impression from Yi that the Korean prime minister was ready to accept Korean-Japanese amalgamation.

On August 16, 1910, Terauchi invited the puppet Korean prime minister Yi Wan-yong to his residence, and for the first time discussed the subject of annexation.[49] The term itself was not used in their conversation. The essential points of the conversations were that (a) Japan and Korea had a similar cultural background and were geographically close to each other, (b) during the two wars within the last ten years Japan had sacrificed thousands of soldiers and millions of yen to protect Korea, and (c) amalgamation of the two countries would not only eliminate many artificial inequalities between Korea and Japan but would also promote the prosperity of the Korean people.

Terauchi suggested that a Korean-Japanese amalgamation should not be interpreted by foreign countries as the results of war or illegal action, but it should be viewed as a voluntary cession of the sovereign right of the Korean emperor to the Japanese emperor. He concluded by saying that Japan would respect the Korean emperor and give him the title of "His Highness the Prince," and the members of the imperial family would also be honored with proper titles and grants. The present members of the cabinet would be rewarded with the titles and grants in accordance with the services rendered for bringing about amalgamation of the two countries. And the Japanese government would employ Korean nationalists in public offices.

Yi Wan-yong, agreeing with Terauchi in principle, expressed his concern over the official name of Korea and the title of the Korean emperor after annexation. He said that Korea should be called Hanguk, and the emperor should be given the title of *wang* (king), because the name and title, even if they are empty words, might prevent the Korean people from making trouble after annexation. During the period of its vassalage to China, Korea had retained the name of kingdom, the ruler was given the title of king, and the people were satisfied. Therefore, if Japan would be willing to treat the emperor as king and to retain the name of Hanguk, the public feelings would be calm and a cooperative spirit would prevail. Terauchi refused. Eventually the name of Korea was changed to Chosun (Chosen in Japanese), and the title of the emperor changed to Yi-wang Dun-ha, His Imperial Highness Prince Yi. Terauchi reported to Tokyo, and the Japanese government drafted the treaty of annexation.

Yi Wan-yong failed to obtain approval from the Korean emperor, but with the help of the emperor's uncle he stole the imperial seal from the palace. The treaty of annexation was signed on August 22 and released on August 29, 1910, under the watchful eye of the Japanese gendarmerie of the Korean peninsula. Thus Korea became a Japanese colony for the following thirty-five years.

CHAPTER 5

THE YI DYNASTY

PAWN OF THE BIG POWERS

KOREA: A BONE OF CONTENTION BETWEEN THE POWERS

Sino-Japanese Clashes (1876–95). After 1860 a number of incidents, such as the French expedition in 1866 and the American expedition in 1871, caused excitement in the Korean government, a government which had continued an absolute isolation policy for more than two centuries.[1]

At this time, the new Japanese ruling class, the Meiji oligarchy, was divided into two groups[2] over the question of when to attack Korea: one group, headed by Soejima Taneomi, the foreign minister, pushed for immediate conquest of Korea; the other group, headed by Okubo Toshimichi, one of the Meiji Restoration movement leaders, opposed on the ground that Japan was still in a transitional stage and financially too weak. This view was supported by Iwakura Tomomi, one of the "liberals," who had just returned from a European tour; he believed that Japanese military action in Korea would not be approved by the Western powers. In effect, however, the Japanese oligarchy was fully agreed as to the necessity of conquering Korea; only the timetable was in dispute.

In 1875 the Japanese government devised a Japanized Western-type treaty policy as a means of forcing the Korean government to open Korea to Japan. In September, the Japanese government dispatched a military mission to Korea and a diplomatic mission to China. The Japanese gunboat *Unyoko*, purchased from England, surveyed the Korean coast, which she had no right to do. The ship was fired upon by the Koreans, and the Japanese retaliated by destroying both the bastion and the defenders of Kanghwa Island near the Inchun harbor, about thirty miles from Seoul.

In the meantime the Japanese special envoy, Mori Yurei, opened diplomatic negotiations with the Chinese government in Peking, presenting a memorandum in which Japan complained about Korea's persistent refusal to enter into official intercourse with her and recounted the recent Korean attack on her surveying ship. Mori also said that the Japanese treaty mission was already under way to Korea, and if the mission was not received in good manner and its demands for a friendship treaty refused, Korea would invite upon itself "an incalculable calamity."[3]

The objective of the Japanese envoy was, however, not merely to complain or threaten, but to obtain from the Chinese government a declaration of Korea's freedom in dealing with non-Chinese powers. To the Japanese government, which was aware of the traditional Confucian relationship between China and Korea, China's assurance of Korean freedom with respect to external affairs was a convenient tool which could be used in breaking the ties between China and Korea.

Mori argued that Korea was not a Chinese dependency, pointing out that China never levied taxes upon her and did not interfere in her internal affairs. But the Chinese representative, Li Hung-chang, being well aware of the Japanese political motives on the Korean issue, avoided any formal declaration of Korea's status in terms of a sovereign state,[4] and the negotiations seemed to be at a deadlock.

Finally, however, Mori and Li found a compromise. Japan indicated her tacit recognition of the special position of China in the Korean peninsula, and China agreed to use her influence to get a courteous reception for the Japanese treaty mission by the Korean government. As the later events showed, the so-called compromise formula was a victory for Japan, because she was the first country to obtain from the Korean government a Western-type commercial treaty.

The "friendship and commercial treaty" was, however, concluded under the military threat of the Japanese government. The Japanese mission arrived in Korea on February 6, 1876, with two battleships and three transportation ships. The Japanese envoy told the Korean official representative that he had brought soldiers and another two thousand would arrive soon. The agreement was signed on February 26.[5] It was composed of twelve articles. Korea agreed to open two additional ports, beside the Pusan port, to Japan; Japan was given the right to survey the Korean coasts and publish the results without restrictions from the Korean government; and the Japanese government was given the right to establish a consulate in each designated port.

The treaty was interpreted in different ways. One Western observer, J. H. Longford, stated that the treaty brought not only the end of Korea's isolation policy but "terminated forever, theoretically at least, its dependence on China."[6] As for China, there were no changes between it and Korea, and the traditional Confucian relationship was maintained by Korea's continued practice of reporting to the Peking government all events in its external relations, including those with Japan. The Japanese government, however, made every effort to have the treaty with Korea "appear as one between equals,"[7] and made Korea appear as a state independent from China so that the Japanese could remain in the Korean peninsula without the further approval of the Chinese government.

To the Koreans, the so-called friendship treaty was an unequal treaty modeled on the Anglo-Chinese treaty after the Opium War and the Japan-American commercial treaty resulting from Commodore Perry's expedition to Japan in 1853. The treaty of 1876 brought many political and economic consequences for Korea. The self-imposed two-hundred-fifty-year isolation came to an end. Similar commercial treaties were concluded thereafter with other Western powers, and Korea was now open to foreign trade. This meant, among other things, that the feudalistic native economic structure began to collapse because of the influence of Western and Japanese capitalism.

The import of Japanese goods soon destroyed the native handicraft industries; the export of Korean agricultural products to Japan through the Japanese merchants caused starvation in the country and general social unrest. Furthermore, the Korean king gave many concessions for the exploitation of natural resources such as mining and fishing rights to foreign companies, especially Russia, Germany, and America. The construction of modern means of communication and transportation was in the hands of foreign investors; almost all foreign legations in Seoul obtained extraterritorial privileges. The peninsula was divided into zones of influence of the various foreign powers, and the native regime was reduced to semicolonial status.

Soon after the conclusion of the commercial treaty Japanese merchants got the upper hand over Korean merchants. They obtained the right to use both Japanese and Korean currency for their trade in Korea. Many of them engaged in moneylending and in running pawn shops. Some of them later became absentee landlords. Japanese merchants formed monopolistic import-export businesses or they imported Japanese manufactured goods to Korea and exported Korean agricultural products to Japan, especially rice and raw materials. No strong native merchant class existed to compete with the Japanese.

In 1882 Korean veterans revolted against the Japanese military reorganization program as well as against the pro-Japanese native cabinet ministers. During the revolt one Japanese military instructor was killed and the Japanese consulate was burned to the ground. The Japanese consulate staff and many Japanese businessmen were compelled to return to Japan. This revolt had the support of the pro-Chinese Korean conservative party, and was helped by some Chinese soldiers stationed in Seoul. This was the beginning of the conflict between China and Japan in Korea.

The revolt ended to the advantage of the Japanese. The Japanese government sent its minister, Habana, back to Seoul with fifteen hundred soldiers. The minister demanded payment for all damage inflicted to Japanese property and also presented a new treaty to the Korean government.[8] The Korean government was to arrest all offenders of the revolt and to prosecute them in the presence of Japanese officials; the Korean government was to pay damages to the Japanese; the Japanese legation was to be given the right to maintain a military force to protect Japanese interests in Korea; and the Korean government was to send an apology mission to the Japanese emperor.

In addition to accepting this treaty, the Korean government was forced to concede further rights to Japanese businessmen in Korea. The business-establishment areas of Japanese in the open ports were extended to fifty square miles; Japanese government officials and their families were given the privilege to travel freely anywhere in Korea.

The most important concession was the right granted Japan to station troops; now Japan could send her military forces to Korea under the treaty agreement at any time under the pretext of protecting Japanese interests.

After the Korean-Japanese treaty of 1876, the Chinese government began to modify her policies toward Korea to compete with the Japanese influence in Korea. During the veteran revolt of 1882, China sent five thousand soldiers to suppress the pro-Japanese faction, and thereafter Chinese forces remained in Seoul. Later, a Sino-Korean commercial treaty was concluded as counterpart to the Korea-Japanese treaty.[9] The new Chinese policy was conducted under the leadership of Li Hung-chang. In pursuance of this policy, early in 1883 Li sent to Seoul P. G. von Möllendorff, who had served with the Chinese customs for a long time, and Chen Shu-tang, who had served as Chinese consul general at San Francisco. The Korean government appointed von Möllendorff as adviser to the Ministry of Foreign Affairs; Chen became commercial agent of the Chinese government in Korea.

Möllendorff concentrated on the organization of the customs service and on general reforms for the industrial, commercial, and financial improvement of Korea. The new Chinese policies were successful because they were supported by the Korean conservatives. The Japanese influence began to decline, and some Japanese businessmen lost their establishments in the Korean port areas.

The Japanese government, however, did not remain idle. Under Japanese sponsorship youthful Korean aristocrats, impressed by the rapid modernization of Japan after the Meiji Restoration, organized a "progressive" party in opposition to the conservatives in power. On December 4, 1884, a Japanese-inspired coup d'etat forced the formation of a pro-Japanese cabinet, but it lasted only three days. The conservative party returned to power under the protection of five thousand royal soldiers and Chinese troops in Seoul. The defeated progressive leaders fled to Japan, and the Japanese minister was recalled.

After this incident, Japan made efforts to recover from the loss of political prestige and economic power in Korea. The Japanese government sent a new minister, Count Inoue, to Seoul with two army divisions. Inoue demanded indemnity for the Japanese properties lost during the political crisis, and also presented a new treaty[10] (the third) to Korea. In January 1885 this treaty was signed. The Korean government agreed to pay an indemnity in cash, made land grants for the construction of Japanese army barracks around the Japanese consulate in Korea, and apologized to the Japanese emperor.

At the same time the Japanese government sent Count Ito to Peking as a special ambassador to negotiate with the Chinese about the Korean issue. Because of the tension between China and France during this time, most Chinese troops in Seoul had to be withdrawn, and Japan was, therefore, in a better bargaining position than in 1875.[11] The main Japanese objective was still to secure recognition of Korea's independence from China. In 1885 Ito and Li Hung-chang signed a treaty at Tientsin,[12] according to which the forces under the Chinese resident as well as the Japanese legation guards were to be withdrawn from Korea. The Korean king was to organize a Korean army, in whose formation neither Chinese nor Japanese were to be employed. In case disturbances in Korea made it necessary for China or Japan to send troops to the peninsula, the country sending them was to notify the other beforehand and in writing of the intention to do so, and the troops were to be withdrawn when the matter was settled.

This treaty placed Japan and China on equal terms in Korean military affairs, leaving open all political and economic problems. The agreement for simultaneous withdrawal of their troops from the peninsula constituted a temporary truce between Japan and China; neither country was ready for a large-scale war over Korea.

After 1885 the Ito-Inoue-directed Japanese policy steadily lost ground in Korea, diplomatically and economically. China sent Yuan Shi-kai to Seoul as the Chinese resident who took charge of diplomatic and commercial affairs between Korea and China. His status was never comparable with that of a diplomatic representative of other countries in Seoul. The Chinese resident had the privilege of being carried from the palace gates to the audience hall and of remaining seated in the presence of the Korean king; other representatives had to dismount at the gates, proceed on foot, and stand when the king was present.

The Korean customs service was drawn closer to that of China by the appointment of Henry F. Merrill as inspector general of Korean customs, as recommended by Yuan. Thus the Chinese resident became the de facto ruler in diplomatic and economic affairs in Korea.

Japanese economic interests declined considerably in Korea from 1885 to 1892, as can be seen in table 1.

Chinese trade with Korea increased from 19 percent in 1885 to 45 percent in 1892; Japanese trade during the same period declined from 81 percent to 55 percent. If this trend was allowed to continue, China would soon surpass Japan. Japan could not wait long, and was prepared to act to end China's supremacy in Korea at the first opportunity.

In June 1894 a peasant revolution under the leadership of the Tonghaks,[14] a semireligious nationalistic group opposed to all foreign interference, Asiatic

TABLE 1. TRADE WITH KOREA[13]
(*in percent*)

Year	*China*	*Japan*
1885	19	81
1886	17	83
1887	26	74
1888	28	72
1889	32	68
1890	32	68
1891	40	60
1892	45	55

or Western, occurred in the southern provinces of the peninsula. The Korean king asked the Chinese government for military assistance, and on July 6 China sent fifteen hundred troops from Tientsin, with seven hundred to follow. In compliance with the Tientsin agreement, the Chinese government notified the Japanese government and assured it that "these troops shall be withdrawn at once, upon the cessation of hostilities."[15] The Japanese government replied on the same day that it was likewise sending troops to protect the Japanese legation and the Japanese residents in Korea. Japan sent six times as many soldiers as the Chinese.

After the rebels accepted the government truce offer, the foreign troops were no longer necessary. Nevertheless, the Japanese government seized the opportunity to ask the Chinese government for cooperation in introducing reforms in the Korean government. The Chinese rejected the Japanese proposal, saying that "even China, whose vassal Korea has always been, would not interfere in the internal administration of the kingdom; Japan, having from the beginning recognized Korea as an independent state, cannot claim any right to interfere."[16]

Japan sent her troops to Korea not to suppress the Tonghaks or to protect Japanese interests, but to destroy the Chinese influence in the peninsula.[17] Before starting war against China, Japan concentrated on the establishment of a pro-Japanese Korean government under the pretext of reforms. On June 26 the Japanese minister in Seoul, Otori, had an audience with the Korean king and presented the following memorandum: "Japan found it necessary, for the mutual welfare of the two countries, to ask that certain radical changes be made in the government and policy of Korea, in consultation with the Japanese authorities. Until these changes are made in a manner satisfactory to Japan the Japanese troops will not be withdrawn."[18]

Two days later Otori demanded within twenty-four hours an answer "whether or not Korea was a tributary of China." To this the Korean government replied by quoting the first article of the Korean-Japanese treaty of 1876: "Korea, being an independent state, enjoys the same sovereign rights as Japan." The reply also contained the quotation of the Korean king's letter to the president of the United States that "in both internal administration and foreign intercourse Korea enjoyed complete independence."

On July 14 Otori presented an ultimatum to the Korean government, demanding that the Korean government, being in charge of an independent state, should order the Chinese troops to leave the peninsula at once, and that the unequal Sino-Korean treaty be abolished. Without waiting for a reply from the Korean government, the Japanese troops in Seoul attacked the royal palace and seized the king. Thereupon a Japanese-dominated Korean government was organized by the king, who now was a prisoner.

On July 24 the "Korean" government issued a decree denouncing the treaties with China and asking Japan's aid in driving the Chinese troops from Korea. Things moved fast: on the following day a temporary agreement between Korea and Japan was signed, by which the Korean government accepted the Japanese reforms, authorized Japanese construction of railroads from Pusan to Seoul and from Inchun to Seoul, and consented to open more commercial ports to the Japanese. In return, Japan agreed to render assistance "for the complete restoration of national independence of Korea."[19] On July 26 a treaty of military alliance[20] was signed with Japan which provided that the Korean government would give every facility for the movement of Japanese troops as soon as Japan started war against China, while the Japanese government promised "to maintain the independence of Korea on a firm footing."

The war actually started when, on July 25, the Japanese sunk the British steamer *Kowshing,* which was transporting Chinese troops. An official declaration of war was proclaimed on August 1 by both the Chinese and Japanese governments.

The Sino-Japanese war lasted from August 1894 to April 1895 and ended in the defeat of China. The peace treaty was signed at Shimonoseki on April 20, 1895. China recognized the "full and complete independence" of Korea, and agreed that "the payment of tribute and the performance of ceremonies and formalities by Korea to China, in derogation of such independence and autonomy, shall cease."[21] Thus the age-old Confucian relationship—Korea's tributary status with China—was ended and the so-called national independence of Korea was guaranteed by the Japanese government.

The Russo-Japanese Rivalry over Korea (1895–1905). The government of Russia had shown an interest in Korea since 1880. A Russo-Korean commercial treaty was concluded in 1882; two years later the Korean government invited Russian officials to help in the reconstruction of the army after the Japanese-inspired coup d'etat intensified anti-Japanese feelings among the Koreans. In 1885 the Russian government attempted without success to secure port concessions from the Korean king for the Russian navy.

During the Sino-Japanese war, Russia avoided any direct military involvement because she was not sufficiently prepared, and because even if Russia had supported the Chinese side, the Japanese would not have withdrawn their troops from Korea.

However, after the war the Russian government showed an active interest in Korea. Japan was forced to renounce her possession of the Liaotung Peninsula by the strong pressure of three powers—Russia, France, and Germany—on the ground that Japanese possession of it "would be a perpetual obstacle to the peace of the Far East." Then the Japanese minister and his staff were charged with plotting to murder the Korean queen, and they were recalled from Seoul. The pro-Japanese Korean cabinet collapsed, and several cabinet ministers were killed by Korean street mobs. In this situation, the Korean king decided to seek political asylum in the Russian legation, and was welcomed by the Russian government. The king reorganized the cabinet by including pro-Russian leaders; Russian trading companies received economic concessions from the king, such as mining and forest concessions along the Tuman and Yalu rivers; Russian officials were invited again as instructors to train the Korean army; Russian financial experts and custom officials became advisers to the Korean government. In March 1896 an agreement was concluded while the Korean king was still in the Russian legation, according to which the Russian government placed "herself in the position not only to control the Korean finance and armed forces, but also, through advice, to direct the policy of Korean government."[22] Thus the Russian influence was clearly in the ascendancy in Korea.

During the period of Russian sponsorship (1896–98), the Japanese government could do little in Korea, and limited itself to preserving its economic interests in the peninsula through agreements directly with the Russian government. The first agreement of this kind was the Weber-Komura memorandum[23] of May 14, 1896 (when the Korean king was still in the Russian legation). The two governments agreed to leave the matter of the Korean king's stay in the Russian legation to his own discretion, but they would advise the king's departure when there were no further doubts about his safety. To insure safety, the Japanese government promised to take measures to control those of their subjects who were known to favor violent action. The Japanese government agreed to recognize the new Korean cabinet as the legitimate government organized by the king "of his own free will." The number of troops as well as the number and location of Japanese telegraph guards in Korea were limited. This agreement constituted a Russion victory over Japan.

The second agreement was the Yamagata-Lobanov treaty[24] of June 9, 1896. Under this protocol, Russia and Japan pledged themselves to respect each other's positions and rights and agreed that only "by mutual accord" would the governments lend money to Korea; they also agreed to permit the creation and maintenance of an armed force and of a native police sufficient to maintain internal order without foreign aid.

Under the Yamagata-Lobanov treaty the Japanese government recovered somewhat from her lost influence in Korea. She could now block Russia as the new sole protector of Korean independence. This treaty, however, became the cause of controversy between the two parties. The Japanese government argued that a loan from Russia, contracted after the treaty, and the dispatch of military personnel to Korea were not in conformity with the agreement; but the Russian government declared that the Russian agreement with Korea to furnish financial and military aid had been signed before the Yamagata-Lobanov treaty.

Fortunately for the Japanese, an incident involving the Russian representative in Korea occurred in 1897; this became known as the incident of Masan, near the port of Pusan, where Russia demanded a "coaling station." The real intention of the Russian government in this area was military—by securing Masan, the Russian naval defense line could be extended from Vladivostok to Pusan and from Pusan to Port Arthur. Thus the Russian sea defense could easily block or restrict Japanese sea power.[25]

While the Masan lease agreement was secretly discussed between Russia and Korea, a Japanese private citizen, Hakuma Fusataro, purchased some of the Russian-claimed lease land and turned it over to the Japanese army. The Russian representative de Speyer was now determined to legalize the lease agreement, and pressed the Korean cabinet for formal approval of the lease. The Korean foreign minister introduced the lease agreement to the cabinet.

When the Russian government could not obtain the lease despite pressure from the Korean cabinet, it threatened to withdraw its financial and military aid from Korea.[26] This threat was gladly accepted by the Koreans. The Russo-Korean bank was closed and the Russian military advisers and financial experts returned to their homeland.

The Japanese government was quick in taking advantage of the Russian diplomatic setback in Korea and signed the Nishi-Rosen treaty[27] on April 25, 1898. Under it the Russian and Japanese governments recognized "the sovereignty and independence of Korea" and agreed "to take no measure in respect to the appointment of military instructors or financial advisors, without arriving beforehand at a mutual agreement on the matter." The Japanese government secured Russian recognition of her interest in the "development of the commercial, industrial, and financial relationships between Japan and Korea." Finally they pledged themselves "to refrain from direct interference in the internal affairs of Korea." The Russian government's formal acknowledgment of Japan's economic interests in Korea left to the Japanese a monopoly of the Korean economy.

After 1898 the Japanese concentrated on three fields in Korea's economy. The financial field was the first. The Japanese established bank branches in Korean cities, ports, and industrial districts. Then these banks obtained the right to purchase gold and silver, to loan money to the Korean government, and to issue bank notes. By a new currency agreement between Korea and Japan, the Korean monetary system was merged with the Japanese system.

Secondly, the Japanese undertook the construction of modern communication and transportation systems. The construction of the Inchun-Seoul railroad, which had been started by an American company but then had not been finished because of capital shortage, was given to a Japanese company. The Pusan-Seoul line was completed by the Japanese just before the outbreak of the Russo-Japanese war. The Seoul-Shinuiju line construction was started during the war, and the Japanese army engineer corps completed the work for military reasons. Thus three important railroad lines which connected Manchuria and Korea were in the hands of the Japanese. Sea transportation business had been a monopoly of the Japanese since the commercial treaty of 1876. Thirdly, the Japanese concentrated on Korea's import and export business.

Korean imports from Japan increased from 50.2 to 73.7 percent, while those from China and Russia decreased from 49.1 to 18.6 and from 0.7 to 0.3 percent between 1892 and 1905. During the same period the Korean exports to Japan, however, decreased from 90.9 to 78.1 percent; exports to China increased from 7.8 to 21.8 percent; to Russia decreased from 1.2 to 0.2.[28]

The most significant factor was the change in Sino-Korean trade relations. The sharp decrease of imports from China and the rapid increase of exports to China put Korea in a favorable position, but in reality, the Japanese export-import business in Korea had monopolized Korean foreign trade. Korea's trade with Russia had always been insignificant.

Japanese nationals in Korea purchased important and strategic property around the open port areas as well as in the interior of Korea; they also secured mining concessions and fishing rights from the Korean government. The Japanese minister in Seoul, Hayashi, made known his government's position by saying that "our policy in Korea consists of our abstinence from all intervention in the internal affairs of this country and to make possible the development of our economic interests."[29]

Yet the Japanese government demanded reforms from the Korean government, sent Japanese military and civilian advisers to Korea, and tried to evade the Nishi-Rosen agreements. The Russian government, despite its setback in 1898, started again to combat the growing Japanese influence and tried to obtain economic concessions from the Korean king. In 1901 the

Russian government secured from him promises regarding further economic concessions by not granting any more mining concessions to any foreigners except Russians. In return, the Russian government promised to furnish capital for the construction of railroads. Besides, the Russian government notified the Korean government of its intention to exercise its option of cutting timber in the Yalu Valley. Later the Russian government sent "frontier guards" to protect her timber properties in that area. Thus Russian forces were stationed in the northern Korean peninsula.[30]

The Japanese viewed this Russian move as an indication that the Russians had no intention of leaving Korea to Japan. Hence Japan began to strengthen her military forces. She also strengthened her diplomatic defenses by signing the Anglo-Japanese alliance in 1902, by which Great Britain recognized Japan's political and economic interests in Korea. To this the Russian government responded by declaring that the Russian-French dual alliance, in existence since 1895, was now to be considered as extending to the Far East.

The Japanese minister at St. Petersburg expressed his government's concern over the Russian advance in the Korean peninsula as follows: "Russia, stationed on the flank of Korea, would be a constant menace to the separate existence of that empire, and in any event it would make Russia the dominant power in Korea. Korea is an important outpost in Japan's line of defense, and Japan consequently considers the independence of Korea absolutely essential to her own repose and safety. Japan possesses paramount political as well as economic and industrial interests and influence in Korea which, having regard to her own security, she cannot consent to surrender to, or share with, any other power."[31]

The backstage political deals based on the Korea-Manchuria trading formula—Russia's freedom of action in Manchuria in exchange for Japan's freedom of action in Korea—continued for six months between the representatives of the two countries. Finally, the Russian government rejected the Japanese offer, negotiations broke down, and war followed.

The Korean government announced Korea's neutrality on January 21, 1904, but it was too weak to avoid involvement in the war. The Japanese government severed diplomatic relations with Russia on February 6, 1904, and two days later Japanese forces began to attack Port Arthur; the next day Russian ships in the Korean port Inchun were attacked by the Japanese navy.

On February 10 the Japanese government formally declared war, and Japanese troops soon occupied the Korean peninsula, ignoring the Korean declaration of neutrality. After two weeks of resistance the Korean government was compelled to sign a treaty of alliance with Japan, by which the Japanese government obtained the right to use Korean territory as a base for military operations. In return the Japanese government again "guaranteed the independence and territorial integrity of Korea."[32] The Korean government also agreed to accept Japanese advisers and reform proposals in the reorganization of the administration.

The Russo-Japanese war officially ended on September 5, 1905, by the signing of the Treaty of Portsmouth[33] through the mediation of the American president Theodore Roosevelt. The defeated Russian government acknowledged Japan's paramount interests in Korea.[34]

Even before the Russo-Japanese war was over, Great Britain and the United States approved Japan's plans in Korea. The British government gave tacit consent to Japan's intention of establishing a protectorate over Korea; Lord Lansdowne's dispatch to the British ambassadors in Russia and France on September 6, 1905, contained the statement that Korea, "owing to its close proximity to the Japanese Empire, its inability to stand alone, and danger arising from its weakness, must fall under the control and tutelage of Japan."[35]

As the Roosevelt-Katsura secret pact on Korea on July 29, 1905, showed, the United States government endorsed Japan's "suzerainty over Korea" in exchange for the pledge that "Japan does not harbor any aggressive designs whatever against the Philippines." William H. Taft, then secretary of war of the United States, stated that "the establishment by Japanese troops of suzerainty over Korea to the extent of requiring that Korea enter into no foreign treaties without the consent of Japan was the logical result of the present war and would directly contribute to permanent peace in the East."[36] Thus international approval was given to Japan's domination over Korea.

THE FALL OF THE YI DYNASTY: FROM PROTECTORATE TO ANNEXATION

In May 1904, two months after the Russo-Japanese war started, the Japanese government declared: "Korea is to become a Japanese protectorate at the proper time; until then, Japan will strive to obtain practical results by giving political, diplomatic, and military protection and by developing Japan's interest in Korea."[37]

Pressed by the Japanese government, the Korean emperor issued a decree in May 1904, abrogating all treaties and concessions previously secured by the Russian government. In August Japan forced the Korean government to accept the appointment of Japanese advisers to the Korean government and to obtain their counsel before any action was taken. Baron Megata was appointed financial adviser, and D. W. Stevens,[38] an American who served in the Japanese foreign office, became adviser to the Korean Department of External Affairs. Kato, another Japanese politician, became adviser to the Royal Household, which was in charge of the affairs of the royal family. The Japanese minister in Seoul was given the privilege of obtaining an audience at any time with the Korean emperor; he was also authorized to supervise the Korean administration, as well as the Japanese advisers.

After the end of the war in September 1905, the Japanese took over the policing of the capital and appointed Japanese police inspectors to every province. Hayashi, the Japanese minister, compelled the Korean government to reduce the Korean army as one of the internal reforms of the Korean administration. The Japanese minister in Seoul thus became the de facto ruler of Korea.

When the Japanese government obtained the consent of the Western powers of her plan to make Korea a protectorate (by the Roosevelt-Katsura secret pact and the new Anglo-Japanese alliance) she moved swiftly toward complete domination of Korea. On November 15, 1905, Ito, a special ambassador of the Japanese emperor, had an audience with the Korean emperor in which he presented demands that amounted to the establishment of a protectorate over Korea, Japan's complete supervision of Korean affairs, together with control over the nation's foreign relations, as described later. The conversation[39] between the Korean emperor and special ambassador Ito has been reported as follows:

> *The emperor:* Although I have seen in the newspaper various rumors that Japan proposed to assume a protectorate over Korea, I did not believe them, as I placed faith in Japan's adherence to the promise of maintaining the independence of Korea which was made by the emperor

of Japan at the beginning of the war and embodied in a treaty between Korea and Japan. When I heard you were coming to my country I was glad, as I believed your mission increased the friendship between our countries. Your demands have therefore taken me entirely by surprise.

Ito: These demands are not my own: I am only acting in accordance with a mandate from my government, and if your majesty will agree to the demands which I have presented it will be to the benefit of both nations, and peace in the Far East will be assured forever. Please, therefore, consent quickly.

The emperor: From time immemorial it has been the custom of the rulers of Korea, when confronted with questions so momentous as this, not to come to a decision until all the ministers have been consulted, and the opinion of the scholars and the common people have been obtained. I cannot, therefore, settle this matter myself.

Ito: Protests from the people can easily be disposed of. For the sake of the friendship between two countries your majesty should come to a decision at once.

The Korean emperor replied firmly: Assent to your proposals would mean the ruin of my country. I will sooner die than agree to them.

Ito's audience with the Korean emperor ended without result. The next day Ito and Hayashi, the Japanese minister, assembled all Korean cabinet members and demanded they accept the establishment of a Japanese protectorate over Korea. The members of the cabinet kept silent more than ten minutes. Then the minister of agriculture, commerce, and industry said: "Is it not rather contradictory for you, Mr. Ito, who advocated Korean independence on many occasions in the past, now to demand an end of Korean independence?"[40] When all members refused to approve the Japanese proposal, Ito demanded a joint audience with them and the emperor.

Finally, the Korean cabinet members agreed to hold a state advisory council with the emperor to discuss the proposal. The council meeting was held at the palace under heavy guard of Japanese soldiers. Hayashi and his subordinate officials also entered the palace and waited in the room next to that where the advisory council's meeting was being held. At the council meeting the members of the cabinet divided into two groups: the opposition group, headed by the prime minister, Han Kyu-sul; and the pro-Japanese group, headed by the minister of education, Yi Wan-yong.

The emperor discussed the Japanese demands with his ministers and attempted to delay a definite answer. But Ito drafted the protectorate treaty, placed Japanese soldiers around the palace, and secured the signatures of five out of eight Korean ministers on November 18, 1905. Prime Minister Han refused to sign.

The treaty[41] consisted of five articles preceded by an important preamble, the last sentence of which read: "The governments of Japan and Korea, desiring to strengthen the principle of solidarity which unites the two empires, have with that object in view agreed upon and concluded the following stipulations to serve until the moment arrives when it is recognized that Korea has attained national strength."

> *Article I.* The Government of Japan, through the Department of Foreign Affairs at Tokyo, will hereafter have control and direction of the external relations and affairs of Korea, and the diplomatic and consular representatives of Japan will have charge of the subjects and interests of Korea in foreign countries.
>
> *Article II.* The Government of Japan undertakes to see to the execution of the treaties actually existing between Korea and other powers, and the Government of Korea engages not to conclude hereafter any act of engagement having an international character, except through the medium of the Government of Japan.
>
> *Article III.* The Government of Japan shall be represented at the court of his Majesty the Emperor of Korea by a Resident-General, who shall reside at Seoul, primarily for the purpose of taking charge of and directing matters relating to diplomatic affairs. He shall have the right of private and personal audience of His Majesty the Emperor of Korea. The Japanese Government shall also have the right to station residents at the several open ports and such other places in Korea as they deem necessary. Such residents shall, under the direction of the Resident-General, exercise the powers and functions hitherto appertaining to Japanese consuls in Korea and shall perform such duties as may be necessary in order to carry into full effect the provisions of this agreement

Article IV. The stipulations of all treaties and agreements existing between Japan and Korea not inconsistent with the provisions of this agreement shall continue in force.

Article V. The Government of Japan undertakes to maintain the welfare and dignity of the Imperial House of Korea.

The last sentence of the preamble and Article V were added by Ito under pressure from the Korean cabinet members. Thus from the Japanese point of view, Japan became the "legitimate" protector of Korea: but the Korean emperor's secret message of November 26, 1905 (revealed by Hulbert, a one-time adviser to the emperor), shows that the so-called protectorate treaty was obtained "at the point of the sword and under duress."[42] The Korean emperor never consented and never signed it. Intimidation was used by the Japanese to secure a majority of signatures from the Korean ministers.

Much to the surprise of the Japanese government, the Korean emperor, in 1907, sent a secret delegation headed by Yi Sang-sul to the Hague Peace Conference to appeal the case of Korea to the world. The emperor's message read: "As the independence of Korea has been known to all the powers . . . we have, for this reason, the right to send delegates to all international conferences . . . . By the terms of the treaty of November 18, 1905, which was extorted from us by force, the Japanese by threat and by violation of all international equity deprived us of the right of direct communication with friendly powers. Not recognizing this act by the Japanese, we hereby appoint delegates for the purpose of making clear to the representatives of the powers the violations of our rights by the Japanese and the dangers which presently threaten our country; and also to reestablish between my country and the foreign powers the direct diplomatic relations to which we are entitled."[43]

The powers participating in the peace conference paid no attention to the Korean delegation and refused to recognize it as representing a sovereign state. The news of the Korean delegation, however, caused much concern to the Japanese government. Resident-General Ito forced the Korean emperor to give up the throne in favor of his fourteen-year-old son. A new agreement, which consisted of six points, was signed on July 24, 1907. In it the resident-general obtained virtually all powers from policy-making to the execution of the governmental functions both domestic and foreign.

The agreement stated: [1] "The government of Korea shall act under the guidance of the Resident General in respect to reform in administration; [2] [it shall] not enact any laws, ordinances, or regulations, or take any important measures of administration without the advance assent of the Resident General; [3] the judicial affairs in Korea shall be apart from the affairs of ordinary administration; [4] the appointment and dismissal of all high officials in Korea shall be made upon the concurrence of the Resident General; [5] the government of Korea shall appoint as Korean officials the Japanese subjects recommended by the Resident General; [6] the government of Korea shall not engage any foreigner without the concurrence of the Resident General."[44]

Outright annexation of Korea was the next step. The plan was launched when the minister of war, General Terauchi, an extreme military expansionist, was appointed as resident-general on May 30, 1910. He believed that "Korea must either be absorbed or decimated." His views were expressed by the Japanese-controlled press in Seoul in these terms: "The present requires an iron hand rather than a gloved one to secure lasting peace and order in this country. Japan is in this country to promote the happiness of the masses. She has not come to Korea to please a few hundred silly youngsters or to feed a few hundred titled loafers. Japan has dealt with Korean malcontents in a lenient way. She has learned from experience gained during the past five years that there are some persons who cannot be converted by conciliatory methods. There is but one way to deal with those people, and this is by stern and relentless methods."[45]

Terauchi was critical of Ito's "conciliatory" policy because it had failed to subdue the native anti-Japanese insurrections. Since the protectorate treaty many anti-Japanese insurrections occurred in Korea. In May 1906, the Righteous Army revolts broke out in many provinces. The intellectuals fanned nationalism and anti-Japanese sentiments through newspapers and pamphlets. In 1908 W. D. Stevens, the pro-Japanese American mentioned earlier, was assassinated by a Korean in San Francisco; in 1909 Ito was killed by a Korean nationalist in Harbin, and the puppet Korean minister Yi Wan-yong's life was threatened by nationalist youths in Seoul. The Japanese military extremists, who controlled the Korean cabinet, thought that "stern and relentless methods" were the only way to deal with the anti-Japanese Koreans and to bring about the annexation of Korea.

Since June 1910 several changes took place in the Japanese cabinet. A Bureau of Colonial Affairs was established under the supervision of the prime minister, and more than six hundred gendarmes were sent to Korea before Terauchi left Tokyo to take over his post as resident-general.

Terauchi arrived at Seoul on July 23 under unusually heavy guard. All vehicles of public opinion, such as newspapers and public meetings, were suspended; several Japanese warships appeared in the Korean ports, and the Japanese police were put on twenty-four hour duty throughout the country. By the end of July the peninsula was under the strict control of the Japanese police. Terauchi now ordered Akaishi Motojiro, commander of the gendarmerie and head of the Korean police, to visit each cabinet minister of the puppet Korean government to investigate attitudes on the intended annexation. None of the ministers opposed it.

On August 22, 1910, the treaty of annexation was signed by the resident-general, Terauchi, and puppet Prime Minister Yi Wan-yong: thus Korea became a colony. The office of the resident-general was replaced by that of the governor-general.

The annexation documents consisted of a proclamation and a treaty. The proclamation explained so-called reforms in the Korean administration.[46] Reforms did not mean needed socioeconomic improvements for the benefit of the Koreans. The Japanese administrative record of 35 years speaks for itself; "reforms" meant the reorganization of the native administration, Japanization of the Korean economy and cultural life, and an educational system in the interest of the Japanese empire.

Article 1 of the treaty reads: "His Majesty the Emperor of Korea completely and permanently cedes to His Majesty the Emperor of Japan all rights of sovereignty over the whole of Korea."[47]

THE REBELLIOUS PEASANTS

Early Peasant Revolts. Since the sixteenth century, peasants had from time to time turned against their masters. The government had no plans for the improvement of the stagnating agricultural economy; the landlords were not interested in introducing new technologies. Tenant peasants continued with primitive farming methods to till the land, which either belonged to the government or to public officials. As a result, agricultural production steadily declined, and the general living standard of the peasants deteriorated.

Several peasant uprisings were caused by floods or droughts followed by famine, but crude exploitation of the peasants by the local officials and official corruption also caused popular uprisings. The discontented peasants took violent action, but usually they lacked organization, leadership, and a systematic program. In all instances, rebellions were suppressed by the regular government armed forces. No peasant revolt was able to set up a new regime, although on many occasions the rebels menaced the authority of the central government. Among the peasant revolts, three uprisings were significant: the Lim Ko-jong revolt, the Hong Kyong-nai insurrection, and the Tonghak revolution.

The Lim Ko-jong Revolt (1562). Butchers were considered members of a "degrading profession" along with bailiffs, traveling singers, basketmakers, female sorcerers, dancing girls, and shoemakers. These occupations were inherited and could not be changed.

Lim Ko-jong was a butcher. He was not allowed to wear a hat, and his clothing was marked by a collar to be recognized by the public. In any social or public meeting he was the last to enter the hall, and allowed to take a seat only when everybody was seated; he was the last man to eat if anything was left over at the community festivals. He was paid in kind by the community, but was always underpaid.

To provide for his family, butcher Lim leased land and engaged in farming to obtain the needed additional income. But according to custom butchers were barred from farming. Therefore his land was confiscated, his father was tortured by the village head and Lim himself was to be next. But Lim killed the village head, fled, and took refuge in a Buddhist temple. After three months he left the temple and organized a band consisting of members of the degraded professions. They raided villages and towns during the nights and plundered the rural areas on market days. They established headquarters in Mount Chilchang in the Ahnsung district, manufactured weapons, and trained combat units. They raided the local *yangban* families and confiscated grains and valuables from them. Then they bribed local government officials with the valuables and distributed the confiscated grains to the poor peasants. This group gained considerable prestige among the lower classes in the Kwansee district (Pyongan province). The peasants called them the Righteous Army, the government referred to them as "butcher bandits."[48]

When this group threatened the authority of the government by blocking communication and transportation lines between the capital and the northern region, the government sent troops to subjugate them. The government forces met strong resistance, not only from the bandits, but from the local peasants too, and during the first few weeks a stalemate resulted. But when the rebels began to split into factions, the government forces suppressed them in 1562.

The Hong Kyong-nai Insurrection (1811). Another peasant insurrection occurred in 1811, caused by economic distress and famine in the northern rural provinces. Epidemics spread in the countryside and dead bodies piled up in public roads. Only one family in a hundred is said to have been able to secure sufficient food. Robbery was rampant. Neither the central government nor the local administration offered relief. During the winter and spring of 1811–12 the poverty-stricken peasants became desperate.

Hong Kyong-nai, a member of a northern *yangban* family, called upon the peasants to strike out against the government by refusing to pay taxes. The peasants and degraded professional classes responded to Hong's call and joined the insurrection. Many local northern *yangban* also joined and helped the rebels economically and politically. These *yangban* were discontent because they had been excluded from the government ever since the Yi dynasty was established as being too "radical" and too "revolutionary." The northern *yangban* believed that if the rebel forces could overthrow the regime, they might have a chance to replace the central *yangban* as a ruling class.

The rebels were led by Hong, who was born in the small town of Nongkang in southern Pyongan province. His family belonged to the local *yangban,* and although he had a chance to advance his social status, he had failed to pass the civil service examination. He was irritated by the squeeze policy of the government on poor peasants and by the corruption of local administrative officials. To overthrow the central government, he organized first a rebel group composed of the lower social classes. He obtained food from discontented local *yangban,* made contact with the opposing political faction in the capital headed by Park Jong-il, and obtained aid from hunters in the Kanggee area of the northern Pyongan province.

Hong established the rebel headquarters in Gasan, a small town in northern Pyongan province, and trained his men as combat forces for three years. Considerable amounts of military supplies and food were prepared. The peasant soldiers worked in the fields during the day and received military training at night. Hong became the de facto ruler in the area, calling himself commander in chief, or generalissimo.[49] He planned to set up a new regime after his soldiers had occupied the capital.

In the fall of 1811, Hong's forces occupied the northern section of the peninsula, that is, north of the Chungchun River. The next objective of the rebels was to occupy Pyongyang, the second largest city in the country. But the government troops launched an offensive and the rebel forces collapsed. Local *yangban* sided with the government, but it took the central government an additional five months to break the rebels' resistance completely.

The Tonghak Insurrection (1894). The most important peasant revolution in Korean history was the Tonghak (Eastern Learning) revolt. As pointed out previously this revolt became one of the causes for the Sino-Japanese war of 1894, because both the Chinese and Japanese governments sent troops under the pretext of suppressing the rebel forces and protecting their legations.

To understand the nature and the meaning of the Tonghak revolt it would be helpful to sum up the socioeconomic and political conditions after the Korean-Japanese commercial treaty of 1876. Korea was still an Asiatic feudal society. Politically the king was the absolute head of the state, but party disputes and reliance upon a big power (*sadae-sasang*) were the predominant political facts of life of the ruling class. The pro-Chinese Min family was the most powerful. Economically Korea was a backward, stagnating country, dependent on a primitive agrarian economy and handicraft industry; a large segment of the economy was under state control. Society was composed of a small minority made up of privileged groups, *yangban,* and the vast number of peasants and degraded professions making up more than 90 percent of the population.

Since Korea was forced to open her door to the foreign powers, her foreign trade increased rapidly; from 1877 to 1881 imports increased eight times; and from 1885 to 1891 exports increased four times. The Japanese, Chinese, and British flooded the country with their merchandise. Foreign-made textiles exceeded all other imported goods. The native handicraft industries were ruined. Rice exported by the Japanese merchants in Korea exceeded all other exports, and shortages in the rural areas became acute, leading to social unrest.

No native merchants who could compete with the foreign merchants existed, and no industrial revolution as in the Western nations took place in Korea. The country faced bankruptcy by the penetration of foreign merchants, especially Chinese and Japanese.

The treasury ran into debt, and the government imposed more taxes on the peasants. Most peasants could not pay the taxes because landlords usually collected rent (which amounted to from 50 to 80 percent of the total harvest of the tenants) before the government tax collectors came around to the peasants. In addition, the total cultivated land area had decreased considerably during the previous two hundred years; the population also had decreased during the same period. Although grain production had declined, rice export to Japan jumped from 0 to 200,000 *suk* (one *suk* equals five bushels).

The Japanese merchants, especially rice merchants and moneylenders, took advantage of the Korean peasants. The peasants, who had no experience in business, needed money desperately to pay their taxes (monetary taxation was adopted in place of taxes in kind) and in many cases sold their grains before the harvest to the Japanese at a lower than market price. The difference was from 50 to 70 percent. Many peasants lost their lands to the Japanese because the Koreans could not pay their debts on the fixed day. The government had no power to intervene. The inaction of the central government and the exploitation by the Japanese merchants aroused anti-Japanese and antiforeign feelings among the peasants throughout the country, especially in the agricultural south.

At this point, the foreign powers, including the United States, Russia, and France, sent forces to protect their legations, nationals, and properties in Seoul. This move caused indignation among the discontented intellectuals, peasants, and lower social groups. The grievances of the masses against the do-nothing regime and the aggressive foreign powers, especially the Japanese, now gathered momentum and the Tonghak-led peasant revolution broke out.

Tonghak is a native religious sect based on a Messianic cult; it was founded by Choi Bok-sool (or Jee-woo) in 1860 in Kyongsang province of South Korea. Choi was born in 1802 in a poor local *yangban* family. Lacking means, he could not obtain a high government position. He spent his youth traveling but finally settled in the Naiwon-am temple and studied Buddhism, Christianity, Taoism, and Confucianism, as well as Shamanism. Refusing to accept any of these religions, he received divine guidance and in a state of religious ecstasy founded a new religion, which he named Tonghak (Tonghak, Eastern Learning, in contrast to Suhak, or Western Learning). Tonghak preached the doctrine of the opening of a New World,[50] which gave hope to the discontented peasants and fanned the peasant revolution. The idea of a new world coincided with the traditional superstitious story of Chunggam-rok, which predicted that "the Yi dynasty will come to an end as soon as it completes its five-hundred-year rule over Korea," and that "a new kingdom will be established by a new ruler in Mount Gainong as a new capital."[51]

The rumor about the rise of a new kingdom spread over the country, and thousands of peasants and lower social groups flocked to join the Tonghak sect. Tonghak intellectuals, discontented with the existing regime, complained about official corruption and about incompetence of the government in domestic and foreign affairs. The government responded by persecution, condemning to death Choi Bok-sool, the founder of the Tonghak, for "misleading the people."

Choi Shi-hong succeeded him as leader. He published a collection of Choi Bok-sool's writings. He reorganized the Tonghak followers into a religious rather than a political organization, and appointed six subdivision heads. Most of them were well-to-do *yangban,* but politically dissatisfied with the central government. Some of them, like Shon Byong-hi, Shu In-ju, and Shon Min-chan, were Confucian scholars, nationalistic and opposed to foreign influence in general, and to the Japanese in particular.

The Tonghak leaders at first attempted to secure redress by passive resistance to the government. In 1893 they petitioned the king and staged a sit-down strike, fasting for three days and nights in front of the royal palace. In doing so, the religious element became secondary to the political protest against the oppressive policies of the government. At this time, unfounded rumors of a general uprising in the south against the native regime and the foreigners reached the capital, and the foreign legations were alerted. The king issued a decree to pacify them, and the leaders of the strike returned to their homes. This was the first of two revolts led by the Tonghak leaders in the capital.

In 1894 a second revolt, sparked by the discontented intellectual Tonghak *yangban* but carried out by the peasants, occurred in rural Kobu-gun, Chulla province. The oppressive policy of the local government officials caused the peasant uprising there. Cho Byong-kap, the head of Kobu county, reconstructed the Mansikbok reservoir with the labor of the local peasants by promising to reduce the rent for the water of their rice paddies; Cho broke his promise and collected extra rice from the peasants for himself. He jailed many peasants who were unable to pay. The Kobu peasants sent three representatives to the county office asking Cho for the release of the prisoners. Cho arrested the three representatives, too.

Chun Bong-jun, a leader of the peasants, stirred the peasants into attacking the county buildings and destroying public documents and government property. They seized some weapons from the officials, opened the government warehouse, and distributed the government-collected rice and other grains to the peasants. Similar uprisings occurred in other places in Chulla province. Chun Bong-jun issued a public statement on behalf of the rebellious masses, which read: "Our uprising has no other intention than to emancipate the masses from their economic and political oppression and to establish a strong national government. We arose to clean up the corruption and tyrannical government officials and to expel all aggressive foreigners from our country. We, the people, have suffered long under the yoke of the *yangban* and government officials; we have been treated like slaves and servants rather than like human beings. We will not stand this any longer."[52]

Within a few days after this proclamation, more than two thousand peasants and underprivileged persons joined Chun's "revolutionary army."[53] A history of this revolution could be divided into two stages: the "civil war" and the anti-Japanese revolution.

The civil war between the rebels and the government lasted from January to June of 1894. The principal targets of the peasants were the government buildings and prisons. Government stores of grains and clothing were distributed freely among the people. Prisoners were set free. During the first two months, the local government forces were defeated by the peasant soldiers at every front. In March the central government appointed Gen. Hong Gaihun as commanding general of the Honam region and dispatched one thousand well-trained troops to Chulla province, equipped with modern artillery. The poorly armed untrained peasant soldiers were no match for them. But the peasant army changed to guerrilla warfare and lured the government troops into the rural areas by retreating from the coastlines. The decisive battle took place in the city of Chunju, the main stronghold of the government forces in the southern section. The peasant soldiers surrounded the city, the governor of Chulla province fled the city, and the government troops surrendered to the rebels. This was the first major military defeat of the central government by the rebels.

The central government issued a public statement[54] as a gesture of conciliation to the rebels and promised remedies for the past wrongs of the local officials. Chun Bong-jun proposed a program[55] to the government as the basis for a truce agreement. The central government accepted the proposal, and hostilities ceased in May 1894. Thus the civil war ended.

The second stage of the peasant revolution—the stage of anti-Japanese resistance—began when the Japanese government sent her troops to Korea in June 1894. As pointed out previously, Japan intervened in Korea to bring about an end to the Chinese influence in Korea, to suppress the anti-Japanese revolution, and to dominate the Korean peninsula.

The Japanese avoided any direct attack on the native peasants for the first three months; instead, they concentrated on an offensive against Chinese forces in the northern peninsula which had been called in by the Korean king. At the end of September, the Japanese won a decisive battle over the Chinese by taking Pyongyang; thereafter the main battle ground shifted from Korea to the Liaotung Peninsula in China. The Japanese did not want to see an early end to the peasant revolution because one of their pretexts for sending their troops to Korea was to suppress it. From the strategic point of view, it was a great advantage to the Japanese to avoid a two-front war—the Chinese in the North and the Korean peasant army in the South. Therefore, the Japanese were satisfied with taking a defensive position in the South and checking the penetration of peasant forces above the Kongju defense line until the Chinese main forces collapsed in the North.

The Japanese offensive against the peasants started in the middle of autumn. The peasant army had established headquarters in Nonsan. A great number of the peasant soldiers were mobilized under the command of Chun Bong-jun in the non-occupied rural area. The battle with the Japanese began at the end of October at Kongju, one of the strongholds of the Japanese southern defense line. The peasant army was forced to retreat; Nonsan, the peasant headquarters, fell to the Japanese, and the peasant forces disintegrated and ceased to exist as an organized fighting force. Chun Bong-jun was arrested by the Korean government and executed in the capital in January 1895.

The revolution suffered from a lack of principles. The immediate objectives of the peasant revolution were the overthrow of the regime and the expulsion of the interventionists, but no long-term objectives—a basic requirement for social revolution—were formulated by the leaders. The leadership of the revolution at first was dominated by the discontented *yangban* intellectuals, and their primary concern was the creation of an indigenous religion, the Tonghak sect.[56] The religious purpose became secondary to the political issue only when the peasants and underprivileged social groups rose against the official oppression and the foreign interventionists. No well-organized and trained revolutionary leadership rose from the peasant class itself, and the whole uprising had to depend on one man, Chun Bong-jun, who had no experience in social revolution. Still, the peasant revolution made a significant contribution; the peasant class itself became a progressive political force by advocating socioeconomic betterment of the lower social groups and by fighting against the native feudal regime and Japanese expansionism. The 1894 peasant revolution also inspired the anti-Japanese resistant movement that occurred following the protectorate treaty in 1905.

THE INDEPENDENCE CLUB

After the Sino-Japanese war, an intellectual political movement started in Korea influenced by Western ideology. An American-educated leader, Shu Chai-pil (who later became an American citizen and assumed the name of Dr. Philip Jaisohn) formed a political debating club called Hyupsung-hai

(Mutual Friendship Society) in Seoul. Students as well as the general public were invited to the meetings, and they discussed current political issues. The main purpose of the club was to study Western politics, especially parliamentary procedures and constitutional laws.

Some members of the club founded a newspaper, issued three days a week, called *Doknip* (Independence), written half in English and half in Korean. The first issue appeared on April 7, 1896. This was the time when the Korean king fled to the Russian legation and formed a pro-Russian Korean cabinet, and when the Japanese government suffered diplomatic defeats because of the direct participation of a Japanese official in the murder of the Korean queen and because of the Japanese withdrawal from the Liaotung Peninsula. On June 7 Shu Chai-pil formed the Independence Club as a reform political party. The immediate concern of the group was the Russian threat to Korean independence.

In February 1897 the Korean king moved from the Russian legation to a new palace which had been built near the American legation. During the one-year asylum the king had made economic concessions to the Russians, such as giving them a lumber monopoly and mining rights. As mentioned before, it was on Russian advice that the Korean king assumed the title of emperor, and that the official name of the country was changed to "Empire of Daehan."

The Independence Club endeavored to achieve national independence without foreign influence and to introduce reforms in internal administration. Under the leadership of Shu, who became an adviser to the king's privy council, the Independence Club raised funds and erected the Independence Arch in Seoul[57] as a symbol of national independence. The club also submitted to the king a reform program,[58] which was signed by 135 members. The essential points of the program were to abandon the traditional idea of reliance upon a big power and to "enforce justice" in the administration of domestic affairs.

The Independence Club also advocated reform by modernization of the administration. The club further called for freedom of speech, assembly, religion, and organization of the people, and for the introduction of modern (Western) education and a free enterprise economy. As to foreign policy, the club stood for national independence without dependence on either Japan or Russia. The club especially opposed economic concessions by the king to foreign powers.

The members of the club were active when the Russian government issued an ultimatum in March 1898 threatening its withdrawal of economic and military aid from Korea. The club denounced the Russian threat and asked the king to accept the Russian offer of withdrawal from Korea. With this popular support, the king accepted. The Russian-Korean bank was closed, and all Russian military and financial advisers returned to Russia. This was the end of the Russian influence in Korea, temporarily at least. For the next two years (1898–90) Korea was able to maintain her independence without direct interference by foreign powers.

The Independence Club thereafter concentrated on internal reform issues and was able to convince the king to accept some of its proposals. In October 1898 a new cabinet was formed in which some Independence Club leaders became members. But the ousted reactionary group urged the king to dismiss the members of the Independence Club from the cabinet. The king reversed his policy, dissolved the cabinet, disbanded the club, and arrested its leaders. The Independence Club held a big mass meeting in the great square before the ancient Big Bell; continuous mass meetings were held day and night in the streets.

The government arrested more members of the club. The reactionary clique hastily organized an "emperor support club" and employed members of the Peddlers Guild to hold counterdemonstrations in answer to Independence Club demonstrations. This led to street fights between the two clubs. Disorder and confusion continued for several days. In the clashes one Independence Club member was killed. The king called the leaders of both sides and asked them to work out a compromise in forming a new cabinet. Yun Chi-ho, the president of the Independence Club and Kim Yung-su, representative of the Emperor Support Club, agreed. The king then bestowed legislative powers on the privy council and increased its members by twenty-five from each of the opposing clubs. Yun was chosen as chairman of the privy council. The reactionary elements were not happy about the Independence Club dominating the privy council and once again asked the king to intervene. The king dissolved the newly formed privy council, ordered again the arrest of the Independence Club members, and forced the club out of existence. Some of the members, including Syngman Rhee, received jail sentences for "antistate activities," and a few of them, such as Shu Chai-pil, took political refuge in Japan or the United States. Rhee came to the United States in November 1904 after he was released from prison.

The remaining leaders in Korea could not take an active part in politics. They merely formed a Constitutional Politics Study Society in 1905, and promoted through newspapers and magazines the concept of popular rights and the theory of constitutional government and parliamentary procedures. After the Russo-Japanese war, they opposed Japanese intervention; their exposure of secret negotiations on the protectorate treaty between the Japanese envoy Ito and the Korean cabinet members was one of their important contributions. The exposé was made in the famous editorial of the *Whangsung Newspaper* protesting the illegal Japanese protectorate and the treacherous members of the Korean cabinet who signed the treaty. The editorial said: "The ministers of our government, who are worse than pigs or dogs, coveting honors and advantages for themselves and frightened by empty threats, trembled in every limb, became traitors to their country, and betrayed to Japan the integrity of a nation which stood for 4,000 years, the foundation and honor of a dynasty 500 years old, and the rights and freedom of twenty million people."[59]

The *Whangsung Newspaper* was immediately suppressed and the editor thrown into prison by the Japanese. The reform movement of the Korean intellectuals had come to an end.

A few final comments on the Independence Club should be added. The club made several contributions to Korean politics; it introduced nationalism, which was based on the rationalistic philosophy of the eighteenth century. Korean nationalism meant, according to the Independence Club, "not to lean on another nation nor to tolerate foreign interference in the national administration." Thus Korean nationalism emphasized only the idea of political independence and ignored the importance of economic and cultural independence. Furthermore, it failed in suggesting how to develop a reasonable, independent foreign policy, which would secure independence. The Independence Club missed the opportunity of proposing to the large powers —Russia, Japan, China, the United States, and Great Britain—an international agreement for permanent neutrality of Korea in the Far East like that of Switzerland.

The members of the club fought for popular rights and the freedoms of speech, assembly, and organization, but failed to introduce the concept of popular sovereignty. Instead, the club accepted the idea of the sovereignty of the king. Therefore the club's mentality was still dominated by traditional emperor worship and by the authoritarian concept in politics.

The club members condemned the protectorate treaty as well as the pro-Japanese Korean cabinet, but they again failed to offer a constructive program: namely, how the Korean people should act against Japanese domination. Statements of public mourning were not enough. The leaders of the Independence Club belonged to the upper social class. They had isolated themselves from the people, especially from the peasants and the degraded social groups. The political reform measures of the club had nothing to do directly with the problems of the lower social groups—the socioeconomic improvement of the majority of the population. Therefore they got no support from the people during the struggle for political reform.

THE ANTI-JAPANESE MOVEMENT (1906–10)

In 1906 an anti-Japanese resistance movement was started by former government officials (civilian and military), patriotic intellectuals, and peasants. The suicide letter[60] of Min Yong-wan, former Korean minister of war, protesting the Japanese protectorate, roused patriotic spirits and intensified anti-Japanese feelings throughout the country. Following the suicide, a declaration of the Korean people's protest against the Japanese protectorate was issued by the representatives of each province (eight at that time), which exhorted the people to strike against Japan, and, if necessary, to die together rather than be slowly killed by the Japanese.[61]

The revolt broke out in May 1906, at Hongju in South Chungchong province. It was called "Righteous Army Uprising against the Japanese Intervention,"[62] and its leader was Min Chong-sik, a former cabinet member. The rebels captured the city of Hongju, but the Japanese suppressed the insurgents by killing eighty and capturing fifty. The next insurrection occurred in North Chulla province in June under the leadership of Choi Ik-hyun, a Confucian scholar and former civilian government official. He sent out messengers to all parts of the country denouncing the protectorate treaty and the establishment of the resident-general, and incited young men, mostly the literati in the provinces. The insurgents captured the town of Shunchang in North Chulla province, but in July 1906 were compelled to surrender to the Japanese. In the meantime, youth groups in Seoul attempted to assassinate five traitors, who had signed the protectorate treaty, but only one, Kwan Jung-hyub, was killed and the rest fled to the Japanese legation.

Again, large-scale insurrections broke out in the summer of 1907 when the Japanese demanded the dissolution of the Korean army. Japanese Resident-General Ito and the military commander Hasegawa requested puppet Prime Minister Yi Wan-yong and Minister of the Army Yi Byong-mu to disband the army. On the morning of August 1, the minister of the army ordered all Korean troops in Seoul to assemble in the drill ground and dismissed thirty-six hundred soldiers. Gen. Park Song-hwan, commander of the first regiment, committed suicide in protest, and this provoked insurrections in the capital by the disbanded soldiers. Street fights between the Japanese regular troops and the Korean soldiers ensued for several hours; then the insurgents were forced to retreat to the country.

In December 1907 insurgents organized a liberation army composed of soldiers, peasants, and the lower social groups. They selected Yangju as their headquarters, and Yi Rin-yong as the supreme commander. Yi appointed five regional commanding generals, dividing the peninsula into five military operation districts for conducting a liberation war against the Japanese administration and nullifying the protectorate treaty. They sent out their secret agents all over the country, including the capital, distributing handbills.

From the later part of December 1907 general insurrections occurred throughout the country. On many occasions transportation and communication lines were severed by the liberation army, and guerrilla warfare was conducted in remote rural areas. The liberation activities concentrated on several aims: to wipe out the Japanese wherever they found them, to destroy Japanese military and police facilities, to cut transportation and communication lines, to assassinate pro-Japanese Korean government officials, and to destroy all pro-Japanese political and social organizations.

In the rural areas the liberationists' activities caused trouble to the Japanese.

In Hamkyong province, the liberation army temporarily occupied most local police stations; the leaders of the liberators ruled these areas until regular Japanese troops reoccupied them. The local people participated in the liberation movement. Residents of Nokdo in South Chulla province participated in the liberation activities; more than two hundred railroad workers in Monhwa county of Hwanghai province also joined.

The Japanese suppressed the insurgents ruthlessly. Any town or village suspected as rebellious was burned and all residents executed without trial. The Japanese organized so-called self-defense corps in each town and village composed of pro-Japanese political and social organizations. This corps was under the supervision of the local Japanese police chief, and if any local resident refused to join the self-defense corps, he was accused of membership in the liberation army.

The Japanese released the statistics shown in table 2 as the result of the five-year activity of the liberation army.

TABLE 2. ACTIVITIES OF THE LIBERATION ARMY[63]

Year	*Number of "rebels"*	*Number of incidents*
1907	44,116	322
1908	69,804	1,451
1909	27,663	953
1910	1,891	147
1911	216	32

During these years, 17 thousand insurgents were killed and 36 thousand wounded; 9 thousand surrendered; 966 pro-Japanese Koreans were killed. Japanese casualties and property damage were not publicized by the Japanese, but the figures must have been large.

The insurgents were defeated, primarily because they had to fight with medieval weapons against a modern army. By 1910 the country was more or less "pacified" by the Japanese, and most surviving insurgents retreated to the mountainous northern provinces and later to Manchuria. There they established the anti-Japanese resistance movement headquarters at many different places inside the Manchurian borders. From there the rebels could easily cross the frozen Yalu and Tuman rivers during the winter. They established a number of military training schools, recruiting cadets among the Korean immigrants in Manchuria, especially in Bookkando. The immigrants were estimated to total about 250 thousand in 1912, and the number steadily increased following the annexation. During the night the well-trained rebels (then called the independence army)[64] crossed the rivers and attacked Japanese police stations, government buildings, and sometimes banks. They also called on wealthy native landlords and demanded cash contributions for the cause of the national independence movement. This kind of guerrilla warfare continued in northern Korea until the Japanese occupied Manchuria and established the puppet state of Manchukuo in 1932.

In addition, at the beginning of the twentieth century, especially after the Russo-Japanese war, a progressive nationalistic movement arose under the leadership of young Koreans. Some of the leading figures of this movement were Ahn Chang-ho (Dosan), Lee Kap, and Lee Tong-hi. They launched what is known as the Patriotic Enlightenment Movement,[65] emphasizing national consciousness, self-governing national independence, and development of national culture. They established many private schools, academic associations, and social organizations in the major cities, such as the Daisung school in Pyongyang, the Shunhung school in Ahnju, the Bochang school in Kwanghwa, and the Research Institute of the Korean Language League. Many nationalistic publications, like the biographies of Gen. Ulji Moonduk and Adm. Yi Shoon-shin, were read widely among young intellectuals. Many foreign works were being translated: the histories of the French Revolution, and the independence of America, Italy, Indochina, and Poland. Public lectures and night schools were opened under the sponsorship of the Patriotic Enlightenment Movement in many major cities. Mass meetings protesting both foreign intervention and the native puppet regime were held throughout the country. But this new nationalistic movement was also suppressed by the ruthless measures of the Japanese resident-general. Many leaders were jailed. All schools, publications, and organizations were forced to close. Some of the nationalistic leaders escaped abroad; among them was Ahn Chang-ho, one of Korea's great patriots, who first fled to China and later to the United States.[66] Hereafter the anti-Japanese resistance movement went underground in Korea. The political refugees abroad, mainly in China and the United States, carried on the movement.

CHAPTER 6

KOREA UNDER JAPANESE DOMINATION

1910–45

POLITICAL SUPPRESSION

Japanese colonial policy consisted of political suppression, economic exploitation, and cultural assimilation. Koreans had no political or civil rights, and high government positions were not open to them; more than 85 percent of the total national wealth was under Japanese control; and no teaching of Korean history, culture, or language was allowed in the schools, where, instead, Japanese history, culture, and language were taught. The Japanese colonial rule over Korea of thirty-five years could be divided into three stages, each of which was significant in establishing certain institutions and procedures: the period of *mudan-jungchi,* or rule by military force; of *munhwa-jungchi,* or "enlightened" (liberal) policy; and of *Naisun-ilche-jungchi,* or "Japan and Korea oneness" policy.

The Mudan-jungchi Period (1910–19). The Japanese government of Korea (government-general, or in Japanese, *Chosen sotokufu*) was administered through a governor-general, a military man, responsible to the Japanese emperor, who appointed him upon the recommendation of the prime minister. He was absolute dictator in Korea—the chief executive, the lawmaker, the commander-in-chief—and he had the right to appoint and dismiss government officials, including the judges. The executive authority of the governor-general included the right to demand the use of armed forces in Korea when he considered it necessary. He also had the right to imprison anyone in Korea for up to one year and to impose a fine of up to two hundred yen, or both, without trial.

Theoretically, the post of governor-general was open to Japanese civilians as well as to military men, but no civilian ever held that post. During the thirty-five year rule, six generals (most of them belonging to the extremist army clique) and one admiral were governors-general. The first two, Terauchi (1910–16) and Hasegawa (1917–19) were the foremost militarists of their day and firmly believed in the use of force in politics.

The structure of the Korean government-general was relatively simple: the governor-general was head of the administration; under him were fifteen thousand staff members of the government. The civil administrator, appointed by the prime minister, was the chief administrative assistant of the governor-general; he was assisted by a secretary, and supervised the government bureaus—home affairs, finance, business, agriculture and forestry, justice, education, and police. In 1943 the bureaus were reorganized and several added, such as monopoly, commerce, mining and industry, and railways.

The commander of the Japanese gendarmerie (military police) in Korea became simultaneously the chief of the Korean national police force, and in each province the local commander of the gendarmerie became the head of the local police until the national police reorganization became effective. In addition to these forces, three army divisions were stationed in strategic places, and two naval bases were established. Thus the police and the armed forces became the chief elements in the power structure of the government-general.

Local administration was split into many subdivisions from the province to the village: Korea was divided into 13 provinces, 20 cities, 218 counties, more than 100 towns, 2,000 townships, and 50,000 villages, and 2 large islands, Chejudo and Ulnungdo. The heads of the provinces, cities, and counties were appointed by the governor-general; the heads of the towns and townships by head of the county. The heads of villages were elected by the people, but they were under the absolute control of the Japanese, usually the police chief of the township. Most heads of the township were Koreans because few Japanese could be found who wanted to work in mountainous or small out-of-the-way places for niggardly wages of less than 20 yen a month. However, Japanese personnel dominated governorships, mayorships, and the headships of counties and towns. In short, the high administrative positions were monopolized by the Japanese, and the Koreans were allowed to hold clerical and minor posts only.

The governor-general created a puppet advisory body, the Central Advisory Council (Chungchu-won), whose members were chosen from native Koreans who had backgrounds of quisling activities during the annexation, and belonged to aristocratic and wealthy families. The council was created as early as September 1910. The sixty-five councilors were selected by the governor-general and appointed by the Japanese cabinet in Tokyo for three-year terms. The council could offer advice only at the request of the governor-general, and then only upon a specific subject. The membership of the council was composed of the vice-governor-general, the only Japanese in the council, who was the president; one vice-president; five advisers; and sixty-five councilors. The technical staff consisted of a chief of the secretariat, a secretary, seven clerks, and seven interpreters. Of the councilors, 24 of the 65 were selected from the provinces and the rest from the capital city; all were either formerly connected with the old puppet government or had business ties with the Japanese.

The main subjects about which the governor-general from time to time asked the council's advice were limited to native customs and beliefs, and never concerned important issues.[1]

The general conditions of public life following the annexation can be judged from the official annual report of 1912, by the Chosen Government-General:

> An association having Confucianism as its object existed in Koshu district, Kokai province, and, showing itself inimical to the public peace by teaching the so-called 'natural-law doctrine', was advised by the authorities concerned to dissolve, which it did in April 1911. Another association, organized by followers of Confucius in Mosan district, was advised on October 11 to dissolve on the same ground. The so-called Communal Association reported its dissolution to the police on April 11, on having been given advice to that effect. In July, a branch office of the business association in Zenshu district was ordered to dissolve as its condition was prejudicial to public peace. The holding of public meetings or the gathering of crowds out of doors was prohibited, except for religious gatherings or school excursions, permission for which might be obtained from the police authorities.[2]

As mentioned, all political organizations and institutions were forced to dissolve on the eve of the annexation. In the autumn of 1911 virtually no social or religious organizations were left to be dissolved, except the Christian and Buddhist churches in Korea. The governor-general was determined to stamp out the influence of Christianity too. One hundred thirty-five native Christian leaders were arrested and charged with a plot[3] to assassinate Governor-General Terauchi. Three of the accused died in prison as the result of tortures; nine were banished without trial; and one hundred and five were sentenced to imprisonment for from five to ten years.

The powers of the gendarmerie, or military police, and the police were not limited to the maintenance of order and the detection of crime but penetrated into every aspect of life of the individual and community, such as in the fields of politics, economic activity, religion, education, public welfare, and health. They were given the right to enter any residence at any time, to arrest anyone without warrant, to serve as prosecutors in the court, and to pass summary judgments on those arrested. More than 16 thousand gendarmerie and police stations with 22 thousand armed regular gendarmes and police and 200 thousand auxiliary gendarmes and police were assigned to control 20 million Koreans. The gendarmes and police outnumbered the teachers, physicians, priests, geomancers, and sorcerers taken together. All government officials, including teachers, were required to wear uniforms and swords during the first decade of control.

In 1912 more than 50 thousand Koreans were arrested by the police and gendarmes; in 1917 more than 130 thousand; and in 1918 more than 140 thousand. The punishments which policemen and gendarmes used were barbarous tortures, like flogging, needle-pinching, or pouring water in the nose. Only 30 to 50 out of every 10 thousand were able "to prove their innocence," about 1200 were "pardoned," and the rest were either fined or imprisoned. The government-general built more prisons than any other buildings in the capital, at the cost of 300 thousand yen, in 1912. Most prisoners in those days were political offenders who opposed Japanese rule.

During the first decade, 1910–19, the Japanese government created a centralized militaristic administration, the government-general, headed by the governor-general. The government-general exercised absolute power over Korea, suppressed virtually all existing native political, social, and cultural organizations, and deprived the Korean people of their basic human freedoms; he also created a puppet institution, the Central Advisory Council, staffed by members of the native aristocratic and wealthy classes as a political tool in support of the Japanese colonial policy. The foundation of colonial exploitation was firmly established by the military and police forces in Korea.

The Munhwa-jungchi Period (1919–30). The second period was known as that of "liberal" administration. During this decade the Japanese government introduced reforms as a means of social and economic domination by cooperation between the Japanese administration and Korean aristocratic landlords.

The change of policy from *mudan-jungchi* to *munhwa-jungchi* was caused by the uprising of the Korean National Independence Movement of 1919 against the ten-year-old Japanese rule and by Japan's domestic needs of Korean natural resources for further industrialization and militarization. The 1919 independence demonstration was the first nationwide uprising against Japanese colonial rule. The Japanese themselves were surprised that the Koreans, who had no arms and were controlled by the Japanese military and police, were strong enough to demonstrate to the world that they wanted to free themselves. More than two million Koreans representing all social and religious groups in the country took part in these demonstrations for more than six months. The Japanese finally suppressed the movement by force. According to Korean sources[4] (Japanese official reports differed), more than seven thousand demonstrators were killed, fifteen thousand wounded, and fifty-two thousand imprisoned.

The Japanese government blamed the uprising at first on ill-informed Koreans who believed in a speedy German victory in the First World War; then they blamed the Bolshevik revolution in Russia as having influenced some Korean groups; finally, they blamed Koreans who misunderstood the meaning of Wilson's principle of self-determination for small nations. However, the Japanese learned two lessons from the uprising: that the overwhelming majority of the Koreans rejected the Japanese colonial rule, and that the Japanese sword alone could not subdue Korean nationalism.

The second factor was more important than the first. Following the First World War, Japan emerged as one of the young imperialistic powers. It considered itself the strongest power in the Far East, in terms of industrial development and military strength. But, like Great Britain, Japan lacked natural resources, raw materials, and food for further industrialization and militarization. Therefore, Japan had to exploit Korea's natural resources and labor power. To achieve this, the Japanese realized that "peace and order" had to be restored in Korea through peaceful means rather than by force alone, because rebellious Koreans would not be economically productive and politically cooperative.

General Hasegawa, one of the most ruthless governors-general, who persecuted thousands of Korean national independence demonstrators, was recalled and Admiral Saito (later a viscount) was sent to Seoul as the new replacement in August 1919. He announced a new Japanese policy, which he called one of liberal and righteous administration, based on the following points: the post of governor-general opened to civilians; nondiscrimination between Japanese and Koreans; simplification of laws and regulations; promptness in conducting state business; decentralization of power; revision of local organizations; respect for native culture and customs; freedom of speech, assembly, and press; spread of education and development of industry; reorganization of the police; expansion of medical and sanitary organizations; guidance of popular thought; opportunity for men of talent; and promotion of good relations between Japanese and Koreans.[5]

Before examining these "reform" measures it should be noted that, even if Saito's statement were taken at its face value, the reform program was not designed for the benefit of the Koreans, but in the interest of the Japanese. There was not much hope for success. Japan itself had been a militaristic authoritarian state granting no political freedom, civil rights, or economic benefits to its own people—how then could it give these rights to the Koreans? Besides, most Koreans were not interested in any reform program introduced by the Japanese administration, because the Koreans' main concern was how to regain their lost independence.

The Japanese government failed in implementing the first point during the thirty-five year rule over Korea: no civilian was appointed governor-general. The governors-general were General Terauchi, General Hasegawa, Admiral Saito, General Ugaki, General Minami, General Koiso, and General Abe.

The promise of nondiscrimination between Japanese and Koreans was never fulfilled. Most Japanese, especially the Japanese officials in the Korean government-general, considered themselves masters of the Koreans. The Japanese administration tolerated discrimination between Japanese and Koreans in every respect; for example, Japanese and Korean policemen who had the same education and the same official rank were paid differently; the former usually received from 20 to 25 percent more. The same was true of school teachers, industrial workers, and business executives. The Japanese residents, mostly government officials and businessmen, segregated themselves from the natives by living in different sections of the urban districts, having better schools for their children, better means of transportation, and better sanitary facilities. Such discrimination also prevailed in Japan. Korean students in Tokyo and other Japanese cities were refused by Japanese landlords the rental of rooms,[6] and the Japanese often used insulting language in addressing Koreans.

"Simplification of laws and regulations" and "promptness in conducting state business" were practiced in order to eliminate unnecessary red tape and to move administrative machinery rapidly from one place to another without delay in case of emergency. For example, under these practices, some of the detailed periodical reports by subordinate officials to the governor-general were eliminated; the provincial governors could appoint or dismiss minor subordinate officials without asking the approval of the governor-general; and school teachers and certain government officials were no longer required to wear uniforms and swords. Obviously these reforms were of no direct benefit to Koreans.

Under the policy of "decentralization of power," police and sanitary officers were placed under the control of the governors of the provinces, who were responsible to the governor-general. Thus the local authorities could use the police at any time without the approval of the central authority. In reality this was nationalization rather than decentralization to meet any local emergency without delay. As described later, the police forces steadily increased and were often used arbitrarily by the local authorities after the decentralization of power.

The Japanese government attempted to induce wealthy Koreans to cooperate with the Japanese by introducing provincial, municipal, and village councils under the reform program of "revision of local organization." The members of the local councils were to be chosen partly in council elections, partly by advisory bodies to the local administration heads, partly by the governors, partly by the heads of the counties, partly by mayors, and partly by the heads of the townships. However, most Koreans did not take part in the council elections. In the provincial council election, the number of council members was fixed by the governor-general, and not by the governors of the provinces. The number ran from twenty-one to forty-five. One-third of the members of the council were appointed by the governor-general upon the recommendation of the governor, mostly from the resident Japanese; the rest were elected. The voting qualifications included ability to read and write Japanese and payment of a minimum in local taxes. Because of these restrictions only a small minority of Koreans could cast their votes compared with Japanese residents. No figures on the provincial council elections were available for 1920, but the municipal council election results show that "the Japanese, who made up only 25 percent of the municipal population, elected 203 council members out of 268."[7] In any event, the councils, although they had no power in the affairs of government, served the political purposes of the Japanese, because a small segment of wealthy Koreans participated in the Japanese administration by their own choice.

Under the name of "respect for native culture and customs," the Japanese administration encouraged Koreans to keep primitive and superstitious customs. It was permitted to have graves in one's own yard as an expression of ancestor worship and to wear mourning dresses for three years after one's parents died. However, the Japanese regime did not allow Koreans to teach Korean history, language, and culture in the schools. This policy was an attempt to keep the Koreans ignorant so that the Japanese could control them easily.

"Freedom of speech, assembly, and press" did not mean much to the Koreans, because any Korean who exercised these rights soon found himself in prison, convicted of having "dangerous thoughts," or of having violated the "public peace preservation regulations." Three native language newspapers were allowed to be published in 1920, but they were under censorship of the Japanese administration; most Korean publishers and editors were thrown into prison at one time or another charged with "antigovernment" writings. No political organization was allowed to exist, and only business, religious, academic (cultural), and sports organizations were permitted. Before these organizations could hold meetings they had to obtain official permission from the local police; and two or three uniformed police officials (sometimes also detectives) were usually present at the meetings. The police officials had the power to arrest any member of the meetings or to dissolve the meetings altogether if in their opinion the meetings did not conform with public peace regulations. In 1930, more than 180 thousand Koreans were arrested, and more than 38 thousand of them were charged with "dangerous thoughts." This was the result of the new "freedom of speech, assembly, and press."

Under the pretext of "reorganization of the police force," the gendarmes now became policemen, and many new police officials were brought from Japan. The official publication of the government-general reported: "To fill the shortage caused by the adoption of a true police system, about 1,500 former gendarmes and about 1,500 police officers and men from Japan were taken into service, in addition to which more than three thousand men were recruited in Japan and a number of auxiliary Korean gendarmes engaged as policemen."[8]

As a result of the reorganization, the Korean police force, composed of police and gendarmes, was increased from 14 thousand to 20 thousand; the Japanese proportion was increased from below 60 percent to 73.3 percent, and the Korean proportion reduced from 41.3 percent to 26.7 percent.[9] The reorganization program did not reduce the arbitrary power of the policemen, which had been much criticized at home and abroad. In fact, police powers were extended to handling both civil and criminal cases. In 1921, for example, 73,262 cases were tried in police court; 71,802 of them ended in conviction. The chief of local police was given authority to impose a penalty of three months' penal servitude or a fine of not more than 100 yen. Nor were the infamous torturing methods, searches, and arrests without authorization abolished.

Regarding "spread of education, development of industry, and expansion of medical and sanitary organizations" more will be said later, but it might be briefly pointed out here that these programs remained promises, because the Japanese basic economic policy in Korea between 1918 and 1930 was the increase of rice production to meet the shortage in Japan. More than 75 percent of the total Korean population were engaged in agriculture and less than 3 percent were classified as industrial workers. In 1929 the food industry occupied first place, and textiles were listed a poor second. Most of the food industry was under Japanese control. Most of the textile manufactures were owned by Koreans. The Japanese industrial development took place in Korea after Japan established the puppet state Manchukuo in 1931.

As for education, in 1930 only half a million Korean children attended primary school, which meant that more than 75 percent of Korean children did not go to school; only one in fifty or sixty Koreans was able to go to high school. There was only one university, Keijo Imperial University, but 75 percent of the student body consisted of Japanese.

The program for "opportunity for men of talent" was an empty promise. In 1910 seven out of the thirteen provincial governors were Koreans; in 1940, one. All administrative positions, including even those of principals of the Korean primary schools, were held by Japanese; Koreans, regardless of their education and talents, were limited to positions of clerks, interpreters, and the like.

As to "promotion of good relations between Japanese and Koreans," it was obvious, as history speaks for itself, that no friendly relations existed between the Japanese masters and the Korean colonials. The Japanese overlords treated Koreans as members of an inferior race, and the Koreans believed that the Japanese were enemies to be expelled from Korea, if not killed.

The Naesun-ilche-jungchi Period (1930–45). During the third stage, the Japanese attempted complete Japanization of Korea under the slogan *Naesun-ilche,* or Japan and Korea Oneness. The Japanese attempted to obliterate all vestiges of Korean identity, especially language and customs, and substituted Japanese for Korean family names. They established Japanese-owned and Japanese-directed industries by building new plants in northern Korea after the pattern of Manchukuo. The political suppression and economic exploitation of Korea was accelerated in this way, and after 1931 Korea became virtually a Japanese war camp, operated as a part of the Japanese total war effort. The Japanese militarists dreamed of establishing the "New Order of Greater East Asia" based on "co-prosperity."

The living conditions of the Korean farmers were described by Governor-General Ugaki in 1933 as follows: "In the poverty season of spring [the farmers] from lack of food would dig out and eat the roots of trees on the mountains and fields or would beg from door to door to keep themselves alive. There are very few Korean peasants who could hope to succeed in the future on account of their poverty in the past and of their suffering in the present. Generally speaking, the reason why we could not remedy these bad conditions and save the farmers from poverty, since the time of annexation, has been the lack of self-confidence among the Korean farmers."[10]

The farmers could only eat part of the rice they grew, because most of it had to be used as payment for rent and taxes. A great part of Korea's rice production was exported to Japan to feed the Japanese. As the official statistics show, the so-called owner-tenants, those who owned land but not enough to feed their families and had to lease land from landlords, fell from 39.5 percent in 1918 to 25.9 percent in 1932; tenants not owning any land rose from 37.7 to 53.8 percent during the same period.[11] The rents ranged from 20 to 80 percent of the total harvest. In addition, the tenant usually paid land taxes, a water bill for irrigation, and had to deliver grain to the landlords. As a result of these excessive payments, the tenants were left with only 18 to 25 percent of the rice crop.

The Japanese industries, heavy and light, developed speedily, but not for the benefit of the Koreans. The industrial development of Korea was based on the Japanese war economy and exploited the Korean natural resources as well as cheap Korean labor. The production of light metals, such as aluminum and magnesium, was pushed; gold production was given top priority because gold was the main means of exchange for oil, copper, iron, and other strategic military materials to be bought abroad, especially in the United States.

The Japan and Korea Oneness policy gave Governor-General Minami, an extreme and cruel tyrant since 1936, the excuse to try to stamp out Korean nationalism, to make wholesale arrests of nationalist leaders, and to suppress all native social, cultural, and religious organizations. According to Japanese sources, the number of arrested persons charged with the breach of "peace preservation" regulations or detained because of "dangerous thoughts" increased from 38 thousand in 1930 to 44 thousand in 1938.[12] When new Sino-Japanese hostilities broke out (the "China Incident of 1937"), the Japanese administration forced Koreans to participate in the "Patriotic Spiritual Mobilization Movement," and organized so-called patriotic units in every village and town under the supervision of the local police chiefs. Soon the Anti-Communist League was formed in Korea under the sponsorship of the government-general, and branches of the league were established in every industrial and business organization, such as trading companies and banks.

In 1938, the governor-general declared that the Japanese language was the national language of Korea; the Korean language was to be no longer taught in any school, public or private. Korean teachers and students were not allowed to speak Korean in the classroom or at public meetings. The main purpose of education was to make Koreans "loyal Japanese subjects." Every Korean was required to memorize and to recite at every public meeting the oath of the Japanese imperial subject: "I pledge myself to be loyal to the Emperor of Great Japan and am ready to sacrifice myself for the glory of the Japanese empire."[13] Emperor worship and Shinto shrine visitations were demanded of Christian and non-Christian Koreans. As a result many missionary schools which refused to worship the emperor as God were ordered to close; many Christians were thrown into prison. The remaining two native language newspapers were ordered to close, and the Koreans were compelled to read only Japanese newspapers and publications. It was at this point that the government-general forced the Koreans to change their family names into Japanese.

After the attack on Pearl Harbor, many wartime emergency measures were taken and all kinds of activities in support of the war were demanded of Koreans. The administration was reorganized into a complete police government under the direct control of the governor-general; under the reorganization the police bureau was composed of the following sections: police affairs, defense (including fire control), economic policy (price control and rationing), and sanitation.[14] In 1941 Korea had more than 60 thousand policemen, which meant one policeman for every 400 civilians. In addition, over 180 thousand men were placed in the so-called auxiliary defense corps, a semi-police force; 24 thousand defense posts all over the country were under the control of these groups.

The Japanese administration forced Koreans to save by taking money from their paychecks and investing it in Japanese war bonds. Labor service was required of every able-bodied Korean, including housewives and students; and work regulations required an eleven-hour day and a seven-day week. Fund-raising and jewel donation campaigns forced Koreans to contribute to the war effort; close to 10 million yen was collected during the four war-years; 25 hundred pieces of jewelry were collected from Korean housewives; and 262 airplanes were purchased for Japan through a special airplane-donation campaign.[15]

The war brought further hardship to the Koreans. The tax rate in 1942 rose to three times that of 1936. More than two-thirds of the Korean rice was shipped to Japan. Eighty to ninety thousand Korean laborers were shipped to Japan every year to work in the war industries and coal mines. The total number of Korean laborers was estimated at one million two hundred thousand in 1942; about the same number of Koreans was forced to immigrate to Manchuria.

The Japanese also began to conscript military-age Koreans in a "voluntary service system." In 1942 they adopted a special military training program to which all physically able Koreans between seventeen and twenty-one were subject; those above twenty-one were under the "voluntary" training program. In 1943 the compulsory conscription law was applied to Koreans and thousands were sent to the front lines as soldiers. Many thousands of Koreans were also sent to the battlefields as coolies for the Japanese troops. Toward the end of the war virtually all schools and churches became military training centers, and even primary school children had to work one or two hours a day for the Japanese.

The Korean people became slaves of the Japanese war lords, and the Korean natural resources were exploited to the maximum to feed the Japanese war machine. This was the meaning of the Japan and Korea Oneness. The result was the end of Japanese rule in Korea.

ECONOMIC EXPLOITATION

In the eyes of the Japanese, Korea was primarily a source of raw materials and a colonial market for their industrial development. Korea was also one of the main sources of food, especially rice, for the Japanese. Japan monopolized Korea's economy after the Russo-Japanese war of 1905.

The Japanese government-general introduced a land survey, a thirty-year plan to increase Korea's rice production, a movement of rural revival for self-sufficiency, and a law on agricultural land. The Japanese constructed a modern transportation and communication system: a railway system (which was second only to that of Japan itself in Asia), highways, a postal system, sea transportation, telecommunications, and streetcars and buses in the main cities. They built first light manufacturing and food industries, and, after the establishment of the puppet state Manchukuo, developed heavy industry like hydroelectric power plants, chemical-fertilizer plants, and metal industries for the preparation of war. During the Second World War the Japanese tried to cannibalize the Korean economy by feeding into it everything that was not necessary for the war.

Japanese Domination of Agriculture. At the time of the Japanese annexation of Korea in 1910, a feudal agrarian economic structure existed, in terms of the economic and social status between landlords and tenants. The landlord was an absolute master, possessing the means of production and the land; the tenant was the servant who had nothing but his physical labor and some primitive agricultural implements. No modern concept of legal contract or agreement on rents of the leased land existed; instead, the age-old share-rent system between landlords and tenants was common. The overwhelming majority of the population were peasants, most of them tenants; agricultural production was the main source of the national income. The legal concept of private land ownership was still in its initial stage, and official arbitrary decisions on disputed land were frequent; no fixed or standard price of land existed. Money was short, and land could be purchased at a low price.

To obtain more rice, the government-general made a comprehensive land survey at a cost of thirty million yen from March 1910 to December 1918. A Land Survey Bureau was organized under the supervision of the civil administrator, the chief administrative assistant of the governor-general. The ordinance of the land survey was composed of fifteen articles of which the following five[16] were important. Article 4: The owner of the land shall register with the Land Survey Bureau of the government-general by a fixed day. Article 5: The landowner, leaseholder, and custodian of the land shall erect a post fence on his own land identifying the landmark; in case of private land, the name of the landowner and the title of the land, and in case of public land, the name of the government agency are to be posted. Article 9: The bureau chief of the land survey shall have authority to make decisions about the owner of the land and boundary lines of the land upon consultation with local land survey committee members. Article 15: The rights of the landowner shall be decided by the court.

In addition, the land survey "led to a revision of the land tax, encouraged the purchase of land because the rights of the owner became more certain, and brought to light lands which had not been taxed before."[17] Korean agricultural statistics became more accurate after the land survey.

The legal concept of private land ownership was not well understood by the public in general and by the peasants in particular. Frequently one piece of land had more than one individual who claimed ownership; in some cases, a government agency (of the old Korean government) or a government official claimed ownership. Under the government-general land ordinance, most of the native *yangban*—the aristocracy—became the legal owners of the land, taking advantage of their social position as literati, who recognized the significance of the ordinance.

Articles 4 and 5 provided that the land registration must be done by "a fixed day." The literate *yangban*, who understood the importance of the time limit, registered their lands with the Land Survey Bureau properly in conformity with the regulations of the ordinance. But the illiterate majority of the peasants not only failed to understand the significance of the time limit, but were not even aware of the existence of the ordinance. Many peasants failed to register their land on time and thus lost it. In some cases, the literate *yangban* registered the peasants' land fraudulently as their own land rather than that of the peasants, and became the legal landowner within the meaning of the ordinance. The government-general confiscated all unregistered peasant land as public property and sold it cheaply to Japanese.

Some peasants found out later that they were not landowners, although they had registered with the proper local government agency. Because they did not know the meaning of the ordinance, they had relied on the official interpreter's honesty for their land registration. Some of the interpreters took advantage of their position and filed the peasants' land fraudulently in their own names.

Some peasants, believing a rumor that registration would mean heavy taxation, refrained from registering, and their lands were confiscated by the government. One of the controversial issues on land ownership was the settlement of common clan property, because members of the clan could not agree among themselves who should be the legal owner of the land. Such disputes arose in well over three thousand cases. Most of them ended to the advantage of the government-general, because the disputed land was confiscated by the government as "confused land" having no legal owner.

According to the official report, lands thus confiscated were estimated at about 62,210 acres of cultivated lands and at 47,430 acres of forest and undeveloped or unreclaimed lands.[18] The government-general also confiscated all former Korean government lands, such as government transportation places, lands of the armed forces, and others. The total confiscated acreage was estimated at more than 325 thousand acres; more than 33 thousand peasants engaged in farming on these confiscated lands.

The total acreage of land confiscated by the government was estimated at more than 681,100 acres; forest and waste lands were more than 22,638,000 acres, which was 58 percent of the total forest and reclamation land of the peninsula.[19] The government-general disposed of the confiscated lands, except for the forest lands, as follows: about 191,100 acres were allocated to the Oriental Development Corporation, and the rest to four Japanese private land companies, Funi, Takakura, Tosan, and Kumamoto. These four companies invested 46 million yen in the land.[20]

How many peasants lost their lands to the government because they failed to register at the fixed time has never been made public. Under the new land policy the native landlords' rights increased enormously because they were protected by law. The landlords were given absolute tenancy rights, and the tenants' "disloyalty" and other causes were sufficient excuses for the landlords to refuse a renewal of the lease of their lands. Thus the landlords now became absolute masters of their own lands and could evict any tenant at any time by demanding excessive rents. Under the old native regime, the cultivation rights of the tenants on the leased lands were protected not by law but by long-standing custom. Few tenants lost their tenancy, and most of them could cultivate the lands as long as they wanted. Since the Japanese administration disregarded native customs, tenants were left to the mercy of the landlords. Neither the tenant's rights nor a fixed rate of rent were recognized by the new land policy. In addition to high rent, which ran from 20 to 80 percent of income (average rent was above 50 percent), the tenant usually paid land taxes. He paid the water bill for irrigation of the paddy field, and delivered the grain if he had to pay rent in kind. He supplied the animal power, seeds, and fertilizers, and he also gave free services to the landlord on such occasions as weddings or funerals. These traditional burdens of the tenant were left intact. As the result of the new land policy the percentage of farmer-owners and farmer-owner tenants (who might be considered an independent peasant class) decreased, but the percentage of landlords and tenants increased. In 1914 the percentage of landlords was 1.8 of the total farm families; of farmer-owners, 20; of farmer-owner tenants 41.1; and of tenants 31.1. But in 1919 the corresponding percentages were 3.4, 19.9, 39.3, and 37.3.[21]

Political implications of the new land policy also were important. The government-general needed close cooperation with the native landlords to obtain an increase of rice production. By protecting the interests of the *yangban* the Japanese insured their acceptance of the new land policy and cooperation on future Japanese colonial policies in Korea. At the time of the annexation in 1910 the Japanese successfully bribed some Korean aristocrats with money and titles;[22] now, in 1918, the Japanese attempted to buy off the landlords with the new land policy. Thus, the land policy killed two birds with one stone: it brought about increase of rice production for domestic Japanese consumption and the cooperation of the Korean upper class.

In 1919, the year after the completion of the land survey, the total acreage of cultivated land was estimated at about eleven million. Statistics were as shown in table 3.

The most significant factor was that, after only eight years of annexation, more than one thousand Japanese had become first-class landlords, equaling the number of Koreans. The overwhelming majority of Korean peasants possessed little more than one acre of cultivated land; and well over a half million peasants became landless—the peasant proletariat—in 1919. Most of them were forced to leave Korea for Manchuria.

TABLE 3. KOREAN AND JAPANESE FARMS IN KOREA[23]
(in *chungbo*: one *chungbo* equals 2.45 acres)

Area	*Number of Koreans*	*Number of Japanese*
Less than 0.5	1,664,000	21,000
0.5–0.99	671,000	7,000
1–2.99	773,000	900
3–4.99	206,000	2,000
6–9.99	110,000	3,000
10–40.99	42,000	3,000
50 or more	1,000	1,000

In 1914 the total production of rice was 14,130,000 *suk* (1 *suk* equals 4.9629 bushels) and the total export to Japan, 1,367,000 *suk;* in 1919 rice production declined to 12,798,000 *suk,* but the export to Japan increased to 2,882,000 *suk.* Per capita consumption of rice in Korea from 1915 to 1919 averaged 0.707 *suk,* and in Japan 1.14. The death rate almost doubled between 1913 and 1918, from 160 thousand to 300 thousand a year; about 50 percent died of malnutrition.[24]

After 1919, the Japanese agricultural policy in Korea could be characterized as "rice priority based on political expediency." Although weather conditions and soils are favorable to diversified cereals such as millet, barley, corn, etc., the Japanese administration concentrated more or less on the single rice crop. Rice suffered more from periodic droughts than the other cereals mentioned, but the Japanese administration disregarded this factor.

In 1919 a thirty-year plan[25] for the increase of Korea's rice production was announced by the Japanese. The rice riots[26] in major Japanese cities in 1919 and a rice-crop failure in Japan were the causes behind this long-term plan. In addition, between 1918 and 1930, the Japanese ruling classes did their best to present Japan to the world as a "have-not" country, under the constant threat of hunger and in need of outlets for her fast-growing population. Thus the rice plan was well received both at home and abroad. The plan made good progress for the next five years; but in 1934 the government-general canceled all agricultural expansion and improvement plans in Korea, because landlords and farmers in Japan protested against the flood of Korean and Formosan rice in the Japanese domestic markets. Between 1930 and 1933 the Japanese agrarian economy faced a depression, partly because of the world-wide depression and partly because of the overproduction of rice in the Japanese colonial areas, Korea and Formosa. Although the plan ended prematurely, the government-general obtained its primary objectives, as shown in table 4.

TABLE 4. RATE OF INCREASE OF RICE PRODUCTION IN KOREA[27]

Year	*Paddy field*	*Rice crop*	*Percentage*
1910	100	100	100
1920	115	145	124
1930	123	183	150

Rice production rose 26 percent between 1920 and 1930, after ten years of the rice-production plan. But as the following table indicates, rice export to Japan increased four times during the same period. Table 5 also shows who benefited from the increase of Korean rice production.

TABLE 5. PER CAPITA CONSUMPTION OF RICE IN KOREA AND JAPAN[28]

Year	*Total output of rice*	*Export to Japan*	*Per capita consumption in Korea*	*Per capita consumption in Japan*
	(in million *suk*)		(in *suk*)	
1918	13.7	2.2	0.68	1.14
1924	15.2	4.6	0.60	1.12
1931	19.2	8.4	0.52	1.30

Koreans consumed their own barley, corn, wheat, and millet and imported other cereals from Manchuria; most Korean farmers sold their rice and bought cheaper cereals. But, as table 6 shows, not only the rice consumption but the consumption of most cereals declined.

TABLE 6. PER CAPITA CONSUMPTION OF CEREALS AND BEANS IN KOREA[29]
(in *suk*)

	1915–1919	*1930–1933*
Rice	0.707	0.447
Millet	0.303	0.325
Barley	0.430	0.411
Beans	0.190	0.142
Others	0.402	0.343
Total	2.032	1.668

The general hardship of the Korean farmer for want of an increase in rice consumption during the twelve years of the rice plan was recognized by Governor-General Ugaki in 1933, who admitted that the Korean farmers had to eat the bark and roots of trees "in the poverty season of spring" even in a good crop year.

The percentage of absentee landlords increased, but the percentage of independent peasants constantly declined. The percentage of tenants increased rapidly, as shown in table 7.

TABLE 7. FARM FAMILIES OF DIFFERENT RELATIONS TO LAND[30]
(*in percent*)

	1918	*1928*	*1932*
Non-farming landlords (absentee landlords)	0.6	0.7	1.2
Other landlords	2.5	3.1	2.5
Farmer-owners (independent)	19.7	18.5	16.6
Owner-tenants (peasants)	39.5	32.3	25.9
Other tenants	38.7	45.4	53.8
Total	100.0	100.0	100.0

In view of all this, even if the thirty-year plan for the increase of Korea's rice production had been completed as originally scheduled, it would hardly have been a scheme for the welfare of the Korean people.

After the abandonment of the rice plan, the government-general worked out a new plan (which also had nothing to do with the welfare of the Korean people). This was the ten-year plan for sheep raising, and the twenty-year plan for cotton production. Korea was to become a source of cotton and wool supplies for the Japanese industry. At that time Japan was more in need of Korean cotton and wool than of her rice.

In 1933, Governor-General Ugaki announced the new plan with the slogan: "Cotton in the South and sheep in the North." Under the twenty-year plan for cotton production about 1,250,000 acres were to be used for 600 million *kun* (1 *kun*=$1\frac{1}{3}$ lb.) of cotton production. The goal for the first ten-year period was to produce 420,000 *kun* from 817,500 acres.[31] This plan also was not completed because the war with China made it necessary for Japan to return to her original plan for the increase of rice. The achievements of the plan were as shown in table 8.

TABLE 8. COTTON CULTIVATION IN KOREA[32]

	1929–1933 (average)	*1939*	*1942 (plan)*
Area, in 1,000 hectares	180.0	252.0	347.0
Crop, in 1,000 metric tons*	28.4	39.6	84.0
Yield, in kilograms per hectare	158.0	157.0	242.0

* In terms of ginned cotton; 3 tons of seed cotton are here considered equal to one ton of ginned.

The increase in cotton production was not impressive; in fact, the 1939 output was far behind that provided for in the plan; the production in that year was to have been 67,300 rather than 39,600 tons. Many Korean peasants were forced to give up their paddy fields to raise cotton. The Korean peasant was forced to sell the cotton to the Japanese at a low price, which was even below the cost of production; over 90 percent of the cotton output was exported to Japan.

The ten-year sheep-raising plan also failed to reach its goal. During this period the number of sheep was to be increased to 100,000; about 3,000 tons of wool were to be supplied by them annually. Actually, the number of sheep increased from 2,675 in 1933 to only 27,000 in 1939, including a number of sheep imported from Australia. A new twelve-year plan was initiated in 1937 with a goal of 500,000 sheep, but the following year the cotton- and sheep-raising plan was superseded by the plan to increase rice.

The undeclared Sino-Japanese war of 1937 caused a shortage of rice in Japan, and the Japanese again worked out a program whereby "it is better to concentrate production of raw materials for industry in China and Manchuria, while Korea should concentrate on production of rice."[33] The Japanese administration pushed the rice output through such means as the improvement of seeds, the use of more night soil, the extermination of pests, deeper autumn ploughing, and harvesting at the appropriate time. No projects for reclamation or construction of irrigation or any other improvement plans were introduced.

The 1939 crop was bad, and less than half of the quota was produced. After the Second World War broke out, armaments absorbed all available resources, and neither the money nor the plans for Korea's agricultural improvement were available. The supply of commercial fertilizer was not adequate; the labor force in the rural areas was drained by military necessities, such as an industrial armament works, mines, road construction, building of airfields, and compulsory conscription. The steel shortage jeopardized the much-needed production of agricultural implements. The general deterioration of agricultural production, especially the rice output, was inevitable during the war; the total arable land acreage was reduced from about 12 million acres in 1938 to 10 million acres in 1943. But rice exports to Japan constantly increased, and virtually no rice was left in the hands of the peasants after they paid taxes, rents, and compulsory rice collections.

Japanese Domination of Industry. Since Japan regarded herself as the workshop of the Far East, Korea was considered, especially before the 1930's, a source of raw materials for Japanese domestic industrial development and a market for the disposition of Japan's manufactured goods. Therefore, such industry as then existed in Korea was confined to the production of light consumer goods and carried on in small plants. Food processing remained the single most important industry, and textile industry was a poor second. These light industries were developed more in the agricultural southern section where the Japanese had first settled; heavy industrial development came later in the North where the major mineral and power resources were.

Immediately after annexation, the government-general in Korea issued the so-called Corporative Law,[34] which provided that the formation of corporations would be permitted by the government-general; and that the government-general would exercise "authority to dissolve any company or corporation which violates the regulations of corporation, public safety, or respected traditional good-business practice." The Japanese administration explained these restrictions as follows:

"A much stricter control and supervision than that exercised in Japan over business conducted by corporations is necessary in the peninsula, partly to guard Koreans lacking in business knowledge and experience against irresponsible schemers, and partly to guard Japanese or foreign capitalists not sufficiently well-acquainted with the real state of things existing in obscure enterprises, so that a healthy development of business activity might thereby be promoted."[35]

The real reason for the restriction was that the Japanese did not wish to introduce industrial development by Koreans but by Japanese in accordance with the needs of Japan by a plan controlled by the government-general. The increase of industry from 1910 to 1920 had been extremely slow, and it was necessitated by the influx of the Japanese and the interests of Japanese commerce and transportation.

The Japanese government-general, however, was interested in mineral production in Korea, and in 1915 issued the Korea Mining Industry Law. A few big Japanese mining corporations were established. These were wartime industries. One of the Japanese *zaibatsu,* the Mitsui Corporation, was active in establishing branches in Korea.

The capital investment of the Japanese in their industries in Korea was increased from ¥10,500,000 in 1910 to ¥59,000,000 in 1917, whereas Korean capital investment was ¥7,400,000 in 1910, and had not increased by 1917.[36]

In 1919 the corporation law was replaced by a new law liberalizing some of the restrictions in the establishment of corporations. In theory, anybody could now form a corporation or industry, because it required only formal registration with the government-general; but in practice, as one Japanese economist, K. Takahashi, said, "The new policy encouraged only small-scale industries working on local raw materials—and even this only after careful investigation by the authorities."[37] Therefore even under the new law industrial establishments were under the supervision of the government-general, and Koreans were discriminated against by the Japanese.

The industrial development policy of Japan in Korea was cautious. First, because the basic Korean economy was agricultural, and commercialization of agricultural production under Japanese domination was one of the prerequisites for industrial development. An increase of grains in general and rice in particular, therefore, was the official policy of the Japanese administration after the annexation. Second, Japan, then one of the youngest capitalist countries in the world, had no surplus capital to invest in overseas industrial establishments. However, during the First World War the Japanese *zaibatsu* —Mitsui, Mitsubishi, Sumitomo, and Yasuda—were able to accumulate capital by war profits, and were ready to invest it in Korea. After 1920, more light industries, especially food industries, textile industries, repair shops, printing plants for government publications, and gas companies were established. *Chosen Keizai Nempo* (Economic Report of Korea)[38] reported the industrial development as shown in table 9.

TABLE 9. DEVELOPMENT OF INDUSTRY FROM 1911 TO 1930

Year	*Number of employees in thousands*	*Number of industries*	*Gross value of industrial production in thousand yen*
1911	14.5	250	19,639
1920	55.2	2,087	179,319
1925	80.3	4,238	337,249
1930	102.0	4,261	363,062

As this table shows, the development of industry began after 1920, and the number of employees increased from 55,200 in 1920 to 102,000 in 1930; the number of industries also doubled, as did the gross value of production.

In 1929, the *Nittei Keizai Nempo* (Economic Report of Japan) classified the capital investment by nationality as follows: Japanese, ¥193,700,000 (62.4 percent); Korean, ¥18,900,000 (6.2 percent); and Korean-Japanese united capital, ¥96,000,000 (30.8 percent).[39] As far as the number of established corporations was concerned, no great difference existed between Japanese and Korean. However 80 percent (dividing the "mixed capital" figure evenly between Korean and Japanese) of the total paid-capital of the corporations was in the hands of the Japanese. This meant that more than two-thirds of Korea's industrial production was produced by Japanese enterprises before the development of modern large-scale industry in Korea.

After establishment of the puppet state of Manchukuo in 1931, the Japanese stressed Korea's industrial development. By this time the ruling military clique had made plans for the conquest of Asia, and considered Korea a link between Japan and the continent. Korea's natural resources as well as Korea's manpower became important to the Japanese war economy.

The most radical changes were the exploitation of the mineral resources, construction of hydroelectric plants, and the establishment of metal and chemical industries in the northern section of the peninsula. The Japanese government-general in Korea granted a special tax exemption to the Japanese entrepreneurs in Korea. No labor legislation existed; wages of industrial workers were less than one-half of the wages in Japan; long work hours, from ten to twelve hours a day, seven days a week, and night shifts without extra pay were common. The industrial raw materials were cheap; indeed, Korea was a paradise for Japanese industrialists.

Korea's coal and water power were important resources to introduce modern industry. One expert has estimated Korea's coal reserves at 42 million tons, anthracite 1,340 million tons, and soft coal 410 million tons. According to 1936 figures the annual consumption of coal was 2 million tons, and coal reserves would last at least eight hundred years. Significantly, the Japanese did not publish the coal production figures after 1936. The output of coal in 1936 was estimated at 2,282,000 tons, and by 1943 would have reached 6,500,000 tons under the five-year plan inaugurated in 1937. All eight big mining companies, including Oriental Development Mining and Mitsubishi Mining, had branches in Korea.

As for water power, the Japanese administration made extensive investigations on three occasions after the annexation. The final investigation revealed a potential of five million kilowatts, including two million kilowatts which could be generated by the Yalu and Tuman rivers alone. If this figure is correct, Korea is one of the world's richest countries in hydroelectric power.

The rapid development of electric power was essential for the establishment of heavy industry based on wartime necessity. The government-general passed a law providing that construction of new stations (after 1932) must be approved by the government; the government reserved the right to exercise general control over all electric stations.

With the exception of one station in Kumipo (Kejiho in Japanese), all 18 power stations were in the hands of private corporations; three of them had a capital of fifty million yen each, thirteen of them ten million yen, and three of less than one million yen each.

None of the Korean entrepreneurs were able to participate in the electric-power development; it became a Japanese monopoly. By 1940 the power stations in operation had a capacity of 710 thousand kilowatts, and by the end of 1943 it was estimated at a million and a half. This meant that a good number of Korean homes could have been supplied with electricity at a reasonable price. But in spite of the development of electric power, only one-eighth of the Korean population could afford electric lights in their homes by 1939, whereas in Japan nine-tenths of the homes were supplied with electricity.

The rapid growth of the mining industry was encouraged by the government-general; large money subsidies were given to the gold producers; tax exemption and subsidies were given to the producers of aluminum and magnesium, both needed for airplane production.

The value of gold production increased from 3.9 million yen in 1923 to 49.9 million yen in 1936 and to 69 million in 1937. A five-year plan for the increase of gold production, adopted by Governor-General Ugaki in 1937, provided a ten ton increase each year to reach seventy-five tons by 1942. Twenty-five million yen for the improvement of mining facilities such as mining roads and electric transmissions were provided in the 1939 budget of the government-general. The only remaining foreign mining company (American), which had operated since 1899 at Unsan, was bought out by a Japanese company. The four gold refineries—Kuhara, Noguchi, Sumitomo, and Mitsui affiliates—were giants with capital of more than ten million yen. The gold pressure was reduced in 1941 when Japan was no longer in need of gold for foreign exchange purposes during the Second World War.

Other mining companies for the production of iron ore were Mitsui, Mitsubishi, and the Japanese Iron Company; for the production of aluminum, the Korea Nitrogen Fertilizer Company and Korea Riken Metal Company. Pig-iron production (no official data were released after 1936) should have reached 800 thousand tons by 1943.

Since 1930, many new monopolistic corporations were organized by the Japanese *zaibatsu*—the houses of Mitsui, Mitsubishi, Sumitomo, Yasuda, the later but powerful Noguchi, and the giant Asia Takushoku Company. Some of them were built on a larger scale than the corresponding enterprises in Japan itself. For example, the Korea Nitrogen Fertilizer Corporation with a capital of 62.5 million yen was the second largest in the world, and in 1938 produced half a million tons of fertilizer in Korea in comparison with only eighty thousand tons in Japan by the same corporation.

The number of Japanese industrial corporations in Korea more than doubled between 1932 and 1939, from 563 to 1,300. The capital (paid) increased more than threefold, from 143.6 million to 510 million yen. In contrast to this, the figure for the number of Korean industrial corporations in 1939 (no data available for 1932) was 2,278, with paid-up capital of ¥122,660,000.[40] Thus the paid-up capital of the average Japanese corporation was six times as large as that of the average Korean corporation. In commerce and agriculture, the share of Korean corporations was about one-fourth; in all others, one-tenth.

As these figures indicate, the industrial corporations with Korean capital in industry were few—only about 5 or 6 percent of all corporations; they were not in a position to compete with the Japanese corporations. In fact, if the Japanese had wanted to destroy completely the remaining Korean corporations, they could have done so easily. But Takahashi said the reason for not destroying the native corporations was political; "If there were no Korean enterprises, the big Japanese capitalists would face masses of hostile Korean workers."[41]

The textile industry, rubber shoe industry, and socks manufacture were in the hands of Koreans; later the Japanese built rayon and other textile plants in the outskirts of the major cities—Seoul, Pyongyang, Inchun, and Kwangju, which competed with the Korean industries. However, all these industries, with no direct relation to the execution of war, suffered from shortage of raw materials, lack of spare parts, disabled machinery, and shortage of labor.

Some of the primitive types of cottage and handicraft industries, such as hand spinning wheels and looms, remained in Korean hands, but they were not operating either, because the Japanese war industry consumed virtually all raw materials necessary for these activities.

The economic development of Korea during the Japanese domination hardly created a Korean economy; it was a Japanese-owned and Japanese-directed economy for the interests of the Japanese empire. The Korean peasants, which constituted more than 75 percent of the total population, continued to live under feudalistic landlords, and their economic and social status remained unchanged. The Japanese-directed agricultural policies were designed to increase rice production for Japanese domestic needs; and during the Second World War more than two-thirds of the Korean rice output was shipped to Japan. The Japanese *zaibatsu* monopolized Korean industry, finance, and banking, and the Koreans were employed as laborers in Japanese business establishments. Few Koreans attained positions of responsibility or wealth, nor did they become technical or skilled workers.

The Japanese "modernized" Korea by constructing government-owned railroads, highways, air lines and telecommunications, but these served merely to further military purposes in northeastern Asia. The Korean currency system was integrated with that of Japan. The financial and banking systems were modernized, because these measures were beneficial to Japan. After 1939, exports to the "yen block"—Japan, Korea, and Manchukuo—accounted for 96.9 percent of the Korean total. Korea under Japanese rule was systematically exploited.

CHAPTER 7

THE ANTI-JAPANESE STRUGGLE

THE INDEPENDENCE MOVEMENT

Modern Korean nationalism began with the anti-Japanese movement, when Korea lost her independence upon conclusion of the protectorate treaty in 1905. The independence movement never ceased to exist both as an organized force and as a nationalistic ideal in the life of the Korean people. It was promoted by two social groups: intellectual middle-class patriots, including former government officials of the Yi dynasty and some Confucian scholars; and leftist intellectuals, later including Communists. However, during the first two decades (1905–25) the intellectual middle-class rightists led the independence movement, carrying out the 1919 Passive Resistance Movement and establishing the Korean provisional government. But after 1925 the left-wing intellectuals were more active in the anti-Japanese resistance movement, and after 1930 a militant group of Communists organized the "People's National Front," together with left-wing nationalist groups, and launched guerrilla warfare against the Japanese forces in Manchuria and North China.

The Rightist Intellectual Middle-Class. After the protectorate treaty, armed resistance by the remnants of the Korean army took place on many occasions throughout the country, but the insurrections were ruthlessly suppressed by the Japanese. However, a new Korean nationalism arose among the young intellectuals, and an independence movement was secretly organized throughout the country. One of the foremost leading figures of the movement was Ahn Chang-ho, who had returned from the United States in 1907.

After his first political speech, before a mass meeting in Pyongyang in 1896, Ahn was recognized as one of the new dynamic reformists and patriots. This meeting was sponsored by the Independence Club, the political reform movement under the leadership of Dr. Shu Chai-pil. Nineteen-year-old Ahn had denounced the official corruption of the Yi dynasty and advocated national strength based on moral force. In 1899 he came to the United States for further study, but he also organized social and political groups among Koreans in San Francisco, such as the Kongnip-hyuphai (Communal Association) and the Korean National Association. A weekly newspaper, *New Korea*,[1] was published under Ahn's leadership for the Korean community in the United States.

When Ahn returned to Korea in 1907, Japanese Resident-General Ito was the ruler of the peninsula and Korea had ceased to exist as an independent state. Ito asked Ahn to cooperate with the Japanese "reform policy" of the Korean administration, and a personal conference between Ahn and Ito was arranged at the request of the latter. Ito attempted to persuade Ahn to form a new cabinet under Ahn's leadership. Ito said that the modernization of Japan should be followed by that of Korea, and eventually of China, stating that Ahn should cooperate with Ito on the reconstruction of Korea first, and then go to China with him to work for the establishment of permanent peace in the Far East. Ahn replied that as Japan was modernized by the Japanese themselves, Ito should let the Koreans reform their country themselves. If the United States of America had imposed the Meiji Restoration, the restoration could not have been successful. Ahn rejected Ito's proposal as a hypocritical and treacherous plot to cajole Korean intellectual patriots into helping Japan.[2]

Instead, Ahn organized the secret Shinmin-hai (New People's Society). Some leaders of this group were military men like Lee Kap and Lee Tong-hi, or patriots like Kim Koo and Lee Sung-hoon. Most of them belonged to the well-to-do middle class, and some of them had been government officials under the Yi dynasty. Each of the eight provinces had one representative who was in contact with the central body of the society. The ordinary members did not know each other. No information is available as to the total membership, but it may be a clue that in 1911 the Japanese government-general arrested more than one hundred suspects of the Shinmin-hai and charged them with implication in the Terauchi assassination plot.

Many members of the Shinmin-hai concentrated on educational work and on establishing Korean business. Among the achievements of the society were the Pyongyang Daisung School, of which Ahn Chang-ho himself was founder and principal; the Porcelain Company in Pyongyang, financed by Lee Sung-hoon, who also became principal of Osan High School; the Taigook Book chain in the major cities; and many hotels throughout the country. Some members worked for newspapers; Yang Ki-taik, for example, became a staff member of the daily newspaper *Daehan*.

Before the annexation of Korea, Resident-General Terauchi, who had succeeded Ito, once again attempted to persuade Ahn Chang-ho to accept the Japanese proposal of a cabinet formed by Ahn in the name of "reform" and "close cooperation" with the Japanese government. Shortly before, in July 1909, the Japanese gendarmerie had arrested most anti-Japanese leaders, including Ahn Chang-ho and his associates (Lee Kap, Lee Tong-nung and others).

Later, as a sign of his good intentions, Terauchi released Ahn and his associates. They assembled at Lee Kap's home and discussed Terauchi's proposal. Lee Kap was in favor of accepting but Ahn was opposed. He said: "Acceptance would mean that we [leaders] would become puppets of the Japanese government."[3]

In Ahn's judgment Japan's annexation of Korea was an accomplished fact and the Japanese resident-general was simply asking the Korean patriots to consent to it by forming a new Korean cabinet. Ahn's answer was the founding of a new national independence movement.

The Korean patriots worked out a plan. One group remained in Korea and continued the program of the Shinmin-hai; a second group (those who might be rearrested by the Japanese) left Korea for abroad where they would carry out their assigned responsibilities in organizing, training, and propagandizing for independence. Ahn Chang-ho and Lee Kap left for the United States but the latter died before arriving; Lee Tong-nung went to Russia, Lee Tong-hi and Lee Si-yong to North China; and Cho Sung-hwan to Peking. Chun Ki-duk, Ahn Tai-guk, Lee Sung-hoon, Kim Koo and others remained in Korea and concentrated on education, publication, and business. The decision of the intellectual patriots of 1909 marked a new era for the Korean independence movement.

Ahn Chang-ho's Theory of Korean Nationalism. Ahn believed that the

Korean independence movement must begin with "national regeneration." In 1913 he organized the Hung Sa Dan (Young Korea Academy).[4]

According to Ahn, Korean nationalism had three objectives: restoration of independence, establishment of a national state based on utilitarianism, and development of a progressive nationalism by the academy. "Utilitarianism" means here "an expression of totality of national welfare."[5] Ahn maintained that individual interest must be sacrificed for the benefit of national interests. Therefore, every Korean should feel that he had a mission to serve the cause of independence.

Ahn advocated a principle of four equalities—racial, political, economic, and educational—and the establishment of a village or community centered on a cooperative economic system. Each individual, he said, must solve his own economic problems by individual efforts in earning his food, clothing, and shelter. A self-supporting economic system, based on the village cooperative unit, would be the first step for the progress of national wealth.[6]

Finally Ahn advanced the idea of "compatriot nonresistance" as a means of solving differences among fellow countrymen for the sake of national unity. The practice of this principle, he said, would eventually remedy age-old factionalism and bring about unity.

Ahn was the first leader who attempted to formulate principles of Korean nationalism. He dedicated himself to the cause of national independence, eventually nearly dying in a Japanese prison in 1938. (He was released from prison because of poor health and died soon after.) His main concern was the cultivation of the national character of the Korean people through the four principal spirits and the three disciplinary measures as set forth by the academy, the new leadership training center for independence. In order to understand Ahn's effort for the cultivation of the national character, a few words are necessary about social conditions prevailing in his day. The Korean people in general, and the ruling class in particular, were losing self-respect and self-reliance. Corruption and factionalism were rampant in the government; "reliance upon a big power," *sadae-sasang,* played a major part in the power struggle between the aristocratic ruling classes; and a handful of traitors were busy selling the country to the Japanese. Thus the Korean people looked like a "mass of loose sand."

Japan had established her military dictatorship, the government-general, in

Korea; the Western powers recognized Japanese domination over Korea; and China and Russia were defeated by Japan both in battle and on the diplomatic fronts. Under these circumstances, an immediate restoration of Korean independence seemed impossible in the near future; so Ahn worked out a long-term plan for the independence movement of Korea. This was the principle of "reconstruction of national character" based on Confucian-oriented ethical principles. He also believed that unless independence was self-obtained it meant nothing.

Ahn's political thinking was influenced by Confucianism; he did not separate politics from ethics. His idea for the reconstruction of the Korean national character was similar to the Confucian teaching of the formation of individual character by the rule of *li,* "propriety": "If you do not learn the rule of propriety, your character cannot be established." The four principal spirits (truth-seeking, deeds, loyalty, and courage) and the three disciplinary measures (knowledge, virtue, and health) roughly correspond with the Confucian five virtues (benevolent love, righteousness, propriety, wisdom, and faithfulness). Confucian political philosophy, which, commonly, is to "cultivate personal virtue, rule the family, govern the state, and pacify the world," was accepted by Ahn in terms of preparation for independence. His program consisted of self- and national-regeneration (first stage), restoration of independence (second stage), the establishment of a national state (third stage), and the development of progressive nationalism (fourth and last stage). The idea of progressive nationalism was added in later years, and it was to be developed by taking only the beneficial elements from capitalism (political democracy) and internationalism (social or economic democracy) in the interests of the Korean people.

The idea of four equalities in politics and the concept of utilitarianism were influenced by Western political ideology, but to Ahn these issues were not very important until Korea obtained her independence. Thus by Western standards, his virtual silence on individual liberty, freedom, and rights (although mentioned in his speeches) but emphasis on the ethical principles could be viewed as the chief characteristic as well as the shortcoming of his political thinking.

His concept of a self-supporting economic system was also rather naïve, or at least idealistic under the existing socioeconomic conditions. It was true that during exile and after his release from the Japanese prison he established model villages in the vicinity of Nanking in China and along the Taidong River and in Hwanghai province in Korea. But these projects failed because of the interference of the Japanese. Even if he had been given a free hand, it is doubtful whether his project could have brought about any beneficial result to the people. Furthermore, his economic plan did not contain fundamental economic policies such as land reform, industrial development, conservation of natural resources, and foreign trade.

THE MARCH FIRST INDEPENDENCE MOVEMENT

The March First Independence movement, a nonviolent demonstration against Japanese colonial rule, was a well-planned, historical program led by middle-class intellectuals. It was the first nationwide peaceful uprising in which everyone participated, peasants, factory workers, students, scholars, clergymen, children, and old men and women. With some exceptions, the demonstrators avoided all physical violence against the Japanese. One foreign eyewitness called it "the greatest example in world history of an organized passive resistance for an ideal."[7]

The Japanese were taken by surprise. They had difficulty in explaining the phenomenon, because despite their spy system and police they were in the dark concerning the nature, purpose, and organization of the movement. In each annual report before the uprising, Japanese propaganda described Koreans as loyal to Japan and happy under its "benevolent rule."

The uprising was caused by the economic exploitation of the Japanese, which made for a miserably low standard of living for the masses in general and for the peasants in particular, by the iron-handed military rule over the Korean people, by the Wilsonian principle of self-determination of the people, and by the success of the Russian Revolution.

During the first nine years (1910–19), the Japanese government-general ignored the people's needs, and the general living standard deteriorated. At the same time, as the result of the land survey, which took eight years and cost thirty million yen, more than 680 thousand acres of cultivated land were confiscated and distributed to private Japanese land companies. More than one thousand Japanese became new landlords in Korea in 1919 (Korean landlords numbered a little more than sixteen hundred); rice export to Japan doubled in the same year despite the decline of rice production; the death rate, as mentioned, doubled between 1913 and 1918, and about 50 percent died from malnutrition.

The Japanese did not develop heavy industry in Korea until the 1930's, but they monopolized light industry, mining, import, and export. Japanese capital investment in Korea's light industries jumped from ten million yen in 1910 to fifty-nine million in 1919, whereas Korean capital investment remained the same during that period. The Koreans could not eat more than a part of the rice they produced, because the Japanese took away so much. Instead, the Koreans were forced to eat millet, beans, and corn which they had to import from Manchuria. The handicraft industries were destroyed by the flood of Japanese-made consumer goods, which were sold cheaply at first to put the natives out of business, and afterward at high prices. During the first decade, the Japanese built railroads, highways, and other means of communication for military purposes or for economic exploitation. Thus Japanese control of Korea reduced the Korean people, with the exception of a handful of aristocrats, to the status of economic slaves. Anti-Japanese feelings, therefore, were strong throughout the country.

To stamp out Korean nationalism Japan set up a militaristic colonial regime and appointed extremist professional military leaders to be governors-general. The first two governors-general, Terauchi and Hasegawa, were firm believers in the theory of force in politics. All native political, social, business, and academic organizations and clubs were dissolved; no native-language newspapers were permitted to publish news without advance censorship and approval by the Japanese; freedom of speech and assembly were abolished for Koreans; and all Korean histories and biographies of eminent national figures were collected from institutions and even private homes and burned.

Higher education and study abroad were almost impossible for Korean youth except for a few sons of wealthy families. Most Korean school-age children were denied education: there were 380 elementary schools for the Japanese in Korea, who constituted less than 2 percent of the total population, but only 400 for Korean children. That is, every Japanese child was able to attend school, whereas only one of ten Korean children could. Worst of all were the attempts at thought control, with the increasing number of political crimes.

The so-called conspiracy case of 1911–12 resulted in over one hundred Korean nationalist leaders—most of them members of the Shinmin-hai, including leading Christians—being arrested and sentenced to five to ten years of prison for allegedly plotting to kill Governor-General Terauchi. The police was given the authority of summary judgment and could arrest any Korean at any time. By 1917 the number of police sentences amounted to more than ninety thousand. One out of every fifty-nine Koreans, including women and children, was flogged by the police in 1918, and two-thirds of the persons given police trials were flogged in 1917.

After the annexation, the independence movement was carried on by two groups of leaders; one group emphasized action, the other preparation and diplomacy. Men like Lee Tong-hi and Hong Bum-do believed in action and waged partisan warfare against the Japanese in mountainous northern Korea; they also established a military school in North Manchuria to train a Korean liberation army. During this period more than a quarter million Korean immigrants lived in that area; many young Koreans received military training, and thousands participated in partisan warfare. During the Russian civil war (1918–22) many Koreans aided the Bolsheviks in their struggle against the White Guards and the Japanese occupation forces.

Some leaders, who believed in preparation and diplomacy, took political refuge in China and the United States, but many leaders remained in Korea. Notably Ahn Chang-ho was very active in the United States—setting up political organizations (such as the Korean National Association and the Young Korea Academy) and publishing a weekly newspaper. These groups attempted to gain sympathy from the Western powers, especially from the United States, for Korean independence during the First World War. Syngman Rhee, who claimed to be a friend of Woodrow Wilson from Princeton days, appealed to him, saying that "Korea should be free from Japanese domination and be placed under the League of Nations' Mandatory Administration until Korea restores her complete independence."[8] The remaining leaders in Korea prepared themselves for an uprising against the Japanese, engaging in religious and educational work since churches, temples, and private schools were the only places where they could work without being suspected by the Japanese.

When the Korean leaders heard about Wilson's theory of self-determination at the opening of the Paris Peace Conference, they thought the time had come to demonstrate their hope for independence. Besides, some young Korean intellectuals, especially the students in Tokyo, were impressed by the "Great October Socialist Revolution in Russia," and believed that the Soviet Union would support the movement against Japanese imperialism.[9]

The Planning and Organization.[10] The central figures of the movement were the leaders of the three religions and several prominent intellectuals, commonly known as the Thirty-three Signers of the Proclamation of Independence of Korea. Fifteen of them were members of Chundokyo (the nationalist Sect of the Heavenly Way), fifteen were Christians, and the rest had no religious affiliations. The initiator of the movement was Son Pyong-hi, the leader of Chundokyo, who, in November 1918, met Lee Sung-hoon, representing the Christians, and Han Nong-wun, representing the Buddhists. They agreed to lead the movement, but the detailed plans for an uprising, the draft of the proclamation of independence, and the establishment of contact with the leaders abroad were assigned to Choi Nam-sun, Choi Rin, Song Chin-woo, and Hyung Sang-youn. In January 1919, the leaders of various groups and organizations met secretly at Son Pyong-hi's residence and worked out the final plans.

They agreed that a mass demonstration was to be carried out on March 3, 1919, the day of the public funeral of the last Korean emperor, who had died on January 20—it was rumored by poison or suicide. Thousands of people had been allowed to come to Seoul to pay their final homage to the emperor. Later the date was moved back two days.

Local committees were organized throughout the country and contacts were made with various social, religious, student, and labor organizations. Specific instructions on how to demonstrate were given: no one was to insult the Japanese, throw stones, or commit other acts of violence.

Student groups made the first public announcement of independence on February 8 at the Korean YMCA building in Tokyo. On March I the thirty-three leaders gathered in the Daehwa Restaurant in Seoul, and at 2 P.M., the scheduled time for the uprising, they signed the proclamation, and then telephoned Japanese police headquarters saying that the independence of Korea had been declared by them, the representatives of the Korean people. They sent a copy of the proclamation to the governor-general. Soon the Japanese police arrived and took them to thecentral police station in Seoul.

At the same hour, more than twenty thousand men and women of every age and social standing gathered at the predetermined points, read the proclamation, and marched along the main streets, cheering and shouting *mansei* ("Long Live Korea"), and waving Korean flags. Similar demonstrations broke out all over the country in defiance of the Japanese authorities. The historical proclamation of independence read as follows:[11]

"We herewith proclaim the independence of Korea and the liberty of the Korean people. We tell it to the world in witness of the equality of all nations, and we pass it on to our posterity as their inherent right.

". . . We take this step to insure to our children for all time to come, life and liberty in accord with the awakening conscience of this new era. This is the clear leading of God, the moving principle of the present age, the just claim of the whole human race. It is something that cannot be stamped out, stifled, gagged, or suppressed by any means."

The proclamation said that the Japanese deprived the Korean people of all basic freedoms, including the right to live and the right of free thought. Restoration of independence would mean the resumption of happiness of the Korean people and would serve the cause of peace in the Far East. The proclamation concluded: "We desire a full measure of satisfaction in the way of liberty, pursuit of happiness, and the opportunity to develop what is in us for the glory of our people."

The declaration incorporated three ideological forces: nonviolent resistance influenced by Western and Eastern religions; the concept of life, liberty, and pursuit of happiness influenced by Anglo-American political thought; and patriotism, or new nationalism, aroused in the conscience of the Korean people as the result of nine years of Japanese oppression.

Demonstrations took place in 211 counties out of a total of 218; more than two million people took part in the uprising over six months. During the first week all schools and shops were closed; factories, including mining and coal, transportation and communication facilities, and public utilities were paralyzed because of a general strike. With a few exceptions, the demonstrators were nonviolent. Many foreign observers noted that "the Koreans gave one of the most extraordinary examples of passive resistance to foreign domination that the world has ever seen."[12]

Suppression. The Japanese in Tokyo and Seoul were shocked and frightened by the sudden and universal demonstrations. Governor-General Hasegawa mobilized all armed forces in Korea and the police force; in addition, the Japanese government sent six thousand soldiers to Korea. The demonstrators were attacked with clubs, swords, bayonets, and guns. Many were killed and church and school buildings were burned. Tens of thousands were arrested. The arrested men, women, and children were whipped thirty times each day for three days. One of the American eyewitnesses wrote: "A few hundred yards from where I am writing, the beating goes on, day after day. The victims are tied down on a frame and beaten on the naked body with rods till they become unconscious. Then cold water is poured on them until they revive, when the process is repeated."[13]

There were incidents of barbaric suppression, including the cutting off of a student's arms and the burning to the ground of a church into which thirty people had been locked.[14] Adequate information is not available on the total number of casualties; the Japanese administration understated the figures, and the Korean sources overstated them. Probably from three to five thousand were killed, about ten thousand wounded, more than twenty thousand imprisoned; more than five hundred private homes, churches, temples, schools, and public buildings were destroyed. More than eleven thousand were still in prison awaiting trial nearly two years after their arrest. The students and the members of the Christian churches and Chundokyo suffered most. Gradually the uprising subsided. But Korean nationalism had been revived in the minds of the Korean people, and the independence movement was continued underground in Korea and openly abroad.

KOREANS ABROAD: THE PROVISIONAL GOVERNMENT

The exiled Korean patriots in Manchuria, Shanghai, Siberia, Vladivostok, and the United States (San Francisco and Hawaii) had been active for the cause of independence since the annexation. The Siberia-Manchuria group concentrated on military action (it was called Mudanpa, or action group) and the Shanghai-United States group emphasized preparation and diplomacy (usually referred to as Munpa, or civilian moderate group).

These two groups established various political organizations: the New Korea Youth Association in Shanghai, the Korean Socialist Party in Siberia, the Korean National Association in the United States, and others. During the uprising in Korea they intensified their propagandist, diplomatic, and fund-raising activities; in Shanghai they sent Dr. Kim Kiusic to the Paris Peace Conference, Lyuh Woonhyung to Moscow, and Chang Duk-soo and Kim Chul to Korea on secret missions to contact the leaders of the uprising; in the United States the Korean National Association sent Dr. Syngman Rhee to Washington and Ahn Chang-ho to Shanghai to meet exiled leaders in China. The Korean Student Association in Tokyo also sent its representatives to Shanghai. The French concession in Shanghai became the center for Korean exiled leaders.

During the time the leaders were assembling in Shanghai, three Korean governments were established in three different places.[15] On March 17, 1919, a Korean People's Congress was held by the representatives of the Korean residents in Manchuria and in Russian territories, and they established a Korean government headed by Son Pyong-hi as president. Syngman Rhee was chosen to be premier, and Lee Tong-hi secretary of war. This government was the product of Lee Tong-hi's group, who had trained military cadets and waged partisan warfare against the Japanese since the annexation. On April 10 Korean residents in Shanghai and the members of the New Korea Youth Association formed another government of exiled leaders, including Shin Kyu-sik, Shin Tai-ho, and Kim Kiusic. They selected forty representatives to form a national legislative body. These representatives chose nine cabinet members: Syngman Rhee as premier, Ahn Chang-ho as secretary of home affairs, Lee Tong-hi as secretary of war, and Kim Kiusic as secretary of foreign affairs. This government was dominated by the moderate U.S.-Shanghai exiled leaders. On April 23 the Hansung (Seoul) government was established in Korea by representatives of the thirteen provinces, who met secretly in Seoul and drew up a provisional constitution providing for a representative form of government and guaranteeing civil rights. They agreed that the members of the cabinet should be composed entirely of exiled

Korean leaders. They selected as cabinet members: Syngman Rhee, head of administration; Lee Tong-hi, premier; Lee Tong-nung, secretary of home affairs; Lee Si-yung, secretary of finance; Kim Kiusic, secretary of education; Mun Chang-bum, secretary of communication; Lu Tong-yun, chief of the general staff; Park Young-man, secretary of external affairs; Lo Paik-rin, secretary of war; Shin Kyu-sik, secretary of justice; and Ahn Chang-ho, secretary of labor. The structure of the government was guided by the principle of a weak presidential executive; the premier was to be the real head of the cabinet, and the president was the formal head of the state.

By July 1919, most exiled leaders from abroad had arrived in Shanghai and were attempting to work out a single Korean government from the three. They faced two problems which caused factional divisions among them. One was Dr. Rhee's earlier appeal to President Wilson for a trusteeship (mandate) of Korea under the League of Nations. This caused the members of the New Korea Youth Association and the Siberia-Manchuria group to oppose Rhee. The other problem was that Rhee made himself known to foreign states as president of Korea without having proper authority. The National Council of Korea (representatives of the thirteen provinces) had not conferred the title of president on him. Furthermore, some of his past activities in Washington were not in conformity with democratic procedures: often he had failed to consult with the members of the cabinet before dealing with financial and diplomatic matters of the Korean government. As a matter of fact, Rhee was still in Washington and did not arrive in Shanghai until December 1920.

In September 1919, the leaders in Shanghai finally reached a compromise formula in establishing a Korean provisional government. They agreed to recognize the members of the Hansung government cabinet as members of the provisional government. However, they drew up a new constitution.[16] The provisional national assembly was composed of the representatives of the thirteen provinces and representatives from the United States, China, and Soviet Russia. The government was to function with separate executive, legislative, and judicial powers. It was to be temporarily situated in the French concession of Shanghai.

On the surface, the new provisional government was a coalition of the Siberia-Manchuria group and the Shanghai-U.S. group, but in reality the latter group dominated: for one thing, the U.S. groups provided the funds for the maintenance of the government, rent of the buildings, and costs of publications and diplomatic activities. It was said that the Siberia-Manchuria group obtained some temporary financial aid from the Soviet government. Without constant financial support from the Korean residents in the United States, especially from the members of the Korean National Association, the maintenance of the provisional government would have been impossible. Secondly, the exiled leaders in Shanghai believed that Washington would eventually become the world diplomatic center, and a small country like Korea should concentrate its propaganda and diplomatic activities in the United States to arouse official and public sympathy for the cause of independence. In short, some leaders thought that if there was no spiritual and material aid for Korea in Washington, there was none anywhere.

However, no foreign government recognized the Korean provisional government in Shanghai; and the Korean delegates' attempts to present the Korean case at the Paris Peace Conference following the First World War ended in failure when the Japanese delegates threatened to withdraw from the conference if the Korean case was heard; members of the peace conference, including the United States, sided with Japan. Thus Korea's hopes for the restoration of her independence were frustrated on both the domestic and diplomatic fronts.

After staying in Shanghai from December 1920 to May 1921, Rhee returned to the United States and never went back to Shanghai. On March 23, 1925, he was officially ousted from the Korean provisional government and charged with usurping authority and using public funds for his own interests.[17] Park Un-sik was chosen to be the president, and thereafter many changes of personnel as well as of the organization of the government took place. The conservative group headed by Kim Koo preserved the name of the provisional government until the end of the Second World War, moving its location from one place to another. The Siberia-Manchuria group had left the provisional government before Rhee.

The main characteristics of the 1919 uprising were that, first, the intellectual middle-class patriots initiated and directed the national-liberation movement, and industrial workers and peasants played a subordinate role, although the majority of the demonstrators was composed of members of the laboring classes. The official report on the occupations professed by 19,535 of those arrested for taking part in the demonstrations showed as follows: peasants (including peasant laborers): 59.4 percent; storekeepers and industrial workers: 11.4 percent; students: 19.9 percent; other occupations: 9.3 percent.[18] The second characteristic of the uprising was that the leadership of the movement stemmed mainly from three religious groups: Christianity, Chundokyo, and Buddhism. The declaration of independence was guided by religious principles concerning the emancipation of the Korean masses from foreign imperialism and domestic feudalism rather than by socioeconomic and political principles. Third, the nonviolent method of protest against foreign rule, which coincided with Gandhi's passive-resistance movement in India, was a realistic and civilized approach.[19] Koreans felt strong enough to demonstrate to the world that they were worthy of freedom.

One of the principal shortcomings of the movement was the lack of a militant and organized leadership. Because of this, the nationalist leaders failed to guide the mobilized masses into a socioeconomic revolutionary movement. From the beginning the thirty-three leaders kept themselves apart from the mass demonstration by their own choice and gave themselves up to the Japanese police as soon as they had read the proclamation of independence. Thus the demonstrations occurred more or less as a spontaneous outburst of nationalism without organized political leadership. After 1919 no militant leaders emerged from the intellectual middle class; the uprising marked the climax of the independence movement led by the middle class. Nevertheless, the 1919 uprising made a great contribution toward the realization of national independence by generating a new nationalism in Korea. Meanwhile, a new political group influenced by Marxism-Leninism began to develop inside Korea, Manchuria, and Siberia. It started to organize an underground liberation movement soon after the uprising.

THE LIBERATION MOVEMENT AFTER THE 1919 UPRISING

Inside Korea. Following the unsuccessful uprising of 1919, the nationalist leaders inside Korea split into two groups: the conservatives and the progressives. The conservative group was composed of native patriotic landlords, well-to-do businessmen, and moderate intellectuals. Many of them were leaders of the uprising who had been released from prison after serving from two to five years. Politically, they were frustrated nationalists; some of them were disappointed about the failure of the uprising, and many discouraged about the Western democratic countries, which not only ignored the appeal of the Koreans at the Paris Peace Conference but more or less approved of the Japanese policy of aggression in the Far East.

In the meantime, the Japanese made a conciliatory gesture by appointing a new governor-general, Admiral Saito, with the policy of a "liberal" administration in Korea. Under Saito's administration, a very limited freedom of speech, organization, and press was granted and even political meetings were permitted to be held under certain conditions.

The conservative Koreans advanced the National Reformation Principles, which advocated the development of the natural and human resources of the Korean nation and waiting for a more favorable opportunity in the future to obtain independence. They said that what Korea needed most was national reformation in every field, political, economic, educational, and religious. Therefore, they advised the younger generation to study more and to prepare for better days, the ultimate goal being self-government.

Some of the wealthy landlords and businessmen provided funds for the establishment of private schools, newspapers, and magazines; the intellectuals organized social and political groups such as the Political Research Society led by Choi Nam-sun, the National Prosperity Society led by Kwan Tai-suk, and the Honam Friend's Society led by Song Chin-woo. The Society for the Encouragement of Using Indigenous Products (Mulsan-changneo-hai) was formed by Cho Man-sik in Pyonyang, and the Self-Improvement Friend's Society (Suyang-dangwoo-hai) was organized by the followers of Ahn Chang-ho, who was then a political refugee in the United States. However, these leaders did not make clear how the ultimate goal—political and economic independence—could be achieved under existing colonial rule.

Later some of the leaders, like Choi Rin and Choi Nam-sun, favored the establishment of a Korean autonomous administration under the aegis of the Japanese empire; and some of the landlords and businessmen as well as one segment of nationalistic intellectuals still actively supported Japanese military expansionism and betrayed the Korean independence movement. Nevertheless, many leaders refused to accept Japanese rule, refused to cooperate, and retired from social and political activities or went to prison.

The progressive nationalists did not share the views of conservative and moderate Koreans, believing that a program of reformation could not be carried out under the rule of the Japanese and would weaken the national consciousness of the people. Some of them favored close ties with the Soviet Union because they thought the Soviets would assist the emancipation movements in general and the anti-Japanese resistance movement in northeastern Asia in particular.

In 1927 the progressive leaders organized a national political group, Shinkan-hai (New Staff Society).[20] It aimed at the awakening of the economic and political consciousness of the people, at unity between the different social organizations, and at the elimination of political opportunism. The officers of the Shinkan-hai were composed of legal, religious, educational, and business leaders. However, each member of the society joined as an individual and not as a representative of his social group. Within a few months after establishment, membership was estimated at more than ten thousand, and branch offices were opened in major cities throughout the country. They concentrated on educational, religious, press, business, labor and legal professions, and achieved a fair degree of unity.

The Japanese administration recognized the Shinkan-hai as a lawful organization but watched its activities closely. Public meetings of the Shinkan-hai were required to obtain permission from the police in advance, and uniformed as well as plainclothes policemen were present at the meetings. The government-general suspected the Shinkan-hai was an anti-Japanese nationalist political group and planned to suppress it at the proper time. In 1929 a new anti-Japanese incident, the student uprising, occurred, and the leaders of the Shinkan-hai were charged with conspiracy in the uprising. Most leaders were arrested and sentenced from two to five years in jail.

Soon after the student uprising, a split within the society appeared between the liberals and leftists on the issue of how to carry out the anti-Japanese resistance movement. The liberals favored legal methods based on lawful procedures; the leftists insisted on the more militant strategy of mobilizing labor, farmer, and student groups, and even going underground if necessary. No agreement could be reached, so in May 1931 the Shinkan-hai was dissolved by decision of the central committee. Thereafter the leftists went underground and worked closely with the Korean Communists; many liberals retired from political activities and remained inactive until the end of the Second World War.

The Student Uprising in 1929–30. The second largest nationwide anti-Japanese uprising after the 1919 uprising was the student strike of 1929–30, which lasted more than five months. High school and college graduates had no chance to be employed because every position of good income was reserved for Japanese. The masses were out of work, and many well-to-do Koreans wasted their time. As one Korean student returning from the United States described it: "All this economic and political pressure led the people to a state of unrest and anarchy."[21]

In addition to this, the Japanese administration set up a discriminatory educational system providing more equipment, libraries, and teaching staffs for Japanese students than for Koreans; the Japanese denied able Koreans the opportunity for higher education in order to rule them more easily.

Japanese students looked down on Korean students. The idea of Japanese superiority over Koreans hampered the development of good relationships between the younger generations of the two nationalities. The Korean students resented the Japanese superiority complex in their private and public relations.

Beginning in 1925, Marx-Leninist ideology began to penetrate the higher educational institutions in Korea, and some of the students, including high school pupils, took part in Marxist activities. Korean students became increasingly politics-conscious and formed highly explosive groups, aware of Japanese attitudes and policies.

On November 3, 1929, a Japanese high school youth in the city of Kwangju insulted a Korean school girl named Park Ki-ok. Korean students watching the scene demanded an apology but other Japanese students ganged up against them. This led to clashes, and the Japanese police intervened and arrested only Korean students. This one-sided treatment caused indignation among Korean students and the general public in Kwangju; the students went on strike and paraded in the streets, singing national songs and shouting *mansei*, "Long live Korea." The news spread throughout the country, and 5 colleges, 170 high schools, and 70 elementary schools went on strike and staged demonstrations for five months. They demanded the release of the arrested students and abolition of the discriminatory educational system.

The police suppressed the demonstrators with the same ruthless methods used in dealing with the 1919 demonstrators. A few thousand students were arrested, 582 expelled from school, and 2,330 suspended for indefinite periods.[22]

Many Korean social and religious organizations sympathized with the striking students, and the activities of the Shinkan-hai were noticeable. The leaders of the Shinkan-hai held an emergency meeting and sent a fact-finding group to Kwangju city, headed first by Chough Pyong-ok, an American-educated college instructor. But he was stopped by the police before reaching the city and forced to return to Seoul. A second mission, composed of lawyers and newspaper correspondents, was able to enter the city and had an opportunity to observe the situation. Thus at the students' trial, Huh Heun and Kim Pyong-no (members of the Shinkan-hai) acted as defense counsels on the students' behalf. Six Shinkan-hai leaders were convicted of "conspiracy" in the student uprising and received jail sentences. Once again the Japanese had suppressed a Korean uprising by force. As a result, the Korean liberation movement was driven underground again.

After 1919 the liberation movement in Korea split into two groups over political ideology and methods. The conservative group lost its leadership to the progressives when the national reformation program failed, and some conservatives became active supporters of the Japanese policy of aggressiveness which began in the 1930's. The split within the progressive group hampered the development of unity, leadership, and coherent revolutionary programs. Following the student uprising the Japanese took once again stern measures to stamp out Korean nationalism. In 1937, just before the Japanese invasion of North China, the government-general dissolved the Suyang-dongwoo-hai, the last organized nationalist political group. But Korean nationalism lived on within the minds of the people, and the national movement was carried on by militant underground leaders.

Outside Korea. Many organized political groups existed outside Korea: most of them at one time or another supported the Korean provisional government in China. In the United States two political groups played a major role, the Korean National Association and the Friends Association (Dongji-hai). The former was organized in February 1909 by the merger of two groups—the Hapsung-hai in Hawaii and the Kongnip-hyuphai in California and other parts of the United States. The main reasons for the merger of the two groups were to support the assassination of W. D. Stevens[23] by two Korean patriots (Chang In-hwan and Chun Myong-woon) in 1908 in San Francisco, and to mobilize the spiritual and financial resources of the Koreans against Japanese domination. The Korean National Association supported the Korean provisional government financially for more than a quarter century and has been publishing two weeklies (in Hawaii and Los Angeles) for more than a half century. According to its original constitution, the Korean National Association promoted educational and business establishments in the Korean community, advocated freedom and equality among the people, looked after the welfare of its countrymen, and devoted itself to the restoration of independence.[24] Membership was never more than a thousand even during its most successful period. Its leaders were moderate intellectuals who came to the United States as political refugees, students, or immigrants in the early part of this century.

Rhee had attempted to organize his own political group as early as 1913, but it was in 1921 that he finally organized the the Dongji-hai in Hawaii. In that year he returned from Shanghai after factional fights within the Korean provisional government. The Dongji-hai set forth three principles:[25] encouragement of the quest for national independence; obedience to the rules and regulations of the Dongji-hai and respect for the official position of its members; and achievement of economic self-sufficiency. Members were pledged to obey unconditionally the orders of the head of the Dongji-hai. A unique provision of the Dongji-hai was that Rhee was elected as permanent or lifetime head on November 23, 1924.[26] (Thirty years later, in 1954, Rhee's Liberal party in South Korea proposed a constitutional amendment providing a lifetime presidency to the assembly for Rhee. He signed it into law although it failed the needed two-thirds majority, saying that "it is the considered opinion of the government that the amendment was passed.")

The Dongji-hai also supported the Korean provisional government in China, at least nominally, and it published a magazine, *Pacific Weekly,* partly in Korean and partly in English. With the support of the Dongji-hai, Rhee concentrated on diplomatic agitation, attempting to present the Korean case to the League of Nations at Geneva in 1932 when Japanese aggression in Manchuria was under discussion. However, he never succeeded in stating his case. During the Second World War his efforts to gain official recognition of the Korean provisional government by the United States also failed. He became a frustrated diplomatic agitator in Washington.

The political disagreements between the Korean National Association and the Dongji-hai continued for many years. In April 1941 the Overseas Korean Resident's Conference was held in Hawaii, attended by representatives of nine organizations in the Hawaiian Islands and in North America. The conference agreed (a) to continue to support the Korean provisional government in China, which at that time moved to Chungking; (b) to establish in Washington an office of the Korean Commission headed by Rhee; (c) to establish the United Korean Committee in America to achieve unified action for the cause of independence, the committee to be composed of representatives of political organizations in the United States and the Hawaiian Islands.

Thus, on the surface, the much needed unity among the political groups was achieved, and Rhee opened his diplomatic activities in Washington. After the attack on Pearl Harbor the Korean Defense Guard was organized among the Koreans in Los Angeles and San Francisco, and the American-Korean Victory Fund Drive was launched.

Soon differences between Rhee and leaders of the Korean National Association developed on how to conduct Korean diplomatic activities. Rhee did not wish any interference in his activities, either in policy decisions or in appointments of personnel for the Korean Commission. This one-man diplomacy was not acceptable to the leaders of the other groups, and in 1943 the coalition broke up with the withdrawal of the Dongji-hai from the United Korean Committee in America.

After the Second World War the Dongji-hai supported the Rhee-dominated Republic of Korea in the South; the Korean National Association supported neither the Southern republic nor the Northern regime on the ground that neither represented the Korean people.

In China, many political groups were organized by political refugees, but most of them were short-lived. In 1930, three rightist groups merged into one political party headed by Kim Koo, the Korean Independence party. The party set forth as its objectives the restoration of independence and the emancipation of the Korean people. Later (when the party returned to South Korea) it adopted as its platform equality in politics, economics, and education.[27]

The Korean provisional government remained inactive until 1930; it was conservative and had little contact with, or support of, the Korean people. In 1932 and thereafter, individual action against the Japanese began under the direction of Kim Koo, head of the provisional government as well as of the Korean Independence party. In January 1932 Lee Bong-chang made an unsuccessful attack on the life of the Japanese emperor in Tokyo; three months later, Yun Bong-kill made an attack on the life of General Shirakawa, the conqueror of Manchuria, when the Japanese celebrated the victory in a parade in Shanghai. At this bombing incident, Admiral Nomura, later the "special peace envoy" to the United States on the eve of the Pearl Harbor attack, lost his left eye, and Foreign Minister Shigemitsu, who later signed the surrender on the battleship *Missouri*, was also injured.

By 1936, liberal and left-wing political groups united and formed the National Revolutionary party,[28] headed by Dr. Kim Kiusic, a liberal, and Kim Won-bong, a moderate leftist and military man. The party concentrated on training revolutionary cadets among young Koreans: sending secret missions to Japanese-occupied areas, including Manchuria and Korea; organizing a Korean volunteer corps, which fought with the Chinese army against the Japanese invaders; and participating in the reunification of the Korean provisional government with the Korean Independence party.

The most important achievements of the National Revolutionary party were the early organization of the Korean volunteer corps when the Japanese attacked North China in 1937, and its participation for the sake of unity in the conservative-dominated provisional government soon after the Pearl Harbor attack.

The Korean provisional government moved to Chungking, the provisional capital of the Chinese Nationalist government, and organized the Korean independence army with the financial support of the Chinese government and overseas Koreans, mainly U.S. residents. A Korean general staff was set up in Chungking, and two Korean generals directed the Korean independence army. Although the Korean force was small in China, together with the Chinese army it waged a determined fight against the Japanese for the independence of Korea. Unity within the Korean provisional government was more or less maintained between the conservatives and liberals until the end of the Second World War. Chairman of the cabinet of the coalition government in 1944 was Kim Koo and vice-chairman Kim Kiusic. The nine other cabinet members represented various political groups.

Immediately after the outbreak of the war in the Pacific, the Korean provisional government attempted to obtain official recognition from the Allied Powers, especially from the United States, as the de facto Korean government, but its efforts "did not elicit more than expressions of sympathy and encouragement from various officials."[29] In the latter part of 1945, the provisional government leaders returned to Seoul from Chungking as civilians and not as members of a cabinet. Each of them cooperated with existing political groups in South Korea: Kim Koo with the rightist Korean Democratic party headed by Song Jin-woo, Kim Sung-soo, and Syngman Rhee; Kim Kiusic became one of the leaders of the middle-of-the-road groups along with Lyugh Woon-hyung and Ahn Chai-hong; Kim Won-bong cooperated with leftist groups such as the Korean National Democratic Front and the (Communist) South Korean Labor party.

THE LEFT-WING ANTI-JAPANESE MOVEMENT AFTER 1919

Inside Korea. A new political force, the socialists, gradually emerged in Korea after the First World War. It was composed of nationalist patriots and of Marxist intellectuals, including university students. In Korea in the 1920's, more than two-thirds of the farm families were tenants and agricultural laborers whose living standards had been deteriorating since the annexation. By 1920 Japanese land companies and individual Japanese owned nearly 45 percent of the paddy fields; private property rights were firmly established and well protected by the Japanese, but neither lease rights of the tenant nor fixed rent rates existed. Under the plan of increased rice production for Japanese domestic needs, the Japanese administration encouraged a system of modern irrigation and land reclamation. This new policy brought heavier burdens to the tenants and small land holders, because they had to pay the bills for irrigation and reclamation in addition to their land taxes and rent.

The Japanese economist Shirushi estimated that after paying rent, taxes, and fertilizer and water bills, the tenants in some provinces were "left with only 18 percent of the rice crop."[30]

The new Japanese agricultural policy brought many serious problems for the peasants. One was that the number of tenants and agricultural laborers increased; many were forced to move to mountainous areas and became squatters on land cleared by burning, *hwa-don* ("fire lands"), or to emigrate, mainly to Manchuria. Another was the increase of tenancy problems. Before 1910, as a matter of accepted practice, tenant farmers were given leases virtually every year. After this date the landlords often refused to renew the leases by demanding excessive rent. This caused disputes and sometimes bloody fights between landlords and tenants.

Following the First World War, Japanese investors became engaged in various industries in Korea, such as food processing, textiles, public utilities, mining, and coal. By 1925 the number of factories exceeded 42 thousand, in which more than 80 thousand workers were employed; the total number of laborers, including those in transportation, communication, construction, and other industries, was more than one million.[31] The average wage of the industrial worker was a half yen (fifteen U.S. cents) a day; average working time was ten hours a day, seven days a week. Nonindustrial workers' wages were less than a half yen a day for a twelve-hour day. Korean laborers got less than half the wages paid to the Japanese, although their productivity was the same. No labor legislation existed; the workers were entirely at the mercy of the employers. Woman and child labor was extensive, because still lower wages were paid to them. More than 30 percent of Korea's industrial production (gross value) was produced by the Japanese industrialists, and more than 75 percent after 1930.

In addition, the Japanese administration introduced an educational system that attempted to Japanize the Koreans by imposing Japanese as the official language of Korea and by prohibiting the teaching of Korean culture, Korean history, and, later, even the Korean language at public and private schools. The unequal salary scales between Korean and Japanese school teachers and public servants, as well as the social discrimination policy, caused intensification of anti-Japanese feelings among the public.

Under the "liberal" administration of Governor-General Saito, some leading Korean nationalist leaders advocated the national "reformation" program discussed before, which in fact was impossible to achieve under existing conditions. The Korean population neither accepted the Japanese policy nor followed the advice of the Korean reformists.

Under these circumstances the progressive middle-class intellectuals and the left-wing patriots organized labor and youth groups. For example, in April 1920 in Seoul the Korea Worker-Peasant Federation was founded as the forerunner of a proletarian movement. In the summer of 1920, many Young Men's League associations were formed, which in 1924 were united into the League of Korean Young Men's Associations. The Korean Women's Association was also organized in 1924. The left-wing Union of Proletarian Comrades was formed in Seoul in 1922.[32]

Korean socialist magazines and newspapers disseminated Marxism and Leninism among the students and intellectuals. *Shin-sanghwal* (A New Life) and *Choson-ji-kwang* (The Light of Korea) were published by the People's Publishing Company in Seoul. As described later, Korean Communist newspapers, like *The First of March* published in Vladivostok and *The Mass* founded by Korean students in Tokyo, were smuggled into Korea despite Japanese attempts to prevent importation. The main themes of the articles were the introduction of Marxism-Leninism and the exposure of Japanese economic exploitation of the Korean people. The articles also were critical of the national reformation program of the moderate Korean nationalists for tending to compromise with the Japanese colonial policy.

The Socialists and nationalists maintained a united front for some time to achieve their common goal—restoration of independence—and cooperated to arouse nationalism among the Koreans. The Japanese suppressed meetings of labor unions and youth associations and banned their publications.

On April 12, 1925, Korean Communists established a Korean Communist party in Seoul.[33] The leaders of the party were Kim Jai-bong, Cho Dong-wook, Chu Jong-kun, and Yu Jin. The party was composed of two Marxist political groups: the Tuesday Association, which was formed in 1924, and the Seoul Youth Association, organized in 1922. The Korean Communist party was approved by the Communist International (Comintern) in March 1926 and was accepted into the Comintern at its Sixth World Congress

(August-September 1928). The Korean Communist Young Men's Association was formed by Park Heun-yong on April 18, 1925, and was accepted into the Communist International Youth in the same year. In 1926 the Korean Communist party in Shanghai united with the Korean Communist party in Korea; thereafter the party concentrated on the formation of a national front with the progressive national group and the labor and student organizations to arouse anti-Japanese resistance.

The party demanded better wages, shorter working hours (eight hours a day and a six-day week), better working conditions, and the right to organize industrial labor unions. It also demanded legal protection of tenants' lease rights in the cultivated lands, low rents (30 percent of the crops), no free services for the landlords by the tenants, and the peasants' right to organize peasant unions. But these demands remained unfulfilled under Japanese rule.

However, on the political front the Korean Communists were to some extent successful in forming an anti-Japanese front with the progressive nationalists. In April 1926 the Communists planned with the nationalists a new nationwide anti-Japanese demonstration on the occasion of the state funeral of Prince Yi. The plan was discovered by the Japanese police, most of the leaders were arrested, and no demonstration took place. In 1929 many members of the Korean Communist Young Men's Association participated in a student uprising; left-wing lawyers and the leaders of the progressive nationalist political group (Shinkan-hai) rendered free legal services for the arrested students.

The Japanese police discovered the existence of the Korean Communist party soon after its formation, and in 1925 the government-general issued a new public-security law. In November thirty Communists were arrested at the city of Shinuiju in north Korea. These first wholesale arrests were a blow to the Korean Communist party because they came within six months of its organization. In 1928 about four hundred Communists, including members of the Korean Communist Young Men's Association, were imprisoned. Thus the Japanese police almost completely destroyed the Korean Communist party. In the same year it was dissolved by the Comintern's Executive Committee because of internal rivalries and because the membership was revealed to the police by the arrested Communists.

Nevertheless, a small militant Korean Communist party remained, and adopted a new program and new tactics applicable to local situations. The Communists took the lead in strikes of fishermen, mining workers, railroad workers, and communication workers. The Communists waged small-scale partisan warfare against the Japanese police stations in the northern mountainous areas. They also concentrated on the leadership training program of the Communist party by sending young Communists to Manchuria and the Soviet Union for militant education on Communist theory and practice. The Korean Communist party reentered the Comintern between 1932 and 1935.

From 1929 to 1940 the Japanese police repeatedly attempted to stamp out Communist activities. In spite of arrests, torture, and execution, the Korean Communists continued their propaganda and organizational work. During the Second World War they carried out anti-Japanese resistance activities in the name of national liberation. At the end of the war the party was divided again into two factions: the Changan faction representing the radical elements, who advocated a proletarian revolution in South Korea; and the Park Heun-yong faction, which insisted on democratic change through legal means in an effort to dislodge the U.S., which was occupying South Korea. The latter group was able to take over the party leadership in South Korea, and Park Heun-yong became secretary of the party. In 1946 the Communist party changed its name to South Korean Labor party, and Hu Heun, left-wing nationalist leader and lawyer, was elected chairman of the new party, with Park Heun-yong as vice-chairman. In 1947 all leftist parties in South Korea united under the name of the Korean National Democratic Front, and the central committee chairmen were four leftist leaders, Lyuh Woon-hyung (moderate leftist), Huh Heun and Kim Won-bong (leftists), and Park Heun-yong (Communist).

Outside Korea. Nationalists and leftists conducted militant anti-Japanese resistance from Manchuria and Siberia, the center of the Korean independent armed forces. Since the annexation large numbers of Korean peasants and political refugees settled in Kando, North China, across the Tuman River; military schools and political organizations were formed there. One of the leaders was Lee Tong-hi, former military official of the Yi dynasty, who established the Shin-hung Military Academy in Kando and the Korean

Socialist party in 1918. Lee is credited with establishing the first Korean Communist party in May 1919 in the Nikolayvsk-Ussuri district, north of Vladivostok.[34] In 1920 a regional committee of the Korean Communist party existed in Khabarovsk to help direct the Korean partisan movement. In the same year the first Korean Communist newspaper began publication; later many leftist newspapers, like *The First of March* (renamed *The Vanguard*) and *Along the Path of Lenin*, were published in Korea.

In 1920 another Korean Communist party was formed by Lee Tong-hi and Han Myung-sei in Shanghai.[35] During the initial period, most Korean Communists were bourgeois intellectuals; later many of them were ousted as inactive. By 1926 only 671, most of them peasants, survived the purge and reorganized the party with active fighters and peasants from the Korean working class.

The most characteristic feature of the Korean Communist party was the emphasis on military action rather than on an economic or social program. As a result, the party had few native Marxist theorists as compared with China and Japan. One of the partisan leaders was Kim Il-sung,[36] the present premier of the North Korean regime. After 1930 Kim concentrated on partisan activities against the Japanese in Manchuria. His main force was composed of Korean immigrants in Kando, Vladivostok, and Manchuria. Kim's partisan movement was successful in areas remote from Japanese occupation. He set up a system of local autonomy for Koreans in Manchuria and cooperated closely with Chinese Communists. A land reform was carried out, partisan cadres were trained, and small-size military weapons were manufactured.

Another partisan movement was organized in Manchuria by Choi Yong-kun and Kim Chek.[37] They established the Chosun Peoples' Revolutionary Army, then called the Eight Route Army and later renamed the Fourth Army. Korean students, intellectuals, and peasants in Manchuria, totaling more than 200,000, formed the Society for the Restoration of the Fatherland.

The two partisan groups merged into the North Korean Peoples' Force at the end of the Second World War and became the nucleus for the forces of the North Korean regime under Soviet military occupation. The three military leaders became dominant figures in North Korean politics.

PART II

THE NEW KOREA

CHAPTER 8

POSTWAR KOREA

1945–48

1945—YEAR OF LIBERATION

At the end of the Second World War, Korea's society was still semifeudal, composed of the privileged and the underprivileged. The privileged group consisted of the landlords, big businessmen, and officials, most of whom had actively collaborated with the Japanese administration and had obtained their positions and wealth at the expense of the people. They were opposed to socioeconomic changes and progress, and upheld the status quo. The termination of Japanese rule forced the rigid semifeudal social structure to change, and the privileged group consolidated its power and wealth behind the Korean Democratic party and the Korean provisional government. As will be seen later, these groups became the backbone of the right wing. (Their immediate concern was to keep the underprivileged group at a distance as much as possible.) The underprivileged group consisted of the vast peasantry (70 percent of the population) and industrial and other workers. They combined with left-wing political groups, the underground anti-Japanese resistance movement, and the Korean Communist party, and became a militant new political power by organizing labor unions of peasants, students, and women. They challenged the supremacy of the privileged group and were determined to emancipate themselves.

When the Japanese, who controlled more than 80 percent of all Korean wealth, left the peninsula in 1945, the prevailing economic conditions could be summed up as follows: industrial production had collapsed; the currency was greatly inflated; the ration- and price-control systems had broken down; war surplus goods that Japanese had stockpiled were flowing into the black market; a large percentage of the public utilities and the means of communication and transportation were inefficient; the factories needed immediate repair and replacement of machinery. Because of the shortage of technically trained Korean personnel even the existing economic machinery was not in full operation.

In addition, the artificial division into an "agricultural" South and "industrial" North crippled the economic structure: the agricultural South needed northern manufactured fertilizer and the industrial North needed southern agricultural products; the light consumer-goods industry of the South depended on the supply of northern electric power as well as semi-finished raw materials, and at the same time the North depended on southern industry for consumer goods. This meant that neither section could have a self-supporting economy.

In the South, the American concept of free enterprise failed to include land-reform measures, nationalization of Japanese-owned property, and effective rationing and price control. Furthermore, the "do-nothing attitude" of the American military government toward the South Korean economy produced economic confusion and social unrest during the first few months.

In contrast, in the North all heavy industries, mines, banks, public utilities, and communication and transportation systems were first taken under the control of the Soviet military commander, and then transferred to the People's Committee, the de facto regime. Public school buildings, hospitals, and estates of Japanese and Korean landlords were also turned over to the People's Committee by the Soviet commander. The People's Committee nationalized them and later distributed the land to the landless peasants in conformity with the land-reform law under the slogan "Only he who tills the land will have the right to own it." Thus, a planned economy under direct Soviet supervision was carried out in the North.

However, it should be noted that the land-reform measures gradually became a empty promise to the peasants when the North Korean Communist regime adopted the collective farm system and the peasants became once again landless.

The Political Situation. Two political groups existed in 1945. The Hanguk Minchudang (Korean Democratic party), which was organized just before the entry of American armed forces into the South, became the core of the right-wing camp, representing the interests of the landlords and businessmen Syngman Rhee, who returned to South Korea from his long residence in the

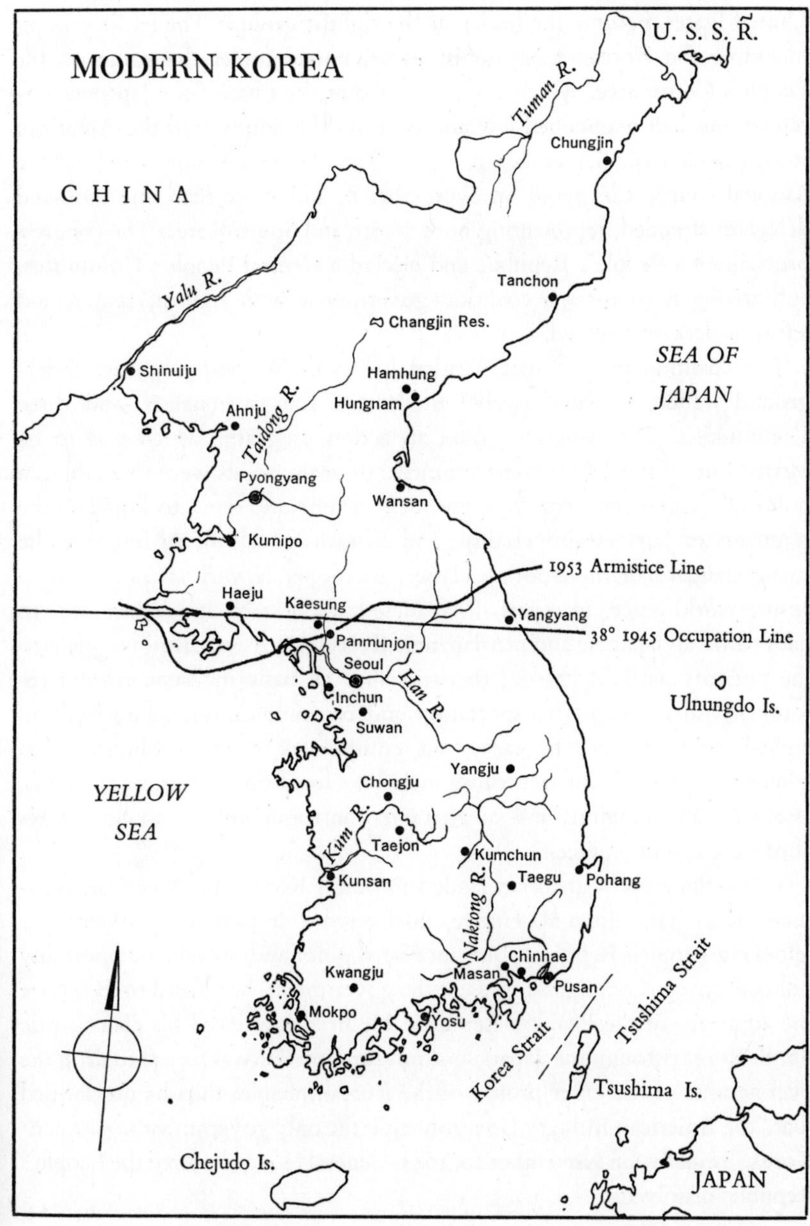
MODERN KOREA
U. S. S. R.
Tuman R.
Chungjin
CHINA
Yalu R.
Tanchon
Changjin Res.
SEA OF
JAPAN
Shinuiju
Hamhung
Hungnam
Taidong R.
Ahnju
Pyongyang
Wansan
Kumipo
1953 Armistice Line
Haeju
Kaesung
Yangyang
38° 1945 Occupation Line
Panmunjon
Seoul
Han R.
Inchun
Ulnungdo Is.
Suwan
Yangju
Chongju
YELLOW
SEA
Kum R.
Taejon
Kumchun
Kunsan
Naktong R.
Taegu
Pohang
Chinhae
Masan
Pusan
Tsushima Strait
Kwangju
Mokpo
Yosu
Korea Strait
Tsushima Is.
Chejudo Is.
JAPAN

United States, became the leader of the rightist groups. The leftist groups, including the Korean Communist party, united under the name of the People's Committee, which was organized at the time of the Japanese surrender and had maintained law and order in the South until the American troops landed on September 9, 1945. The People's Committee called a national congress in Seoul on September 6, and more than one thousand delegates attended, representing both North and South Korea. The congress proclaimed a People's Republic and elected a Central People's Committee, authorizing it to form a coalition government with rightist, center, and leftist leaders represented.

The coalition government, headed by Lyuh Woon-hyung, an underground leader, included twelve moderates, four nationalists, and three Communists. The congress passed an action program[1] which was to be carried out by the coalition government. Its main points were to establish a politically and economically independent democratic state; to liquidate the remnants of Japanese imperialism and Korean feudalism; to improve the living standard of the laboring classes; to cooperate with states abroad to ensure world peace; to repeal all Japanese laws, decrees, and regulations; to nationalize all Japanese and pro-Japanese Korean lands and distribute them to the peasants without charge; to nationalize all basic industry, natural resources, and means of transportation and communication; to establish an eight-hour workday; to carry out compulsory primary education; to guarantee basic human freedoms, including freedom of expression, press, assembly, and religion; and to guarantee universal suffrage to both sexes above the age of eighteen.

When the American forces landed in South Korea, the American commander, Lt. Gen. John R. Hodge, discovered a de facto government, the left-wing People's Republic. But since he was not authorized to support any political group claiming to represent the government, he refused to recognize the authority of the People's Republic. He first announced his plan to rule South Korea through the Japanese administration but was forced to drop the plan because of the bitter protest of the Korean people; then he proclaimed that "the American Military Government is the only government in southern Korea."[2] Finally, on November 20, 1945, General Hodge ordered the People's Republic dissolved.[3]

The American military government, which was not acquainted with the Korean situation and had no expert on Korea on its staff, had trouble from the beginning. Only conservatives and American-educated Koreans, including Christian leaders, were willing to cooperate with the American authorities. But even the support of the conservative political group was temporarily withheld as a result of the Moscow Agreement of December 1945, which amounted to a five-year trusteeship of Korea. The Korean provisional government organized a general work stoppage and mass street demonstration in protest against the Moscow Agreement; it attempted to take over the police and judicial system by proclaiming the Korean provisional government as the only legal government. The work of the American military government was more or less stopped for three days, because many Korean employees of the military government participated in the demonstrations. However, the leftist groups, which first joined the street demonstrations with the rightists in protest against the Moscow Agreement, came out in support of the agreement after receiving instructions from North Korean Communist leaders. Thus the Moscow Agreement was the first open power contest between right and left. In the meantime, the popularity of the American military government reached its lowest ebb, because the American-supported rightists opposed the Moscow Agreement and the leftist groups, whose People's Republic had been dissolved by the military government, came out in support of it. The strength of the right was impressive but the left continued to enjoy a popular following: the *Christian Science Monitor*'s correspondent reported that "the so-called People's Republic, composed of Socialists and Communists, enjoys far more popular support than any other single political grouping."[4]

The entry of Russian combat troops into North Korea on August 12 and its immediate occupation of land above the 38th parallel had given a great advantage to the leftists. On August 20 the Korean Communist-sponsored "preparatory committee" was organized to cooperate with the Russian command. A few days later, a People's Committee was formed in every village, town, and county as the representative body of the Korean people. With the approval of the Soviet command, the People's Committee maintained law and order, and from the latter part of August took over the normal administrative powers from the Soviet command, functioning as a de facto government in North Korea. The committee purged pro-Japanese Koreans from political, economic, and social positions. Some of them escaped to South Korea.

In October the Bureau of the Central Committee of the Communist party of North Korea was formed under the leadership of Gen. Kim Il-sung, who had returned from Manchuria. Thirty-year-old Kim was treated as a national hero and became the most militant revolutionary leader leftist Korea had ever had.[5] Under Communist control, North Korean trade unions, peasants' union, and the Democratic Women's Alliance were organized. Besides the Communist party, the Chosun Minchudang (North Korean Democratic party) headed by the patriot Cho Man-sik, and the Chundokyo party (of a native religious sect) were also organized, but they were under the indirect control of the Communists.

In North Korea a Soviet military government similar to the American military government in the South was never formally established. Instead, the Soviet command permitted the Korean Communists to carry out all political activities and administrative works under the supervision of Soviet political officers. On this aspect the late George M. McCune said: "The Russians avoided much criticism by hiding behind the Korean regime even though Russian control was only thinly veiled. But there was considerable evidence that the Russians did permit the Koreans of their choice to exercise real authority, whereas in the American zone, the Korean employees of Military Government were allowed little power and no authority."[6]

Division of the Country. Contrary to a widely held view that the division of Korea was another secret agreement engineered at Yalta, the 38th parallel was agreed upon by a small group of staff planners of the State and War Departments in Washington, D.C.[7] With the Soviet declaration of war on Japan on August 8, 1945, and the entry of Russian combat troops into the northeastern tip of Korea, military occupation of Korea by Soviet Russia seemed an accomplished fact. The American State and War Department planners were therefore working on a directive for the surrender of Japan to the Supreme Commander for the Allied Forces, General MacArthur. The directive was approved by President Truman on August 13. Copies of the directive were transmitted to the heads of the British, Soviet, and Chinese governments and approved by them. In conformity with the directive, the Soviet commander accepted the Japanese surrender north of the 38th parallel and the American commander south of it.

Secretary of State Byrnes said that "for the purpose of military operations the occupation of Korea was divided north and south of latitude 38 into Soviet and American areas."[8] Professor Leland M. Goodrich expressed his views as follows: "It is interesting to speculate why Stalin was willing to accept the division of Korea since Soviet forces were in the position to occupy the whole territory. Possibly the Soviet leaders figured that their chances of sharing in the military government of Japan would be improved thereby."[9]

American interest in postwar Korea seemed mainly political. The United States wanted to prevent the occupation of all Korea by the Soviets; occupying southern Korea, she would have as strong a voice as the Russians on the issue of Korean independence as promised by the Cairo and Potsdam declarations. In addition, the pressure of United States armed forces in the Korean peninsula would limit further Soviet expansion in East Asia, especially Japan.[10]

In contrast, the Russian interest in Korea appears to have been not only political but also economic and geographical. The geographical factor is important. Korea borders on Russia along the Tuman River in the northeastern peninsula, and Vladivostok is only one hundred miles away from North Korean ports. Because of this, Russia has considered Korea as a part of her strategic defense line in East Asia. Russian political interest in Korea has been demonstrated since tsarist times: the Russians interfered in Korean internal affairs soon after the Sino-Japanese war (1894–95) in supporting the pro-Russian Korean leaders who were in power, and obtained economic concessions from the Korean king. The first military showdown between Japan and Russia for the control of Korea took place in the war of 1904–5, which ended in Russia's defeat. However, Soviet interest in Korea increased after the Bolshevik Revolution: the first Korean Communist party was organized in Siberia in 1918 with the help of the Soviet Communist leaders, and Siberia, where more than 200,000 Koreans resided, became a base for the Korean revolutionary movement against Japanese rule. During the Second World War many Koreans, including Kim Il-sung, joined the Russian army and fought against the Axis. The Soviet government concurred in the Cairo Declaration of 1943 and the Potsdam Declaration of July 1945, which promised Korean independence "in due course." The economic factor is as important as the political and geographic factors in the long-term Soviet policy toward Korea. With a Soviet-directed industrialization plan, a close economic tie between northern Korea, southeastern Siberia, and Manchuria would be possible. If such a plan materialized, the three areas would become a giant industrial zone for the Socialist bloc, able to challenge the rest of the world, especially non-Communist Asia.

Therefore, Soviet interest in Korea is understandable, and a Korean government friendly to Moscow would be beneficial to Russia in many ways. Although American interest in Korea has been less explicit than that of Russia, the United States stood firm not to allow Soviet-oriented Korean Communists to seize power in South Korea. Thus in the postwar period the Korean peninsula became once again a friction spot of power politics between two opposing blocs.

The two-zone division extends to all phases of Korean life—economic, political, cultural, and social. Korea comprises 85,000 square miles and has a population of over 34,000,000. The southern zone comprises 37,000 square miles with over 25,000,000 people; the northern zone 48,000 square miles with 10,000,000 people. Although the cultivated acreage in each zone was almost equal—about 6,000,000 acres each—South Korea was the "rice and barley" zone, producing more than 60 percent of the total output, whereas North Korea traditionally has been the "millet and corn" zone, producing more than 70 percent of millet and 90 percent corn. The South could be characterized as a light-industry zone, manufacturing 74 percent of the total output of the country; the North as the heavy-industry zone, producing 84 percent. The North has rich mineral resources, timber, and potential electric power; the South lacks all of these. Thus the two zones are economically complementary. Under the division neither part can by itself establish economic independence. Prospects for the ultimate attainment of a normal living standard for the impoverished Korean people are dim as long as the two parts remain apart.

Conflicting political ideologies along with the opposing economic systems brought new antagonisms between northern and southern Koreans. Factionalism had existed in Korea ever since the period of the Three Kingdoms (58 B.C.–A.D.668). During the Yi dynasty (1392–1910), factionalism was strong among Confucian aristocrats at the court and used as a means of keeping northern Koreans out of government positions. Even today Southerners describe their northern neighbors as "uncouth but ambitious rebels," and the Northerners refer to Southerners as "scheming and lazy."

Since the division of the country the Northern Communist propaganda machine has denounced the Southern leaders as the "running dogs of American imperialism"; the Southern politicians, on the other hand condemned the Northern leftists as "traitors, who sell the country to Russian Communists." The Soviet government was determined to install a Communist-dominated Korean government, even as the United States government insisted on a pro-American Korean regime. As a result, in the North the pro-Russian Korean Communists virtually monopolized political power, and in the South pro-American politicians, civilians, and military personnel succeeded in establishing themselves as the ruling class. The old idea of *sadae-sasang*, reliance upon a big power, was revived.

Social differences based on the land system had long existed between North and South Korea. South Korea has three times as many acres of rice land, so that small farms with many tenants have been characteristic; North Korea, being a dry-field area, developed large farms and a high percentage of self-supporting, landowning farmers. Consequently, landlordism was not as powerful in the North as in the South; the feudalistic social structure was more or less intact in the South, and land reform there was needed more than in the North for social progress.

In the postwar period the influence of the American concept of individualism in the South and the Soviet concept of the totalitarian society in the North caused rapid social changes. In the South the family-centered semifeudal social structure has been in transition toward a Western-oriented, individualistic democratic society; in the North the family-centered society is being transformed into a regimented Socialist society under state control.

American culture has influenced South Korea, especially those who became wealthy through American aid during the Syngman Rhee administration. The members of this class go to American movies, have cocktail parties, dance to American music, and read American books, newspapers, and magazines; they also build Western-style houses and drive American cars. The South Korean government introduced the American educational system; and the teaching of English and of Western civilization and culture occupies a major part of the curriculum.

The North Koreans have followed Soviet-oriented Socialist ways. Communal life in rural areas has been put into practice. The people there work together, and stay together as one economic unit according to the commune system, and their children stay in nurseries while they work in the fields. Individual freedoms and liberties are restricted. The children study Marxism and Leninism in school and the adults at public meetings and in evening schools. The teaching of the Russian language and of Russian culture occupies a major part of the school curriculum. Thus the political, economic, social, and cultural unity of the Korean people based on the same history and culture is gradually disappearing.

THE MOSCOW AGREEMENT

The first major commitment concerning Korea's independence was made at the Cairo Conference, December 1, 1943, by President Roosevelt, Prime Minister Churchill, and Generalissimo Chiang Kai-shek. The joint declaration reads: "The foresaid three great powers, mindful of the enslavement of the people of Korea, are determined that in due course Korea shall become free and independent."[11] On behalf of the three powers, the U.S. State Department worked out a tentative program of three points: (a) An "interim international administration of trusteeship" should be established, either under the authority of the proposed international organization or independently of it; (b) the four powers, the United States, Great Britain, China (Nationalist), and the Soviet Union, should become the sponsoring countries in such an administration; and (c) after the capitulation of Japan a military government should be established on "the principle of centralized administration with all Korea administered as a single unit and not as separate zones."[12]

At the Yalta Conference in February 1945, the Soviet Union agreed to the trusteeship idea in principle. However, there is no record of any discussion on the question of the division of Korea into two occupation zones and the establishment of a military government. In May 1945, when Stalin discussed Far Eastern matters with Harry Hopkins, personal representative of President

Truman, the Soviet government reaffirmed its promise to enter the Pacific war against Japan as agreed at Yalta. On August 8 the Soviet government declared war against Japan and made public its support of Korean independence "in due course," adhering to the Cairo Declaration.

In conformity with the American-drafted Japanese surrender directive, North Korea was occupied by Soviet armed forces, South Korea by the United States army. However, the American commander, General Hodge, and the Soviet commander, General Shtikov, could not agree on relaxation of travel restrictions between the two zones and on the establishment of a unified economic and administrative machinery for all Korea. Hence the issue was placed before the Council of Foreign Ministers at a conference in December 1945 in Moscow. An agreement was reached there between the foreign ministers of the United States, Great Britain, and the Soviet Union to implement the Cairo Declaration. The Chinese Nationalist government later joined the Moscow Agreement. This agreement[13] was composed of four articles: (a) There was to be established "a provisional Korean democratic government which shall take all the necessary steps for development of the industry, transport and agriculture of Korea and the national culture of the Korean people"; (b) a joint American-Soviet commission, representing the two commands in Korea, was to be established and its primary responsibilities were to assist in the formation of a provisional Korean government through consultation "with the Korean democratic parties and social organizations"; (c) with the participation of the Korean provisional government and democratic organizations, the commission was to work out measures "for helping and assisting [trusteeship] the political, economic, and social progress of the Korean people, the development of democratic self-government, and the establishment of the national independence of Korea"; the proposals of the commission were to be submitted, following consultation with the provisional Korean government, for joint consideration "of the four powers for the working out of an agreement concerning a four-power trusteeship for a period of up to five years"; (d) "a joint conference of the representatives of the two occupational commands should be held within two weeks to consider urgent economic and administrative matters as well as the measures for permanent coordination."

Korean reactions to the "in due course" independence and four-power trusteeship for five years were various: disappointment and opposition at first but later support by leftist political groups and disapproval by the right wing. When the Cairo Declaration on Korea was announced, the Korean people, who were looking forward to immediate independence, opposed the idea of "in due course." They demanded immediate independence because Korea had been an independent state for more than four thousand years and had its own history, culture, and language; Korea's natural resources and agricultural economy would be self-supporting; Korea, they argued, had a high degree of literacy and maintained local autonomy even under Japanese administration. They also pointed out that through the Christian church a good percentage of the population had learned democratic procedures governing their church affairs; and through the long anti-Japanese movement many Koreans became able politicians as well as trained administrators. For example, the Korean provisional government, which was formed in 1919 after the March First Independence Movement, was one of the oldest exile governments in world history. Moreover, thousands of Koreans had joined the anti-Japanese underground movement and carried out guerrilla warfare in Manchuria and on the Chinese mainland. They further argued that the phrase "in due course" was not in conformity with the principles of the Atlantic Charter, especially that of "self-determination of small nations."

The trusteeship plan was violently opposed by the rightist political and social organizations in South Korea, and it was soon clear that any American attempt to put it into effect would drive the rightists into open hostility against the United States. Facing this situation, the official American view of the trusteeship plan became more liberal and flexible. Secretary of State Byrnes stated that "the Joint-American Commission, working with the Korean provisional democratic government, may find it possible to dispense with a trusteeship: it is our goal to hasten the day when Korea will become an independent member of the society of nations."[14]

In contrast, Soviet policy became rigid on the issue of trusteeship, insisting that all outstanding Korean problems should be solved in conformity with the Moscow Agreement. In the meantime, the Korean leftists supported the Moscow Agreement, saying that trusteeship meant assistance by the four powers for political, economic, and social progress of the Korean people.

Finally, the Moscow Agreement became a scrap of paper when the United

States government submitted the issue of Korean unification to the U.N. General Assembly in September 1947, and the assembly passed a majority vote rejecting the Soviet counterproposal for the withdrawal of all foreign troops from Korea and the leaving of the unification problem in the hands of the Korean people themselves.

THE MILITARY OCCUPATION OF SOUTH KOREA (1945–48)

Characteristics of the American Military Government. Military government by its nature is authoritarian: its primary responsibility is to maintain law and order. Military authorities from the beginning of their careers are taught to make quick decisions which determine victory or defeat, advance or retreat, and therefore they have no patience with slow democratic procedures. Therefore, the occupation and administration of a Korea that needed thoroughgoing socioeconomic and political reforms was no easy task for the American military. In general, the American military administrators were not trained for such a complex political job. In addition, there were practically no training programs for the American army in the Korean language or on Korean problems, such as existed for Japan and Germany.

The primary duty of the American forces in South Korea was to demobilize the Japanese army and to liquidate the Japanese administration on the one hand and to uphold law and order on the other. South Korea was placed under the jurisdiction of Gen. Douglas MacArthur, commander-in-chief of the United States forces and Supreme Commander of the Allied Powers (SCAP). General MacArthur issued an order, Proclamation No. 2, which said that anyone who committed "an action with the aim of destroying public peace or order, and deliberately performs action hostile to the Allied troops will, according to the decision of a Military Occupation Court, be sentenced to death or any other punishment which the Court determines."[15] Lt. Gen. John R. Hodge was appointed commander of the American armed forces in South Korea and Maj. Gen. Archibald V. Arnold military governor.

When the American forces landed in South Korea on September 8, 1945, a newly formed "People's Republic" offered its services to the American commander, but the offer was turned down for two reasons, as mentioned before: first, the American commander was not authorized to recognize any

Korean political organization which claimed to be a de facto government; second, the commander thought that the People's Republic was a Communist-controlled group. Finally, General Hodge established the American military government in South Korea and urged the Koreans to cooperate with it. However, only right-wing conservatives responded to the general's appeal. Some of them were political refugees from the Japanese who had lived in the United States and China; others were well-to-do property owners who had remained in Korea and cooperated with the Japanese administration either willingly or unwillingly. American military authorities had to depend on these conservative English-speaking Koreans, who often oversimplified the political and economic situation to protect their status. In this sense, the American military government could be characterized as a "government of interpreters."

The Search for New Political Leadership. Upon establishment of the American military government in South Korea, the American policy of impartiality toward Korean political groups shifted to favor the right-wing groups. In October 1945 the American commander appointed eight influential Koreans—property owners and talented nationalists—as advisers to the American military governor. Most of them were the leaders of the conservative Hanguk Minchudang (Korean Democratic party), which had come into being only two days before the U.S. forces landed. Many high posts in the military government also were filled by members of the Korean Democratic party: for example, Kim Yong-mu, a Japanese-trained lawyer, was appointed chief justice of the Supreme Court; Chough Pyong-ok, an American-educated teacher and newspaperman, became head of the police department; and Chang Taik-sang, a British-educated son of a big landlord, became police chief of Seoul.

At the request of General MacArthur, Dr. Syngman Rhee, who had lived more than thirty years in Hawaii and Washington, returned to Seoul in October 1945 as political adviser to the American command; soon after, the leaders of the Korean provisional government flew into Seoul from Chungking as "private citizens." A mass meeting to welcome Syngman Rhee was held in Seoul, and on this occasion General Hodge introduced Rhee to the South Koreans as a great patriot, a great leader, and a "home-coming national hero"[16] after long-continued exile abroad. Rhee told the Korean people, "Trust me, follow me, and unite for the cause of complete independence."[17]

Rhee and the right-wing Korean provisional government leaders headed by Kim Koo worked to mobilize all conservative forces and weld them into one political group. Soon the Korean Democratic party joined the Rhee–Kim Koo group. In February 1946 the rightist group called for an emergency national assembly and passed a 27-point national program based on "principles of political, social, and economic and educational justice for all." They also recommended to General Hodge a plan for the establishment of a "Representative Democratic Council" as an advisory body to the American commanding general. General Hodge accepted the plan and appointed twenty-three council members. Rhee was chairman, and Kim Koo and Kim Kiusic (moderate leader of the Korean provisional government) vice-chairmen. The overwhelming majority of the members of the council were right-wing conservatives, including big landlords and some former collaborators with the Japanese, so that liberals and leftists like Lyuh Woon-hyung refused to participate.

Critics of the council compared it to the Central Advisory Council of the Japanese administration, a pro-Japanese political institution during the war. During the council's existence of several months, it never became an effective agency of the American military administration because it was not in any sense a representative body of the Korean people pursuing the interests of the people, and because of a developing disagreement between Rhee and General Hodge on the problem of unifying rightists and moderates. General Hodge believed that strong political unity between the rightist and moderate groups was necessary to present a political force controlled by the right wing at the forthcoming U.S.–U.S.S.R. Joint Commission, but Rhee refused to cooperate with the moderates, insisting they were "Communist influenced" and working for the interests of the Soviets. Finally Rhee took independent action. In the middle of the joint conference the right-wing groups staged anti-Soviet demonstrations, adopting the name of Anti-Trusteeship Committee and demanding immediate independence.

The tension between Hodge and Rhee reached the breaking point when Rhee announced a visit to Washington with the intention of presenting the

Korean problem personally to the State Department and to the United Nations, "going over his [Hodge's] head."[18] At this point, the American military authorities, including the military governor, Maj. Gen. Archer L. Lerch, came to the conclusion that it would be better to let Rhee go to Washington with his own plan, and decided to "leave him alone." In the meantime, the American authorities decided to support the moderate political groups headed by Kim Kiusic in place of the rightist groups. Thus the military administration appeared to have found new leadership in South Korea at the end of 1946.

THE SOUTH KOREAN INTERIM ASSEMBLY

The hope for immediate unification of Korea became remote when the U.S.–U.S.S.R. Joint Commission adjourned indefinitely without reaching an agreement. This meant that in each zone the occupying authorities had to take measures to improve the existing political and economic structures. A new constructive plan was much needed in the American zone, because economic deterioration and social unrest as well as political confusion prevailed. More industries were closed down than could be put back into production because of the shortage of raw materials, power, and trained personnel; the price of goods had risen 100 percent since the American forces landed, while wages had gone up only 25 percent; the failure of the joint commission increased the antagonism between rightists and leftists, because the latter blamed the former for the collapse of the commission, and rightist youth groups began to terrorize leftist leaders. The first violent strikes, Communist-led rice riots, took place in all southern provinces, the strikers demanding land and rice for the peasants.

Against this background, the American occupation authorities announced their "Koreanization programs": establishment of a Korean legislative assembly and, later, of a Korean interim government. As a first step toward Koreanization, the military government proclaimed Ordinance No. 118,[19] which stated that the assembly should be composed of forty-five elected members and forty-five members appointed by the American commanding general, and that the assembly should enact ordinances, subject to the approval of the military governor, on matters affecting the general welfare. The election, the first in Korea's history, would be held in November 1946. The ordinance further stated that the primary objective for the establishment of the assembly was to provide the Koreans with a greater voice in policy-making matters on their own affairs, under the supervision of the military governor. However, foreign affairs and some economic matters (such as Japanese property) were not under the jurisdiction of the assembly.

The American plan for the creation of an assembly was denounced by rightists and leftists alike, but for different reasons. The rightists under the control of Rhee and Kim Koo wanted a "self-conducted election" without supervision by the military government. They also advocated the withdrawal of all foreign troops from Korea, so that a nationwide general election could be held without interference by foreign powers. The leftists said the American plan would hamper reunification, and was a device for the extension of the American military government in South Korea; instead, they demanded a reopening of the U.S.–U.S.S.R. Joint Commission.

The moderates supported the plan. They organized a coalition committee of liberals and leftists, excluding Communists. Some of the leaders of the committee were Kim Kiusic, Ahn Chai-hong (liberal nationalist), and Lyuh Woon-hyung (leftist). The committee recommended to General Hodge, and he accepted, the following five points as conditions for cooperation with the plan: (1) appointing the forty-five members of the assembly after consultation with the coalition committee; (2) introducing drastic reforms in the police system; (3) purging the former Japanese collaborators from the military government; (4) cleaning up widespread official corruption; and (5) restricting before the election the terrorist activities of the rightist youth groups conducted under the pretext of anti-Communism.

In November 1946 the election was held, but there was not universal suffrage. Only tax payers and property owners were entitled to vote. It was an indirect election—passing in four stages from village, town, county, to province—and the number of seats open was different according to the province. Only the capital city of Seoul selected three assemblymen. In most cases, the village headman acted as spokesman for his constituents; the village voters cast their votes according to his instruction. In the urban areas, intimidation, mob action of the youth groups, and bribes played a dominant part in electing assemblymen.

Dr. Kim Kiusic, chairman of the coalition committee, requested that General Hodge invalidate the elections on the ground that "leftist candidates were handicapped by current police investigations."[20] General Hodge ordered the opening session of the assembly postponed until an investigation of the election irregularities could be made. He also ordered a new election in Seoul and in one province, but the new vote did not alter the results. Finally, he disqualified the three assemblymen who were elected from Seoul city, because of their pro-Japanese records. All of them were leaders of the Korea Democratic party: namely, Kim Sung-soo, Chang Duk-soo, and Kim Doyun.

The results[21] of the elections were as follows; fifteen seats to the Korean Democratic party; fourteen seats to the National Society for the Rapid Realization of Korean Independence (Rhee's party); two seats to the Independence party (Kim Koo's party); twelve to candidates who claimed to have no party affiliations but were rightists; and two seats went to the left-wing party.

In December General Hodge announced the names of the forty-five assemblymen. Political orientations were these: seventeen rightists, seventeen moderates, and twelve leftists. No member of the Communist party was appointed; and Lyuh Woon-hyung (moderate leftist) declined to accept the appointment, saying that the assembly would not serve the cause of reunification. This meant that sixty seats from a total of ninety went to rightists, sixteen to moderates, and fourteen to leftists.

It could be said that General Hodge's appointments better represented existing political conditions than the results of the "election." However, the rightists, especially Rhee's clique, were critical of Hodge's appointments because the majority of the appointed assemblymen were leftists. Rhee and Kim Koo did not run for the assembly, and they were not included in the nomination list of the coalition committee. Hence they were excluded from the American-sponsored Koreanization program.

The Structure and Activities of the Assembly. Before the opening of the first session of the assembly the military governor had difficulties with the rightists. More than twenty rightist assemblymen boycotted the preliminary session on December 11 in protest against orders by Hodge which disqualified a few rightist members of the assembly. The military governor changed the original three-fourths quorum rule of the assembly to a simple majority quorum rule. Thus the assembly opened its first session on December 12 with only fifty-two members out of ninety present. Dr. Kim Kiusic was elected chairman of the assembly, and Choi Dong-hi and Yun Ki-sup were elected vice-chairmen. All were members of the Korean provisional government in China and claimed to be moderates. The assembly established fourteen standing and special committees, such as defense, external, police and internal, education and welfare, and investigation. The majority of the committee chairmanships went to the moderate leaders.

Although the moderates held the committee chairmanships, the assembly was dominated by the rightists, who were able to block any legislative bill contrary to their interests. Perhaps the most important and pressing problems at this period were the land reform, the franchise law, special legislation for punishment of collaborators, and the five-year trusteeship provision of the Moscow Agreement.

For the first two months the assembly failed to do any constructive work and appeared to be a debating group. In February 1947 the military governor wrote a letter to the chairman of the assembly stating: "The primary purpose of setting up the Korean Interim Legislative Assembly . . . was to provide the means by which the Korean people themselves could enact an ordinance providing for universal suffrage and a legislative assembly to succeed the temporary assembly. . . . It is my hope that a universal suffrage law and the provision for a legislature completely elective in nature can be enacted sufficiently early to provide for the actual seating of the members of the new legislative body not later than June 30."[22]

The assembly did not act on the universal suffrage legislation for three months. It was first passed in June but the military governor had to return it to the assembly for revision because of some undemocratic features contained in the bill. In September the assembly completed the bill[23] and sent it to the governor who approved it with his signature. Some of the features of the bill were: (a) voting age to be twenty-three or above and no residence requirements for either candidates or voters; (b) two hundred assemblymen to be elected from the 150 electoral districts; (c) voters required to write the name of the candidate on the ballot; and (d) the term of office to "continue until such time as the provisional government of united Korea is established." This law never became effective because the elections supervised by the United Nations took place under the U. N. election law, as will be discussed later.

The second important piece of legislation was the passage of the special act concerning the punishment of collaborators. The act was composed of twelve articles, which covered the definition of collaborator as well as penal provisions (running from five years of imprisonment to death).

The much needed land reform act was considered by the assembly but could not pass because of opposition by the conservative majority. On the other hand, the rightist assemblymen were able to bring the trusteeship issue to the assembly, in spite of objections from the American commanding general. The rightists passed the antitrusteeship resolution by 44 to 1 over the protests of the moderates and leftists, who absented themselves from the final voting. The resolution repudiated the Moscow Agreement and advocated the creation of an independent unified government through general elections without supervision by foreign powers. It also criticized General Hodge, stating that "regardless of the fact that Koreans strongly object to the provision for trusteeship of Korea in the Moscow Agreement, General Hodge understands that signing the 5th Communique of the Joint Commission means supporting the Moscow Agreement in full. This is a distortion of the general will of the people. We hereby point out the unreasonableness of this contention and oppose it strongly."[24]

The moderates did not take part in the antitrusteeship resolution, because they believed that the four-power trusteeship contained in the Moscow Agreement was not to be considered a mandatory clause, and that a future Korean government established through the U.S.-U.S.S.R. Joint Commission would have the right to reject the trusteeship. They also placed confidence in the earlier statement by Secretary of State Byrnes that the joint commission, working with the Korean provisional democratic government, "may find it possible to dispense with a trusteeship."

During its less than two years' existence the assembly spent much time in discussing problems not important for the general welfare. The work of the assembly was interrupted by the submission of the Korean problem to the United Nations General Assembly and the subsequent arrival in Seoul of the

U.N. Temporary Commission on Korea in January 1948; its supervision of the new election made unnecessary any further legislative work by the assembly.

THE SOUTH KOREAN INTERIM GOVERNMENT

A broad directive for Koreanization from Washington to the occupational commanding general in South Korea stated that "administrative control should be transferred to Koreans as soon as they are able to qualify." Accordingly, in August 1946 General Hodge "requested the Military Government to turn over actual operation of all departments of government to Koreans," except for the "operation of the Material Control Corporation, Property Custody, and the Civilian Supply Program." Hereafter, the Korean counterparts of the military officials, who had acted as interpreters, became directors, and the American military officials remained as advisers. Early in 1947 all American advisers moved from the capitol building and set up offices in other quarters.

The military governor nominated Ahn Chai-hong, a moderate nationalist and the sole voter against the antitrusteeship resolution in the assembly, as civil administrator, that is, chief executive; the nomination was confirmed by the assembly, and he took the oath of office in February 1947. Ahn was given authority to appoint department heads and provincial governors, and Korean became the official language used in government documents. "South Korean Interim Government" (SKIG) replaced, as the official government name, "American Military Government." The structure of the executive branch of SKIG was based on the structure of the American military government. The military governor was still head of the government, and under him the Korean civil administrator "directed" the activities of the departments and of the offices of the central and local administrations. The reorganized administrative structure was as follows: Under the direct control of the military governor were National Price Administrator, National Labor Board, National Food Administration, Controller of Commodities, Coordinator of Civilian Supply, and the Korean Economic Advisory Board. Under the civil administrator were 13 departments: interior, security, police, education, transportation, labor, commerce, public works, agriculture, health and welfare, communication, finance, and foreign affairs; and three offices—public information, civil service, and general administration. Each department was subdivided into bureaus, sections, and units.

The structure of the local administration remained the same as under Japanese rule: the province was subdivided into county, township, and village. The provincial governor was appointed by the central authority, and the head of each individual subdivision was appointed by superior officials, namely, the governor and the head of the county.

The Koreanization program did not transfer real authority to the Koreans. Although the civil administrator was given appointment power, he could not exercise it without prior approval by the American military governor. Even low-ranking positions, like the bureau chiefs or section heads of a department, could not be appointed by the Korean authorities without approval of American advisers.

The American advisers held a specially tight grip on financial matters: every item of expenditure and income in each department had to be countersigned by them. Brig. Gen. Charles G. Helmick, then acting military governor, explained that the transfer of financial authority had not been made because "the policy of finance is so closely tied up with responsibility of government," and "a great deal of money from the U.S. is being used to further the civilian goods program, the import of fertilizer, and the import of grains," so that "a control of finance must be maintained."[25]

Despite the creation of a Korean legislature and executive, the American command and the military governor retained veto power and the authority to appoint key personnel, promulgate ordinances, and determine major policy. The American advisers, who numbered more than three thousand, of which twenty-five hundred were military and five hundred civilian, tightly controlled the operations of each department, particularly in the selection of personnel and in financial matters. Control was exercised by requiring that any directives and decisions be countersigned by the advisers. Thus the Koreanization program was characterized by planning which was initiated and controlled by Americans.

SOUTH KOREAN POLITICAL PARTIES

In South Korea three political groups existed: rightist, leftist, and moderate.

The major rightist groups were united in the Antitrusteeship Committee; the leftist groups operated under the Korean Democratic Front; and the moderates were united in the Coalition Committee. The moderates formed the government party for about two years, and had the support of the American military government. In 1948 the rightists were able to seize power in South Korea because they supported the U.N. elections sponsored by the United States, which were held on May 10.

The Character and Activities of the Rightist Groups. The rightists represented the interests of the big landlords, collaborators, and profiteers. These three groups had not only cooperated with the Japanese, but had themselves exploited the Korean people during the Japanese administration. The leaders were extreme conservatives, representing the right-wing members of the Korean provisional government. Most of them, like Syngman Rhee and Kim Koo, had resided for more than a quarter century abroad, mainly in the United States and China.

The rightists paid lip service to democracy and styled themselves nationalists and patriots. In their party platform they even advocated land reform and nationalization of former Japanese property. In doing so, they presented themselves to the American military authorities as democrats, labeling other groups, especially the People's Republic group, Communists.

Upon the recommendation of the rightists, the American military authorities, who were not well acquainted with the Korean situation, appointed many former officials and Japanese collaborators to key positions in central and local government: the police was completely in the hands of Japanese-trained Korean officials.

More than a dozen rightist groups flourished during the American occupation period; the following three were the most powerful and the best organized. The Korean Democratic party was formed on the day the American forces entered South Korea by Song Chin-woo, a nationalist and former president of the *Dong A* newspaper, and his brother-in-law Kim Sung-soo, a big landlord and founder of Bosung College, which later became Korea University. The National Society for the Rapid Realization of Korean Independence was established by Syngman Rhee. The Korean aristocracy (feudal landlords), profiteers, and collaborators during the Japanese rule, as well as right-wing fascist youth groups, supported Rhee's society. The Korean Independence party was founded by Kim Koo (leader of the right-wing group in the provisional government) in Shanghai in 1930. The rural Confucian landlords, wealthy businessmen, and terrorist youth groups supported this party.

The political activities of the rightist groups were intensified when Syngman Rhee and Kim Koo returned from their long exile. For the first few months, the Korean people treated them as national heroes, affectionately calling Rhee "Gukbu" ("Father of Korea") and Kim "Revolutionary Patriot." The landlords, profiteers, and collaborators donated large sums for political funds and luxurious mansions for Rhee and Kim. Soon they became the leaders of the conservatives in South Korea and started to challenge the liberals and leftists. At first the rightists had attempted to gain popularity by opposing the Moscow Agreement and insisting that the Korean provisional government, as the legally constituted government, included within its jurisdiction North Korea. When these efforts failed because of the opposition of the American military authorities, they called an "emergency national assembly," in which all rightist groups were represented, and adopted a 27-point national program based on "the principle of political, social, economic, and educational justice for all."[26] They also proposed, and the American commanding general accepted, a plan for the establishment of a representative democratic council as an advisory body to the military governor. As mentioned previously, the council never functioned, partly because liberals declined to become members and partly because of disagreements between General Hodge and Rhee on the unification issue.

Hereafter, Rhee and Kim Koo concentrated on the antitrusteeship movement in South Korea and tried to sabotage the work of the U.S.–U.S.S.R. Joint Commission. As soon as the first joint conference adjourned without reaching agreement, Rhee advocated the establishment of a national government in South Korea and urged the people to suppress the Korean Communists and to fight for unification, using force if necessary.

When the joint commission was reopened in 1947, Rhee and Kim Koo announced through the press that they would not participate as long as the commission insisted on fulfillment of the four-power trusteeship provision. They also demanded the immediate withdrawal of foreign troops from

Korea so that the Korean people could conduct a "free" national election. Antitrusteeship mass demonstrations inspired by rightists took place in front of Duksoo Palace, where the conference was being held, and mobs of youths stoned the car of the Soviet delegation. At the same time, as a "precautionary measure," the South Korean police arrested hundreds of leftists and Communists. Lyuh Woon-hyung, former head of the People's Republic, was assassinated by terrorists on a Seoul street. Thus the antitrusteeship demonstrations were converted into anti-Soviet and antileftist riots.

When the second joint commission broke down and the United States submitted the Korean unification problem to the U.N. General Assembly, the Korean Democratic party and the National Society for the Rapid Realization of Korean Independence supported U.N. elections in South Korea. But Kim Koo's party, Korean Independence, refused to participate in elections on the ground that they would hamper efforts at reunification. Thus Rhee became the unchallenged rightist leader and formed the Republic of Korea on August 15, 1948.

The Moderate Groups. The Democratic Independence party was organized under the leadership of Kim Kiusic (chairman of the interim legislative assembly) and Ahn Chai-hong (civil administrator of the interim government). As mentioned above, it was a government party, receiving American backing until the end of 1947. The leaders were liberals. The major provisions of the party platform were: (a) establishment of a national coalition government through the U.S.-U.S.S.R. commission; (b) free distribution of former Japanese land to landless peasants and nationalization of heavy industry; (c) purgation of former collaborators with the Japanese and release of political prisoners arrested since the liberation; (d) reorganization of the police along democratic lines; and (e) protection of the four freedoms—from fear, from want, of speech, and of religion.[27]

The primary concern of the leaders was to bring about unity among the dissenting political groups and to achieve unification of the country. They attempted to solve the first problem by forming a coalition committee, but their efforts failed, because the extremists on the right and the left refused to participate. Only Lyuh Woon-hyung (moderate leftist) was willing to cooperate, but he was soon assassinated. The moderates supported the Moscow

Agreement by their participation in the joint commission. But they opposed the U.N. elections in South Korea proposed by the United States because such elections would permanently divide the country, because the Northern Communists would also conduct and establish a separate government, and because no adequate efforts had been made by Korean leaders to unify themselves. Therefore, the moderates suggested that a conference of political leaders from the North and South precede the U.N. elections.

On this issue agreement between the American military authorities and the moderates could not be reached. Finally, Kim Kiusic resigned from the chairmanship of the assembly and attended the North-South leaders conference, which was held on April 22 and 23 in Pyongyang, today the capital of the Northern regime. Ahn Chai-hong also resigned as civil administrator, stating that his service was no longer useful since the United States was determined to carry out the U.N. elections in South Korea and that therefore hope or funification had faded.

Many moderates, including Kim Kiusic, retired from active politics when the two separate governments were established in 1948. Thus the liberal democratic political movement came to an end.

The Left-Wing Groups. The three major leftist groups were the South Korean Labor party (former Communist party) on the extreme left, headed by Huh Heun, a Japanese-trained lawyer; the Labor People's party, organized by the members of the former People's Republic group and headed by Lyuh Woon-hyung; and the Korean People's Republic party (former National Revolutionary party formed in China during the Japanese invasion of North China in 1937), reorganized by the left-wing leaders of the Korean provisional government under the leadership of Kim Won-bong, former defense minister of the provisional government. The three chiefs of the leftist groups became the central-committee chairmen of the Korean Democratic Front, which acted as one party.

Early political activities of the leftist groups in Korea might be briefly reviewed. When the German forces surrendered to the Allied Powers the Korean underground leaders believed that a Japanese defeat would follow soon. When the Soviet Union declared war on Japan, they held a secret meeting with right-wing nationalist leaders (such as Song Chin-woo and

Kim Sung-soo) to discuss the establishment of a Korean government. Lyuh Woon-hyung, representing the underground groups, proposed that a self-governing body including students should be organized to maintain law and order when the Japanese forces collapsed, and that a Korean government should be formed consisting of representatives of the underground movement and of revolutionary political and social organizations which had been fighting the Japanese.

Song Chin-woo, representing the conservative nationalist groups, however, felt that the organizing of youth groups was premature and that the present Korean provisional government in Chungking should become the national government of all Korea.

When the Japanese emperor proclaimed the surrender, Governor-General Abe conceded to Lyuh the power of preserving order in Korea and asked for a guarantee of the safety of a quarter million Japanese until they left Korea. Lyuh demanded the following, which Abe conceded: (a) the release of political prisoners; (b) three months' food for the Korean people by a release of army supplies; (c) an agreement to refrain from intervening directly or indirectly in Korean political affairs; (d) an agreement not to interfere with the mobilizing and training of Koreans for preserving public peace and order.[28]

On August 17 a Preparatory Committee (later changed to People's Committee) was organized under the leadership of Lyuh; he was elected chairman and Ahn Chai-hong vice-chairman. Soon local preparatory committees were also established in villages, towns, counties, and provinces throughout the country. In the South these committee members maintained law and order until the American forces landed. As mentioned previously, on September 6, just two days before the landings, the committee called a Congress of People's Representatives in Seoul, and proclaimed the People's Republic of Korea. Two months later the American military authorities outlawed the republic, insisting that the American military government was the only government in South Korea.

From the beginning of 1946, all left-wing political activities were carried out in the name of the Korean National Democratic Front. They announced two political programs, one for immediate objectives and one for long-term objectives.[29] The former contained six points: (1) support of the Moscow

Agreement for unification; (2) establishment of a coalition government based on the democratic parties, excluding pro-Japanese groups and landlords; (3) nationalization of the Japanese and pro-Japanese Korean-owned properties and basic industries; (4) land reform based on the principle of free distribution of land to the landless peasants; (5) purgation of collaborators and profiteers; and (6) an eight-hour working day. The long-term objectives were not spelled out other than to state the goal of "realization of socialism."

The first political action of the leftist group was the so-called People's Rally to support the Moscow Agreement as a counteraction to the rightists' antitrusteeship movement. In doing so, ironically, the leftists and the American military government appeared to "stand together" for the Moscow Agreement. But since the failure of the first joint commission, the leftists determined to oppose the American policies, while the military government was determined to suppress the leftist activities "whenever they reached proportions threatening the maintenance of peace and order."

From the summer of 1946, there spread throughout South Korea strikes and demonstrations, primarily provoked by pressing economic hardships. The general price index rose to more than eighty times that of 1945, while wages went up only fifteen times. Unemployment increased every month when factories closed down because of the shortage of raw materials and electric power. Under the compulsory rice-collection system, farmers were forced to sell their rice at a price that was lower than the cost of production.

In September 1948 more than forty thousand railroad workers went on strike demanding wage increases and liberal labor legislation. Soon the other communication and transportation workers joined the strike, and high school and college students demonstrated in the streets for better facilities and better teachers. In October the tenant peasants went on strike in protest against the compulsory rice-collections and the high rates of rent for their farm lands. The government called this strike the October Rice Riots, and the leftists called it the October Peasant Revolution.

The first peasant strike occurred in Taegu, North Kyongsang province, and spread to almost all southern provinces. The rioters, ranging from several hundred to as many as ten thousand, overran police stations and seized local government buildings. The strikes lasted more than a month and involved more than two million people. According to official reports, in the Taegu riot alone more than fifty policemen and the same number of strikers were killed. The total number of casualties was not made public. The military government declared martial law and arrested hundreds of leftists and thousands of strikers. More than five hundred leaders were charged with disturbance of the peace and convicted by the military court.

In March 1947 the so-called Twenty-four-hour Flash Strike took place in fifteen major cities; more than twenty thousand industrial workers and twenty thousand peasants joined. The police arrested twenty-seven hundred leftist leaders. On August 3 a leftist political riot was also scheduled. This was the date of a memorial service for Lyuh Woon-hyung, who had been killed by terrorists, but an early police roundup of the leaders prevented the riot. At the end of 1947 a thoroughgoing campaign against the leftists led to the arrest of virtually all leaders and sympathizers; a few were driven underground or escaped to the north. The late G. M. McCune commented: "The policy of suppression of the leftist agitation was understandable and in many respects necessary under the circumstances, but lack of a more vigorous constructive policy to encourage democracy served to weaken the position of democratic and liberal elements."[30] The political consequence of the anti-Communist suppression through the Japanese police strengthened the anti-democratic reactionary forces in South Korea.

CHAPTER 9

THE FOUR NATIONAL ISSUES

Between 1945 and 1948, South Korea passed many milestones of history: the Moscow Agreement, the U.S.-U.S.S.R. Joint Commission, the United Nations' supervised elections, and the North-South Political Leaders' Coalition Conference. Each of them was concerned with the problems of the unification and independence of Korea, so that each political leader had to take a position for or against them. In each decision the political future of each politician was at stake.

The Moscow Agreement. The Moscow Agreement for the unification and independence of Korea was formulated by the foreign ministers of the United States (Byrnes), the Soviet Union (Molotov), and the United Kingdom (Eden) on December 27, 1947; later Nationalist China joined. The agreement consisted of four articles according to which Korea would be under "a four-power trusteeship for a period of up to five years." The joint American-Soviet commission, representing the two commands in Korea, was to assist in the formation of a provisional Korean democratic government through consultations with "the Korean democratic parties and social organizations."

Right-wing nationalists, especially the long exiled Korean provisional government group, launched the anti–Moscow Agreement movement (also known as antitrusteeship movement). They issued a statement saying that since Korea had governed itself for centuries a four-power trusteeship was an insult. They called a general strike of all workers for the military government and staged mass demonstrations in Seoul in which "No Trusteeship" banners were displayed.

The antitrusteeship movement turned into an anti-Communist movement when Secretary of State James Byrnes made a radio speech declaring that to the American government "trusteeship" meant only aid and assistance.[1] Syngman Rhee took the view that "aid and assistance was not what the Soviet Union had in mind," and warned the Korean people that "an immediate effect of the Moscow Agreement would be to extend Russian influence directly over the whole peninsula."[2] The Moscow Agreement, nevertheless, was supported by leftist leaders and their parties, and soon moderate leaders also supported the agreement. They argued that Korea had been liberated by the Allied Powers and that unification of the country was possible through cooperation between the United States and the Soviet Union. Dr. Kim Kiusic, moderate and former vice-chairman of the Korean provisional government in China, declared that the primary task of the U.S.–U.S.S.R. Joint Commission was to assist in the formation of a provisional Korean government so that it would have the right to reject or accept the trusteeship system. Therefore it was pointless to raise the issue of acceptance or rejection of trusteeship at this time. Thus leftists and moderates united in supporting the Moscow Agreement and the forthcoming joint commission.

The U.S.-U.S.S.R. Joint Commission of 1946–47. To discharge its duties according to the Moscow Agreement, the joint commission convened on March 20, 1946, at the Duksoo Palace in Seoul. Maj. Gen. Archibald V. Arnold was the chief American delegate and Col. Gen. T. F. Shtikov, commanding general of the Soviet armed forces in North Korea, was the chief Soviet delegate. The main issue was the problem of consultation with the democratic political and social organizations of Korea.

General Shtikov insisted that any party representatives who had ever expressed criticism of the trusteeship should be ineligible for consultation in forming the proposed Korean provisional government. The American delegate objected to the Soviet position on the ground that such a policy would deny the rights of free speech and insisted that invitations be sent also to groups opposing the Moscow Agreement.

The Soviet delegate wanted to prevent the rightist leaders who opposed the Moscow Agreement, especially Syngman Rhee, Kim Koo, and their associates, from participating in the provisional Korean government, and hence refused to consult with them; but the American delegate was determined to include them. Thus the commission adjourned indefinitely on May 6 without agreement.

Eventually, communications between Secretary of State George C. Marshall and Soviet Foreign Minister V. M. Molotov resulted in a compromise formula on the question of consultation with Korean political parties and social organizations. The following three points[3] were agreed upon: (1) Consultations were to be held with all democratic parties and social organizations who fully accepted the Moscow Agreement. (2) If any representative was hostile to the Moscow Agreement or to one of the Allied Powers, the joint commission by mutual agreement could demand that the party appoint another representative in his stead. (3) Persons, parties, or social organizations which after having signed the declaration of Communique No. 5[4] instigated demonstrations against the joint commission, one of the Allied Powers, or the fulfillment of the Moscow Agreement were to be excluded from further consultation with the joint commission. The decision on the exclusion of such persons, parties, or social organizations was to be made by the two delegations within the joint commission.

Both sides yielded somewhat from their previous stands: the Soviet Union accepted rightist Korean groups which had previously opposed the Moscow Agreement but now declared their support and ceased their opposition; the United States retreated from its stand on freedom of speech by agreeing that any Korean groups or leaders who actively opposed the agreement should not be consulted.

Disagreement between the two delegations became obvious when they investigated "ghost parties" and organizations which existed only on paper. In the Russian delegate's view,[5] only 119 out of 425 groups in South Korea were qualified to be consulted; the rest were declared "ghost organizations," or rightist groups which had shown little disposition to cooperate with the joint commission.

The real deadlock, however, occurred when the Soviet delegation insisted that twenty-four rightist groups said to be members of the antitrusteeship committee should be excluded from consultation. These groups had refused to renounce their opposition to the Moscow Agreement and the joint commission. The Soviets declared that these groups, mostly followers of Rhee and Kim Koo, should be admitted for consultation only if they withdrew from the antitrusteeship committee. The American delegation rejected the Russian proposal.

In July Major General Brown, chief of the American delegation, issued a unilateral press release[6] revealing the points of disagreement. He charged that the Soviet delegation wished to eliminate many of the groups submitting questionnaires either on grounds that they were not genuine social organizations or that they did not support the Moscow Agreement. Then he released the Soviet delegation's proposed list of parties and organizations qualified for consultation with the commission, as shown in table 10.

TABLE 10. SOVIET LIST OF GROUPS TO BE CONSULTED BY JOINT COMMISSION

South Korea:	rightist groups—	74
	leftist groups—	34
	center groups—	11
North Korea:	all leftist—	28

The totals were seventy-four for the right wing, sixty-two for the left wing, and eleven for the center.

In an effort to break the deadlock, on August 12 the American delegation recommended that oral consultation be abandoned and that a call for a free election for a national legislature be made instead. The Soviet delegation offered a counterproposal which accepted the abandonment of oral consultation but advocated the formation of a provisional assembly which equally represented the North and South and was composed "only of those groups who fully support the Moscow Agreement." This plan was rejected by the American delegation on the same grounds as before—that it was undemocratic in its violation of the freedom of the Korean people to express their opinion.

The discussion of the Korean problem was then transferred to the capital cities of the two major powers. On August 26 the United States government asked the Soviet Union to settle the Korean issue through a four-power conference of the United States, the Soviet Union, China, and the United Kingdom. The Soviet Union turned down the plan on the ground that it would violate the Moscow Agreement of the three powers.

In order to oppose the Moscow Agreement and the joint commission's work, Rhee and his followers launched the antitrusteeship movement throughout South Korea. The movement can be divided into two stages: the initial stage from December 1945 to the end of 1946, and the second stage from February 1947 to September 1947. In the early part of 1946, Rhee formulated two plans of action to carry out the movement: one was the formation of the National Society for the Rapid Realization of Korean Independence, the other was the advocacy of self-government for South Korea alone if a unified national government was impossible owing to Soviet influence in North Korea. The society set forth three main objectives: establishment of an independent national government, abrogation of the Moscow Agreement (especially the four-power trusteeship system), and immediate withdrawal of all foreign troops from Korea. The society refused to participate in the joint commission because its success would mean that a unified Korea would be placed under the four-power trusteeship in accordance with the Moscow Agreement.

When the first joint commission failed on May 6, 1946, the leftists charged that the rightists tactics of sabotage were primarily responsible. They also attacked Rhee's proposal of self-government, charging that the rightists were preparing for a separate government in South Korea which would hamper the efforts for unification. The rightists, in turn, accused the leftists of being puppets of a foreign power.

On May 12 the National Society for the Rapid Realization of Korean Independence held a meeting in Seoul Auditorium, where it denounced Soviet Russia and the left-wing political leaders and advocated that "the Korean people should establish their government by themselves regardless of where it is located."[7] Crowds of people paraded down the main streets of Seoul, and some of the youth bands stoned the leftist party headquarters and their newspaper buildings.

The moderate groups appealed to both sides. Following suggestions of the moderates, General Hodge invited Rhee, Kim Koo, Kim Kiusic, and Lyuh Woon-hyung to unite in an advisory coalition committee. The former two leaders rejected the invitation, but the latter two accepted it and cooperated with the American military government.

Hereafter ill feelings between General Hodge and Rhee became acute.

Hodge warned that "no solution for Korea was possible without Russian cooperation," and that Rhee should refrain from criticism of Russian intentions, cease to oppose the Moscow Agreement of which the United States was one of the contracting parties, and stop denouncing the U.S.-sponsored South Korean interim assembly as an undemocratic and left-wing-dominated body. Dr. Oliver wrote about the relations between Hodge and Rhee as follows: "When I arrived in Korea on June 2, 1946, General Hodge told me that 'Syngman Rhee is so much the greatest Korean statesman that he may be said to be the only one, but because of his persistent attack upon Russia he never can have a part in any government which the United States may sponsor in Korea.' "[8] Oliver also said: "Rhee first tried to persuade Hodge to abandon his plan [establishment of a South Korean interim assembly] and was told brusquely that the general did not intend to permit Rhee to 'seize power.' "[9]

The cordial relations between Hodge and Rhee broke down because American authority could not tolerate or approve of Rhee's terrorist tactics; and Hodge believed that Rhee's primary concern was to assume power on his own terms. Rhee believed Hodge had softened toward the leftists, and that Hodge's appointment of forty-five assemblymen from a list presented to him by the moderates (the coalition committee) was undemocratic and an attack on his political leadership. That is, Rhee now realized that Hodge rejected his political leadership and supported the moderates, Kim Kiusic, Ahn Chai-hong, and Lyuh Woon-hyung.

Rhee launched a six weeks' speaking tour to capture public opinion for his side. The main themes of his speeches were the need for establishment of a national government (in South Korea alone if necessary), complete suppression of "the radical elements" (meaning socialists and Communists), organization of a protective youth corps, and opposition to the four-power trusteeship.[10] About the same time Kim Koo also made a speaking tour in South Korea advocating the same ideals as Rhee. When the relations between Hodge and the rightists had reached their lowest ebb, Kim Koo and his associates announced that the provisional government, which had been formed following the March First Independence Movement of 1919, was the only lawful government of Korea and asked the people to support it. This was his answer to the plan of the American military authority to set up a South Korean interim government under the leadership of moderates, with Dr. Kim Kiusic as chairman of the assembly, Ahn Chai-hong as civil administrator, and Kim Yong-mu as chief justice of the Supreme Court.

Rhee, by now a frustrated politician, decided to return to the United States to present his plan to Washington and the United Nations, thus going over the American military authority's head. On December 1, 1946, he sailed from Inchun for Tokyo, where he visited his old friend General MacArthur, who provided Rhee passage on a military plane to the United States.

Rhee's main arguments in Washington were that Hodge's appointment of forty-five middle-of-the-road assemblymen was an "undemocratic procedure," that the American military authorities in South Korea were soft on Communists, and that the Korean people, except a minority of Communists, opposed the Moscow Agreement. Rhee suggested that the United States sponsor the establishment of a separate government, even if it had to be confined to South Korea, because in his judgment "it should by this time be abundantly clear to everyone that Russia would not agree to the establishment of a free government for all Korea."[11]

In February 1947 Rhee formed what was known as "a strategy council," composed of Dr. Robert T. Oliver, John W. Stagger, Jay Jerme Williams, Col. M. Preston Goodfellow, Col. Emory Woodall, Keveren Frederick Brown Harris, "Col." Ben Lim (Rhee made the military rank to suit his own convenience), and Miss Louise Yim. They formulated the following six-point program[12] and presented it to the State Department as well as to the United Nations General Assembly:

1. Election of an interim government for southern Korea, to serve until the two halves of Korea can be reunited and a general election held immediately thereafter;

2. Admission of this interim government to the United Nations and permission to negotiate directly with the Russian and United States governments concerning the occupation of Korea;

3. Consideration of Korean claims for reparations from Japan to aid in the rehabilitation of the Korean economy;

4. Granting of full commercial rights to Korea, on a basis of equality with other nations;

5. Stabilization of Korean currency and establishment on the international exchange;

6. United States security troops should remain in southern Korea until the two foreign armies of occupation simultaneously withdraw.

The program did not impress the State Department because the South Korean interim government had already been established under the sponsorship of the American military government in December 1946; and also there was a good possibility of reopening the second joint commission for unification, for Marshall and Molotov had reached agreement on the consultation issue; namely, that all Korean leaders, including those opposing trusteeship, would be consulted. According to Rhee, only Gen. John R. Hilldring, the assistant secretary of state for occupied countries, was in favor of the six points, feeling there was "no reason why South Korea should not be allowed to organize a free government as a counterbalance to the controlled regime the Russians established north of the 38th parallel."[13]

Rhee hastily returned to Korea in April. There were two reasons for this. First, during his stay in the United States Kim Koo was taking charge of the antitrusteeship movement and also agitating for an independent government, and his views were different from Rhee's. Kim Koo wanted to reestablish the sovereignty of the provisional republic of 1919 even though such action would be hostile to the United States. Rhee thought that such a unilateral move would have disastrous results for both the United States and Korea. When Rhee returned, Kim Koo resigned from the chairmanship of the provisional government, and Rhee took over.

The second reason for Rhee's return was the unexpected renewal of the second joint commission. As Dr. Oliver wrote, "Rhee was greatly disheartened by this development, for he did not expect Russia to agree to a reunified and independent Korea and he did fear that the renewal of the talks would block any progress toward establishment of a government in South Korea."[14]

In short, Rhee returned to Seoul to take over the chairmanship of the provisional government from Kim Koo and to block negotiations of the joint commission for the unification of Korea, because these threatened to hamper his own plan—establishment of a separate government in South Korea under his authority.

The second stage of the antitrusteeship movement began when the majority of the South Korean interim assemblymen passed the Antitrusteeship Resolution in January 1947. The resolution opposed General Hodge's support of the Moscow Agreement because his position was contrary to the Korean people's absolute opposition to the trusteeship provision, adding that "restriction of the freedom of opinion of the parties and organizations invited to be consulted by the joint commission would mean imposition of trusteeship over the Korean people in defiance of the principle of freedom of speech guaranteed by the Atlantic Charter."[15]

Thirty-five right-wing political groups who had signed Communique No. 5 canceled their signatures. They blamed the moderate leaders for dominating the coalition committee and for misleading the people. They also issued an antitrusteeship statement,[16] which said: "We have trusted the Allied powers . . . when they were talking about trusteeship over our people; we believed that at least our right to express ourselves as individuals or parties on trusteeship would be protected and that we could exercise self-determination in full, including the right to reject the trusteeship. With this understanding we signed Communique No. 5; but now we realize we have been deceived."

The statement went on to say that "the trusteeship agreement between the three powers should be viewed neither as a treaty nor as binding international law as far as the Korean people are concerned, but as a high-handed measure of the Allied Powers in violation of Article 3 of the Atlantic Charter. . . .

"Are the Allied Powers going to establish a so-called provisional Korean democratic government with the minority of the trusteeship supporters, who are traitors to the Korean national independence movement?"

The statement concluded by appealing to the governments of the United States, Soviet Union, United Kingdom, and China to annul the trusteeship.

On January 24, 1947, the Antitrusteeship Independent Struggle Committee (Bantak Doknip Toojang Imwonhai) was formed; Kim Koo was elected chairman and Syngman Rhee chief adviser. In the name of the committee a five-point action program[17] was distributed to the rightist patriotic organizations.

On February 4 a three-man delegation (Cho So-ang, Lee Woon-yung, and Lee Woo-sam) called on General Hodge on behalf of the antitrusteeship committee.[18] General Hodge was cool and urged them to cooperate with the joint commission, which would reconvene in May. Later he also pointed out that "the Moscow Agreement is an 'immutable law' which no one can change."[19]

Shortly thereafter, the leaders of the antitrusteeship committee split into two groups: One, headed by Chang Duk-soo, was ready to cooperate with the joint commission; the other, headed by Kim Koo and Syngman Rhee, advocated establishment of an independent government in South Korea. Chang was assassinated by a rightist police officer. Kim Koo was called to the witness stand when the murder trial was held by the American military court, but he denied any connection with Chang's assassination.

In the early part of 1947, the right wing, especially the antitrusteeship committee movement, was showing signs of internal weakness. The relationship between Rhee and Kim Koo had cooled after the pro-Rhee group had defeated Kim's plan to declare publicly "the authority of the provisional republic" as the legal government, and had removed Kim from the chairmanship of the provisional government in favor of Rhee. On the other hand, the moderates became stronger in terms of their organizations and of the followers of their programs. Because of their willingness to cooperate with the joint commission and to support the Moscow Agreement the moderates received American backing as the "government" party.[20]

When the second joint commission convened on May 21, Kim Koo and Rhee declared that "they would reserve their decision on participation in the activities of the Joint Commission until the meaning of 'trusteeship' and 'democracy' as used by the Commission became clear."[21] However, the right-wing Democratic party had finally decided to participate in the joint commission in spite of warnings from the Kim Koo–Syngman Rhee groups that once a party signed Communique No. 5 and participated in consultation it would not be in position to oppose trusteeship. Rhee issued a series of public statements opposing the joint commission.[22] His main arguments were that (a) the joint commission did not guarantee the freedom of opinion of the Korean people, (b) the government sponsored by the joint commission would be a mixed government in violation of the self-rule principle, (c) an independent national government was only possible after the withdrawal of the two armed occupation forces, (d) the government and public opinion of the United States were in favor of establishing an independent government in South Korea.

During the joint commission sessions Rhee and Kim directed rightist groups, some of them terrorist, and instigated antitrusteeship demonstrations in defiance of the ban on mass demonstrations against the Moscow Agreement by the American commanding general. The Young Men's Association, a right-wing terrorist group, was ordered dissolved. But on June 23 student groups held a mass demonstration against the joint commission by taking advantage of the official homecoming for Shu Yun Bok, a marathon champion. They stoned the Soviet delegates, who were attending the joint conference at Duksoo Palace in Seoul and demanded[23] immediate abolishment of the trusteeship system, guarantee of a national general election, recognition of the independent government sponsored by Rhee and Kim Koo as the government of Korea, and support of the Rhee-Kim plan.

On July 19 Lyuh Woon-hyung, one of the leading compromise candidates in the provisional government sponsored by the joint commission and head of the 1945 People's Republic, was assassinated by terrorists in Seoul. On July 26 Soviet delegates were stoned again. Plans for a left-wing mass demonstration as a countermeasure to rightist political activities on August 3 (the date of a memorial service for Lyuh) did not materialize. During August the South Korean police vigorously pursued a campaign against leftist leaders.

The arresting of a great number of South Korean left-wing leaders by the Seoul city police was made the issue of sharp exchanges between chief delegates Brown and Shtikov: Brown charged that the Soviet delegate was attempting to interfere in the internal affairs of the American zone while he was a "guest" in Seoul; Shtikov charged that the unwarranted "anti-people's action" was designed to disrupt the work of the commission.

About this time the United States government considered a new course of action to replace the Moscow Agreement, either submitting the Korean problem to the four powers (U.S., Soviet Union, United Kingdom, and China) or to the United Nations General Assembly. The antitrusteeship committee held that the new course meant the abandonment of the Moscow Agreement and expected that a general election under the supervision of the international body would be held. This was one of the major victories of the antitrusteeship committee—especially a personal triumph for Rhee. Hereafter Rhee's political fortune began to rise again.

The United Nations' Resolution. As early as March 1946, the Korea case was submitted to the United Nations General Assembly by a delegate of the Korean Representative Democratic Council. This appeal was Rhee's idea. But since no member of the United Nations was willing to sponsor the appeal on behalf of Korea, it was not brought to the attention of the General Assembly. The appeal[24] demanded that the Cairo Declaration and the Potsdam Declaration should be immediately implemented, that all American and Russian military forces should be withdrawn from Korea, and that the interim Korean government should be admitted to membership in the United Nations.

The appeal further requested that the American military government in South Korea be terminated and a Korean civilian government be established. In the event of a delay in the withdrawal of Soviet authorities from North Korea, the American military forces should be retained, under Lt. Gen. John R. Hodge, "until the Russian forces withdraw."[25]

On September 17, 1947, General Marshall, U.S. secretary of state, introduced the Korean problem to the U.N. General Assembly; on October 17 a formal American proposal was made by Ambassador Warren Austin; and on November 5 the Political and Security Committee voted forty-six to zero for creation of a United Nations Temporary Commission on Korea. On November 14 the General Assembly adopted the resolution by an overwhelming majority vote without the participation of the Soviet bloc.

The provisions of the United Nations resolution[26] were (a) the establishment of a temporary commission consisting of representatives of Australia, Canada, China, El Salvador, France, India, the Philippines, Syria, and the Ukrainian Soviet Socialist Republic; (b) the holding of an election in Korea not later than March 31, 1948, to choose representatives for a national assembly, which, in turn, would establish a unified government; and (c) the consulting of the U.N. Commission with the newly established government concerning the national security forces and the dissolving of all military or semimilitary formations not included therein, the taking over "the functions of the government from the military commands and civilian authorities of north and south," and the arranging "for complete withdrawal of foreign armed forces from Korea, if possible within ninety days."

The Soviet bloc objected to the United Nations resolution sponsored by the United States because an election in a Korea occupied by foreign powers would not be a true reflection of the Korean will, because Korean delegates from both North and South should be invited and their desires heard before adoption of the resolution, and because the United Nations was not competent to deal with the problems of Korean independence.[27]

The United Nations Temporary Commission on Korea (UNTCOK) convened at Duksoo Palace in Seoul for its first meeting on January 8, 1948, without the participation of a representative from the Ukrainian Soviet Socialist Republic.

The commission failed to get permission to enter North Korea, and hence was unable to fulfill the obligation imposed on it by the United Nations resolution. This failure raised legal doubts within the commission as to its status. Chairman Menon, therefore, reported to the Interim Committee of the General Assembly on the internal political situation of Korea and asked for a further resolution.

On February 26, 1948, the United Nations Interim Committee adopted the resolution "that the United Nations Commission on Korea proceed with the observance of election in all Korea, and if that is impossible, in as much of Korea as is accessible to it."[28]

According to Menon's report[29] to the interim committee, the majority view of the U.N. Temporary Commission was that "the formation of a separate Government in South Korea will not facilitate the twin objectives laid down in paragraph 5 of the Resolution, namely the attainment of the national independence of Korea and the withdrawal of the occupying troops." Therefore some of the delegates felt that "it will be unrealistic to treat any scheme of election in South Korea, even though that scheme may apply theoretically to all Korea, as national." The chairman of the commission, Menon, expressed his view on the Korean problem as follows: "I feel that, if only the Koreans are left to themselves—not merely in name but in reality—they will work out their own salvation and establish their own democratic government."

Within the commission there were sharp disagreements on the decision of the interim committee. The Australian delegate, for example, favored postponement of a U.N.-sponsored election, because all political parties except those of the extreme right would boycott it; the Canadian delegate felt that the resolution of the interim committee was unwise and unconstitutional; and the Syrian delegate insisted that the commission should have authority to reject any election it found conducted in an "unfree" and "fettered" atmosphere. The final vote was five to three in favor of carrying out the interim committee's decision.

The aim of the United Nations resolution, the unification of Korea, seemed impossible because the Soviet Union refused to cooperate. However, the American plan paved the way for the abandonment of the Moscow Agreement and for the formation of a separate government as the result of the U.N.-supervised election in South Korea, the cherished objective of Syngman Rhee.[30]

Significantly, support of the election came from only two extreme rightist parties—Rhee's group (the National Society for the Rapid Realization of Korean Independence) and the Korean Democratic party headed by Kim Sung-soo, one of the big landlords. The two parties justified their support of a U.N. election in South Korea by saying that South Korea had two-thirds of the total population, that a separate election would be the first step toward unification of the country, and that a separate election would be necessary at the time because of the noncooperative attitude of the Soviet government.

Nevertheless, many political parties and social organizations, including the middle-of-the-road Democratic Independence party, the rightist Korea Independence party, and all leftist parties (such as the South Korea Labor party, the Laboring People's party, and the Revolutionary party) opposed the setting up of a "national" government in South Korea. The opposition leaders before Subcommittee 2 of the commission said that a so-called national government in South Korea was a contradiction in terms, because, geographically, it would exercise authority over less than half the area and only two-thirds of the population of Korea; and politically, it would "inadequately reflect the general will because the elections, leading to the formation of such a government, are likely to be boycotted not only in the North but by most parties in the South as well."[31]

Few Koreans believed that the formation of a separate ruling body in the

South, even if invested with the prestige of a national government, would ultimately result in a unified independent Korea; it seemed more likely that it would perpetuate the division and cause a civil war. Three of five national leaders in South Korea—Kim Kiusic, chairman of the South Korean interim assembly; Kim Koo, former chairman of the Korean provisional government in China; and Ahn Chai-hong, civil administrator of the U.S.-sponsored South Korean interim government—held this view and opposed the U.N. election in South Korea. Kim Kiusic told the U.N. Temporary Commission:

> Any Korean who talks about a South Korean . . . government will be condemned by history because once that term is used, the Communists in the North under the direction of the Soviet Union will establish a so-called people's republic. . . . Then you will have two . . . governments in this small space of 85,000 square miles. . . . Once such a thing occurs . . . it will be permanent; and then you are responsible for perpetuating the division of Korea.[32]

As an alternative to the U.N. election, the three leaders proposed a meeting of the leaders of the North and South to find ways of bringing about unification of the country by the Koreans themselves. This suggestion was rejected by the American military commander, who later denounced the meeting as a Communist political plot. Kim Kiusic resigned the chairmanship of the South Korean interim assembly and announced that he was preparing to attend the forthcoming North-South political leaders' conference, which is described later.

When Ahn Chai-hong failed to persuade General Hodge to agree to the coalition conference, he submitted his resignation as civil administrator. Kim Koo anounced that he was planning to participate in the conference. Subsequently, more than fifty political leaders and forty different political and social organizations in South Korea announced their desire to participate. This all brightened Rhee's political future, for no powerful challenger to Rhee remained in South Korea, and the United States and the U.N. favored his plan for a separate government in the South.

In spite of the propaganda of the United States military government and Rhee's appeal to South Koreans for support of the U.N. election on May 10, only two extreme rightist parties and their affiliated groups offered active support; the overwhelming majority of the South Korean political and social organizations—rightists, moderates, and leftists alike—boycotted the election, because "it would perpetuate the division and cause a bloody civil war."

Officially, the election was held under the supervision of thirty staff members of the U.N. commission in an area of more than forty thousand square miles, where more than seven million registered voters resided. But actually, "in order to uphold law and order during the election," General Hodge authorized the police (about ten thousand men) to mobilize about one million members of the Community Protective Corps, which was formed in April 1948. A uniformed policeman and stick-carrying youth bands (members of the Community Protective Corps) guarded each polling place and the residences of the candidates.

On May 9 the American military authority also sent its own election observation team, composed of one civilian and one army officer each, into each of the two hundred election districts. On election day many districts reported that unidentified youths and policemen checked each qualified voter's home and asked whether he had voted.

Approximately 75 percent of all eligible voters cast their ballots. One hundred ninety out of 198 elected assemblymen belonged to the Rhee and Kim Sung-soo parties and their affiliated groups. According to the figures released by the South Korea interim government, 589 persons, including policemen, government officials, candidates, and civilians, were killed during the election. Many incidents were reported of pressure and intimidation by police and terrorist groups during registration of candidates for the assembly and voters for qualification. Some U.N. delegates returned to Seoul from an observation tour in rural election districts with the information that "one reason for the very high registration was a threat by the police to withdraw individual ration cards from Koreans who did not register."[33] The most notable incident occurred in Syngman Rhee's district. Rhee had picked a safe district in Seoul, and did not expect any other contestant in the election. The election law did not require the candidate's residence. Choi Nong-chin, an American-educated physical education instructor and former chief of the Investigation Bureau of the police department of the United States military government in South Korea, decided to run against Rhee, and presented his documents to the District Election Committee. But the committee refused to accept them, saying that Syngman Rhee had already filed his candidacy. Choi protested and obtained assurance from the American military authority that he was entitled to have the same chance to run as anyone else. When Choi for the second time attempted to file his application for candidacy, Rhee's youth band beat him and threatened to kill him. Choi's complaint[34] was rejected by the National Election Committee, which was dominated by the Rhee and Kim Sung-soo clique.

Rhee was chosen as speaker of the South Korean Assembly on May 31, 1948. Three months later, in August, the assembly elected him president of the Republic of Korea.

The North-South Political Leaders' Coalition Conference. As early as December 1947, Dr. Kim Kiusic, leader of the middle-of-the-road group, had suggested a conference of political leaders from the North and South to discuss the unification of the country.[35] Kim Koo, a rightist, Lyuh Woonhong, a socialist, and many other political and social leaders supported the plan. On February 16, 1948, a letter[36] signed by Kim Kiusic and Kim Koo was sent to two Northern Korean leaders, Kim Il-sung, then chairman of the Provisional People's Committee, and Kim Du-bong, head of the Labor party in North Korea. The letter proposed a conference to discuss unification and the formation of a democratic national government.

The Northern Korean leaders accepted the idea but suggested that the conference demand withdrawal of all foreign troops from Korea before the national elections, support "opposition to a separate election in South Korea," and demand "complete elimination from the conference of all reactionary politicians who have been attempting to divide the country and people."[37]

On behalf of the political and social organizations which supported the idea of a conference, the North Korean People's Committee issued a formal invitation to more than forty different political and social groups in South Korea.[38] Pointedly, Syngman Rhee and Kim Sung-soo were not invited. This invitation was immediately denounced by the American commander, General Hodge, as an illegal and misleading Communist plot. The rightists condemned the conference as Soviet oriented.

The overwhelming majority of the public[39] and newspapers expressed their support for the conference, which was scheduled for April 22 and 23 in Pyongyang, the present capital of North Korea. It was argued that the conference might pave the way for the reunification of the country and the avoidance of national tragedy. Kim Kiusic, spokesman for the South Korean delegates, stated five points[40] as the basic principles of the conference:

1. Opposition to dictatorship and striving for democracy;

2. Opposition to monopoly capitalism and the favoring of a private property economy;

3. Striving for the establishment of a unified government by a general election;

4. Opposition to concession of military bases to foreign powers;

5. Demand for a public announcement of the withdrawal of American and Soviet troops from Korea on a fixed date.

As described later, the bulk of these points was adopted by the conference as "the Conference Resolution."

The conference was attended by 545 delegates, of whom 360 came from the South. Nationally known delegates from the South were Kim Kiusic (moderate), the chairman of the South Korean interim assembly and head of the National Independence Federation; Kim Koo (rightist), former chairman of the Korean provisional government and head of the Korean Independence party; Hong Myung-hi (liberal and writer), head of the Democratic Independence party; and Lyuh Woon-hong (socialist), head of the Social Democratic party. The Northern delegates included General Kim Il-sung, chairman of the Northern Korean People's Committee; Kim Du-bong, head of the Labor party (formerly called the Communist party); Choi Yong-kun, head of Chosun Democratic party; and Kim Dail-hyun, head of Chungwoodang.

After two days, the conference issued a joint communique,[41] making the following four points:

1. Demand for the immediate and simultaneous withdrawal of foreign troops from Korea in conformity with the proposal made by the Soviet Union;

2. Opposition to civil war and demand for peaceful unification of the divided country without interference of foreign powers;

3. Demand for the organization of a democratic government by a na-

tional political conference representing all sections of the Korean people;

4. Opposition to separate elections in South Korea.

This communique was signed by the leaders of fifteen political parties and social organizations of the North and twenty-six parties and organizations of the South. The conference also passed a resolution opposing dictatorship, monopolistic capitalism, and the establishment of foreign military bases in Korea.

Dr. Kim Kiusic and Mr. Kim Koo issued a special statement[42] upon their return to Seoul. They declared that Korea could be unified by the Korean people on the basis of the withdrawal of the two occupation armies; the organization of a provisional government by a national political conference immediately after the withdrawal of foreign troops; and the adoption of a national constitution and formation of a united national government by representatives to be chosen through a national election.

The unification efforts by North and South Korean leaders were abortive, however, because two opposing approaches to the unification issue existed between the power blocs as well as between the Korean leaders. As already mentioned, it was at this time that the Soviet Union proposed "withdrawal of all foreign troops from Korea, leaving the Korean affairs in the hands of the Korean people," a proposal which paralleled one of the main principles of the conference's declaration. However, the United States took the position that the Korean unification problem should be solved through U.N.-supervised elections.

General Hodge said of the South Korean leaders who attended the conference, "They were blind men who had been baited by the Communists."[43] Rhee denounced the conference: "The conference serves the cause of Soviet political objectives . . . and some of the leaders are ignorant of the Soviet communizing plan of Korea as well as the whole world."[44]

Some Koreans argued that the conference benefited leftist political aims because a so-called second coalition conference was convened late in June 1937 (without the participation of Kim Kuisic, Kim Koo, and many other leaders who attended the first conference), with the aim of establishing a Korean "Democratic People's Republic" as a counterpart to the Republic of Korea in the South. The Communist-dominated Democratic People's Republic came into being on September 8, 1948, in North Korea, and the leftists claimed it as the legal government of Korea. They further observed that even if the conference of April had been successful in bringing about the unification of the country by establishing a coalition government, including rightists, leftists, and moderates, Korea might have become the Czechoslovakia of the Far East.

Other Koreans insisted that Korea had been artifically divided by the wartime Allied Powers for temporary military expediency and gradually had become a pawn of power politics between the two power blocs in the Far East.

CHAPTER 10

THE FIRST REPUBLIC UNDER SYNGMAN RHEE

CHARACTERISTICS OF RHEE'S POLITICS

Syngman Rhee,[1] the former president of the Republic of Korea, was one of the controversial politicians of our time. There have been two views on the character of Rhee's politics. Some Koreans and foreign observers admired him as a great political leader. Dr. Robert T. Oliver, one-time political adviser to Rhee, described him as "a catalyst of democracy in Asia" and as "one of the epicenters of his age—a symbol, a magnet, a target; and also a prophet and a statesman as well."[2] Lt. Gen. Van Fleet, the former commander of the Eighth Army in Korea, admired him "as one of the greatest thinkers, scholars, statesmen, and patriots of our times."[3] The writer of the Liberal party's manifesto (Rhee's own party) in 1955 stated that Syngman Rhee, "the founding father of the Republic of Korea, is one of the most perspicacious and outstanding leaders in the free world."[4]

In contrast, the *Manchester Guardian* described him as a "dictatorial, ambitious, reactionary, irresponsible, and bloody-handed politician."[5] Owen Lattimore denounced him as a "little Chiang Kai-shek."[6] Lt. Gen. John L. Hodge, commanding general of the U.S. armed forces in South Korea from 1945 to 1948, told the United Nations Election Commission: "He [Rhee] will, no doubt, make an effort to direct the voting in certain areas by high-powered campaigning and possibly by means of which we do not approve. If we do not watch, he will attempt to mislead Koreans in the interpretation of the election law and confuse the country people."[7]

During Rhee's first term as president, two vice-presidents, Lee Si-yong and Kim Sung-soo, resigned, protesting Rhee's ironfisted dictatorial methods in handling state affairs. Sir Winston Churchill commented on Rhee's unilateral action in releasing twenty-six thousand North Korean prisoners of war: "I was shocked by the action of Rhee; England would never fight to conquer North Korea for Syngman Rhee."[8]

Let us turn to some of Rhee's own public statements. As mentioned before, the first meassge to the Korean people in 1945 when he returned from the United States was: "Trust me and follow me and unite together."[9] He opposed the Moscow Agreement on Korea because it contained a four-power trusteeship of Korea for a period of five years; and he also refused to participate in the U.S.-U.S.S.R. Joint Commission in 1946 and 1947 on the ground that it would work toward a unified provisional Korean government in conformity with the Moscow Agreement. Instead, he demanded immediate withdrawal of all foreign troops and a national election without interference by any foreign powers in order to establish a single national government.

In December 1946 Rhee issued a statement saying that "on my returning to Korea I advocated unification . . . so that we could drive the Russians from the North. America is our friend; we must fight those who are not our friends. As soon as the time comes, I will instruct you. Then you should be prepared to shed blood."[10]

In 1948 he supported the U.N. resolution on Korea providing for a temporary commission to observe elections in South Korea.

On March 1, 1950, the anniversary of the 1919 declaration of Korean independence, Rhee, who in August 1948 had been elected president of the Republic of Korea, said: "Despite advice given by friends from across the seas not to attack the foreign puppet in North Korea, the cries of our brothers in distress in the North cannot be ignored. To this call we shall respond."[11]

In May 1952, during the Korean war, Rhee jailed fourteen assemblymen and proclaimed martial law in order to amend the constitution, saying, "I have no constitutional authority to do this, but the will of the people transcends the constitution."[12]

In October 1954 he made a public statement urging the national assembly to pass another constitutional amendment—namely, the lifetime presidency clause.[13]

In 1956 he ran for a third term in the name of "the will of the people." In February 1959 the eighty-four-year-old Rhee ran again for a fourth term, because he had "not completed the task of unification," which he said was his life-time duty. His method of unification was that of force, on the ground that the Communists respected only force.

In his public statements he advocated "liberty," "independence," and "the will of the people," and he attempted to identify himself as a democratic leader and patriot. But in his conduct of domestic affairs he was a dictator who suppressed political freedom and eliminated almost all his political adversaries by authoritarian tactics. He reduced the national assembly to a rubber-stamp organization, and he used mob violence and police intimidation in support of his program and his election. On the international level, he attempted to undermine unification based on the United Nations resolution on Korea whenever it conflicted with his own political interests.

Rhee's Ilmin-jui, The One-People Principle. In 1948, two months after the establishment of the Republic of Korea, Rhee pronounced *ilmin-jui*[14] to be the basic governing principle of the new state. This is the only major statement of Rhee's political philosophy and is therefore cited here at length, frequent repetitions being omitted. Rhee declared:

> I advocate *ilmin-jui,* the one-people principle. With this principle I will set forth my national policy. We, the Korean people, have a long national history as one race and we have always been together as one people, not two. Therefore, we, the Korean people, should be one people in all situations. But vicious distinction between high and low society and between the rich and the poor has divided the people one against another.
>
> Moreover, geographical sectionalism and discrimination based on sex have caused the Korean people to depart from oneness. . . . Many men of learning have been worrying about this misfortune of the country; and a farsighted philosopher, Lee Taik, pointed out the grave fault in our political life by saying that 'unless we abandon the system of lineage for public office and the distinction between lord and subject, there will be no political justice.' Hong Dai-yong [nineteenth-century scholar] advocated 'the abolishment of class distinction between rich and poor.'
>
> These doctrines were rejected by strong traditional political forces, and without reformation of any kind we emerged into the last period

of the Yi dynasty, the modern era. After the Kapshin-ran and Kapoo-ganchang revolts, class distinction was officially abolished, but actually never disappeared under the strong monarchy; especially the economic structure remained unchanged. During these revolts Korea was invaded by a foreign power.

When I was busy with the activities of the Independence Club, the country was heading toward collapse; loss of sovereign power was just a matter of time. When Korea actually lost her sovereignty to the foreign power, I thought of the future of the Korean people and my sadness was overwhelming. However, I had one belief—*ilmin-jui,* the one-people principle.

By first giving up the concept of geographical sectionalism we should develop a strong feeling of oneness; next, let us not talk about discrimination based on sex. . . . Efforts to eliminate divisions between high and low social statuses and between the rich and poor are now being made.

The two words *ilmin* have been the alpha and omega during my fifty years in the national independence movement. Although I know the world situation has been unkind to us in the past, the thirty-eighth parallel division has broken my heart. How many years have passed now since we were forced to live separated from one another? Our hope is in international justice for an orderly and reasonable solution of our national problem, but we must do our best to solve our problems ourselves. All Koreans prefer unity to division. The true national feeling, which has flowed from north to south, from south to north, will survive regardless of the many obstacles created by the great powers. We must open the closed line that separates us from one another. . . . Let us make *ilmin-jui* the national policy of our new rising state.

Our forefathers formulated the one-people principle as national policy in the early days. At one time a section of our territory was lost to the Han dynasty of China and it was known as Han-gun but later was reincorporated. At another time, Silla [southern Korea] and Koguryo [northern Korea] opposed each other during the T'ang dynasty of China, but, again, the two parts joined eventually. . . .

Our race is one; therefore our national territory, national spirit, our treatment of each other, our national politics and national culture are to

> be one. If we have failed in making ourselves one in any of these in the past, we must succeed as soon as possible. In the meantime, if there is any obstacle to this development of oneness, we must stamp it out at once. *Any individual action contrary to oneness must be eliminated.* Our race will be aroused by this idea of oneness. Separatists will not dare join in the oneness movement. Remember this: if we are divided we will die and if we unite we will survive; that is, we will die separated and we will live united.

Rhee's *ilmin-jui* can be characterized as *nationalistic monism.* No differing views in politics, domestic and foreign, are allowed, for the sake of "oneness" and national unity. Hence, individual rights and freedoms, the essentials of democracy, are not recognized. The political result of *ilmin-jui* during the ten years of the Rhee administration was the establishment of a patriarchal dictatorship based on a semifeudalistic society.

Rhee called for "economic and social equality" as a means of achieving *ilmin-jui*—not equality in the sense of rights, freedoms, and the welfare of the people, as understood by Western democratic societies. His interpretation of equality is revealed by his veto of the Land Reform Bill of 1949, which the overwhelming majority of the people supported in the hope of eliminating the sharp divisions between landlords and peasants. It is further revealed by his approval of the so-called new National Security Law of 1958, which abridged the constitutionally guaranteed civil rights of the people and transformed Korea into a police state.

One might argue that Rhee's predominant concern was praiseworthy in that it was unification of the country. But, of course, all Koreans, regardless of party affiliation, were in favor of unification. And every Korean had the right to express his views on unification without fear of intimidation by the government. But Rhee advocated unification by force, arguing that "the Communists respect only force;" and views on peaceful unification were treated as heresy. The years of political tragedy in South Korea were mostly the result of *ilmin-jui,* nationalistic monism.

Rhee's Political Tactics. Rhee believed in force as a political tool and was convinced that means justify ends.[15] He saw in power (physical force) the substructure of politics, and in legal and moral forces and public opinion the superstructure.

Rhee formulated his own political tactics, which one might call "triangle operation" and "priority politics." His triangle can be constructed as in table 11.

TABLE 11. RHEE'S "TRIANGLE OPERATION"

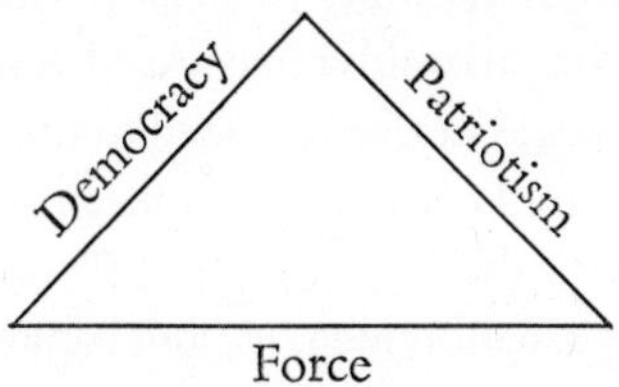

Rhee seldom mentioned force except when he was talking about unification. He first stressed such terms as "will of the people," "mandate of the people," and "people's sovereign rights and freedoms" as being the essence of democracy. Next he emphasized the necessity of unconditional patriotism for the sake of "democracy" and for national unity. Then he branded opposition leaders as Communists or fellow travelers. Finally, he used force—intimidation, police power, terroristic youth groups—as a means of subduing opposing political forces. As described later in detail, he used these tactics on many occasions: the constitutional amendments in 1952 and 1954, all elections (including the presidential and assembly elections), and the new National Security Law legislation in 1958.

Rhee had two political aims: one, to keep his power over all opposition in South Korea; two, to unify the country during his lifetime. Since he insisted that the second aim should be accomplished on his own terms, he identified Korea's interests with his own. As a result, he was a ruthless, irresponsible, and arrogant politician when his authority was challenged. He was so preoccupied with the two aims that he treated as secondary such vital matters as economic reforms, reconstruction problems, development of democratic parliamentary procedures, educational reforms, and social welfare. He vetoed the land reform legislation of 1949 because he depended on the support of the landlords, who had been the absolute masters of the peasants for centuries. He gave to his followers much of the vested property formerly owned by

Japanese; a great portion of the United States economic aid was misappropriated to bolster Rhee's political funds. The economic dependence of South Korea was acknowledged by Secretary of State Dean Acheson as early as 1950 when he stated before Congress that "the Republic of Korea government would fall within three months if economic assistance were not provided" by the United States government.[16]

Rhee reduced the national assembly to a rubber-stamp body by intimidation of antiadministration assemblymen. As described earlier, when he realized in 1952 that he would not be reelected to the presidency by constitutional procedures, he declared martial law on the ground that some assemblymen had connections with the North Korean Communist regime, and arrested fourteen anti-Rhee assemblymen. He also banned the Voice of America and circulation of *Newsweek* and *Time*, which carried unfavorable comments on his actions. Then he threatened to pull out from the battlefront one division of the South Korean army in order to force the passage of the constitutional amendment calling for presidential election by popular vote.

Rhee appointed his own men to every key governmental position, gradually making himself the absolute patriarchal dictator of South Korea. Political favoritism and the spoils system were institutionalized, and official corruption, graft, and usurpation of authority became common practices. The spoils system and favoritism had served Rhee well in retaining his power—his first political aim.

About his second aim, the unification of Korea on his own terms, he was explicit on many occasions. For instance, on December 30, 1949, at a press conference Rhee said:

"In the coming year we shall all unanimously strive to regain the lost territory . . . through our own efforts."[17]

Rhee opposed bitterly the truce negotiations between the representatives of the United Nations forces and the North Korean–Chinese Communist forces. To undermine the peace negotiations, he ordered the release of twenty-six thousand anti-Communist North Korean prisoners of war in the midst of the negotiations, threatened to resume the war with South Korean armed forces alone, and advocated the immediate resumption of war after the Geneva conference of 1954 failed to reach an agreement for the unification of Korea. In his visit to the United States in 1954, Rhee urged the United States government to join South Korea in war against Russia.[18]

THE U.N.-SPONSORED REPUBLIC OF KOREA

The United Nations Temporary Commission on Korea consisted of representatives from Australia, Canada, Nationalist China, El Salvador, France, India, the Philippines, and Syria; the delegate of the Ukrainian Soviet Socialist Republic declined to become a member of the commission, because no representative of Korea had been invited to attend the United Nations debate. The commission held its first meeting in Seoul on January 9, 1948. Immediately doubts arose as to its legal authority to observe the Korean election, because it failed to establish contact with the Soviet commanding general in North Korea as would have been necessary according to the resolution. In addition, the majority of South Korean political leaders—rightists, moderates, and leftists—also opposed the election, because the Soviet-boycotted Temporary Commission could not observe the election in North Korea and therefore the unification problem would not be solved. Under these circumstances, the chairman of the commission, Dr. K. P. S. Menon, returned to the United Nations headquarters to receive new instructions from the Interim Committee of the General Assembly. On February 26, 1948, the Interim Committee adopted another resolution without participation of the Soviet bloc, stating that "the United Nations Temporary Commission on Korea [would] proceed with the observance of elections in all Korea, and if that is impossible, in as much of Korea as is accessible to it."[19]

Thus the Interim Committee authorized the commission to hold a separate election in South Korea. Three members of the commission voiced objections: the delegate from Australia held that since all Korean political and social organizations except the two extreme rightist groups would boycott the elections, the commission should withdraw; the Canadian delegate thought the resolution unconstitutional, because it contradicted the original purpose of the United Nations resolution; the Syrian delegate stated that the commission should reject elections held in an "unfree atmosphere." But the three were outvoted by the five members favoring the elections, which were to be held on May 10.

As mentioned before, to provide orderly elections the American military command authorized the Korean police, which had a force of ten thousand, to deputize one million men of the Community Protective Corps, which had been organized under the supervison of the police department to prevent any moves by leftist groups on election day. Election-observation teams of the U.S. military government, which included one army official, were sent out to each election district. The U.N. election-observation team was composed of only thirty staff members of the commission.

As a result of these elections 190 out of 200 seats of the assembly were taken by the two extreme rightist groups, the National Society for the Rapid Realization of Korean Independence and the Korean Democratic party. After the election the commission left for Shanghai to prepare a report for the forthcoming United Nations General Assembly. On December 12, 1948, after almost four months, the Republic of Korea was proclaimed in the South. The United Nations General Assembly declared that "lawful government has been established in South Korea where the Temporary Commission was able to observe the elections. . . . This is the only such Government in Korea."[20]

The Organization of the Republic of Korea. On May 31, 1948, the national assembly elected Syngman Rhee chairman of the assembly. The assembly had to work rapidly because the United States government planned to terminate its military government by August 15. Rhee appointed members of a constitutional drafting committee. The constitution was adopted on July 2 in the assembly after little debate.

The most important feature of the constitution[21] was the authority of the president. It provided that the national assembly elect the president and the vice-president, and the president in turn select the prime minister with the approval of the assembly. Article 57 gave the president almost unlimited power in time of crisis, and the president was also given authority to appoint all justices of the Supreme Court. The position of the prime minister under the constitution was that of "first" minister, having no real authority since his tenure also depended on the pleasure of the president like that of the other ministers. Therefore, the president, not the prime minister, was the head of the state, as well as the real head of the government.

The assembly elected Rhee president, and eighty-year-old Lee Si-yong, former member of the Korean provisional government and one of the old Korean nobility, vice-president. Rhee then nominated Lee Youn-yong, a former minister of the Methodist Church and acting chairman of the Korean Democratic party, prime minister, but the assembly rejected the nomination. Kim Sung-soo, head of the Korean Democratic party, was favored by a large number of assemblymen, but Rhee was not interested in nominating him. Finally, a compromise candidate, General Lee Bum-suk, a graduate of the Whampoa Military Academy in China and a strong believer in authoritarian government, was made prime minister. Eleven cabinet members were then chosen; most of them had received their higher education abroad.

The prime minister and defense minister, General Lee, had been the head of the Korean National Youth Corps after his return from China in 1945. The Youth Corps was similar to the Nazi and Kuomintang youth groups. A number of the youth corps combined to form the nucleus of the South Korean army. General Lee was a strong anti-Communist and opposed to any negotiation with the Northern regime.

Foreign Minister Chang Taik-sang, a graduate of the university of Edinburgh, had been chief of the Seoul metropolitan police and a notorious prosecutor of liberals and left-wing leaders through brutal police measures during the era of the American military government. Minister of Internal Affairs Yun Chi-yung had studied in the United States. He had been a private secretary to Rhee and belonged to a wealthy family. The police were under his control. Minister of Commerce Louise Yim, a graduate of the University of Southern California, had been principal of a girls' high school and had served as head of the Woman's Democratic party and as a representative of the so-called Korean Democratic Assembly (an unofficial body established by Rhee) at the United Nations General Assembly in 1947–48.

Minister of Education Ahn Ho-sang, a graduate of the University of Mannheim in Germany, was a professor of philosophy and later became an influential right-wing leader. Minister of Finance Kim Do-yun was a graduate of American University, Washington, D.C. Minister of Transportation Min Hi-sik, a graduate of the University of Nevada, had held the same position in the South Korean interim government; he was an antilabor unionist who used police-state methods to suppress strikes. Minister of Justice

Lee In, a Japanese-trained lawyer, had been chief prosecutor under the South Korean interim government. Minister of Social Affairs Chun Chin-han, a graduate of Waseda University, Tokyo, was the organizer of a right-wing labor union. Minister of Agriculture Cho Bong-am, a former Communist, was the only cabinet member who favored a land-reform program aimed at breaking landlord holdings. Minister of Communication Yun Suk-koo was not known to the public and had no experience in communications work. Rhee appointed Chough Pyong-ok, a graduate of Columbia University and a former director of the police under the American military government, to the post of goodwill ambassador in Washington, London, and Paris. Chang Myun, an American-educated high school principal, was appointed Korean ambassador to the United States.

Most cabinet members belonged to wealthy aristocratic families. None of them was a recognized national leader. Most members of the Rhee cabinet had no administrative experience in Korean politics. More than half of them had studied in Western countries, and the rest had been educated in Japan and China. The most noticeable figures among the cabinet members were Prime Minister Lee Bum-suk and Foreign Minister Chang Taik-sang, known for their dictatorial and police-state suppression of liberals and left-wing leaders during the American occupation. Rhee's goodwill ambassador Chough Pyong-ok had also been a notorious prosecutor of leftists as the head of the police department under the American military government.

The strongest criticism was that Rhee's cabinet members were all from wealthy Southern families; no Northern Koreans were included although many able individuals were available. (Many of them had escaped from the North and had held high positions under the American military government.) Rhee continued the traditional policy of exclusion of North Koreans from the central government, which had been practiced by the Yi dynasty for five centuries. The constitution and the government of the Republic of Korea was Syngman Rhee's own handiwork, reflecting his personality. The government became a one-man regime.

RHEE FACES INTERNAL AND EXTERNAL TROUBLES

Soon after the formation of the government, factional rivalry developed within the cabinet. In less than four months, Rhee removed three ministers.

Foreign Minister Chang was dismissed because he was a potential challenger to Rhee, and the minister of internal affairs and minister of social affairs were removed as the result of personal ill feelings between them. Rhee also found that he had to fight the national assembly, which was dominated by the Korean Democratic party and independents. These two groups had also been excluded from cabinet positions, and they attacked Rhee's favoritism as well as his police state methods in dealing with the opposition. Rhee ordered the arrest of ten assemblymen, including the vice-chairman, who had been critical of the administration's policy. Seven newspaper offices were closed and a dozen editorial writers jailed, because they had criticized the administration's methods in dealing with the national assembly. The assembly called for resignation of all cabinet members by a vote of 89 to 59 the first time, and 82 to 61 the second time; but Rhee ignored the demand.[22]

In November 1948 a Communist-inspired armed rebellion occurred in the port of Yusu, situated on the southern coast two hundred miles south of Seoul. Many villages and towns in that area fell to the rebels before the government sent troops to suppress the uprising. More than eighty-nine thousand persons were arrested.[23] South Korea was then shocked by the news of the sudden assassination of Kim Koo by an army officer—Kim was not only considered a patriot but also the only strong political rival of Rhee.

Rhee faced more trouble when the national assembly election of May 1950 drew close. First he attempted to postpone the election until fall in order to strengthen his position by organizing youth groups and increasing the police force. His attempt was thwarted by the United States State Department, which threatened to cut off economic aid if the election was not held in May. The election itself was disastrous for the rightist parties in general and for Rhee's own group in particular. Rhee's group dropped from 56 seats to 12 and the Korean Democratic party from 78 seats to 28, out of a total 210 assembly seats. The independents and the moderate groups won a majority. The United Nations Commission, which observed the election, reported to the General Assembly as follows: "The new Assembly with some 130 Independents out of a total 200 seats convened on 19 June 1950 in a hopeful atmosphere conducive to continued progress in the building of an effective representative government in an economically healthy state. The initial sessions have indicated determination to tackle the Administration in a critical spirit for its numerous shortcomings."[24]

The new election meant, among other things, that Rhee was reduced to being a lame duck president; he was in office only because the president's term had been set at four years. It was abundantly clear that Rhee would not be reelected.

Soon after the election, Rhee confronted a new problem: the peaceful integration of the North Korean regime, which was supported by some South Korean assemblymen. The new South Korean assembly was dominated by fewer conservatives than the previous one, and a majority of assemblymen were against the administration. Many assemblymen believed that their major task was to find ways of reunifying the country without civil war, which Rhee and his principal ministers had often advocated.

The North Korean regime, knowing the feelings of the South Korean assembly, accelerated its peace campaign. On June 7, 1950, the Northern regime proposed a unification formula in the name of the Central Committee of the United Democratic Front of the Fatherland of Korea. The essential proposals were (a) that a general election be held from August 5 to 8 in both the South and the North and a united supreme legislative body be formed by the elected representatives; (b) that the first session of the supreme legislature be opened on August 15, the fifth anniversary of the liberation; (c) that, in preparation for the above, a political conference representing the political and social organizations of both parts of the country be convened on July 17, either at Kaesung or Haeju. The proposal also contained two provisoes: eight South Korean political leaders, including Syngman Rhee, Lee Bum-suk, and Kim Sung-soo, should be excluded from the political conference, because of their record of thwarting unification; and interference by the United Nations Commission on Korea should not be allowed.[25]

On June 11 a peace team composed of three members of the Central Committee of the United Democratic Front of the Fatherland of Korea was sent to the South Korean national assembly. Upon crossing the 38th parallel, they were arrested by the police, and nothing was heard from them thereafter. The Rhee government dismissed the peace offer as a Communist plot.

The Northern regime advanced another unification proposal on June 19, six days before the military invasion of the South. The proposal urged (a) that unification of the country be secured by merging the Supreme People's Assembly of the northern People's Republic and the national assembly of the southern republic into a single all-Korean legislative body; (b) that the all-Korean legislative body thus created draw up a constitution for establishment of a single government; (c) that the eight "traitors" mentioned in the first unification proposal be arrested; and (d) that the United Nations Commission on Korea leave Korea immediately.[26]

Since 1948 the Northern regime had been taking the initiative for unification with considerable popular support throughout the country, while the Southern regime had been taking a negative attitude and was without a definite policy to counter Northern proposals. It was also clear that the Northern regime had sufficiently built up its military for unification by force, as they demonstrated in the successful military occupation of almost all of South Korea until the U.N. forces landed in Inchun in September 1950. Contrary to the boasts of South Korean Defense Minister Shin Sung-mo on November 1, 1949—"We are strong enough to march up and take Pyongyang within a few days"—the Southern Korean regime had not prepared for any military attempt at unification, as was proved at the beginning of the Korean war when the Southern army lost the capital city within two days. Many Koreans believed that without United States intervention South Korea would have been overrun by the Northern forces within a week, and Rhee would have fled to Hawaii in 1950 and not in 1961.

RHEE AS AN IRONFISTED RULER

Rhee's first term as president was to end on August 15, 1952, and he knew that he would not be reelected by the antiadministration assembly. In May, in the middle of the war, Rhee pressed the assembly to act on a constitutional amendment—to change the election of the president from an assembly vote to a popular vote. The assembly rejected the amendment. Thereupon Rhee declared martial law on the ground that some assemblymen had connections with the Northern regime, and arrested the fourteen assemblymen who had led in opposing the constitutional amendment. At the same time, he ordered the police to jail all antiadministration elements throughout South Korea; he banned all anti-Rhee newspapers and foreign news media, such as Voice of America broadcasts and distribution of *Time* and *Newsweek* magazines—all on the charge of news distortion. Pro-Rhee "youth groups" broke up mass meetings sponsored by civic leaders to protest Rhee's illegal actions, and many of the leaders were beaten up by these hoodlums.

Vice-President Kim Sung-soo resigned in protest against Rhee's dictatorial and brutal methods. Kim was the second vice-president to resign; the first elected vice-president, Lee Si-yung, had resigned for similar reasons, as will be recalled.

The United Nations Commission on Korea issued a statement saying that "it could not ignore Rhee's actions in view of the fact that the free people of the world are making enormous sacrifices in men and resources to preserve the freedom of the Korean people." But Rhee, unmoved, said: "Don't interfere in the internal affairs of the Republic of Korea, or get out of Korea." Then he announced his intention to pull out one army division from the front line if necessary for the passing of the constitutional amendment. When he received a critical note from President Truman, he responded, saying, "I know you don't like me but I don't care." He threatened to dissolve the assembly if it did not accede to his wishes. He admitted that he had no constitutional authority to do this, but he justified his actions by saying, "The will of the people transcends the constitution." He would change his mind if he received "a mandate from the people."[27]

The constitutional amendment was then passed in the assembly, only pro-Rhee assemblymen being present—guarded by police acting under martial law. Rhee was promptly reelected president by "popular vote," and became the ironfisted ruler of South Korea for the next ten years.

Rhee Organizes the Liberal Party. After the bitter experience concerning the constitutional amendment, Rhee realized the necessity of having a political party under his control which could dominate the assembly. Thus, after the 1952 presidential election, Rhee urged political, social, labor, youth, and economic groups that had been supporting him in the past to form a political party. In November more than 190 representatives of pro-Rhee groups assembled in Pusan, the provisional capital during the war, and decided to establish a new political party, ironically called the "Liberal" party.[28] At that time no definite party platform or party principles were announced, but the party leaders accepted Rhee's *ilmin-jui*, which declared that the

Korean people belonged to one race and therefore "national politics and national culture are one" and "any individual action contrary to oneness must be eliminated." Later, when the party leaders announced the objectives and platform of the Liberal party, they professed the ideals of social justice, political morality based on democratic procedures, the establishment of a free-enterprise economic system, and anti-Communism. The party platform pledged better education, benefits for the laboring class and peasants, aid for rapid development of industry, and reorganization of the administration based on the principles of efficiency and simplicity.

The structure and functions of the Liberal party were roughly as shown in table 12.

TABLE 12. STRUCTURE OF THE LIBERAL PARTY

President: Syngman Rhee

Party Central Executive Staff (One general administrator and seven departments)	Central Legislative Committee (10-15 members)
Seoul branch	Party caucus in the assembly composed of the assemblymen
District branch	Provincial branch
Section branch	City branch and County branch
	District branch

The structure of the Liberal party and the party functions were based on one man, President Sygnman Rhee, who had the authority to veto party policies, personnel changes, and appointments. For example, the central legislative committee was entitled to formulate party policies and to elect the members of the central executive staff, but all these had to be approved by the party president before becoming effective. The central executive staff was to work under the supervision of the central legislative committee. Each branch was allowed to hold a unit conference, and the party annual conference was comprised of delegates from all units, that is, from sections, districts (including counties and provinces), and Seoul city.

The second man of the party, next to the president, was the chairman of the central legislative committee, Lee Ki-pung, who also had been the chairman of the assembly. Lee had been one of Rhee's henchmen for many years. He acted as a middleman between the Liberal party and the assembly because of his positions as chairman of the central legislative committee of the party and speaker of the assembly. But actually he carried the same message from Rhee to both the party and the assembly. The Liberal party was thus totalitarian in structure and functions; authority came from the top, and every member of the party had to obey party decisions without reservation. Party membership was estimated at about one million during its nine-year existence, from 1952 to 1961.

The Liberal Party and the 1954 Elections. Elections for the assembly were held in May 1954. There were two rightist parties, the Liberal and the Democratic. Many candidates ran as independents or nonpartisans. From Syngman Rhee's point of view, the 1954 election was important as being the first national election since he organized his own party. His second term was to expire in 1956 but he could not run again because of the constitutional limitation of two terms for any one person.

The main proposal in the Liberal party's campaign platform was the amendment of the constitution—the removal of the two-term limitation. In addition, the platform proposed that all important national problems be decided through referendum rather than in the assembly, that the government be given the right to dissolve the assembly, and that a free and competitive economic system be established. All Liberal party candidates for the assembly had to be approved by Rhee after recommendation by Lee Ki-pung; they were required to sign a written pledge promising to vote for the constitutional amendment, so that Rhee could run again for president in 1956. There were 270 Liberal party candidates to contest 203 seats in the assembly.

Then Rhee and his men worked out the campaign strategy. Rhee ordered his home minister, who controlled the police, to purge three opposition party leaders, Shin Ik-ki (leader of the Democratic party), Chough Pyong-ok (one-time goodwill ambassador and former home minister), and Cho Bong-am (vice-chairman of the assembly and former minister of agriculture). As a result, Shin Ik-ki could not even visit his home district (a little town 15 miles east of Seoul) because of police intimidation and threats from youth groups. Cho Bong-am was disqualified by the Central Election Committee because he could not get one hundred people to sign his registration petition (many of his original signers had been persuaded by police to withdraw their names). Chough Pyong-ok's campaign manager was in jail in Taegu on a charge of making illegal payments to petition signers.[29]

Two independent candidates for assemblymen were under arrest on charges of using abusive language in criticizing administration policies, and fifty Democratic and independent candidates withdrew their candidacy for reasons of personal safety, which meant police intimidation or threats from Rhee's youth groups. More than thirty-five newspapermen were under arrest because they printed the story of the death of an independent campaign worker in Pusan.

Most of the Liberal candidates obtained their campaign funds from high government officials as well as from the Bank of Korea. They were also well provided with campaign facilities, such as free transportation, public buildings for speeches and meetings, and police protection. The other party candidates were not even free to make campaign speeches, because of threats and intimidation from pro-Rhee groups, including the police.

In the election more than eight million voters cast their votes to elect 203 assemblymen. The Liberal party candidates won 109 seats, the Democrats 15, and independents 79 seats. Significantly the Liberal party failed to rally the much-needed two-thirds majority in the assembly, which would be a workable majority to put through domestic or ordinary bills. Rhee's campaign tactics of suppression had not completely succeeded. Two out of three of those candidates most objectionable to Rhee, Shin Ik-ki and Chough Pyong-ok, were elected by an overwhelming majority over Rhee's candidates. This was a manifestation of the people's repudiation of Rhee's dictatorial methods. One noteworthy point in this election was the increase in the strength of independents, who had avoided any party affiliations. Their votes were vital for Liberals and Democrats because neither had a two-thirds majority. Therefore, soon after the election the Liberals and Democrats made great efforts to win the support of independents.

The Liberals' Strategy for Amending the Constitution. The Liberal party leaders worked out three tactics to win over the independents to their side. One was to invite them to become members of the Liberal party by promising them positions, such as membership to important committees or the chairmanship of the assembly. When this method failed, they tried to intimidate the independents, charging them with election fraud. Several independent Democratic assemblymen were placed under police investigation for similar charges. The third tactic was the threat of a so-called third force (middle-of-the-road group). The story of the threat of a third force originated with a member of the Democratic party, but the Liberal party in power took political advantage of it.

Briefly, in the midst of the debate on the constitutional amendment in the assembly, Ham Dai-hun, director of the propaganda section of the Democratic party, issued a statement entitled "The Threat of a Third Force within the Democratic Party."[30] He said (a) that the third force is composed of the (members of the Korean National Youth Corp, North-South coalition leaders, and Communist sympathizers as well as some Democratic party members; (b) that the political theory of this group is based on coalition government and neutralism; and (c) that Shin Ik-ki, the chairman of the Democratic party, had held a secret meeting in New Delhi, with Cho So-ang, one of the leaders of the moderate group in North Korea, when Shin was on the way home from Queen Elizabeth's coronation ceremony. The statement also mentioned the secret meetings in Pusan between the representatives of the North Korean groups and Shin Ik-ki's followers to discuss how to organize a strong third-force party; because the third force had so deeply penetrated the Democratic party, Ham suggested it should be dissolved. When this was rejected, he withdrew from the Democratic party.

The debate on the amendment of the constitution was interrupted by Ham's story of the threat of the third force. The Liberal assemblymen brought the matter to the assembly for debate and investigation. After spending more than a week on charges and countercharges between Liberals and Democrats, the assembly called three witnesses to testify: Ham Dai-hun, Kim Dong-sung (who accompanied Shin Ik-ki as one of Rhee's representatives to the coronation ceremony of Queen Elizabeth), and Shin Ik-ki himself.[31] On the basis of their testimony the assembly found no evidence indicating the threat of a third force. Finally, the assembly agreed to submit the matter to the departments of justice and interior for further investigation. But the department never took any action. Ham was placed under police protection and nobody was allowed to see him.

The political consequences of the incident were important: Ham's public statement was a political bombshell for the Democratic party in general and Shin Ik-ki in particular, because Ham Dai-hun, a recognized party leader, left the party denouncing its close ties with the Northern coalition leaders controlled by the Communists; and the leadership of Shin as party chairman was weakened if not lost, and his popularity with independents in the assembly also decreased.

When the Liberal assemblymen first introduced the constitutional amendment, there was no hope for the Liberals of securing the necessary two-thirds majority in the assembly. Rhee warned in the press about the danger of the third force and denounced the neutralization-of-Korea movement as "a Northern Communist plot"; then he charged that the third-force members had been receiving financial aid from abroad and were aiming at the overthrow of the Republic of Korea. Thus Rhee supported indirectly Ham Dai-hun's view on the threat of the third force. In this point, the Liberals attacked the Democrats, labeling them leaders of the third-force movement. As a result, the antiamendment movement led by the Democrats was sidetracked, and some independent assemblymen were persuaded by the Liberals to support the amendment. Through these tactics the Liberal party was able to increase its membership in the assembly from 109 to 136, which was exactly a two-thirds majority.

The assembly resumed debate on the constitutional amendment. After much sharp debate between the Liberals and opposition Democrats and independents, the amendment bill came to a final vote on November 27, 1954. It was defeated by one vote. That evening many Seoul newspapers issued extra editions on the defeat of the amendment, and the government radio station also announced the fact that the amendment had been defeated by one vote.

However, the next day the director of public information issued a statement that the "constitutional amendment was carried by the assembly, because the needed two-thirds majority was 135 and not 136." The government spokesman further explained that "a two-thirds majority of 203 is 135-1/3, but the fraction could not be counted, and 135 was therefore the needed majority."[32] Vice-Chairman Choi Soon-ju apologized that "he had erred in saying that the amendment had failed," and submitted his resignation.

At once fighting broke out in the assembly hall between the proamendment and the antiamendment assemblymen, and more than sixty assemblymen left the assembly hall in protest against the vice-chairman's statement. The remaining Liberal party assemblymen and one independent carried a motion that 135 was the needed two-thirds majority for 203 seats, and the amendment bill was sent to Syngman Rhee for his signature. He signed the bill, saying, "It is the considered opinion of the government that the amendment carried."[33]

The "Threatening Document" Incident. The public was shocked that the constitutional amendment was passed. The press, the Korean Bar Association, and many university professors as well as civic leaders were critical of the administration's view that 135 (not 136) constituted a two-thirds majority. In the assembly the opposition Democrats and independents organized a Constitutional Defense Comrades Association and resolved to carry out the fight until the amendment was invalidated. They prepared to take the issue to the Supreme Court. Twelve dissatisfied members of the Liberal party announced their withdrawal from the party, and some of them joined the Constitutional Defense Comrades Association. Thus the administration was under attack from all directions after the spurious amendment of the constitution.

On December 18, 1954, a sensational event, the "threatening document" incident, took place. Two unidentified men delivered to the residences of six assemblymen a document wrapped in a copy of *Dong A Ilbo,* the Democratic party newspaper. The six assemblymen were the leaders of the Constitutional Defense Comrades Association, four of them Democrats and two independents. According to the six assemblymen, the document was sent by the Northern Communist regime. It proposed a conference between North and South political leaders to discuss unification, and demanded that Syngman Rhee and the United States government be excluded from this coalition conference. The six assemblymen turned the document over to the police for investigation. The assembly set up a six-man special investigation committee of its own to find out the true nature of the incident.

Soon the two men who had delivered the document were arrested by the police. They revealed that two military police officials had ordered them to deliver the document to the six assemblymen. Then the assembly committee called Lt. Col. Kim Chin-ho to the witness stand. It ascertained that the distribution of the document had been arranged by the provost marshal to test the political beliefs of antiamendment assemblymen, and that the military police believed it their duty to "exterminate such antigovernment elements."[34]

The committee called Provost Marshal Lt. Gen. Won Yong-duk as a witness. He admitted that he had ordered the distribution of the document to the six assemblymen, because "it was necessary to know their loyalty to the Republic of Korea." He further admitted that he had done this without consultation with the minister of defense. He believed, he said, that the provost marshal was a "special soldier" who could be excused from the existing army regulations forbiding interference in political affairs.[35]

The special committee made a report to the assembly stating that one of the immediate objectives of the military police was to suppress the newly formed Constitutional Defense Comrades Association, because it was, in their opinion, an antigovernment organization. The assembly then passed a resolution calling for the punishment of Won Yong-duk.

The administration had been silent up to this time, but as soon as the assembly's resolution was made public the administration's version of the incident was announced. The director of public information, Kal Hong-ki, stated that the document had been sent by the Northern Communist government to stir up the South Koreans on the issue of unification, and that the document had first been seized by the American Army intelligence office and later was turned over to the South Korean military police. The information director went on to say that in the document a few names of South Koreans were listed: therefore, it was the "administration's opinion that the document should be distributed to those individuals who were known to be middle-of the-roaders, because the government wanted to know their exact attitude on the issue of unification through coalition."[36] Then the director denounced the resolution of the assembly on the ground that opposition party assemblymen had turned the incident into a political attack against the administration.

Syngman Rhee supported the provost marshal. The matter, in his opinion, should be closed without further discussion in the assembly.[37] The anti-amendment assemblymen, especially the members of the Constitutional Defense Comrades Association, were frightened by Rhee's support of the provost marshal's action and did not further oppose the amendment of the constitution.

Suppression of the Press and Academic Freedom. The administration was determined to eliminate all opposing views of the constitutional amendment. *Dong A Ilbo,* one of the oldest and most influential newspapers in Korea, had been critical of administration policies in domestic and foreign affairs and strongly opposed the constitutional amendment. It carried the story of the threatening document as well as the committee report on the six assemblymen. The editorial comments on the incident were critical of the administration's attitude.

Three weeks after the incident, the *Dong A Ilbo* carried an article entitled "Puppet High-Ranking Circles Are Waiting," in which the paper attacked high government officials for not making their own decisions but waiting for instructions from President Rhee in every matter.[38] On March 17, 1955, the director of public information charged the *Dong A Ilbo* with violation of the national security law. In the government's view, the article insulted the head of the state by using the word "puppet" in reference to government officials under the president's supervision; such an article did not serve the best interests of the state. The *Dong A Ilbo* was suspended for a month.[39]

In April the Department of Education issued an order to stop publication of a constitutional law book, which was prepared by Professor Han Tai-yun, on the ground that his views on the two-thirds majority issue would hamper the creation of a unanimous opinion among the people. Professor Han had expressed the view that whenever the question of a two-thirds majority arose in the assembly the minimum necessary number for a constitutional amendment would be 136 as long as the assembly seats numbered 203, and therefore the new provision of the amendment itself would not seem valid. At first Han attempted to defend his views by invoking the protection of academic freedom, guaranteed in Article 13 of the constitution. Later he agreed to strike out the offending part of the book, which was then published.[40]

CHAPTER 11

RHEE SETS UP A POLICE STATE

THE 1958 ELECTIONS

Rhee Runs for a Third Term. Rhee secured himself a third term when the Liberal-dominated assembly changed the constitution through an arbitrary maneuver, as discussed in the preceding chapter. Rhee's political strategists started the presidential campaign as early as January 1956. Rhee announced in Seoul that he was undecided whether he would seek reelection. Rhee declined to announce his candidacy either directly or through his party; he wanted to create an atmosphere in which he could tell the Korean people that he would reluctantly accept the nomination for a third term, bowing to "the will of the people." Such a gesture would also make the American public think he was indispensable.

On March 4, 1956, four Liberal party leaders visited Rhee and told him that the party would nominate him for the presidency at the party convention. Rhee replied that he was determined not to seek another term, but added that "public opinion should be respected in the nomination of the presidential candidate."[1] Rhee said he would not run because a president should withdraw after two consecutive terms of service, because he was more than eighty years old, and because he felt responsible that the country was still divided.

Nobody, however, took Rhee's assertions seriously. If he believed that two consecutive terms was the democratic practice, he would not have forced the assembly to change the constitution in 1954, permitting the first president —but no others—to seek the presidency for any number of terms.

As soon as Rhee's announcement was made public, a government-directed "spontaneous movement of the people" in support of a third term for Rhee took place throughout South Korea. The Seoul police reported that within two weeks 4.7 million people had joined the movement and had held over one thousand mass meetings. Some organizations issued statements urging Rhee to stand for reelection.

Rhee still played coy. When people from rural areas came to Seoul and stayed day and night in front of Rhee's residence petitioning him to reconsider, Rhee issued the following statement: "I cannot permit people to suffer in cold weather. . . . I ask my fellow countrymen to . . . go home and write me a letter."[2] Then he ordered the immediate installation of special mail boxes at the railroad stations and at the corners of every main street in cities throughout South Korea.

Now the trade union announced its plan for a two-hour work stoppage of streetcars in Seoul and a possible general strike if Rhee continued to refuse a third term. Rhee appeared before the crowd and said: "I had no desire for personal honors or public office but I am always thinking of our nation. . . . Please give me time to think over your request."[3]

Before making a final announcement, Rhee was interviewed by William Randolph Hearst, Jr., publisher and editor-in-chief of the Hearst newspapers. Rhee said: "My people know my life is theirs. Anything they want I will do. If they want me to commit suicide I will. If they want me to be with them I will be with them. They know I'll do anything, but . . ." Hearst reported: "At this point President Rhee broke down. . . . His lips moved without words. Tears welled in his eyes."[4]

The dramatic final hour arrived on March 23. Rhee "yielded to the will of the people." He stated: "For the past 17 days since I announced my decision not to run for a third term, I have been besieged by representatives from all parts of the country urging me to reverse my decision. More than 22,000 letters and petitions signed by more than 3 million people and approximately 8,000 telegrams representing various organizations have overwhelmed me. . . . I realized that I could deal with such persistence only by giving up my own wishes and following the will of the people. Therefore, reconsidering my previous decision, I accept the nomination for another term as president of our Republic."[5]

Thus the nomination farce ended. The presidential campaign opened in the name of "clean and free elections." Rhee announced a three-point campaign program: no individual or organization should spend large sums of money to campaign for Rhee's reelection because he would consider any such action a reflection on him and an insult; any candidate for the presidency should spend in this and all subsequent elections a maximum of one million *hwan* (about two thousand dollars); and the voters should insist that the assembly create a House of Councillors, or upper house.

The Liberal party adopted as its campaign platform the themes of unification, victory against communism, development of democracy, and establishment of a self-sustaining economy. Then the party nominated Lee Ki-pung, chairman of the assembly, as Rhee's running mate. The members of the party pledged themselves to win more votes for Rhee than he had received four years previously, and predicted Rhee would get at least 6 million votes, and Lee Ki-pung 4.5 million votes out of a total 9 million. In the meantime, the government paper, *The Korean Republic,* said that Rhee would not conduct an active campaign for reelection since the outcome of the election was obvious. The Liberal party and the government alike advocated "a clean and free" election.

The party and the government then mobilized all sympathetic organizations and agents and prepared posters, leaflets, and movies on behalf of Rhee and his running mate; they were allowed to use government-controlled radio stations and other public facilities, such as school buildings and auditoriums. In addition, the leaders of the Liberal party worked out two new plans. One was that the presidential election was to be held more than two weeks earlier than the previous ones to "avoid the busy farm season." This plan would be doubly beneficial to the Liberal party, because more farmers would vote for the candidates of the Liberal party and also the opposition party candidates would not have time to campaign, as most South Korean newspapers commented. The other plan was the postponement for twenty more days the recess of the assembly. According to the election law, the assemblymen and the members of the local council were required to register with the Central Election Committee in the event of taking an active part in the campaign for their candidates. Therefore, during the twenty days recess period, all assemblymen were freed for engagement in the presidential campaign. The party in power naturally could take more advantage of this opportunity than the opposition.

As the election day approached, the methods of the Liberal party became more obvious. Rhee's lieutenants denounced the Democratic party's vice-presidential candidate, Chang Myun, as pro-Communist, because he had allegedly attempted to run for president against Rhee in 1952 with campaign funds provided by the North Communist party. The Democratic candidate for the presidency, Shin Ik-ki, was unable to make his campaign speeches because the government refused to give him permission to use public buildings or grounds for his rallies. Cho Bong-am, the Progressive party candidate for the presidency, had to hide to excape terrorism by pro-Rhee youth groups; the houses of him and his campaign manager were destroyed and their belongings stolen. As the United Press reported on May 15, 1956, the oppostion candidates "were placed virtually outside the realm of the protection of the law." Chang Myun, who ran against Rhee's running mate, had to go "into hiding on election eve because of fears for his safety."[6] As described later, Shin Ik-ki, who ran against Rhee, died in the midst of his campaign, and Rhee's reelection was secured even before the voting.

The Election Results. Before commenting on the election results, two factors in South Korea are worth mentioning. One is that all opposition candidates for president and vice-president had been important public officials since the republic was established. All of them were appointed by Rhee. Dr. Chang Myun served as the first ambassador to the United States and later as prime minister. Cho Bong-am was a former Communist, but because of his anti-Communist activities since 1945 Rhee appointed him minister of agriculture and forestry in his first cabinet; Cho was elected to the assembly twice and served as vice-chairman. Shin Ik-ki was vice-chairman when Rhee was elected chairman after the election of May 10, 1948, held under U.N. supervision; and Rhee appointed Shin as his personal envoy to the coronation of Queen Elizabeth. Therefore, most of Rhee's political foes had been his friends at one time or another. As long as they supported Rhee, they were safe. However, if anyone attempted to challenge Rhee's leadership and power, that person was marked for elimination from South Korean politics.

The other factor was that in the presidential election no substantially different issues were involved. All candidates claimed to be gallant anti-Communists and advocated unification, democracy, and a self-supporting economy. The only difference between the Liberals and Democrats was that the former favored a strong presidential form of government, and the latter a cabinet system responsible to the parliament. In foreign policy, all favored close alliance with the Western powers, especially with the United States.

The election results surprised everyone, including Rhee himself.[7] He received less than 55 percent of the total votes, or 5,046,437 out of 9,068,247; the hiding candidate Cho Bong-am obtained more than 2,000,000 votes (22.5 percent), and the dead Democratic candidate Shin received more than 1,800,000 votes (19 percent), in spite of the government warning "not to vote for a dead person." Perhaps the most significant fact was that more than 70 percent of the total population were farmers, and the rural areas were under the absolute control of the police; therefore Rhee won the election with the farm vote. Rhee lost in the urban areas; for example, in Seoul, Rhee polled only 205,235 votes against 284,359 for his dead opponent candidate Shin. Rhee also failed to carry Taegu, the third largest city in South Korea. In this sense Rhee appeared to be a president of the farmers; or, as the New York *Herald Tribune* put it, Rhee is "still a symbol to the farmers but his power has dwindled in the more politically aware urban areas."[8]

The defeat of Rhee's hand-picked running mate was the first decisive blow to Rhee's leadership since he had seized power in South Korea. After many disputes over the irregularities in counting votes in Taegu, the stronghold of of the Democratic party, Lee Ki-pung finally conceded defeat, and the opposition Democratic vice-presidential candidate, Chang Myun, won the vice-presidency for the first time in his party's history. Thus the 1956 presidential elections could be characterized as the people's repudiation of Rhee.

The Election for the Assembly. For the first time, the two major political parties campaigned for the national assembly with different platforms on the major issues.[9] Following the 1956 presidential election, the Liberals in power were concerned with the possibility of the vice-president's succession to the presidency in the event of the eighty-year-old Rhee's death or disability. Therefore the Liberal party adopted a proposal for a constitutional amendment in its party platform, stating that the president and vice-president should be elected from the same party, as in the United States. The Democrats wanted the present system continued because the vice-president, Chang Myun, had been a member of the Democratic party and elected on the Democratic ticket, but for their party platform they adopted the establishment of a cabinet-type executive in which the premier would be the head of the administration and the president would only be the formal head of state.

As for unification of the country, the Liberals once again advocated a "U.N.-supervised election for North Korea alone," arguing that South Korea had U.N.-supervised elections in 1948 and the Republic of Korea was recognized as the sovereign state of Korea. The Democrats came out for unification through nationwide (North and South) elections under U.N. supervision. This coincided with the U.N. resolution proposed by the United States. The Democrats also called for abolition of the Home Ministry as a first step to neutralize the police in politics. The Liberals wanted the present police system under the Home Ministry continued. The Democrats called for tax reforms to increase national revenues and a reduction of the armed forces; the Liberals advocated an increase of armed forces, atomic weapons, and no tax reform.

The most controversial issues during the campaign were the proposed constitutional changes and the way to unify the North and South. The Democrats denounced the Liberals' proposal for constitutional changes as a scheme to maintain political power in their hands and to eliminate the possibility of Chang Myun succeeding to the presidency. The Liberals condemned the Democrats' unification plan as denying the sovereign authority of the Republic of Korea over all Korea.

The elections were held with many irregularities and with coercion by the Liberal party. The most notorious election episode was the so-called uncontested victory of Lee Ki-pung, who was an unsuccessful candidate for vice-president in 1956 and then chairman of the assembly. Lee was considered by the Liberals a successor of Rhee's and the second man in the Republic of Korea.

The executive committee of the Liberal party worked out a strategy to assure the reelection of Lee to the assembly. As early as August 1957 the members of the executive committee had attempted to make a deal with Democratic leaders by proposing "a free constituency" for the head of each party. According to this plan, each party would not run a candidate in the district where the opposition party leader was expected to run. The Democratic party leaders were not interested in the plan, but the Liberals had decided not to put up candidates in three districts where the Democratic leaders would run, hoping the Democrats would do the same thing. In March 1958 the Democratic party put up its candidate in the Sudaemun-ku district in Seoul where Lee Ki-pung had filed his candidacy. Thus the idea of a free constituency was rejected by the Democrats.

The Liberals unsuccessfully attempted to force Lee's opponent out of the race, denouncing him as "not qualified." Thirty minutes before the registration deadline, Lee withdrew his name from the Sudaemun-ku district and filed his candidacy in another district, Lichun, which is situated in the southern part of Kyonggi province and has a population of ninety thousand. In the Lichun district, two candidates had already registered with the Central Election Committee. But soon the local Liberal party candidate canceled his candidacy in favor of Lee Ki-pung, and the opposition Democratic candidate was forced by the local police to withdraw his name. Lee had finally secured a "free consituency."[10]

The results of the election were: 126 Liberals elected out of 236 candidates, 43 percent of the vote; 79 Democrats out of 199 candidates, or 32 percent of the vote; 27 independents and one candidate from the Unification party.[11] As in the 1956 presidential election, the party in power made its best showing in the rural areas, where the police had great influence on the election; in urban areas the Democrats were strong, especially in the capital where only one Liberal was elected, the remaining 16 seats going to Democrats.

Although the Liberals won the election with a majority, it was far from the two-thirds majority needed to pass a constitutional amendment. Even if the Liberals had been able to swing all independents to their side, they would still not have secured the two-thirds majority. Hence the Liberals had to give up hope for a constitutional change through legal means.

Another important factor was that the voters had shown their dissatisfaction with the record of the so-called independent assemblymen; their previous seventy-nine seats were reduced to twenty-seven; the voters clearly did not trust the independents, who shifted from one party to another when it served their interests. Perhaps the most significant point in this election was that the people, especially the urban population, had expressed their discontent with the party in power even under pressure from the administration. Many observers believed that this trend would encourage the development of a two-party system in South Korea.

SOUTH KOREA BECOMES A POLICE STATE

Thought Control and Censorship. Although the constitution guaranteed freedom of the press and academic freedom, the government frequently censored newspaper articles, jailed reporters, editors, and publishers, and closed newspapers for political reasons. In 1957, the Ministry of Education issued a "list of books considered subversive" and banned their publication and import. For years the International Press Institute (IPI) refused South Korea membership on the ground that it had no free press.

The Liberal-controlled assembly passed the press provisions of the election law in 1957, despite the protest and opposition of the Korean Newspaper Editors' Association and the Democratic party. Under this law, the owners and editors of newspapers, magazines, and other publications were forbidden to print election news when it was evident that the owners or editors expected to receive gratuities from political candidates. The newspapers were restricted from reporting "false facts in order to have certain candidates elected or not elected."[12] Any violator of this regulation would "be punished with penal servitude or confinement not exceeding three years or fined not more than 300,000 Hwan."[13]

Soon after the 1958 assembly elections, two reporters and one magazine writer were arrested by the Seoul police for their articles. A *Korean Times* columnist, Chang Su-yong, was arrested because an article by him contained the following sentences:

> The revolt in Lebanon and the coup d'etat in Iran were the manifestations of the people's will, and the Democratic landslide in the Seoul elections last May was the expression of the people who were dissatisfied with the status quo.[14]

Hahm Suk-heun was arrested for writing in the monthly magazine *Sasanggye* that "Koreans are a people without a country, because the North Communist regime calls the South Korean government an American puppet, while South Korea calls the North Korean regime a Russian puppet."[15] Choi Won-kak, a *Dong A Ilbo* military affairs reporter, was jailed for his exposure of the "reduction plan" of the Southern armed forces.[16]

Freedom of thought was likewise curtailed. Under the order against "subversive" book and motion-picture censorship, Seoul police seized hundreds of volumes of so-called subversive literature, arrested five book dealers, and closed five bookstores in Seoul alone. Yun Keun-il, a twenty-year-old sophomore in political science at Seoul National University, was arrested by the police for writing on social democracy in the university bulletin and for casual private conversations with friends on the peaceful unification of Korea.[17]

All three newsmen's writings and views were based on facts, and were neither false nor subversive. But the government could not tolerate views opposing Rhee's administration. The arrest of the young student was outrageous; the police not only encroached on academic freedom but frightened the campus intellectuals. This incident made it clear that every college campus was being watched, either by secret police or by informers; nothing was exempt, not even class lectures or private conversations between friends and between professors and students.

Political Persecution. To understand the meaning of the 1958 political persecutions, it is necessary to review briefly some of the preceding political murder cases. The first political victim was Song Chin-woo, one of the founders of the Democratic party. Song, a nationally known patriot, was one of the rightist leaders in Korea in 1945. He was assassinated by a young terrorist on December 21, 1945, but the political situation was so confused at that time that even today no clear evidence is available as to which faction was responsible for the assassination. The second political victim was Lyuh Woon-hyung, a moderate leftist and at one time the head of the leftist People's Republic, established before United States forces landed in Korea. He supported the Moscow Agreement and the U.S.-U.S.S.R. Joint Commission, and became one of the leaders of the coalition committee, working for the establishment of a coalition government between rightists and leftists to bring about the unification of the country. Lyuh was shot dead by a rightist terrorist on July 19, 1947, while the joint commission in Seoul was still negotiating for unification. Next, the rightist Chang Duk-soo, educated in England and the United States and one of the leading figures in the Democratic party, was killed by a uniformed South Korean police official in

December 1947. He was considered the leader of the cooperative faction within the rightists and supported the joint commission for unification. At that time the Rhee and Kim Koo faction opposed the joint commission.

The next political victim was Kim Koo, an extreme rightist; he was the head of the Korean provisional government until 1945 and the founder of the Korean Independent party. Kim was the only remaining rightist rival of Syngman Rhee in 1949. He was killed by a South Korean army lieutenant. None of the political murderers was punished in any real sense: some of them were freed after a few months in jail; some escaped to Japan; the lieutenant became a lieutenant colonel a few years later.

When Rhee came to power in South Korea, he did not tolerate political rivals even within his own administration. As mentioned before, three out of the four vice-presidents resigned before their four-year terms ended; only one vice-president, eighty-five-year-old Ham Dai-young, served his full term. The last vice-president, Chang Myun, a Democratic party leader, was forced into confinement at his home after a police-inspired assassination attempt on September 2, 1958, less than three weeks after he took office. (Chang resigned during the April Student Revolution in protest against Rhee's strong-arm tactics in suppressing the student demonstrators.) Nor did Rhee tolerate any individuals, groups, or political parties which disagreed with him on how to unify the country. As pointed out, Rhee wanted unification by force on the ground that the "Communists respect only force." But many Korean leaders believed that peaceful unification was the only alternative to war, and supported the U.N. resolution—nationwide free elections under U.N. supervision.

After the 1956 presidential election, the administration resumed more vigorously its attack against individuals and parties who had advocated peaceful unification at one time or another. A government spokesman said that such strong measures were necessary because the North Communist regime had taken a so-called peace offensive which aimed at the destruction of the Republic of Korea.

But many observers disagreed with the government's views. Rhee's power was weakened as a result of the two elections (the presidential and the legislative) and he was anxious to eliminate all opposition forces before they became too strong. The Progressive party's strong stand for peaceful unification provided Rhee the opportunity. In 1958 the Seoul police arrested most of the Progressive party leaders and charged them with violation of the old national security law. The charges by the government were (a) that the peaceful unification plan of the Progressive party was identical with the North Korean plan and would jeopardize the existence of the Republic of Korea; (b) that an article by Cho Bong-am (head of the party) which appeared in the October issue of *Chungang Jungchi* (Central Politics) was subversive because it advocated all-Korean elections as a means for unification; (c) that Cho Bong-am illegally possessed weapons and secret documents, including a copy of a letter written to Kim Il-sung, North Korean Communist premier; and (d) that Cho received forty million *hwan* from North Korea for his presidential campaign funds.[18]

Even before the formal court trial, the office of public information withdrew the publication license of *Chungang Jungchi,* and soon it canceled the registration of the Progressive party as a legal party. Thus the party and its publication were outlawed. At the trial all leaders of the Progressive party declared the charges nonsense. Kim Tal-ho, the sole Progressive party assemblyman, challenged the legality of the prosecutor's assertion that the mere advocacy of peaceful unification was a reason for arrest. Kim argued that it was not "peaceful unification" but "unification through a march toward the North" which was contradictory to the standing policy of the government. He pointed out that the existence of a pact between the Republic of Korea and the United States which prevented South Korea from undertaking unilateral military action against North Korea was the most eloquent proof of the righteousness of those who advocated peaceful unification.

The prosecutor demanded the death sentence for Cho Bong-am and Yang Myong-san, and prison sentences ranging from life to ten months for the other members. The court sentenced Cho and Yang to five years in prison and four others to a few months. The others were acquitted. The prosecutor immediately appealed to the Seoul Appellate Court. In the meantime, about two hundred members of the anti-Communist Youth Association held a mass demonstration, protesting the milder sentences. In December 1958 the Seoul Appellate Court handed down severe sentences to all arrested members of the Progressive party, charging them with "espionage activities and violation of the national security law." Cho and Yang were given death sentences for treason, and eighteen members received prison sentences from one to twelve years. The Supreme Court upheld this judgment, and Cho and Yang were executed in 1959.

The persecution of the Progressive party leaders, primarily because they advocated unification in terms that coincided with those of North Korea, could perhaps be understood better in relation to the motives of the party in power rather than court rulings. The sentiment for peaceful unification as the only alternative to war was strong among the Korean people, especially among the intellectuals and the opposition political leaders, including the Democrats. As mentioned before, it was about this time that the North Korean Communists drew up a peaceful unification program for political propaganda. As a result, Rhee and his Liberal party took the position that they were surrounded by two political enemies, political rivals within and hostile Communists without. At this point, dictator Rhee devised two political strategies: trying for treason the leaders of the Progressive party and drafting a new national security law.

The National Security Law. The controversial new national security bill was drafted by the minister of justice in June, approved by the State Council in August, and submitted to the Judicial Committee in November 1958. It was passed by the party in power, the Liberal party, after three hundred policemen and thirty regular guards had driven eighty opposition assemblymen (Democrats and independents) from the assembly chamber on Christmas Eve 1958.[19] It became law on January 15, 1959, twenty days after the president's signature.

The reason for a new bill, a government spokesman said, was the inadequacy of the existing security law to cope with Communist conspiracy and Communist infiltration from North Korea, for it allowed many legal loopholes for the Communists and their sympathizers. Syngman Rhee supported the new bill, saying that "its only purpose is defense against Communist conspiracy and treachery. It does not abridge or curtail any of our freedoms."[20]

Nevertheless, the opposition Democrats, independent assemblymen, and many social organizations, including the Korean Bar Association and the

Korean Newspaper Editors' Association, opposed the bill: the Democrats' strong opposition was primarily political, based on the fear that the Liberal party wished to perpetuate its political power under the pretext of upholding national security, instead of concentrating on the job of meeting any real danger of Communist subversion; the Newspaper Editors' Association opposed the bill on the ground that articles twelve, seventeen, and twenty-two would restrict the freedom of the press; and the Bar Association condemned a part of the bill (chapter eleven) as an encroachment on civil rights and therefore unconstitutional.

The security law consisted of three chapters, subdivided into forty articles. The first chapter (articles one to five) made clear the purpose and scope of the law, including the meaning of *national secret* and *enemy*. The following articles are significant:

ARTICLE 1

The purpose of the present law is to safeguard national security and interests by supplementing and amending the provisions concerning penalties and criminal procedure applicable to (1) associations, groups, and organizations which aim to subvert the state in defiance of the constitution; and (2) activities for the attainment of such aims.

ARTICLE 4

"National secrets" as used in the present law shall mean any document, drawing, other material, fact, or information required to be kept secret from foreign governments and the enemy in the interest of national defense. Such secrets can cover political, economic, social, cultural, or military affairs.

ARTICLE 5

"Enemy" as used in the present law shall mean any association, group, or organization defined in articles 6 to 8 which takes, or attempts to take, military action.

Chapter two (articles 6 to 31) defined what constitutes criminal action and set penalties. Some of the important articles are:

ARTICLE 6

Any person who organizes an association or group with the intent of presenting it as a government or of subverting the state in defiance of the Constitution shall be punished as follows: (a) the death penalty or life imprisonment for ringleaders and staff members; (b) not more than ten years of penal servitude for ordinary members.

ARTICLE 7

Any person who forms an organization operated for, or under the directive of, an association or group mentioned in the preceding article shall be punished as follows: (a) the death penalty or life imprisonment for ringleaders and staff members; (b) life or not less than three years of penal servitude for those in leading positions; (c) not more than seven years of penal servitude for ordinary members.

ARTICLE 12

1. Except for the cases mentioned in the preceding articles, any person who collects information on political, economic, social, cultural, and military affairs of the state with intent to benefit the enemy shall be punished by penal servitude not exceeding ten years.

2. Any person who collects information on government or public officers, political parties, social associations, or any individual person with intent to benefit the enemy shall be punished in the same manner as provided in the foregoing paragraph.

ARTICLE 22

1. Penal servitude not exceeding ten years shall be visited upon any person who publicly defames constitutional organs through meetings or by dissemination of documents, sound recordings, drawings, pictures, or any other medium of expression in behalf of, or under the directive of, an association, group, or organization defined in articles 6 to 8.

2. The constitutional organs referred to in the preceding paragraph are the president, chairman of the national assembly, and chief justice.

Chapter three (articles 12 to 40) stipulated rules of special procedure for criminal suits against offenders of the security law. Some of the articles are:

ARTICLE 26

A judge of a district court, on request of the judicial police, may approve only once the extension period under Article 202 of the Criminal Procedure Code, when he considers that there exist reasonable grounds for the continuation of the investigation with respect to the crime defined in Article 19 of the present law.

ARTICLE 40

Officers, warrant officers, and noncommissioned officers of the military intelligence agencies may investigate crimes falling under the provisions of articles 10 and 11 and paragraph 1 of Article 18 of the present law, in accordance with the provisions of the law and the Criminal Procedure Code.

To sum up: (1) The purpose of the national security law was protection of the security and interests of the Republic of Korea from the subversion and infiltration of the North Korean Communist regime (Article 1); (2) The definition of *national secret* and the meaning of *enemy* were very broad; the former included "any document, drawing, other material, fact, or information" which should be kept secret in the interests of national security; the latter included any subversive association, group, or organization defined in articles 6 to 8; (3) It was a criminal action to collect information on "government or public officers, political parties, social associations, or any individual person with intent to benefit the enemy" or for a subversive organization, group, or association. This crime was an *Absichtsdelikt*—a crime in which the offender is conscious of the purpose. The allegation or dissemination of false or distorted facts intentionally to "disturb the public mind" and to "benefit the enemy" also constituted a crime (articles 12 and 17); (4) Defamation of constitutional organs constituted a crime (Article 22); (5) As Article 26 stipulated, the police was virtually given the right to extend the detention period of crimes defined in Article 19; (6) Article 27 recognized the probative value of the investigation record prepared by the police officer. (It had been a general principle of criminal procedure that the protocol by the police officer in which the statement of the suspect was recorded could be adopted as evidence only if the suspect or his attorney admitted the contents in court); (7) Article 40 authorized the military intelligence agencies, under the prosecutor, to investigate civilians who had committed crimes falling under the provisions of articles 10 and 11 and paragraph 1 of Article 18.

The security law was so loosely drawn and sweeping, covering almost all phases of the citizen's daily activity, that it could easily be abused. In fact, the Liberal party used it as a means of suppressing opposition in national elections and whatever opposition was offered by the Democrats and independents in the assembly.

Along with the security bill another significant bill was passed by Liberal assemblymen without the participation of the minority assemblymen—the bill to abolish the age-old local autonomy system. Henceforth chiefs of the lowest administrative unit were appointed by the heads of the *myun* (township), who, in turn, were appointed by the provincial governor on recommendation of the county chiefs. County chiefs and mayors were appointed by the president on recommendation of the provincial governor through the minister of home affairs, who controlled the police and was responsible to the president. The provincial governors and the mayor of Seoul were appointed by the president.

Through this appointment system most local offices were filled by the members of the Liberal party and its sympathizers. The system increased the practice of political favoritism in state affairs. The instituting of a centralized political power structure in place of a local-autonomy system was a manifestation of the authoritarian character of the Liberal party. Soon Rhee announced that he would seek a fourth term because he had "not completed the task of unifying Korea." This meant, first, that Rhee and the Liberal party were preparing for an indefinite one-party dictatorship, and, second, that any efforts at peaceful unification would be fruitless, for Rhee believed that "Communists respect only force." This was the meaning of the new national security law in South Korea, unconstitutionally foisted on the people.

CHAPTER 12

THE KOREAN WAR

Causes of the War. The causes of the Korean war must ultimately be sought in the history of the Korean people, a people who lived in a Confucian feudal society in which the gentry exploited the lower classes. The Japanese, during their thirty-five year domination, kept the Korean feudalistic social setting intact and used it for their own interests. Landlords were well protected and enjoyed privileges, but the majority of the people were forced to work either as serfs of landlords or as slave laborers in Japanese industries.

Even after liberation from the Japanese in 1945, when Korea was divided into two zones and occupied by the United States and the Soviet Union, most people were still compelled to live under either the old feudalistic system in the South or the regimented totalitarian regime in the North.

The Korean people have been fighting against native feudalism and foreign domination for centuries. The first large-scale insurrection against the corrupt ruling class occurred in 1811 and is known as the Hong Kyong-nai revolt. The rebellious "people's army" was composed of discontented small aristocrats and peasants. At one time they occupied the northern section of the peninsula and threatened the capital, but they were eventually crushed by the central government. The second revolt was against the decadent Yi dynasty and took place in 1894. The rebel forces were composed of peasants and led by the Tonghak, a semi-religious group opposed to foreign intervention. They seized a large part of the southern peninsula and marched toward the capital. The central government asked the Chinese government for help, and Chinese troops were immediately sent. The Japanese government also announced that it was sending troops to Korea, although they were not requested by the Korean government. This situation precipitated the Sino-Japanese war of 1894–95, from which Japan emerged as the new master of Korean affairs. In the meantime, the Korean government arrested and executed the Tonghak leaders, and the revolt collapsed.

The March First Independence Movement in 1919 was the first national liberation movement against Japanese colonial rule. It was led by middle-class intellectuals and religious leaders, but almost all social groups, including students, peasants, and industrial workers, participated in the struggle. Koreans in the United States, China, the Soviet Russia, and elsewhere supported the movement, and in 1919 the Korean provisional government was formed in Shanghai. The independence movement, however, was suppressed by Japanese bayonets.

The second largest uprising against Japanese rule was the student strike of 1929, triggered by an incident between a Japanese high-school boy and a Korean school girl. Many social and religious groups sympathized with the striking students and rendered legal and financial support. The uprising was put down ruthlessly by the Japanese police.

Anti-Japanese resistance was carried on by underground leaders inside and outside the peninsula during the Second World War. The Korean people expected immediate independence when Japan surrendered to the Allied Powers, and were disappointed with the division of the country and occupation by the two powers. Many Korean leaders, including rightists, moderates, and leftists, made every effort to unify the country by peaceful means; before the establishment of the two governments in the South and North, political leaders held a conference in Pyongyang, but it failed because of the opposition of the power blocs, the United States and the Soviet Union.

The immediate cause of the war was the belief of the North Korean regime that the time was right to extend its rule into the South. This belief was based on a statement by Senator Tom Connally, chairman of the Senate Foreign Relations Committee. He said in May 1950 that Korea was not a "part of the American Defense perimeter in the Far East."[1] The North Korean regime interpreted this to be a nonintervention policy on the part of the United States in case of a Northern invasion.

The Eve of the War. May 1950 was election time for the assembly of the Republic of Korea. All political parties, except the outlawed underground Communist party, known as the Labor Party of South Korea, participated in the election. The two largest parties in the previous assembly, Rhee's pro-government party and Kim Sung-soo's opposition party, suffered heavy losses: the former dropped from 56 seats to 12, the latter from 78 to 28. The most significant gains were made by those moderates who had boycotted the 1948 elections supervised by the U.N. They won 130 seats out of a total 210. The new assembly convened on June 19, less than a week before the outbreak of the war.

At this time, the North Korean regime outlined a peaceful unification program to the South Korean assembly. The plan was based, first, on the merger of the Supreme People's Assembly of North Korea and the national assembly of South Korea into a "a single all-Korean legislative body" purged of all politicians opposed to peaceful unification, including Syngman Rhee and Kim Sung-soo; and, second, on the immediate expulsion of the U.N. commission on Korea from South Korea. The North Korean regime sent a three-man peace delegation team to the South Korean assembly, but they were arrested by South Korean police and never heard from again.

On June 19 Rhee told the assembly, which was dominated by assemblymen favoring unification, that "we refuse to compromise with or make any concessions to the Communists. That would be the road toward disaster."

The United States Far Eastern policy appeared to be changing at about that time. John Foster Dulles, then adviser to the secretary of state, went to Seoul at the invitation of President Rhee, and told the South Korean assembly on June 19: "Today . . . in the front line of freedom, under conditions that are both dangerous and exciting . . . you are not alone . . . so long as you continue to play worthily your part in the great design of human freedom."[2] Dulles stayed three days in Seoul and made a one-day inspection tour along the 38th parallel. On his way home he spent several days in Tokyo visiting General MacArthur, supreme commander of the Allied Powers. At that time a military conference was held by MacArthur in Tokyo, with Gen. Omar Bradley, head of the U.S. Joint Chiefs of Staff, and Secretary of Defense Louis Johnson attending. Very little was made public about what they discussed, but some observers believe that the conference produced the reversal of the earlier American strategic position, according to which "Korea was not part of the essential American defense perimeter in the Far East."

It would seem that South Korean authorities knew that a North Korean attack was planned for June. As early as January and February of 1950 the chief of the South Korean Army had informed the U.N. commission that the heavy buildup on the 38th parallel was a sign of impending invasion. On May 10 the South Korean Defense Minister Shin Sung-mo stated at a press conference that North Korean troops were "moving in force toward the 38th parallel and that there was imminent danger of invasion from the North."[3] In the same month President Rhee warned that "May and June may be the crucial period in the life of our nation."[4] The leading American military commentator, Hanson Baldwin of the *New York Times,* reported "a marked building of the North Korean People's Army along the 38th parallel beginning in the early days of June."[5] But the imminent danger of a North Korean attack was not confirmed by the chief of the U.S. Military Advisory group in South Korea, Brig. Gen. William L. Robert, or MacArthur's intelligence chief, Maj. Gen. Charles A. Willoughby, or the U.N. commission on Korea, which made an inspection tour along the 38th parallel on June 24 just a few hours before the outbreak of war. On the contrary, the U.N. commission reported that "there was no sign of the imminent invasion."[6]

In any event, it is clear that at this time the North Korean regime was well prepared to unify the country either by peaceful means or by force. Thus it was striving for a commanding position to dictate unification in any way it chose to the South Korean government, which was faced by political and economic crises, and would be in no position to reject any North Korean challenge.

The Northern Offensive. North Korean ground forces supported by Russian-made tanks and artillery crossed the 38th parallel early in the morning of June 25 and advanced rapidly without much resistance from South Korean forces, which had often been described by American military advisers as "the best army in Asia." South Korea's capital, Seoul, was in the hands of the North Korean army within four days. President Rhee and top government officials fled Seoul long before the Northern army's entry. Rhee left behind a recording of his voice which was played even after Seoul had fallen: he appealed to the people to fight against the Northern army until the last man, and he assured them that Seoul would be defended by the loyal armed forces of the Republic of Korea; he also asked the people not to leave the capital.

In the confusion a South Korean officer ordered the destruction of the Han bridge before the retreat of the South Korean army had been completed: as a result, many soldiers and much military equipment plunged into the Han River.

According to the story of an eyewitness who stayed in Seoul during the occupation by the Northern army, the behavior of the occupation army was courteous on the surface, but the treatment of American and Rhee sympathizers was shocking: they were tried at so-called public people's courts, and when the judge pronounced them guilty they were shot to death in public. The Northern regime organized spy networks at all levels, which even reached into individual families. The population in general lived in fear and suspicion.

During the period of the Northern occupation, some prominent political and military leaders, including Dr. Kim Kiusic, Ahn Chai-hong, Kim Hyo-suk (minister of interior in the Rhee administration), and General Song Ho (former chief of staff of the South Korean constabulary during the U.S. military government), had cooperated with the Northern regime. All of these leaders were taken to North Korea before the U.N. forces recaptured Seoul.

After the fall of Seoul, the South Korean and American military forces set up a defensive line in the Taejon area. But American ground forces under the command of Maj. Gen. William F. Dean, former military governor of South Korea, were completely defeated at Suwon by the North Korean forces. Even the personal heroism of the American commanding general failed to save the situation. General Dean was reported as missing in action and later listed as a prisoner of war.[7]

The next line of defense was Kumchun, but this line also broke without much fighting, and the city surrendered. Within six weeks the Northern army occupied all of the Southern peninsula except for a beachhead extending for two hundred miles along the natural defense line formed by the Nakdong River, Taegu, Pohang, Masan, Chinhae, and Pusan. South Korean and U.N. troops were able to hold this line until the U.S. Marines landed in Inchun on September 15. After the arrival of the Marines, the tide of the battle began to turn, and the offensive of the North Korean army collapsed. They retreated in great confusion.

The failure of the North Korean offensive to be completely successful can be explained in various ways. As the area of occupation was extended, the North Koreans faced great difficulties equipping the front-line soldiers with adequate military supplies. The transporting of supplies required a great deal of manpower and could only be done at night because of air attacks by U.N. forces. Crossing the three big rivers—Han, Kum, and Nakdong—was difficult and time consuming for the North Korean troops, since they had to cross at night in small boats. They suffered heavy casualties each crossing. From the beginning, the North Korean forces had not the sea and air power to match the U.N. forces; their offensive depended on ground forces.

On the other hand, the Northern army had a few advantages over the South Korean forces. They were well equipped with Russian-made tanks, artillery, and rifles. Most of the commanding officers had experience in guerrilla warfare in Manchuria against the Japanese after 1931: many of them had fought with the Red Chinese army, and some of them had fought with the Russian army during the Second World War. The North Korean soldiers were well trained in military tactics and political ideology; they considered themselves professional soldiers of a revolutionary army. Korea is a hilly and mountainous country, and modern mechanized warfare is difficult. Guerrilla-type military tactics worked well.

The United Nations' Intervention. On June 24, 1950, the American ambassador in Seoul, John J. Muccio, sent the following cablegram to the State Department: "According to Korean Army reports which are partly confirmed by the Korean Military Advisory Group field adviser, North Korean forces invaded the Republic of Korea territory at several points this morning. . . . It would appear from the nature of the attack and manner in which it was launched that it constitutes an all-out offensive against the Republic of Korea."[8]

The message reached Washington about 9:30 P.M., and at 3 o'clock in the morning of the next day, the 25th, the deputy United States representative to the United Nations, Ernest A. Gross, informed Trygve Lie, secretary-general, about the Korean situation. Gross also requested a meeting of the

Security Council, since the attack "constitutes a breach of the peace and an act of aggression."[9]

The United Nations Security Council met at 3 P.M. on the 25th without the representative of the Soviet Union, who had been absent from council meetings since January in protest against the presence of the Chinese Nationalist representative. The council declared the action of the North Korean forces "a breach of the peace" and called for immediate cessation of hostilities"; it requested the North Korean authorities "to withdraw forthwith their armed forces to the thirty-eighth parallel," asked the United Nations Commission on Korea to submit recommendations, and called on all members of the United Nations for assistance.[10]

Military Aid to the Republic of Korea. President Truman, who was spending the weekend in his home town in Missouri, flew back to Washington on Sunday afternoon, June 25th. In the evening, the president met in Blair House with his principal advisers, including the secretaries of state and defense and the Joint Chiefs of Staff. In that meeting it was decided to move the Seventh Fleet from the Philippines to the Formosa Straits, use naval and air forces to assist and protect the evacuation of American civilians from South Korea, and furnish arms to the Republic of Korea.[11]

A second Blair House meeting was held on the evening of June 26. At noon of June 27 the White House released the historic statement that the United States president had "ordered United States air and sea forces to give the Korean Government troops cover and support."[12] The United States was also to increase military aid to the Philippines and French Indochina, and to use the Seventh Fleet to neutralize Formosa. General MacArthur, Far Eastern commander-in-chief, was authorized to employ U.S. naval and air forces against North Korean forces north of the 38th parallel.

The president justified his actions on the ground that the United Nations Security Council had called upon all members to render every assistance. He pointed out that "the attack upon Korea makes it plain beyond all doubt that Communism has passed beyond the use of subversion to conquer independent nations and will now use armed invasion and war."[13] He went on to say that "in these circumstances the occupation of Formosa by Communist forces would be a direct threat to the security of the Pacific area and to

United States forces performing their lawful and necessary functions in that area." Therefore he had ordered the Seventh Fleet to "prevent any attack on Formosa," declaring that the determination of the island's future status "must await the restoration of security in the Pacific, a peace settlement with Japan, or consideration by the United Nations."[14]

Secretary of State Acheson explained U.S. military action in Korea before the Senate Armed Services and Foreign Relations Committees by saying that "the attack on Korea was . . . a challenge to the whole system of collective security, not only in the Far East, but everywhere in the world. . . . If we stood with our arms folded while Korea was swallowed up, it would have meant abandoning our principles, and it would have meant the defeat of the collective system on which our own safety ultimately depends."[15]

It would seem that the United States military decision on Korea was based on two considerations. First, the North Korean attack was judged to be a part of overall Communist strategy, approved by Peking and Moscow in advance. Second, the attack was a direct challenge to the United Nations system of collective security.

At 10:45 P.M. on June 27, eleven hours after President Truman had ordered American military aid to the Republic of Korea, the United Nations Security Council adopted the United States draft resolution. The Security Council recommended that "the Members of the United Nations furnish such assistance to the Republic of Korea as may be necessary to repel the armed attack and to restore international peace and security in the area."[16]

Views on the actions taken by the United States and the United Nations differ. Professor Hans Kelsen in *The Law of the United Nations* states:

"Under Article 39 the Security Council may make recommendations or take enforcement measures in accordance with Articles 41 and 42. But in its resolution of June 25, the Security Council did neither make a recommendation nor did it take an enforcement measure." The United States military action on June 25, Kelsen said, "was justified as an assistance to the United Nations in the execution of the Security Council's resolution of June 25, 1950. Only after this order was issued by the United States President the Security Council adopted a resolution by which an armed intervention by a member of the United Nations against North Korea could indeed be justified."[17]

I. F. Stone wrote in *The Hidden History of the Korean War* that when President Truman "ordered United States air and sea forces to give the Korean Government troops cover and support he was in effect imposing military sanctions before they had been authorized by the Security Council." Thus the United States military action on June 25 became a *fait accompli* before the United Nations Security Council.[18]

Professor Leland M. Goodrich, in *Korea: A Study of U.S. Policy in the United Nations,* commented that the United States military action "was completely in accord with the spirit of the Charter and the intention of its authors that in case of a flagrant breach of the peace, collective measures should promptly be taken to restore peace before any attempt at peaceful settlement of the dispute"[19]

The Soviet Union took the position that the war was started by an attack of South Korean troops. It asserted that the United States military action interfered with the internal affairs of the Korean people and that therefore the United States armed forces should have been immediately withdrawn from Korea. The resolution of the Security Council was said to be illegal because a representative of Nationalist China had participated in its adoption.[20]

Some observers believed that the action taken by the United States and the United Nations Security Council to be hasty compared to action taken in similar incidents, like the Dutch assault on the Indonesian Republic and the Arab attacks upon Israel. The Security Council had not made a genuine effort to ascertain all the facts and exhaust all means of peaceful settlement: for example, the Security Council could have sent a fact-finding committee, or invited the parties to present their cases, as Article 32 of the U.N. Charter stipulates.[21] Most members of the Security Council accepted the Korean war as a *fait accompli* and U.S. intervention became a "matter of emergency."

The United Nations' Counteroffensive. In accordance with the Security Council's resolution[22] of July 7, President Truman appointed General MacArthur Supreme Commander of United Nations Forces. On July 15, President Syngman Rhee authorized MacArthur to command the land, sea, and air forces of the Republic of Korea.

In addition to the Republic of Korea, 16 nations contributed troops to the U.N. forces in Korea. About two-thirds was contributed by the United

States. By services, the United States contributed 50 percent of the ground troops, the Republic of Korea 40 percent; of the naval forces, the United States 85 percent, the Republic of Korea 7.5 percent; of the air force, the United States 93.4 percent, the Republic of Korea 5.6 percent. In 1952 the total number of U.N. troops in Korea was estimated at 450,000, of which, it is clear from the figures above, the contribution of other United Nations members was very small indeed.

The U.N. counteroffensive started at the time of the United States Marines' amphibious landing at Inchun in the middle of September.[23] At that time the U.N. forces at the Pusan beachhead broke through the Nakdong river line of the North Korean army and attacked north to join the U.N. forces in the Inchun area. North Korean resistance collapsed on every front and retreated in disorder. Seoul was recaptured, and on September 19 General MacArthur entered the capital. Within a couple of weeks U.N. forces reached the 38th parallel. Then they were faced with the question of whether they should cross the parallel.

The United States government took the position that the June 27 resolution of the Security Council authorized the U.N. commanding general to cross the parallel.[24] The Indian government excepted, the other members of the United Nations did not seriously dispute this interpretation. The representative of India warned that crossing the parallel would bring Communist China into the conflict. During the latter part of September, U.N. forces crossed the parallel. On October 1 General MacArthur issued a proclamation calling for the unconditional surrender of North Korea.[25] It should be noted that MacArthur did this without waiting for instructions from the United Nations.[26] The North Korean regime rejected the surrender terms and retreated further north. On October 20, Pyongyang, capital of the Northern regime, fell to U.N. forces. Six days later, advancing South Korean troops reached the Yalu River, the natural boundary line between Korea and Red China. At this time the main forces of the North Korean army had ceased to exist, and major northern cities and towns as well as industries had been completely destroyed. Thus the "home-by-Christmas" offensive of General MacArthur appeared to be nearing its successful end.

Communist China Sends "Volunteers." On September 29 the Associated

Press had reported from Moscow that "the Soviet Union, which like Communist China, borders on North Korea, would unquestionably take a grave view of any effort by United States or Allied forces to push up beyond the 38th parallel";[27] on October 3 a *New York Times* dispatch from Hong Kong called attention to the danger of Chinese entry into the war because of the "important economic as well as political and military stakes of the Peking regime in North Korea."[28] The first official warning of possible intervention by Communist China was made by Premier Chou En-lai in an address on the first anniversary of the Central People's Government of the People's Republic of China on October 10, 1950; China would not "supinely tolerate" an invasion of North Korea.[29]

On October 29 Peking radio stated that "the MacArthur advance to the frontiers [poses] a threat to Manchuria" and called on the Chinese people "to support the Korean people against American imperialism."[30] On the same day the South Korean army intelligence reported that forty thousand Chinese Communist troops had crossed the border to join in the defense of the border along the Yalu River; two days later MacArthur's headquarters confirmed the entry of Chinese Communists into the war.

The Chinese version of the entry into the Korean conflict was told by Wu Hsiu-chuan, representative of the Central People's government of the People's Republic of China, before the United Nations Security Council at Lake Success, New York, on November 28, 1950. He charged that: (1) President Truman's statement of June 27 ordering the Seventh Fleet to "prevent any attack on Formosa" was "armed aggression against Chinese territory," since "Taiwan is an inseparable part of the territory of China"; (2) "from August 27 to November 10, 1950, the military aircraft of the United States aggression force in Korea have, ninety times, violated the territorial air of Northeast China"; (3) "the civil war in Korea" was started by the United States puppet government in South Korea, and the United States armed intervention in the Korean war had "directly threatened Chinese security and such threat had increased as the United Nations forces reached the Yalu River, which separated the two countries only geographically." Under such circumstances, the Chinese representative said, "The Chinese cannot afford to stand idle. . . . The Chinese people are volunteering in great numbers to go to the aid of the Korean people." He continued: "The

Chinese People's Republic sees no reason whatever to prevent voluntary departure for Korea to participate, under the command of the government of the Korean People's Democratic Republic, in the great liberation struggle of the Korean people against United States aggression."[31]

The exact day of entry of the so-called Chinese volunteers into the Korean battlefronts is not known, but by the first part of November 1950 Chinese fighting units were already along the Yalu fronts. The United Nations November 24 offensive, known as MacArthur's "Home-by-Christmas" campaign, met with strong resistance from the Communists. Furious battles were fought between United Nations and Communist forces, and finally the Communist troops forced the United Nations forces to retreat from the Chungjin reservoir. This was the first major breakthrough of the Communist counteroffensive. On December 24 the Tenth Corps of the United States Army was evacuated by sea from Hungnam and Wansan harbors. Thus the northeastern front of the United Nations collapsed. On the western front, the entire Eighth Army of the United States was pushed back from the Yalu River area and retreated south. Pyongyang was recaptured by the Communists, and on January 5, 1951, Seoul fell again into the hands of the Communist army. All United Nations forces were pulled out of the Seoul area through Inchun harbor just before Communist troops entered the capital.

Stalemate. The Communist side halted their offensive in January 1951 and appeared to want "a de facto cease fire," as indicated by the lack of further advance south into the peninsula. By the middle of March U.N. forces improved their positions and launched a counteroffensive. They retook Seoul in the same month without resistance by Communist forces. All Communist troops retreated orderly to just above the 38th parallel and set up strong defensive lines there. The United States government viewed this as an indication of a desire for cease-fire. At this time the majority of the other members of the United Nations with armed forces in Korea were opposed to again crossing the parallel. Upon the initiative of the United States government, the other fifteen governments having troops in Korea agreed to issue a statement saying that they were ready to invite the Communist side "to a cease-fire and to settle outstanding political problems by negotiation."[32] On March 20 General MacArthur was informed of the plan and instructed not to let U.N. forces cross the parallel before diplomatic effort toward settlement could be made. But on March 24 General MacArthur, without authorization from President Truman, issued a statement "inviting the commander-in-chief of the enemy forces to confer with him regarding the means by which the political objectives of the United Nations in Korea might be achieved without further bloodshed."[33] The Communist side rejected this at once. On March 26 South Korean patrols crossed the 38th parallel for a second time. Four days later the First United States Armored Column also crossed the parallel, and in April other members of the United Nations armed forces followed.

In the meantime, General MacArthur "threatened direct military action against Communist China." He was also in favor of using Chinese Nationalist forces from Formosa in the Korean war, as revealed in his letter to Congressman Martin, then Republican leader of the House of Representatives.[34] Such actions led to President Truman's decision on April 11, 1951, to remove MacArthur as the supreme commander of the United Nations forces in Korea. General Matthew B. Ridgway was immediately promoted to MacArthur's former position.

The Communists attempted to launch two major offensives against the Allied forces in the latter part of April and middle of May, but on both occasions suffered heavy losses and pulled back to the 38th parallel. After these attempts both sides seemed to realize that neither side could achieve a military victory; nor did they want an all-out war over the Korean issue. Thus both sides wished to stop the fighting and come to the negotiating table.

The Armistice Negotiations. On June 23, 1951, Jacob Malik, the permanent representative of the Soviet Union, said on the United Nations radio program "The Price of Peace" that negotiations "should be started between the belligerents for cease-fire and an armistice providing for the mutual withdrawal of forces from the 38th parallel."[35] Two days later, *The People's Daily,* mouthpiece of the Chinese Communist government, endorsed the Malik proposal; they demanded the complete withdrawal of all foreign troops from Korea and a chance for the Korean people to settle their own problems. On June 27 Andrei Gromyko told the American ambassador in Moscow that the "cease-fire should be strictly military" and that political and territorial problems should not be involved in the discussion.[36] The members of the United Nations having armed forces in Korea accepted the Russian cease-fire proposal: on June 30, General Ridgway, supreme commander of the United Nations forces, sent the cease-fire offer[37] over the armed-forces radio to the commander-in-chief of the Communist forces in North Korea. The cease-fire was accepted and signed by Kim Il-sung, commander-in-chief of the North Korean army, and Peng Teh-huai, commander of the Chinese volunteer forces.

The truce negotiations[38] began on July 10, 1951, at Kaesung. The United Nations delegation was headed by Vice Adm. C. Turner Joy, U.S. Navy, and the Communist delegation by Gen. Nam Il, North Korean Army. It took more than two weeks for both sides to agree on the truce agenda. It was finally agreed to fix a military demarcation line, to come to a concrete agreement for the realization of an armistice, to settle the question of prisoners of war, and to make recommendations to the governments of the countries concerned in preparation for discussions of political matters.

It took four months to reach an agreement on the fixing of the demarcation line. During this period the negotiations were suspended on two different occasions because of alleged violations of the neutrality of the conference zone of Kaesung. Negotiations were resumed at a new location, Panmunjom. The Communist side insisted that the 38th parallel should be the demarcation line, while the United Nations delegation insisted on the actual line of battle, which was north of the parallel. Finally, on November 27 a demarcation line was agreed upon.[39] As for a supervisory organ to carry out the terms of armistice, both sides agreed to have an inspection team composed of Sweden, Switzerland, Poland, and Czechoslovakia.

It was recommended that "within three months after an armistice has been signed and effective, a political conference of a high level of both sides should be held by representatives appointed respectively to settle through negotiation questions of withdrawal of all foreign forces from Korea, the peaceful settlement of the Korean questions." They agreed that the Republic of Korea should be included as one of the participating members of the political conference.[40]

The prisoners-of-war issue blocked the truce for more than seventeen months. The Allies insisted that, "while all prisoners of war should be released, repatriation should take place in accordance with declared wishes of the individual prisoner," and the choice of the individual should be made voluntarily under the supervision of an international organ. The Communists wanted all prisoners of war to be released and returned to the country from which they came.[41] Neither side yielding, the deadlock refused to be broken.

The parties finally agreed on the following formula:[42] (1) prisoners who refused to return to their home countries (estimated at about 47,000) would be placed in custody of the neutral nations, India, Poland, Czechoslovakia, Switzerland, and Sweden; (2) Indian troops would be placed as guards of nonrepatriated prisoners in South Korea; (3) Communist representatives would be allowed to persuade them to return home during a four-month period; (4) the nonrepatriated prisoners after four months would be referred to a postarmistice political conference; and (5) the fate of the remaining nonrepatriated prisoners would be decided by the U. N. General Assembly.

The formal signing of the armistice agreement was interrupted by Rhee's release of Communist prisoners on June 18, 1953. Rhee threatend "to go it alone" and march North to unify the country if the armistice agreement, which he had opposed from the beginning, was signed. The Communists demanded immediate return of all released war prisoners and assurances that the Republic of Korea would respect the armistice agreement. The United Nations command promised to "make every effort to obtain the cooperation" of the Rhee government and would "establish military safeguards to insure that the armistice terms are observed."[43] In the meantime, President Eisenhower sent Assistant Secretary of State Walter S. Robertson to Seoul to make an effort to bring Rhee into line by assuring him of the continuation of United States military and economic aid to South Korea after the armistice. On July 11 Rhee agreed not to sabotage the armistice agreement.[44] Finally, as a result of one of the longest truce neogiations in the history of war, the armistice agreement was signed on July 27, 1953.

Nobody won in the Korean war—everybody lost. The total casualty toll on both sides was close to 3 million: Allied casualties were 1,400,000; Communists casualties 1,500,000. The civilian casualties were well over 1 million; 5 million were left without means of livelihood; 100,000 war orphans and

300,000 war widows were left behind; and in South Korea 50 percent of all physical facilities, such as houses, schools, hospitals, and industries, were destroyed. No adequate information is available on North Korean war damage, but it is estimated that 75 percent of physical facilities were destroyed and the civilian population was diminished from 8 to 4 million.

CHAPTER 13

THE STUDENT REVOLUTION AND THE SECOND REPUBLIC

The Student Revolution of April 19, 1960, which ended Syngman Rhee's 12-year-old ironfisted rule, is a highlight in the struggle for liberty in the annals of Korea. The Rhee regime fell because of official corruption, favoritism, political oppression, and fraudulent elections. All these were practiced in the name of anti-Communism and in the guise of patriotism.

The student uprising first took the form of protests against government interference in academic freedom during the presidential campaign. Then it developed into mass street demonstrations. Finally the students demanded new elections and actually succeeded in ousting eighty-five-year-old Syngman Rhee from power on April 26. The collapse of the Rhee regime recalls Lord Acton's statement that "absolute power corrupts absolutely,"[1] and contravenes Machiavelli's idea that means justify ends.

BACKGROUND OF THE STUDENT REVOLUTION

Since the liberation from the Japanese in 1945, Korean society had been in transition from a family-centered semifeudal society to a Western-oriented, individualistic democratic society. Korean society today can be divided into two classes: the haves and the have-nots. The former is a small privileged group, including profiteers, political opportunists, and high government officials, both military and civilian. The latter is composed of peasants, industrial workers, white-collar workers, and intellectuals, embracing more than 85 percent of the population. The overwhelming majority of South Koreans (twenty-two million people in 1960) were poor, with a per capita income estimated at no more than fifty dollars a year. The reasons for this poverty are the stagnation of agriculture and industry under the old feudalistic system, the crude colonial exploitation by the Japanese for nearly a half century, the artificial division of the country at the 38th parallel into an "agricultural south" and an "industrial north," and the three years of war that cost South Korea one million lives and three billion dollars' damage to cities, towns, and villages.

After the armistice was signed on July 27, 1953, foreign aid to South Korea began its rise to a total of $2.2 billion, the overwhelming portion of this from the United States. The largest amount of this aid went into the political funds of the Liberal party and was for the personal benefit of party leaders and high government officials, including Rhee and his wife. American aid created many Korean millionaires and sustained many corrupt practices, but failed to raise the living standard of the people. South Korean big businesses became the monopolies of a handful of rich Koreans, who were loyal to Rhee. No Korean middle class existed, and the line between rich and poor was sharply drawn.

THE POLITICAL BACKGROUND

In 1960 the Republic of Korea had two major political parties, but in reality the Rhee-dominated Liberal party was in absolute control of local and central government, with a clear majority in the national assembly. Both Liberals and Democrats were conservative, anti-Communist, and pro-Western (especially pro-American); no fundamental differences in this respect existed. Both parties had factional groups struggling for power, but they maintained loose coalitions until the 1960 elections. The difference between the Liberals and Democrats was that the former favored a strong presidential form of government and the latter a cabinet type of government responsible to parliament.

The Liberal party unaminously renominated Syngman Rhee for the presidency and Lee Ki-pung for the vice-presidency at the party convention. The Democratic party, after a fight between Chough Pyon-ok and Chang Myun, nominated Chough for president and Chang for vice-president. The Liberal party together with government officials, notably the ministers of justice, interior, and public information, worked out the tactics for the presidential campaign. Chief of Public Information Jun Sung-chun ordered the Catholic newspaper *Kyung Hyang Shinmun* closed, charging the newspaper with having printed a "false report" beneficial to the Communists.

Soon after opposition candidate Chough entered Walter Reed Hospital in Washington for a major operation, a new election day, March 15, two months sooner than usual, was announced by the State Council under the pretext that an early election would be convenient for the farmers since May is the rice-transplanting season. The Democrats denounced this opportunistic move. Conveniently for the Liberal party, Chough died in the hospital and left Rhee unopposed. Therefore, the real contest was for the vice-presidency, and Rhee was determined to see the hand-picked Lee Ki-pung elected. Rhee turned down a request by the Democratic party for a delay in the elections so that they could nominate a new candidate for the presidency.

As election day came closer, the government mobilized the police and army as well as terroristic youth groups: the police were placed on twenty-four-hour duty throughout South Korea; the Counter Intelligence Corps was used to "persuade all servicemen to vote for Rhee and Lee Ki-pung"; and nine youth groups were reorganized into one "Anti-Communist Youth League" under the leadership of Liberal party assemblyman Shin To-whan. Minister of the Interior Choi In-kuy urged all government employees to take an active part in the elections in supporting Liberal party candidates although such activities were a violation of the law concerning public employees; and he also sent out directives to local government officials stating that all public halls, athletic fields, and other facilities, such as school buildings and playgrounds, should be opened free of charge to campaigners of the Liberal party only. Even bus and taxicab services were suspended in many cities and towns by order of the local authorities, usually the district police chiefs. Under these circumstances, the opposition candidate, Chang Myun, often found himself unable to find a meeting place at which to give his speeches.

Meanwhile, the strategists of the Liberal party designed a plan to secure a landslide victory for Rhee and Lee Ki-pung. A week before the elections the Liberals sent out millions of model ballot sheets, identical to the actual ballots on election day, under the pretext of "rehearsing" in the rural areas, where more than 60 percent of the qualified voters resided and where police controls were the most complete. In the rehearsals, teams of nine men practiced marking the model ballot sheets for candidates Rhee and Lee Ki-pung. On election day the nine-man teams were subdivided into teams of three men each, and these teams entered the polling place together and watched to make sure each person voted for the Liberal party.[2]

A few days before the elections, many terroristic activities took place: at the southern port city of Yosu the Democratic party treasurer was beaten to death with wide iron bars; in Kwangju a young Catholic leader, who had been supporting Chang Myun, was stabbed to death by the local chief of the Anti-Communist Youth League; in Suwon, not far from Seoul, a 17-year-old student was arrested by the police on his way to hear a Democratic campaign speech.

On the other hand, as described later in detail, in Taegu, the third-largest city in South Korea, more than one thousand high school students conducted antigovernment demonstrations for the first time, because Sunday classes forced them to keep away from a Democratic rally. In Seoul, after a Democratic rally on March 5, two hundred students clashed with policemen because they shouted for free elections; twenty of them were jailed.

THE STUDENT DEMONSTRATIONS

First Stage: The High School Demonstrations.[3] Most school authorities, public or private, became political tools in the 1960 presidential election: the schools encouraged the students to attend Liberal party rallies, but kept the same students away from Democratic party campaign speeches.

On February 28 (Sunday) in Taegu City, the Democratic vice-presidential candidate Chang Myun was scheduled to make his campaign speech. Three days earlier, three high school principals asked all students to attend school on the coming Sunday for "special programs," such as taking examinations in Kyungbok high school (changed to a free motion picture program when the students opposed examinations on Sunday), rabbit hunting for Taegu high school, and sports for Busok high school.

The representatives of the student bodies of the three high schools protested against these programs, and when they could not change the minds of their principals they made plans of their own: peaceful demonstrations demanding academic freedom. On Sunday afternoon eight hundred Kyungbok high school students marched in Taegu's streets shouting "Academic Freedom!" About an hour later, more than two hundred Taegu high school students joined the demonstration, rejecting the pleas of their principal and teachers "not to join the street demonstration against the government." The demonstration lasted for more than four hours, cheered by the general public. The police attacked the students with clubs and sticks, injuring twenty and arresting two hundred fifty. The governor of North Kyungsang province and the mayor of Taegu condemned the student demonstration as "mob action" and demanded that the principals and teachers resign.

When the news of the Taegu student demonstration spread, high-school demonstrations mushroomed in other cities. Perhaps the most significant demonstration occurred in Masan, South Kyungsang province on March 15. It developed into a massive demonstration against the government. Masan was a stronghold of opposition to Rhee's Liberal party: in the 1956 elections, its voters gave half their votes to the Progressive party candidate and many voted for the dead Democratic candidate. Thus Rhee received less than 40 percent of the votes in Masan. The leaders of the Liberal party were determined not to let that happen at this election. A strong anti-Democrat, Shin Do-sung, who had been expelled from the Democratic party, was appointed the new governor of the province; and the police chief and the mayor of Masan schemed to bring about a landslide victory for Rhee and Lee Ki-pung through bribery, police, and terroristic youth groups. As revealed later, the police chief printed fake Communist leaflets. Shortly after the polls closed on election day, it was announced that the Liberal party candidates had won by a ratio of three to one. Masan voters did not believe this. Democrats marched through the streets charging fraud and calling for a new election; a thousand people from the general public, including many high-school students, joined them, demanding nullification of the fraudulent election. They clashed with police and seventeen demonstrators were killed and more than two hundred arrested. Seven of the dead were high-school students, one of them sixteen-year-old Kim Chu-yul. Kim's body was missing and the police claimed for more than three weeks they knew nothing about it. Eventually the body was found floating near the beach of Chungan-dong, in the southern part of Masan; the corpse's head contained a fragment of one of the tear gas shells that police had used to put down the demonstrators; the police had stuffed one of the fake Communist leaflets in his pocket.[4] The Korean Bar Association published a report charging the police with having thrown Kim's body in the sea.

The incident shocked the country. Thousands of angry citizens of Masan flocked to the building where Kim's corpse lay and demanded "to take it to Seoul and show it to the National Assemblymen." When the authorities refused, the crowd stoned the city hall, police stations, the local office of the Liberal party, and the home of the mayor. Thousands of the demonstrators were arrested and more than thirty were killed by the police. Now high-school demonstrations broke out in three other southern cities, and the general public joined them demanding freedom and a new election. The government, including Rhee, condemned the Masan "riots" as "the work of the Communists."

Second Stage: The University Demonstration. Before the Masan incident some members of the Korea University Student Association discussed demonstrations against the government. No agreement was reached at this meeting. However, when they heard of Kim Chu-yul's death they unanimously agreed to demonstrate. At Korea University more than three thousand students met on the campus and read a declaration protesting the government action. Then they marched from the campus to the national assembly building shouting against "corruption," "dictatorship," "murderous police system" and "fraudulent elections." When they reached the building the students presented three resolutions[5] to the minister of interior, asking for an immediate reply. The minister turned down the resolutions. The students refused to obey the university president's plea to break up, and staged a sit-down demonstration in front of the building. Hundreds of Seoul policemen and plainclothesmen encircled the demonstrators. Finally, a Democratic assemblyman, Lee Chul-sung, a graduate of Korea University, persuaded most of the students to return to their campus; the others were forced away by the police.

The students returning from the assembly building to the campus were attacked by about a hundred political hoodlums, agents of the Liberal party, with iron sticks, fire hooks, and knives, under the cover of policemen. About a dozen students and some reporters were injured.

The news of the Korea University demonstration and of the hoodlum attack on the demonstrators sparked the next day's mass demonstrations in the capital. Thousands of students marched to President Rhee's mansion demanding new elections, and thousands rushed to the residence of vice-president-elect Lee Ki-pung to demand his resignation; others demonstrated in front of the Supreme Court and the national assembly building demanding the retirement of their members from public life. Most Seoul high school and even grade school students joined the street demonstrations; and thousands of their parents followed the demonstrators from one place to another encouraging them. On many occasions, the general public mingled with the demonstrators, denouncing "dictatorship" and "the murderous police."

The police first used tear gas to put down the demonstrators; then they fired on them, killing dozens every day and injuring hundreds. Several thousand students were arrested and beaten by the police. The angry demonstrators responded by attacking the police stations and setting fire to the residences of Lee Ki-pung and the leaders of the Liberal party. They also destroyed the headquarters of the Anti-Communist Youth League (Rhee's private organization) as well as the progovernment Seoul Daily Newspaper building.

Rhee now imposed martial law in the major cities throughout South Korea. The Republic of Korea had the appearance of a country torn by civil war.

The United States State Department issued the strongest statement yet to Rhee's government, denouncing "the repressive measures unsuited to a free democracy" and demanding that "the Korean government . . . take necessary and effective action aimed at protecting democratic rights of freedom of speech, of assembly, of the press, as well as preserving the secrecy of the ballot and preventing unfair discrimination against political opponents of a party in power."[6] Thereupon Rhee's whole cabinet resigned. The eighty-five-year-old dictator found himself in the worst position of his twelve-year rule in South Korea.

In vain he tried to save the deteriorating situation by announcing his willingness to "divorce" himself from the Liberal party and to "serve the nation as its executive at the head of its administration." Neither the students nor the general public were impressed by Rhee's promises, and more demonstrations erupted throughout South Korea, demanding the resignation of Rhee himself. The martial-law commander, Army Chief of Staff Lt. Gen. Song Yoo-chan, ordered his soldiers not to fire on the demonstrators and instructed the police to release all arrested students and not to arrest any more without adequate cause.

Vice-President Chang Myun, with four more months to go in office, resigned on April 23, protesting the Liberals' "continuance of suppression and tyranny." Rhee was told by his former foreign minister and prime minister, Pyun Yung-tae, that "the students had accomplished what the rest of us could not," awaken a consciousness of individual liberty; the March 15 elections, he said, "were rigged systematically and outrageously," and "vice-president-elect Lee Ki-pung should voluntarily retire from politics."[7] Thus Rhee had to make his final decision.

Third Stage: The Professors Join. In the midst of the political crisis, more than 250 university professors joined the antigovernment movement and marched down Seoul streets. The professors had known of the corruption of Rhee's administration for a long time, but they had refrained from saying so openly for fear of reprisals. Now that their students had taken their lives in their hands by speaking out, the professors believed it time to act. Prof. Lee Sang-en, one of the leaders, said: "If we remain spectators during all this student uprising we must disqualify ourselves as educators—talking about social justice, democratic rights, and the like."[8]

The professors were shocked by the government accusation that the student demonstrations were the "work of the Communists" and "a plot of the opposition party." This charge meant that the thousands of students who participated in the demonstrations would be charged with treason under the National Security Law if the Rhee administration remained in power.

Leaders of the antigovernment movement viewed Rhee's so-called divorce statement—his promise to sever himself from the Liberal party and devote himself to the interests of the people—as a maneuver to deceive the people. Meeting secretly, the professors representing four leading universities in Seoul agreed to issue a public statement supporting the student demonstrations as justifiable, and to hold a mass meeting for professors to decide whether to join the student demonstrations.

On April 25, 258 professors attended an open meeting in the faculty building of the Medical College of Seoul National University, adopted a fifteen-point declaration,[9] and decided by a majority vote to march in the street demonstration. Headed by elderly professors and shouting for a new election, the professors marched three miles through the main streets of the capital to the assembly building, despite the martial law. According to press reports, more than fifty thousand students and a hundred thousand Seoul citizens followed the professors, cheering and singing the national anthem. Hundreds of armed soldiers stood by and made no attempt to interfere with the crowd following the marching professors. When the demonstrators reached the front of the assembly building, Professor Lee Hyang-nung, the oldest among them, read the fifteen-point declaration before the crowd; then they dispersed. There was no incident or violent act during the professors' demonstration. For the first time in Korean history, the professors had revolted against tyranny.

Rhee's Regime Falls. Rhee was now attacked from all directions. On April 26, 136 assemblymen out of 233 demanded Rhee's resignation of the presidency and called for nullification of the March 15 elections and for creation of a parliamentary system with a prime minister elected by the assembly—this last to be accomplished by revision of the constitution. The United States State Department warned for the second time within a week through Ambassador Walter McConaughty that "this is no time for temporizing."[10] In the meantime, the representatives of the sixteen nations which had fought for the South in the Korean war issued a joint statement urging "an early resolution of the situation in a manner which would permit the orderly functioning of democratic government."[11] Thousands of students, including grade-school children, marched once again to Rhee's mansion shouting for him to resign. The American ambassador again called on Rhee, and this time the Korean martial-law commander as well as the U.N. Forces commander were also present. The martial-law commander arranged a meeting between Rhee and the representatives of the demonstrating students. As reported later, the commander and the minister of defense told Rhee, "There is no hope for restoration of order unless you resign."[12] The student representatives were told that Rhee was considering stepping down. After visiting Rhee, Ambassador McConaughty said he was convinced that "the authorities are earnestly working toward redressing the justifiable grievances of the people." He further went on to say that "this is a day that will long be remembered by the Republic of Korea and its many friends abroad."[13] In Washington, D.C., Korean Ambassador Yang Yu-chan resigned because he had been wrong in believing that the wave of antigovernment rioting in South Korea was Communist instigated.[14]

Under these pressures Rhee was forced to make a public statement once again on April 26: "I will resign from the presidency if the people so desire."[15] The news electrified first the capital, then the whole peninsula. Millions of people cheered, overjoyed by the victory brought about by the students. Rhee's statue in the Pagoda Park in downtown Seoul was brought down and displayed in a victory parade as a symbol of the final fate of tyranny. On April 27, 1960, Rhee sent his formal resignation to the national assembly.

The victory had not been won cheaply: 183 students were dead; 6,258 were injured—more than 200 of them permanently maimed. Vice-President-Elect Lee Ki-pung (Rhee's right-hand man), his wife, and his two sons—the first son was adopted by Rhee—committed suicide in the annex building of Rhee's mansion on April 28.

Characteristics of the Student Revolution. The characteristic feature of the revolution was the revolt of the younger generation against the older generation—the ruling class. The ages of the high school students in the antigovernment movement ran from fifteen to nineteen: the leaders were seventeen and eighteen years old. This shows that high school students had not received Japanese colonial education—they were from one to three years old when Korea was freed of Japanese domination in 1945. This also means that they were only five to eight years old when the Korean war broke out in 1950, so that they were not old enough to understand that the nature of the war, democracy versus communism, was the result of the artificial division of the country by foreign powers.

The South Korean government introduced American-oriented democratic education, and the teachers taught the theoretical concepts of individual dignity and human freedom along with the idea of academic freedom both in public and private institutions. But the political society under which the students lived was entirely different—a corrupt authoritarian regime.

Most high school teachers were from thirty to forty years old, and had received, partly or entirely, Japanese education, with its emphasis on duty to superiors and conformity with the existing social order rather than thought about social, economic, and political issues. Since the liberation from Japanese domination, a limited number of teachers, mainly administrators (principals and superintendents), had the opportunity to acquaint themselves with the democratic educational system through government-sponsored inspection tours abroad. Therefore most high school teachers were still Japanese-trained and their mentality and teaching methods had not sufficiently changed to the new American-oriented liberal education. The same had been true in the higher institutions, colleges, and universities. The educational system in South Korea had been in a stage of transition from the old to the new. Moreover, the teachers had been under political pressure from the Liberal party in power during the past twelve years: they were not only asked to support government policies but had been called upon to campaign actively for the Liberal party in every election. Under these circumstances, the teachers were forced to talk about academic freedom and democracy in the classroom and at the same time to ask the students to support the Liberal party. The students were called upon on numerous occasions to participate in "spontaneous" rallies in support of one government policy or another, but they were denied the right to raise their voice against government policies. It was natural that the students regarded their teachers as hypocrites.

The ruling class in South Korea, until the Student Revolution, consisted of the leaders of the political parties, high officials, legislators, high-court judges, and the high military officials. With the exception of Syngman Rhee, all of them had received Japanese educations and their ages were well over fifty. Some of them did their graduate studies in the United States and England. Many had participated in the independence movement at one time or another during the thirty-five years of Japanese rule. Since 1945, however, none of them had real popular support as national leaders because they did not fight for the interest of the people, but for their own.

When Rhee seized power in South Korea, most political leaders supported his policies and many served as cabinet members or representatives abroad. Some first worked closely with Rhee but in later years distinguished themselves by disagreeing with him. One of them was Chang Myun. He was a high school principal in Seoul until 1945; he was one of the South Korean assemblymen appointed by Gen. John R. Hodge during the United States military occupation period. In 1948 Rhee appointed Chang first ambassador to the United States, and then prime minister. During the 1952 constitutional amendment crisis, Chang became one of Rhee's political enemies, accused of seeking the president's office with the support of "certain groups" in the United States. Chang joined the Democratic party and in 1946 won the vice-presidency over Rhee's running mate, Lee Ki-pung. However, Rhee never consulted with vice-president Chang and even refused to see him. When on April 23, in the midst of the student uprising, the Vice-President resigned in protest against the rigged March elections, Rhee remarked angrily: "I hate getting into a fight with him. He's dirty . . . evil . . . and it is all my fault. I created him. I made him ambassador to Washington and prime minister."[16]

The students revolted against Rhee's corrupt society, but politically they took no sides and supported none of the contending leaders. The student revolution suffered from lack of principle, leadership, and militant organization. The revolutionary leaders, including the revolting professors, cried for social justice, truth, liberty, and democracy, but they failed to spell them out in exact terms; nor did they advocate new political and economic reform programs. Consequently, no new political forces or parties that could challenge the supremacy of the old political forces emerged from the student movement. What the students accomplished was the ousting of Syngman Rhee and a few of his lieutenants, the opening of the Liberal party's closed political door to the Democrats (who seized power for the first time since the establishment of the Republic of South Korea), and the regaining of the people's lost political freedoms. The restoration of political freedom for the twenty-five million South Koreans was the most significant achievement of the student revolution.

THE SECOND REPUBLIC UNDER THE DEMOCRATS

A New Party Movement. In 1954, following the amendment of the constitution, a new party movement under the leadership of the Democratic party started. More than sixty assemblymen, most of the members of the Constitutional Defense Fraternal Association, recognized that the Democratic party had been too weak to compete with the Liberal party, and therefore wanted to establish a genuine two-party system by reorganizing the several existing minority political parties into the one opposition party. The aim of the new party was to introduce a parliamentary system in place of the strong-president system.

In January 1955 a conference was held by representatives of all minority parties and various social and religious groups: some of the major groups participating in the conference were the Korean Democratic party, the Constitutional Defense Fraternal Association, the Young Korean Academy, Catholic Church groups, and the Socialists. The representatives of the conference organized a committee to draft new party principles and party membership regulations. Soon the committee members on economic policy and party membership split into two groups: the conservatives favored a free competitive economy and exclusion of Socialists from membership, while the progressives insisted on a planned economy and open membership allowing the Socialists to become members of the party. But all agreed that known Communists, rightists, and corrupt officials should be barred from the party. On economic policy and admission of Socialists no agreement could be reached, so the committee was dissolved.

The conservatives now organized a new committee and declared their determination to run the new party without the progressives. On July 17, 1955, a Preparatory Committee Conference for organization of the new party was convened with 168 delegates: of these, 33 were incumbent assemblymen, including members of the Korean Democratic party and independents; 34 were former assemblymen, including a few former members of the Liberal party; and more than 100 represented various social and religious organizations. No progressives were invited.

Leading personalities of the conference were Shin Ik-ki and Chough Pyong-ok, representing the old guard of the Korean Democratic party; Chang Myun (John Chang), representing the Catholic group; Kwak Sang-hoon, who represented the independents in the assembly; and Chu Yo-han, leader of the Young Korean Academy. The conference passed a resolution to create a new political party named the Democratic party based on the following objectives and principles: Achievement of national independence based on the principle of self-government and the practice of democratic principles.[17] The party principles contained twenty-five articles, which can be summarized in three points: (a) introduction of a cabinet form of government with parliamentary supremacy; (2) introduction of a free competitive economy; and (3) promotion of peaceful international relations by cooperating with democratic states.

The conference condemned Communism, corruption, and abuse of power by the executive branch of the government. The final action of the conference was the election of seven committees, of which the six-man secretariat was the most important. Four of the six party secretaries were chosen from the former Korean Democratic party, and Shin Ik-ki succeeded as chief of the new Democratic party. Thus the leadership of the Democratic party was dominated by the former Korean Democratic old guard, while the second positions of the party were filled by the moderates, who belonged to the Young Korean Academy and the Catholic group. This meant that the Democratic party did not represent the peasants and industrial workers. Neither the intellectuals nor the liberals participated in the party. Therefore, the Democratic party, too, as the Liberal party, had to depend on support from the upper social class.

Establishment of a Parliamentary Cabinet System. Following the fall of Syngman Rhee's government, the Democrats and independents passed a constitutional amendment which established a parliamentary cabinet system by an overwhelming majority, 208 to 3. The amendment[18] weakened the authority of the president and increased the power of the cabinet under the head of a prime minister. The president was no longer the head of the executive branch of government; he had no power to veto bills passed by parliament; and he was not allowed to belong to a political party after he was elected president. The fixed term of his office was five years, with an additional consecutive term possible.

The office of vice-president was abolished; in the event of a presidential vacancy, the line of succession was: president of the House of Councilors, speaker of the House of Representatives, and prime minister. The prime minister became the real head of the executive branch of government. He was appointed by the president with the approval of the House of Representatives (usually the prime minister is the head of the majority party), and he could select the cabinet ministers from the legislative members of his own party or outside, and the president confirmed the appointment as a matter of formality. The prime minister could issue executive orders in time of crisis, which formerly was the prerogative of the president. The prime minister and his cabinet were responsible to the parliament for their policies and actions. In the event of a vote of nonconfidence by the House of Representatives, the cabinet must resign en bloc or dissolve the house within ten days.

The House of Representatives was given more or less exclusive legislative power; the House of Councilors was a consultative body in the legislative process. It elected the president jointly with the House of Representatives. If the two houses disagreed on a bill the House of Representatives had the final decision.

The revised constitution guaranteed the independence of the judicial branch by providing for the appointment or removal of justices by a group of judges confirmed by the president. It also guaranteed fundamental human rights and freedoms more clearly than before by refraining from such ambiguous reservations as "as specified by law" which appeared in the old constitution. Local autonomy was restored by the revised constitution, and a constitutional court was established to interpret the constitution.

New elections. The assembly passed a new law for the election of the members of the parliament. The caretaker government headed by Huh Chung announced July 22, 1960, as the election date. The election law lowered the voting age from twenty-one to twenty, reduced deposit money for the candidates, lowered the age of the upper-house candidates from thirty-five to thirty, stipulated political neutrality of the armed forces and government employees (including the police force) during election campaigns, and spelled out severe punishment for election frauds. According to the election law, the parliament was composed of 233 representatives and 58 councilors.

As soon as Rhee was ousted from power, the Liberal party rapidly disintegrated. Most of the Liberal members of the assembly ran for reelection as independents; some of them formed a new political party, the Constitutional Politics party. Many leaders of the Liberal party went to jail because of the March election frauds.

Following the student revolution many new progressive parties, such as the Popular Socialist party, the Korean Socialist party, and the National

League of Progressives, were organized, and advocated a planned economy, social welfare, and peaceful unification. But because of rivalries, they failed to form a united front to meet the challenge of conservative power. None of the progressive parties was based on mass support in the rural or urban areas, so that most of them could be characterized as idealistic intellectual parties. None had sufficient campaign funds.

The Democratic party was the only well-organized party left that was capable of conducting a successful campaign, but as will be seen later the interparty factionalism between the old guard (the former Korean Democratic party clique) and the young group (known as the Chang Myun faction) was so deep-seated that it was doubtful how well they would be able to govern, even if they did get into power.

At the close of the registration day (July 2, 1960), more than 1,562 people had filed as candidates for the House of Representatives: 305 were Democrats, 54 Liberals, 1,010 independents, 154 Progressives, and 12 members of the Korean Independent party. The total number of candidates for the House of Councilors was 214: 61 Democrats, 131 independents, 12 Liberals, 7 Progressives, and 1 member of the Korean Independent party.

The actual platforms of the parties were not substantially different from one another: all of them pledged themselves to clean up corruption, oppose dictatorship, promote economic reconstruction, protect human rights, and continue a pro-American, anti-Communist foreign policy. All parties wanted peaceful unification, but the conservative parties favored free nationwide elections under U.N. supervision while the progressives advocated elections supervised by neutral nations.

The election campaigns were conducted in a fairly free atmosphere in comparison to previous elections. Martial law, proclaimed during the student revolution, was lifted. The chiefs of the army, navy, air force, and marine corps reaffirmed neutrality on Constitutional Day, July 17. The U.N. Commission for Unification and Rehabilitation of Korea increased its observation teams from five to ten. The police were instructed not to interfere with election campaigns or voting. On election day, July 29, more than eleven million people cast their votes, which was about 82 percent of the eligible voters. Although according to the statement of the office of the attorney general there were more than 900 violations of election laws and indictments of 120 persons, there were much fewer than during previous elections held under the Rhee regime. Foreign observers, including the U.N. commission and the United States embassy team, commented that the election "was free and honest" despite "isolated incidents" of violence.[19]

The House of Representatives had 233 members elected: 172 Democrats, 54 independents, 4 progressives (3 Popular Socialists and 1 Korean Socialist), 1 Unification party member (Rightist), and 2 Liberals (both of them were in jail pending trial for election frauds). Councilors numbered 58: 31 Democrats, 21 independents, 4 Liberals, 1 Popular Socialist, and 1 member of the National League of Progressives. The election constituted a landslide victory for the Democratic party.

The Democrat-controlled parliament (the first bicameral legislative body) was convened on August 8. The House of Councilors elected George Paik, independent and former president of Yunsei University, as president; Democrat Kwak Sang-hoon was elected chairman of the House of Representatives. The parliament's first order of business was to select, within five days, a president who would then nominate a prime minister. After much factional struggling over the position of president and prime minister between the old guard and young group or moderates, a compromise was reached: Yun Po-sun, leader of the old guard, became president, and Chang Myun, leader of the moderates, prime minister. On August 12 Yun was elected president by 208 votes out of 250 in the joint session, which was more than the necessary two-thirds. The next day Yun was inaugurated.

On August 16 President Yun, contrary to the agreement between the old guard and the moderates, nominated his fellow old guard Kim Do-yun as prime minister, by-passing Chang Myun. The House of Representatives, however, rejected Kim by a vote of 111 to 112, with one invalid, out of 227 votes. The necessary simple majority was 114. The defeat was the result of an alliance of the Democratic party moderates and the independents. On August 18 President Yun nominated Chang Myun as prime minister. Chang was approved by a vote of 117 to 107, with 1 abstention, out of 225. This was a very small victory for the moderates over the old guard, won with the help of independent votes.

On August 23 Chang organized a fourteen-man cabinet with one old guard, two independents, and twelve moderates from among his own followers.[20] Minister of Foreign Affairs Chung Il-hyung was an American-educated former minister of the Methodist Church and had served as director of civil service under the American military government as well as under the South Korean interim government. He had been one of the leaders of the Young Korean Academy, a moderate group of the Democratic party; and he had been a member of the South Korean assembly since 1948 and was reelected to the House of Representatives in the last election.

The minister of education was Dr. Oh Chun-suk, an American-trained educator who had served as director of the educational department in the South Korean interim government. The minister of interior was Japanese-educated Hong Ik-pyo, who had served as a member of the Constitution Draft Committee and had been elected twice to the assembly.

Minister of Defense Hyun Suk-ho, a graduate of the Keijo Imperial University during the Japanese administration, had been a government official for many years with different positions during Japanese domination. He was considered one of the brain trust of Prime Minister Chang.

The minister of justice was Cho Chai-chun, a graduate of the Japanese Chuo University and an attorney who had served as governor of north Kyongsang province in the South Korean interim government. He had been a spokesman for the Democratic party as the head of the propaganda section of the party.

Minister of Finance Kim Yung-sun graduated in law from Keijo Imperial University and had been a government official for many years during the Japanese administration. He had no experience in finance.

The minister of reconstruction was Chu Yo-han, a China-educated writer who had been an editor-in-chief of *Dong A Ilbo* and *Chosun Ilbo*. He was one of the leading members of the Young Korea Academy as well as of the Democratic party. He became another member of Chang's brain trust.

The minister of commerce and industry was Lee Tai-yong. He was a graduate of Keijo Imperial University and had been a government official during and after the Japanese administration, occupying such positions as bureau chief of financial affairs of the Department of Communication and trustee of the Korean Electric Company. He had been an assemblyman for more than four years during Rhee's regime and had been reelected to the House of Representatives.

The minister of agriculture and forestry was Park Jae-hwan, a graduate of Doshisha University in Kyoto, Japan.

The minister of health and social affairs was Shin Hyun-don, a graduate of Seoul Medical College and a physician.

The minister of transportation was Chung Hyun-ju, a graduate of the Japanese Chuo University, who had been a member of the assembly twice and had served as chairman of the Constitutional Draft Committee. He was the only old guard cabinet member but later terminated his relationship with the old guard.

Minister without portfolio Kim Sun-tai was a graduate of Nihon University and had been a lawyer. He had served as a judge of a district court.

The minister of communication was Lee Sang-chul, a graduate of Meiji University in Tokyo. He had been a newspaperman and had no experience in government work.

Chief Cabinet Secretary Oh Yi-yong was a graduate of Business College in Kobe, Japan, and had been head of the Korea Trust Bank. He also was a member of Prime Minister Chang's brain trust.

Prime Minister Chang announced new foreign and domestic policies:[21] the holding of a general election throughout Korea under the supervision of the United Nations to reunite the country; the reopening of negotiation between Korea and Japan to establish normal diplomatic relations; and the establishment of diplomatic relations with neutral Afro-Asian countries. The administration favored a complete reorganization of the police force so that it would be politically neutral, the reorganization of the administration for simplification and efficiency, the adoption of the principle that government positions should be filled in accordance with individual ability, the prosecution of the ring leaders of the March 15 election frauds and of profiteers and tax evaders during the Rhee administration, and the restoration of local autonomy. The new administration also outlined its economic policies: rapid development of heavy industry, especially of electric power plants, fertilizer plants, and coal and mining industries; and establishment of a National Reconstruction Service for road building, land reformation, water-resources development, and rural-community development. To carry out this plan the administration called for more foreign aid, private capital investment, and a reduction of the armed forces.

The general reaction to Chang's administration was unfavorable from the beginning. The old guard, as was to be expected, denounced the administration as being a bureaucratic institution dominated by Japanese-trained officials, and attacked Prime Minister Chang for "thinking more about his personal friends than about the nation." They threatened to pass a nonconfidence vote against the administration. Criticism of the administration also came from a faction within Chang's own group, the "juniors," who had been excluded from cabinet posts although they had played an important role in obtaining votes from the independents to elect Chang prime minister. They charged that the administration was weak, and that it was composed of Chang's friends. They threatened to form a new political group.

Even the general public was critical of the administration, because it appeared incapable of carrying out the promised socioeconomic reforms. The public was also disappointed with the Democratic party leaders in parliament, because they engaged in factional fights. Less than ten days after Chang had formed his cabinet, the Democratic party split into three groups: the old guard headed by Kim Do-yun, the unsuccessful candidate for prime minister; the Chang Myun group, backed by the Young Korea Academy and Catholic members; and the "junior" group composed of the young Democrats who were dissatisfied with the other two factions. (Later this group again divided into old guard juniors and new faction juniors.)

Chang again tried to bring about party unity by reorganizing his cabinet as a coalition. In September a coalition cabinet was formed consisting of five old guards in the ministries of defense, reconstruction, health and social services, transportation, and communication; Chang filled the remaining posts with the previous ministers. Thus the new cabinet was composed of five old guards, two independents, and eight of Chang's own group.

The old guard was not satisfied with the new cabinet and charged that the new government was still dominated by Chang's friends. Some die-hard old guards insisted on the establishment of a separate party and formed the New People's party with Kim Do-yun as chief. More than eighty members of the House of Representatives joined this party, most of them former Democrats. About the same number of Democrats, loyal to Chang's administration, remained in the Democratic party. The New People's party became strong opposition for the government.

The local elections held in January 1961 indicated that the people were discontented with the administration: nearly half of the qualified voters did not vote and independent candidates defeated the candidates of the New People's party and the Democratic party. The government party, the Democrats, suffered most.

The coalition government collapsed when the old guard recalled its five cabinet members, of which four responded. Prime Minister Chang then formed his third cabinet from members of his own party in addition to two pro-Democratic independents. But this third cabinet was the weakest of all. Factionalism within the Democratic party had not been overcome, and many of the "junior" group leaders refused to accept posts in the cabinet.

The prime minister appealed to the people for their support of the administration and asked to give it time to fulfill its promises—"its revolutionary tasks." As a new administration policy, the government announced a five-year plan for economic reconstruction. But before the administration had a chance to put the new policy into practice, a coup d'etat on May 16 brought the Second Republic to an end.

Characteristics of the Second Republic. The Second Republic came into being as a result of the student revolution which brought to an end Syngman Rhee's twelve-year-old dictatorship. As mentioned before, the revolution was a revolt of the younger generation against the older generation—that is, against the corrupt and incompetent ruling class. One of the shortcomings of the revolution was that no new political forces or parties which could challenge the supremacy of the old political forces emerged from the student movement. Consequently, the Second Republic was established and dominated by one of the old political forces, the Democrats. This meant, among other things, that the Second Republic was not a government of the people by the people, and for the people; it had no genuine political and economic reform programs to further the interests of the people.

All top positions went to Koreans educated in the United States or England: Yun Po-sun, a graduate of Edinborough University, was president; Chang Myun, a graduate of Manhattan University, was prime minister; and Chung Il-hyung, another American university graduate, was minister of foreign affairs. None of them was a nationally recognized political leader: most of them had been school teachers during the Japanese administration. They had begun to participate in politics after liberation in 1945; all of them had originally supported Syngman Rhee and served in his administration but gradually had become his political foes.

Twelve out of fourteen cabinet ministers had graduated from universities under Japanese control, and many had worked with the Japanese administration. One-third of the ministers were law and political science graduates of Keijo Imperial University. All fourteen cabinet ministers had worked at one time or another with the American military government as well as with the Republic of Korea. They were the trained and experienced bureaucrats.

However, under the military government and the Rhee administration most of them had been "underdog bureaucrats," because they spoke no English, which was one of the conditions for becoming a higher official in the military government. Many of them had been members of the Democratic party, opposed to Rhee's Liberal party. Following the establishment of the Second Republic, all became heads of departments, and many became corrupt and practiced political favoritism.

The factionalism in the Democratic party caused the split of the party into two groups. Thereafter, the main concern of Chang's administration was how to survive by securing a simple majority vote in the House of Representatives in the event of a nonconfidence vote. He neglected to carry out the socioeconomic reforms.

CHAPTER 14

THE MILITARY COUP D'ETAT

Economic and Political Conditions on the Eve of the Coup. In less than one year the Second Republic became so corrupt and incompetent that economic deterioration, social unrest, and political instability were rampant.[1] In April 1961 more than four million city dwellers representing 28 percent of the total working labor force were unemployed. Business and industry stagnated because of shortages of capital and electric power: industrial production declined 75 percent, and many small and middle-sized business establishments went bankrupt. Meanwhile, living costs went up; the price index had risen 30 percent since the Student Revolution the year before. In the rural areas, more than five million farmers were desperate—caught between crop failures and payment of exorbitant interest on loans (in some cases as high as 80 percent per year). Large numbers of the rural population were on the brink of starvation.

As the first anniversary of the Student Revolution approached, a rumor of another uprising circulated. The number of newspapers and periodicals had mushroomed from 592 to 1,380 during the previous ten months, and some of the irresponsible ones attacked everything and everybody. Some left-wing papers stirred up anti-American sentiments and advocated pro-Communist policies of unification. Antigovernment demonstrations led by the Socialist party and student organizations took place in many major cities in protest against a new government bill—"the provisional special law against Communism." Organized hoodlums, acting as political agents for Rhee's administration, reappeared in the major cities, threatening the general public and demanding money through blackmail. Dancing halls, bars, coffee shops, and movie theaters proliferated; stores were filled with imported luxury articles for the rich. The haves and have-nots had never been divided more sharply. The administration was unable to cope with the mounting social unrest and the dissatisfaction of the people. The police were too weak to keep law and order.

Politically the Chang administration was confused. As pointed out previously, Chang had been elected prime minister by a three-vote margin in the Democrat-dominated House of Representatives, and the Democratic party was split by a number of factions. Chang changed his cabinet several times, appointing some faction leaders to posts; but the changes brought more factionalism and destroyed the continuity of the administration.

The prosecution of the wrongdoers (including the ringleaders of the rigged election of March 15 and the illegal profiteers of the Rhee administration) was not as thoroughly carried out as the administration had promised. The Democratic party's election promises to accomplish the goals of the April revolution—cleaning up corruption and establishing political democracy and economic reconstruction—became empty words.

The people's disapproval of the Democratic administration was demonstrated in the local elections, which were held less than four months after the new administration came into power: about half of the voters stayed home on election day, and most of Chang's candidates lost. The incompetence of the national legislative body was also demonstrated when the students wounded during the April revolution seized the chairman's rostrum and demanded the dissolution of the House of Representatives unless factional fights were stopped and work done for constructive legislation.

The administration suffered also in diplomacy. The negotiations with Japan to improve relations were almost broken off because Japan insisted on carrying out its commitment to send Korean residents in Japan to North Korea. And the Japanese economic mission to South Korea was called off because of strong anti-Japanese demonstrations throughout the country. The United Nations for the first time invited North Korean representatives to take part in the debate on the Korean issue in spite of opposition by the South Korean government.

It is against this background that the rise of the unification movement in South Korea has to be discussed. The Council for Independence and National Unification was formed by the Socialist parties, the student organizations, the Association for Permanent Neutralization of Korea, and the labor unions.

Some members of the New People's party (old guard of the former Democratic party) joined. Many intellectuals were interested in U.S. Senator Mansfield's idea of a solution to the problem of Korean unification through neutralization on the Austrian pattern.

The council demanded an opening of trade between North and South and exchanges of cultural missions, sports teams, and newspaper correspondents before any formal discussion on the unification issue; in due time a free general election should be held to unify the country.

On May 5 the National Student League for Unification passed a resolution stating that a North-South Student Conference should be held on May 20 in Panmunjom by delegates of the students of the two sections. Later, a national rally was held in Seoul to send off the South Korean student delegates to the conference.[2]

The North Korean government announced that it would support the student conference and invited the South Korean student delegates to North Korea, guaranteeing their personal safety and freedom to travel anywhere in the North. The South Korean government vacillated. It hesitated to suppress the student unification movement because the student demonstration of April 1960 had brought down the Rhee regime and had brought the Democrats into power, yet the Chang administration did not have the courage to support the student movement because it was afraid to be charged with aiding a "Communist-oriented political plot."

The Coup. Information on the military coup of May 16, 1961, is still incomplete. But it is possible to put the inside story together from newspapers, personal observation, and some official publications.[3] The original plan for the coup was worked out by nine young army officers, ranking from lieutenant to major general, soon after the rigged election of March 15, 1960. Their aim was to overthrow the Syngman Rhee regime. However, the plan was temporarily postponed when the April Student Revolution brought about the downfall of the Rhee government. The leaders of the coup expected that an honest and efficient new government would follow after the revolution. But when the new administration became as corrupt and weak as the previous one, the nine officers met again in secret to evaluate the situation. They recruited 250 officers of all ranks and decided that "their duty was to carry out a military revolution to save the country from eventual Communist domination."

According to one source, the coup was to be carried out on April 19, the first anniversary of the Student Revolution, but was changed to May 1961. May 13 was the fixed day, but it was delayed three more days. May 16 was considered the best time because the North-South Korean Student Conference was scheduled for May 20 in Panmunjom, and the coup was to be carried out before the conference.

The chief engineer of the coup was a forty-four-year-old major general, Park Chung-hee, then vice-commander of the Second Army. He received his military training in the Manchukuo Military Academy and the Japanese Imperial Military Academy; he was discharged with the rank of first lieutenant from the Japanese army at the end of World War II; after returning to Korea he entered the Korean Military Academy, and later he also received an advanced training course at the U.S. Artillery School, Fort Sill, Oklahoma.[4] He was not a party man during the Rhee administration, and he seldom attended the popular American cocktail gatherings; he was considered one of the few Korean military officers who did not take part in corrupt practices.

There were more than a dozen young army officers under General Park, known as members of the eighth graduating class of the Korean Military Academy; they acted as Park's advisers. Until 1963 Col. Kim Chong-pill (a nephew of General Park), chief of the Central Intelligence Service, was the second man of the junta.

As a matter of strategy, General Park used Lt. Gen. Chang Do-young, who had been appointed army chief of staff by Prime Minister Chang Myun, as leader of the coup d'etat, forcing him at gun point during the early hours of the upheaval to pretend to lead the uprising. At 3 A.M. on May 16, about 3,500 soldiers (less than 0.5 percent of the armed forces), including infantry, marines, and paratroopers, moved into Seoul. They occupied all important government buildings and met practically no resistance. When the paratroopers entered Bando Hotel, they found that Prime Minister Chang had escaped. President Yun was detained in his official residence and three out of fifteen ministers (foreign, defense, and communication) were arrested. At 5

A.M. Lt. Gen. Chang Do-young announced by radio that the Republic of Korea's armed forces had taken over the government, because "we can no longer trust corrupt and incapable politicians."[5]

A six-point revolutionary pledge, which will be discussed later, was announced. Martial law was declared in the name of the chairman of the military revolutionary junta, General Chang. Both houses of the national assembly and all provincial legislatures were dissolved; all political parties, social organizations, student organizations, and labor unions were outlawed; all newspapers and publications were subject to censorship; the currency was frozen; all seaports and airports were closed; all travel abroad by Koreans was banned; a dusk-to-dawn curfew was imposed; and the arrest of the prime minister and his cabinet members was ordered.

On May 18 Prime Minister Chang emerged from his hiding place, announcing that "I and the cabinet have decided to resign, assuming moral and political responsibilities for what has happened. . . . It is our sincere hope that no blood will be shed."[6] Next day President Yun also announced his resignation. But the president was immediately forced to withdraw his resignation by the military junta, which wanted to avoid international difficulties. The retention of the president as head of state would relieve the military junta of the need to obtain recognition from the United States and other governments.

Attitude of the U.S. Government. The official attitude of the United States government, as in the case of the Student Revolution, was a decisive factor in the success of the military coup. Since the Korean war, the South Korean armed forces had been under the authority of the United Nations command; these forces had been given only two days' supplies of ammunition and gasoline at one time since the truce in 1953; the Korean First Army, the strongest army in the South Korean armed forces, took a neutral position during the coup, abiding by the order of the U.N. command.

General Magruder, commander of the United States and the United Nations forces in Korea, issued the following statement on May 16 at 7 A.M.: "I request all soldiers under my command to support the duly recognized government of Korea headed by Prime Minister Chang Myun. . . . I also urge the Korea military chiefs to use their authority and influence to see that control is immediately turned back to the governmental authorities so that order is restored in the armed forces."[7] On the same day Marshal Green, chargé d'affairs at the U.S. embassy in Seoul, said, "I wish to make it emphatically clear that the United States supports the constitutional government of the Republic of Korea elected by the people last July."[8]

In Washington the State Department spokesman, Lincoln White, expressed the view that the two statements were "entirely within the scope of their authority but the situation is so fluid and unclear that we are unable to make substantive comments on it."[9] On May 18 Acting Secretary of State Chester Bowlcs said that he assumed the United States would recognize the junta as a *fait accompli* since "we can't run the world or move in and out of situations as an omnipotent power."[10] On the same day, the Korean ambassador to the United States, Dr. Chang Lee-wook, submitted his resignation.[11]

There was no sign of opposition to the military junta, and the public generally took an attitude of indifference. Only a few individuals and social groups voiced support of the junta. Under these circumstances, the junta became the de facto government of South Korea.

The Structure and Objectives of the Military Junta. When the military junta seized power, it was composed of only five army generals. Soon this number increased to fourteen, including air, navy, and marine corps generals. At that time, Gen. Chang Do-young became the chairman of junta and Gen. Park Chung-hee vice-chairman.

The junta proclaimed the Law Regarding Extraordinary Measures for National Reconstruction, by which the Supreme Council for National Reconstruction was established as the ruling body of South Korea.[12] The Supreme Council was composed of thirty-two officers on active duty, six lieutenant generals, five major generals, eight brigadier generals, and seven colonels.

As a policy-making organ for the Supreme Council, six standing committees were established and placed under its jurisdiction.

For executive functions a military cabinet was formed: General Chang became chief of the cabinet and was later replaced by Gen. Song Yoo-chan (Song, retired from the army, lived in the United States before the coup d'etat took place.) Only three out of fifteen cabinet members were civilians.

Provincial governors and city mayors were replaced by military men, and the heads of government-owned enterprises were also replaced by generals and colonels. Mostly military men were appointed as new diplomats, from ambassador to consul general. By decree of the Supreme Council for National Reconstruction, a Revolutionary Court was established to try "anti-state or counter-revolutionary activities." Thus the Supreme Council for National Reconstruction became the supreme governing organ in South Korea, exercising executive, legislative, and judicial power on behalf of the Republic of Korea. The Supreme Council was to exercise these powers until "the establishment of a government following the composition of the National Assembly by means of a general election to be held after the completion of the task of the May 16 Military Revolution."

The military junta announced a revolutionary plan of six points known as "Revolutionary Pledges."[13] These were (1) opposition to Communism, (2) strengthening of relations with the United States, (3) elimination of corruption, (4) development of a self-sustaining economy, (5) national unification, and (6) eventual restoration of civilian government.

General Park, who succeeded to the chairmanship of the Supreme Council for National Reconstruction after purging the Gen. Chang Do-young clique, declared that in order to achieve those objectives the military junta "had to adopt exceptional measures to seize the reins of power by force and turn over the legislative, administrative, and judicial powers exclusively to the revolutionary government."[14] On August 12, 1962, General Park made public the fact that the military junta would turn over the government to civilians in the summer of 1963. After retiring from the army, General Park ran for president in 1963 as a civilian and was elected.

"Cleaning Up" Measures. The junta suspended the constitution of the Second Republic of Korea and announced that South Korea would be ruled by the decrees of the Supreme Council for National Reconstruction. The junta dissolved all fifteen political parties and 230 social, labor, and student organizations. Within the week the junta seized power, more than twenty-two thousand persons were arrested: among them more than two thousand were charged with being Communists, including some members of the

Chang cabinet as well as members of the socialist parties; more than five hundred teachers and one hundred students were accused of being leftists, because they had advocated peaceful unification with the North Korean regime.

All outdoor and indoor assemblies and meetings were forbidden. All publications were censored by the junta. More than nine hundred newspapers and news agencies and magazines were outlawed; only eighty-two newspapers and news agencies were permitted to continue operation. More than 150 newsmen were charged with violation of the press decree, and arrested. The junta fired more than forty-one thousand government employees as corruptionists, draft evaders, concubine keepers, and politically incompetent public officers.

The junta assumed the authority to hire and fire teachers and to change curriculums in private and public schools. College and university professors and instructors were required to submit an annual treatise or research product to secure reappointment or promotion. Teachers had to retire at sixty. As a result, more than 500 teachers, including 107 professors and many college and university presidents, lost their positions. Entrance examinations for high school, university, and college were to be conducted by the Ministry of Education; the number of university and college students was reduced to 50,000 from more than 100,000. Bachelor degrees were to be given to those who passed examinations conducted by the Ministry of Education, which would be held nationwide on a certain day. Seventy percent of the students were required to take vocational training courses, and 30 percent liberal arts.

In 1962 seven colleges and universities were closed, and twelve university presidents dismissed on charges of financial mismanagement. Several colleges and universities were forced to merge with big universities; for example, the Pusan Fishery College and the Pusan Teachers College merged into Pusan National University. No political activities are allowed for students and teachers. All students were required to wear school uniforms.

More than thirty heads and managers of big corporations were placed under arrest and charged with profiteering and tax evasion. Many bank presidents were arrested on the ground that they loaned or gave away money to political party leaders during the elections. As a result, hundreds of big and small enterprises suspended operations. The South Korean economy plunged into chaos at the end of 1961. Later most of the businessmen were released when they promised to cooperate with the military government's reconstruction plans.

Hundreds of coffee shops, bars, and dancing halls were ordered closed; the sale of foreign cigarettes and luxury articles was prohibited.

The Junta Launches Reform Measures. In an article entitled "Directions of the National Movement" General Park stated one of the basic reform principles of the junta: "economy first and democracy second."[15] Park wrote that the reconstruction of the economy was "a basic and prerequisite condition for a genuine free democracy that guarantees man's freedom and dignity."[16] He went on to say that the objective of the national movement was to achieve "social justice" and to build "a welfare state for the greatest benefit to the greatest number possible."[17] To achieve these objectives, he said that "the economy must be subject to planning and adjustment by the state" and that efficiency of management and modern technology must be introduced as "an absolute necessity"; he emphasized public responsibility and the duties of the citizen rather than individual freedoms and rights, because a rapid modernization of South Korea "must rely on cooperation in democratic government and establishment of a planned economy."[18]

The junta announced a series of drastic reforms covering politics, economics, social structure, and education. The junta concentrated, however, on two major fields, economic reconstruction and moral regeneration. The junta stated that "Korea's economic order will continue to be free and competitive with strong government participation" and that the military government "intends to prevent business monopolies detrimental to the public welfare and to enhance with positive measures the economic conditions of rural and fishery communities."[19] The ultimate goal of the military revolution was to establish a welfare state so that the "basic needs of all people can be satisfied."[20]

Immediately following the coup d'etat, all bank deposits were frozen, grain prices were controlled by decree, and relief grains were distributed to needy families. The military government adopted a new budget system based on the reduction of nonessential expenditures and the increase of constructive projects; a new tax system became effective—taxpayers were to file tax returns voluntarily, and optional tax assessments were abolished. To eliminate tax evasion, the government made public all the taxpayers who were delinquent during the previous administration. The government banned the import of luxury articles (such as foreign cigarettes) and encouraged the use of native products. Interest rates of savings deposits were increased to make saving attractive.

A decree covering "usurious debt settlements" invited farmers and fishermen to lessen their burdens by reporting their debts to the government; the government then made low interest loans available to them. A new fertilizer supply system based on exchanging fertilizer for grain became effective, and the farmers were enabled to get necessary fertilizer.

In the industrial field the government concentrated on the rapid development of hydroelectric power plants, coal, and fertilizer plants. To reduce operating costs and to increase efficiency, the three government-owned electric companies merged. The government also provided loans to small and medium-sized enterprises to develop middle-class business.

The government also announced a five-year plan to start in 1962. As will be discussed more thoroughly later, the general objectives of the plan were to step up the rate of economic growth 7.2 percent annually, lay a foundation for further economic development, reduce unemployment, and lower the nation's deficit on external accounts. The total capital investment was estimated at $2.5 billion, the government sector accounting for about 46 percent, the private sector for 54 percent; native capital resources accounted for 72 percent and foreign investment for 28 percent. The allocation of the capital was 42.1 percent for light industry, 41.5 percent for heavy industry, and 16.4 percent for agriculture, forestry, and fisheries. The government emphasized that the first five-year plan would endeavor to build an industrial base principally through expansion of energy production, with the major emphasis laid on electric power and increase of agricultural production.

The junta launched a seven-point "moral regeneration" program[21] to encourage an austere life, inspire diligence, promote a creative and productive life, respect native customs, enhance national morality, and improve individual physical fitness. To carry out this program, the junta established a National Reconstruction Movement headquarters in Seoul under Dr. Yu Chin-o, president of Korea University. More than eighty-five hundred civic leaders were appointed by the junta as staff members of the movement, and everyone was asked to join in this "spontaneous movement in a spontaneous society." The movement was to be organized in block units in every city, town, and village throughout the country, and one member of each family was to be present at the meetings. College students were also asked to participate in the movement, and so-called voluntary student bands were sent out to the countryside to explain the seven-point program to the farmers.

Views of the Military Take-Over. The nature of the military coup has been judged in two ways.[22] Some see nothing but a reactionary power move led by a handful of military opportunists who suffered from a lack of revolutionary theory. Therefore, the military coup is not seen as either a political or social revolution. The so-called six-point revolutionary pledge is nothing new, because the corrupted Rhee government had advocated the same things —anti-Communism, elimination of official corruption, development of a self-supporting economy, and unification of the country by force; the deposed Chang Myun administration also advocated practically the same, and in fact a five-year economic development plan was adopted by the Chang government under its "economics-first policy."

According to this view, the seven-point moral regeneration program is not new either. Since the liberation in 1945, religious, educational, and political leaders have continually launched "new-life movements" based on the principles of individual responsibility in private and public life and an austere and honest life. Thus both the junta's six-point pledge and its seven-point program are said to be repetitions of former plans.

The junta criticized Chang's Democratic administration as corrupt and incompetent. Official corruption has been, no doubt, a widespread disease in South Korea. But the army officers were perhaps the most corrupt sector of the government during the Rhee and Chang administrations. However, when it was found that the seven junta-appointed officials of the Investigating Committee on Illegal Profiteers were paid off with 2.7 million dollars by businessmen, all seven were indicted by the Military Court. Soon after this case, another five army generals and one vice-admiral were found guilty by the Military Court of making illegal profits.

Factionalism and nepotism also were widespread in the armed forces. During the Rhee administration most high military officials, including the army chief of staff, the commanding general, and the provost marshal, acted as political agents for the Liberal party and, in every election, were known as "political generals."

The military government retained close ties with Syngman Rhee's supporters. Many former officers under Rhee returned to new positions: Kim Yu-taik, former Korean minister to Japan, was appointed minister of finance in the military cabinet; Cho Chin-man, the new Supreme Court chief justice, served as minister of justice under Rhee; the new premier, Song Yoo-chan, was army chief of staff under the Rhee regime; Rim Byung-gik (Bean Rim), chief adviser of the Korean delegation to the United Nations, was ambassador to the United Nations in the Rhee government; and Gen. Chung Ill-kwan, the Korean ambassador to the United States, was former army chief of staff and ambassador to Turkey under Rhee. Thus, according to the first view, the junta regime was dominated by two reactionary groups: a young and ambitious military fascist group and an authoritarian civilian clique. The South Korean economy was controlled once again by the giants who had become millionaires during the Rhee administration through illegal profits and had been condemned by the military government.

The second view accepts the military coup d'etat as the inevitable historical result of thirteen years of complete failure in democratic government. During the more than two thousand years of recorded history, the Korean people lived in a rigid feudal society. As a result, until the end of World War II the people had never had an opportunity to participate in politics. After the establishment of a democratic form of government, the majority of the people were not prepared to exercise properly the freedoms and rights that maintain a democratic system. At the same time, the political leaders lacked the experience and ability to run a democratic government. They fostered corruption, favoritism, and factionalism, abusing their positions and public funds.

The April Student Revolution overthrew the corrupt Rhee government, but the new Chang government became equally corrupt. During the Chang period the left-wing-dominated unification movement became strong, but the government had no power to curb it. According to this view, the coup d'etat was inevitable under these circumstances for the following reasons: (1) the armed forces were the only organized power to take over the government; (2) only the armed forces were capable, by training, of reorganizing the administration into one based on efficiency and integrity; and (3) only the armed forces were strong enough to suppress Communist infiltration and subversion. Those who hold this view argue that the only possible alternative to the military coup at that time would have been a Communist take-over of the Republic of Korea by peaceful unification or by subversion. Therefore the military take-over was "a necessary evil" to save the country from Communism.

General Park explained that "the May 16 military revolution is like a medical operation" to cure a sick person: "This revolution is designed to perform a full-dress operation for the revival of the freedoms and rights of the state and the people at a time when the nation is confronted with a total destruction and the people's rights are miserably trampled down." He went on to say that "a medical operation is not a pleasant recreation, but to sacrifice a cause for the attainment of a greater cause can be pardonable as a necessary evil."[23] Thus, according to General Park's view, the coup d'etat aimed at saving Korea from the Communists and at establishing a true democracy.

However, many Koreans take a dim view of the military take-over. The coup meant a backseat for democracy in South Korea. Under the nose of the United States military command, a handful of Korean army officials trained by the United States seized power in the name of patriotism and anti-Communism, and established an absolute military dictatorship, ruling twenty-five million people by decree. The individual freedoms and rights, the essential elements of democracy, which the military government had claimed as its goal, were completely denied under its rule.

The Korean people asked: Who are the sick persons requiring an operation? They believed that the majority of Koreans were in good health and needed no surgery and that the small ruling class, composed of privileged civilian and military groups from the Rhee and Chang administrations, were the sick ones. The real patients were the rulers, not the ruled.

CHAPTER 15

SOUTH KOREA'S ECONOMY

The Predominantly Agrarian Economy. Korea has had an agricultural economy for centuries. Under the land nationalization system of the Yi dynasty, the land belonged to the state in theory, but in practice the aristocratic Confucian bureaucrats retained control of the land as landlords and exploited farmers through taxation and rent in kind.

Following the Korea-Japan Commercial Treaty (the Kanghwa-do treaty) in 1876, many Western countries, including the United States, Britain, Germany, France, and Russia, concluded commercial treaties with Korea. Korea became an open market for contending capitalist countries. But the Japanese, being on the ground first, enjoyed many advantages. Japanese merchandise poured into the Korean peninsula without restriction, because in the treaty the Yi regime had agreed not to impose tariffs on Japanese goods. Many Japanese merchants in Korea engaged in usurious practices and gradually became big landlords by seizing farm land when the owners could not pay their debts.

Following the annexation of Korea in 1910, the Japanese government-general itself became the largest landowner as a result of the Land Survey Project, which took away land from Korean farmers.[1] The government-general then sold the lands at low prices or gave them away to Japanese land corporations and to private Japanese. During the thirty-five years of Japanese rule, Japanese landlords gained possession of more than 25 percent of the best land. The semifeudal tenancy system remained: the relationship of landlord and tenant was that of master and servant; land lease rights were not recognized for tenants; and 75 percent of the population were farmers, of whom 50 percent were tenants.

Agricultural production accounted for about 46 percent of the gross national product. More than one-half of agricultural products, mainly rice, was exported to Japan. Therefore, during the Japanese administration the Korean agrarian economy continued to be based on feudal landlordism and primitive cultivating methods.

Japanese War Industry. The Yi dynasty made no attempt to develop industry and commerce during its five-hundred-year rule. The modern industrial revolution never took place in Korea, and no native merchant class or business establishments came into being. Hence when foreign merchandise poured into the peninsula, the native handicraft industry went completely out of business.

For the first two decades (from 1910 to 1930), the Japanese were not interested in the industrialization of Korea. They wanted to turn the peninsula into an exclusive market for their industrial products. Japan also needed Korea's raw materials for its industry; Korea's mineral resources, such as anthracite and lignite coal, iron ore, copper, tungsten, gold, and silver, were exploited at a high rate with the help of Japanese government subsidies. At the same time, industrial facilities were developed for supplying consumer wants, for processing raw materials, and for manufacturing component parts for final assembly in Japan. The major emphasis was placed on the development of food-processing plants, like the rice-refining factories in southern Korea; on the development of chemical factories, such as the fertilizer plants in northern Korea; and on the development of textile mills in central Korea. The foodstuff industry became the first-ranking industry, constituting 57.1 percent of the entire Korean industrial capacity.

For military purposes the Japanese administration concentrated on the construction of railway transportation and communication facilities which linked Korea to northern Manchuria. During the next decade—that of the 1931 Manchurian "Incident," the 1937 Sino-Japanese War, and the 1941 Pacific War—Korea's economy was rapidly adapted to Japanese wartime needs. Major emphasis was placed on the development of the munitions industry, the development of the heavy chemical industry, and on the construction of a giant hydroelectric plant, utilizing the Yalu River in northern Korea. In the meantime, the production of light metals—aluminum and magnesium—was encouraged by tax exemption and direct government subsidies. Gold production also was boosted during this period because

Korean gold was one of the main sources of foreign exchange needed for strategic military materials from abroad. As the war progressed, consumer goods industries were virtually at a standstill and began to deteriorate.

In 1945 Japan came into practically full possession of the Korean economy: Japanese nationals possessed 85 percent of the total wealth of Korea; 96.9 percent of export and import trade was in the hands of Japanese; Japanese capital investment in consumer industry was 90 percent, in heavy industry 99 percent.[2]

The Unnatural Postwar Division of Korea. The Korean peninsula covers 85,285 square miles, roughly the size of Minnesota. It is surrounded by the major powers of Asia—Japan, China, and Russia, each interested in controlling the peninsula because of its strategic location in the Far East. The total population is about thirty-six million, of which twenty-eight million are in the South.

Because of mountains and hills, only one-fifth of the land can be cultivated. Generally, mountainous northern Korea is referred to as the industrial zone, having rich mineral resources and potential hydroelectric power; southern Korea is referred to as the agricultural zone, blessed with rich soil and mild climate. The Korean peninsula has about fifty-four hundred miles of coastline; good harbors are on the south and west coasts but few on the east coast. Korea has a variety of mineral deposits; it is the world's fifth largest gold producer and has considerable amounts of coal and copper. It is lacking in petroleum. Many Korean economists maintain that the natural resources of the peninsula could be developed so as to make the country self-sufficient.

The division at the 38th parallel destroyed national unity, brought war, and produced many other tragedies. One of the most serious results of the division has been the crippling of the economy, because neither zone can by itself establish economic independence.[3] Northern Korea, as mentioned above, produced 86 percent of the heavy industry output, while southern Korea produced 75 percent of the light industry output. The south had almost three times as large an area of irrigated rice land as the north. The consumer-goods industry of the south depended on northern electric power and semifinished materials; in return, the north depended heavily on southern consumer products. The southern farmers depended on the chemical fertilizers produced in the north, while the north needed rice from the south. Thus the two zones were complementary and interdependent. This means, then, that as long as the peninsula remains divided it will be difficult, if not impossible, for Korea to attain a normal standard of living.

Economic Confusion during U.S. Occupation (1945–48). When the U.S. Army landed at Inchun on September 9, 1945, South Korea was in a state of economic collapse. As a result of the breakdown of the Japanese economic system when the Japanese retreated from Korea, industrial production had collapsed, currency had become inflated, the Japanese rationing and price system had broken down, Japanese war surplus goods had disappeared into the black markets, and public utilities and communication and transportation systems had become badly depreciated and in need of repairs or replacement. Technically trained personnel both in operation and management were lacking.

Moreover the population of southern Korea had increased by heavy immigration of northern political refugees and repatriates from China and Japan. Between 1945 and 1948 the population jumped by 20 percent to nearly twenty million in an area of thirty-seven thousand square miles. Many were on the edge of starvation.

The American military authorities set forth three economic objectives: revival of industrial production to the prewar level; efficient operation of public transportation and communication systems, especially the railroad; and increase of the electric-power output.[4] To achieve some of these objectives, coal was imported from Japan and commercial fertilizer from the United States. In the meantime the military government adopted a policy of compulsory grain collection and of rationing to meet the food shortage in the urban areas. The military government also introduced a relief program for South Korea called GARIOA (Government Appropriation for Relief in Occupied Areas) and distributed surplus civilian goods. United States aid to South Korea amounted to $310 million during the three and one-half years of occupation.

One of the principal problems of the occupation authorities was how to dispose of former Japanese property. The Japanese government-general and Japanese nationals owned about $1,500 million worth of property, which included industrial, commercial, financial, mining, and transportation enterprises, and also farm lands and public buildings. This Japanese property posed many legal and administrative problems. In addition, there were political implications, because the Korean people believed that the Japanese property, whether private or public, was obtained by exploitation of Koreans and Korean natural resources; and that, therefore, this property should be used for the benefit of the Korean people as a whole. Even many right-wing political groups favored public ownership of Japanese-owned industries, and distribution of Japanese-owned land through a land reform. All left-wing groups, as might be expected, demanded free distribution of land to the landless peasants at once, and immediate transfer of all Japanese property to the "People's Republic," which was established in Seoul before the American army landed. Under these circumstances, the American military government promulgated a series of ordinances: the December (1945) ordinance stated that the title to Japanese property "was vested in the American Military Government which would hold them on a custodial basis in behalf of the future government of Korea."[5] Soon the Office of the Property Custodian was established and entrusted with general responsibility for the care and administration of Japanese property. The Material Control Corporation was set up and given authority to take charge of all surrendered or abandoned Japanese movable or tangible possessions, such as army supplies and equipment, warehouse stocks of foodstuffs, building supplies, clothing, and household items. The Oriental Development Company, a giant Japanese corporation, changed its name to New Korea Company and took charge of all former Japanese farmlands. The Department of Commerce of the military government assumed jurisdiction over former Japanese extractive and manufacturing establishments; the Department of Finance was responsible for the Japanese bank and insurance property; and Japanese private railroads were placed under the authority of the Department of Transportation. Local property custodian officers were created and empowered to take care of Japanese property in local areas. It took almost one year to complete the creation of these administrative organs; one and a half years passed before a final policy regarding the disposition of vested property was established; and it took more than two years for the military government to make a comprehensive survey of vested property. During this time, industrial plants deteriorated further, and a great amount of consumer goods and personal property was sold at the black market through profiteers. Most industries were idle because of the lack of electric power, raw materials, and trained personnel. According to an official report in 1946, industrial production averaged only 20 percent of capacity; some recovery took place during 1947, but it took until 1949 (the American military government came to an end on August 15, 1948) before industry "commenced to show general signs of improvement."[6]

Agricultural production was also down in 1946, because chemical fertilizers from North Korea were unavailable to southern farmers; the average yield per hectare planted in rice was only 1.67 metric tons compared with 2.04 metric tons in 1941. The farmers were able to cultivate only 70 percent of available farmland. Inflation became acute and prices rose sharply. Japanese currency notes in August 1945 totaled 8,000 million *hwan,* by the end of 1946 18,000 million *hwan,* and by the end of 1947 nearly 33,000 million *hwan.* The 1945 price of rice rose eighty-five fold by March 1946, while wages went up only seventeen fold.[7] The main reason for the rapid rise of the price of rice was that speculators, seizing upon opportunities for quick profits, bought up stocks of goods in short supply, by taking advantage of the inadequate price-control measures of the military government.

In March 1947 the military government finally declared that vested property "should be sold as soon as responsible and efficient purchasers could be found."[8] But the military could not find qualified Korean investors, primarily because the political uncertainty caused by the division of the country discouraged Korean businessmen from engaging in long-term private investments. Most businessmen were interested in speculation and short-term projects. Next the military government tried to sell certain types of holdings to private concerns as physical assets. For example, the government announced that mining rights and mining property classified as "small businesses" were to be sold by the property custodian "to prevent the disposition of unprotectable assets to promote utilization by Korean capital."[9] This plan also was unsuccessful. The American attempt to encourage a private free-enterprise economy in South Korea failed.

At this point the military government finally came to realize that the future Korean economy must be other than free enterprise, and kept all major industrial plants and establishments under the control of the property custodian. As a result, the military government transferred more than 90 percent of all modern industry in South Korea to the Republic of Korea as vested property in 1948. Perhaps the only successful action of the American military government concerning the South Korean economy was the disposition of Japanese agricultural land that had been entrusted to the New Korea Company. About 600,000 acres of land were sold to 500,000 tenant farmers, the cash price being three times its average yearly production. The purchase price was to be paid in 15 years without interest, and a farmer could pay 20 percent of a normal crop each year.[10]

A Trial for Planned Economy under Rhee. The general economic situation of South Korea in 1948 was not much better than that of 1945. South Korea lacked electric power, raw materials for industry, capital formation, and technology. Inflation was becoming worse; prices of consumer goods were still rising; profiteering on government contracts, black-marketing, and graft were sources of wealth for a handful of businessmen. The industrial output was still down to 20 percent of its prewar level and the outlook for industrial development was grim, particularly after the power shutoff by North Korea. South Korea's industrial composition in 1948 was: textile manufacturing as the leading industry; chemical and foodstuff industries came second, but most plants were of medium or small scale; metal and machine industries came last. Thus heavy industry was in its initial stages, and light and consumer-goods industries were predominant.[11]

Agricultural production improved somewhat in 1948 compared with that of 1945. This was mainly because of the import of fertilizers from the United States, although many farmers still suffered from lack of fertilizers and inadequate irrigation systems.

South Korea's economy was based on planning. The constitution of the Republic of Korea provided that heavy industries, public utilities, and foreign trade be controlled by the government (Article eighty-seven). It also provided for land reform, stating, "Farm land shall be distributed to those who work the land themselves" (Article eighty-six). However, Article eighty-seven provided for private enterprise, saying that "when required by public necessity, enterprises shall be licensed to private individuals."

In 1948 sixty-nine enterprises, former Japanese industries and public utilities, were under government control; fifty-two were managed directly by the government and seventeen by government-appointed managers as semiprivate enterprises. The government enterprises were placed under the jurisdiction of the executive branch; the president of the republic exercised virtually dictatorial power in management, appointment of directors, policy-making, and disposition of property. On the other hand, the legislative branch was given only so-called price-proposing power, suggesting prices for the products of government enterprises.

In December 1948 the government planned a long-term economic rehabilitation program by signing an economic aid agreement between the Republic of Korea and the United States. According to this agreement, the program was to be carried out in the United States through the Economic Cooperation Administration (ECA), and in the Republic of Korea by the newly established Interim Foreign Aid Administrative Bureau. ECA funds for South Korea amounted to $200 million by the time the Korean war broke out in June 1950.

Accepting American aid, the Republic of Korea agreed to balance its budget, to control inflation, to economize in government expenditures, and to increase foreign trade; it also assumed responsibility for developing industries as rapidly as possible and making efforts to increase production in government-owned industries.

The rehabilitation program started well: construction of three railroads was begun to provide access to coal areas not previously reached by rail; a moderate powerplant project was initiated; a number of irrigation and land reclamation projects were completed; and, also, a cement plant, tungsten and mining industrial projects, and fertilizer plants had completed the planning stage of construction.

As a result of these efforts, some economic progress was made in South Korea. Food production increased; consumer goods production also increased somewhat, although it was still far short of even minimum domestic needs; coal production increased about 40 percent by the middle of 1950. The per capita gross national output 1948–50 reached the post–World War II high of eighty-six dollars.[12]

Yet economic stability in South Korea was not attained. South Korea lacks mineral resources. This forced an expansion of agricultural production as the only means of gaining exchange to purchase the necessary importations. But the increase of agricultural production was only possible by using costly imported fertilizers since no chemical fertilizer plant existed in South Korea at that time. Therefore a great share of U.S. aid was spent for commercial fertilizer and foodstuffs, instead of for reconstruction of industries. Moreover, the Republic of Korea had to support a large military force to oppose the Northern Communists after the withdrawal of the American troops. It was estimated that more than 50 percent of the national budget was spent for the military. The South Korean economy was dominated by one man, President Rhee, who abused the economy for political purposes. For example, Rhee appointed his political favorites, who knew nothing about business, as directors and managers of government-owned enterprises. The profits went either into the directors' pockets or into Rhee's political funds. At every election time, the Seoul Electric Company and the Bank of Korea were the main sources of Rhee's campaign funds. The foreign-aid fund was handled by Rhee personally. As all evidence indicated, Rhee was not interested in economic reconstruction but in the setting up of a strong police state by doubling the police force in order to secure his power. Rhee twice sabotaged the implementation of the land-reform law.

The total dependence of South Korea's economy on American aid was expressed by Secretary of State Dean Acheson in 1950 before Congress: "The Republic of Korea's government would fall within three months if economy assistance were not provided."[13]

The Wartime Economy. The Korean war accelerated the decline of the South Korean economy and drove it into bankruptcy. It disrupted normal economic activities and brought unparalleled destruction to the country. The cost of the hostilities, in terms of personal loss and human suffering to the Korean people, is not measurable. The physical damage to industrial installations, transportation systems, public utilities and buildings, housing, rice fields, and irrigation and flood-control facilities has been estimated at more than three billion dollars.[14] The heaviest damage was suffered by the industries on the western coast, particularly those in the Seoul-Inchun industrial area. Many industries were completely ruined, others were damaged from 50 to 80 percent. During the war agricultural production was reduced considerably because of fertilizer shortage, lack of labor, damage to irrigation, and loss of farm animals. There were more than a million civilian casualties; more than a half-million children were orphaned; five million people lost their homes and properties.

Inflation ballooned: the banknote currency of 71,383 million *hwan* at the end of 1949 rose to 650,135 million *hwan* in the middle of 1953. The national debt assumed astronomical figures; the 1953 revenue deficit alone was 42 billion *hwan*.[15]

Foreign aid, mainly from the United States, saved South Korea's economy from complete collapse. As will be discussed later, direct military aid from the United States was estimated at $5 billion during the three-and-a-half-year war. Civilian aid through organizations such as the United Nations Korean Reconstruction Agency (UNKRA), Civilian Relief in Korea (CRIK), and Armed Forces Assistance to Korea (AFAK) amounted to more than $6,000 million during the war. The greater share of civilian aid was used for immediate relief to the war-stricken people, the rest for the rehabilitation of schools, hospitals, health centers, and orphanages.[16]

During the war only the tungsten and gold output increased, and that after the conclusion of the Tungsten Agreement between the United States and the Republic of Korea. Japanese imports dominated the South Korean market during the war years. As a result, the postwar Japanese economy recovered considerably from its war damage.

Free Enterprise Economy after the Korean War. Following the truce agreement in 1953, the economic reconstruction problems in South Korea were enormous and confused. Nearly 90 percent of industry was idle—raw materials, electric power, and manpower being in short supply; agricultural production was down, unemployment up, and inflation out of hand; per capita output was less than fifty dollars a year. More than 70 percent of the total population in South Korea was still engaged in farming; yet only about half of the total value of the national output was in agriculture. The agricultural economy provided the means of livelihood for more than 70 percent of the population and had to feed twenty-two million. The average acreage per farm-family was 2.5 acres, but one-third of the families owned less than one acre.[17]

In the face of this situation, the Republic of Korea adopted a free-enterprise economy in place of a planned economy. There were two reasons for the change. Many Korean economists and politicians favored free enterprise and blamed the planned economy for having destroyed the middle class and brought about official corruption and graft. Furthermore, the planned economy system was not attractive to private foreign investment. In the 1954 election, both the Liberal party and the opposition Democratic party advocated free enterprise in their party platforms.

The official policy of the U.S. government also supported free enterprise in South Korea. Three congressmen, headed by Charles B. Brownson, chairman of the International Operation Subcommittee, arrived in Seoul in October 1953 and blamed the low production in South Korea on government ownership of the basic industries; as a remedy they proposed that the constitution be amended so that commercial activities by both private and foreign investors could be encouraged.[18] In 1954, at the request of President Eisenhower, three governors, John Fine of Pennsylvania, Allan Shivers of Texas, and Dan Thornton of Colorado, visited South Korea to evaluate the progress of rehabilitation of the war-ravaged economy. They also recommended that the South Korean government "increase efforts to stimulate private enterprise and private foreign investment through the establishment of sound monetary reforms."[19]

Shortly thereafter, the South Korean assembly passed a constitutional amendment providing licenses to exploit mines, marine resources, water power, and other economically available natural powers for limited periods.[20]

In 1954 the Economic Agreement between the Republic of Korea and the United States was signed, by which Korea agreed "to encourage private ownership of investment projects."[21] Subsequently, government-owned enterprises were denationalized: more than fifty industries were sold to private concerns. Most of them, however, were sold with political strings attached by the Rhee administration. Only members of the Liberal party or sympathizers of the Rhee administration were given the privilege of purchasing them.

The administration also concluded a series of contracts with foreign private companies: for example, the right to construct a fertilizer plant and an electric power plant was given to American companies, and construction of a cement plant was awarded to a Danish firm. The largest contract was an electric plant; the $30-million project was awarded to the Pacific Bechtel Corporation of San Francisco.[22]

Since no safeguards were set up against Rhee's parceling out of national resources and the government-owned enterprises to Koreans and foreign favorites for political patronage, the South Korean economy was converted to private enterprise within a short period in the name of economic reconstruction. Nevertheless, many stubborn problems remained. Industrial production was highly uneven; high-powered and ultramodern equipment furnished by ICA and a small number of skilled workers sometimes coexisted with antiquated methods and tools in the same industry; capital and modern entrepreneurial talent were lacking, and growth depended on foreign capital and management; industrial composition was still dominated by light industry—the ratio was 22 to 78 percent. Furthermore, economic decisions were often made for political considerations, which resulted in favoritism and illicit profit by high government officials, party leaders in power, and businessmen. The question of how much and what kind of industrialization would be economically sound for South Korea was never seriously studied by either government or private business.

For a six-year period (1954–60),[23] no substantial economic progress was made through the free-enterprise system. At a 1955 constant market price, the 1960 gross national product had risen by only 2.3 percent. Agricultural products increased somewhat; the rice crop in 1960 was 2,294,000 tons as compared with 2,143,000 tons in 1954. The increase of the rice crop was attributed mainly to fertilizer. However, construction of the fertilizer plant was not completed even in 1960 (the original target was 1957).

There was no increase of the farmers' income, and their living conditions remained the same as before; most of them were short of food from spring until harvest time. In 1960 industrial production declined, because of the political change caused by the April Student Revolution, the revision of the exchange rate (from six hundred *hwan* to thirteen hundred *hwan* for one dollar), and the trial of illegal profiteers during the Rhee administration. There was a small increase in power output, totaling about 1,697 million kilowatts, but still far below the requirement for industry.

The Foreign Investment Encouragement Law, which granted many privileges to foreign investors, such as a five-year waiver in full of corporation tax, a three-year waiver in full of personal income tax, and a five-to-eight-year waiver of all custom duties, failed to bring foreign private investment to South Korea; for economic and political conditions in Korea were unattractive except on a short-term contract basis, as in the construction of power and fertilizer plants. Thus South Korea not only suffered from an acute shortage of capital for industrialization but also from an acute shortage of entrepreneurs—men able and willing to assume top management responsibility and, at the same time, willing to risk a substantial amount of money in backing up their judgment. Consequently little free enterprise developed in South Korea.

As mentioned before, foreign aid played an important part in South Korea's economy: without it the whole economy would have collapsed. From 1953 to 1960 alone, South Korea received more than two billion dollars in aid, mainly from the United States. About 50 percent of the aid produced local currency which was used to underwrite part of the budget of the South Korean government. More than 50 percent of the national budget was spent for defense—South Korea maintained a standing army of more than 600,000, the fourth largest army in the world. Furthermore, American aid created Korean millionaires and sustained official corruption during the Rhee and Chang Myun administrations.

CHAPTER 16

PROBLEMS OF SOUTH KOREA'S ECONOMY

LAND REFORM

Historical Background. Agriculture provides livelihood for 70 percent of the Korean population and has been the source of about half of Korea's exports. According to Japanese statistics of 1938,[1] before the Second World War the arable land of Korea amounted to 12 million acres.[2] About 62 percent of the cultivated land was owned by ninety-three thousand landlords, about 3 percent of the three million farming population. Only 18.1 percent of the farm families owned their own land; 23.9 percent were semitenants, that is, they owned some of the land and rented the rest; 51.8 percent were tenants; 2.4 percent were squatter farmers on *hwa-don* (fire lands); and 3.8 percent were farm laborers. Seventeen percent of the farmers cultivated more than 6 acres, while 38 percent cultivated less than 1.2 acres.

The same Japanese statistics show that agricultural income accounted for 45.8 percent of the gross national product, which was a little more than three billion yen (about one billion dollars). The occupational classification of the population was: 73.6 percent farming, 7 percent commercial activities, 3.9 percent professions, and 3.1 percent industry; the rest—12.4 percent—were engaged in a variety of other occupations.[3] The per capita value of production of farmers was 83 yen (a little over $27), while that of all other workers was about 133 yen (over $44).[4]

In 1938 Korea produced 120 million bushels of rice annually[5] and exported half of it to Japan. Japanese landlords and the government owned 18 percent of the farm land in Korea; they were absentee landlords, living in urban areas. The rate of rents ran from 50 to well over 70 percent in kind; the tenants were sharecroppers and had no lease rights.

The age-old feudal relations between tenants and landlords continued during the Japanese administration; the tenants worked as servants of the landlords and lived as virtual tenant slaves, as eternal debtors to the master landlords. Three-fourths of the tenanted land was owned by Korean landlords.

After the division of the country in 1945, there were about 5.5 million acres of arable land in South Korea,[6] of which about 500,000 acres of paddy lands and 150,000 acres of dry lands belonged to former Japanese landlords.[7] Generally, the fields of South Korea were divided into paddy fields used for rice crops, and the dry or upland fields were used for other crops; the former covered about 3 million acres, the latter 2.5 million acres. Rice has traditionally been the most important agricultural product of South Korea.

All South Korean political parties, including those on the extreme right and extreme left, supported land reform, but the methods they advocated were different.[8] The leftist parties demanded confiscation of former Japanese-owned land and native landlords' lands without compensation, and its distribution to landless tenants free of charge. They argued that the Japanese had been nonproductive exploiters of the tenants; without speedy land reform there would be no socioeconomic progress and no development of democratic society in South Korea. The conservative parties insisted on the principle of "confiscation with compensation to native landlords and free distribution to the tenants." They said that most Korean landlords had been patriotic nationalists and were entitled to compensation for their properties. The rightists proposed a land reform based on the principle of "purchasing and selling of the land," which meant that the government would buy the native landlords' lands at a fixed price but would confiscate former Japanese-owned land without compensation and sell it to the tenants. They argued that the Korean landlords should be compensated in order to create a class with sufficient liquid assets to undertake the financing of Korea's industrial development. This would mean that the Korean landlord class would become a class of industrialists and financiers.

The American military authorities took the position that land reform should wait until the establishment of a provisional government for all Korea,[9] and that if a land law was enacted by a South Korean national assembly while the military government was in power, the landowners should receive compensation.

The property owners who dominated the South Korean assembly were slow to pass land reform legislation—too slow even for the military government, which finally promulgated ordinances nos. 173 and 174 to create the National Land Administration to sell the former Japanese holdings to Korean farmers.

The American "Land Reform." The American military government held about 700,000 acres of former Japanese land, which included about 600,000 tenant families who cultivated the land and paid one-third of the crop to the military government according to the terms of the 1946 rent-reform law.[10] The Americans who took charge of the land sale were former employees of the U.S. Department of Agriculture. The group was headed by Dr. Clyde Mitchell, administrator of the National Land Administration (former New Korea Company). They spent almost three years planning the land sale, including the preparation of forms and documents, as well as the training of the seven thousand Korean employees of the Land Administration and related agencies.

The farms were surveyed and assessed; on each day of the sale the administration transformed ten thousand more parcels of land. Sales were made only to tenants who had actually been farming the land. Each piece of land was sold for three times its average yearly production; the purchase price was to be paid in 15 years, without interest; a farmer could pay 20 percent of a normal crop each year, or he could pay off faster if he was able to do so. No tenant or single buyer was entitled to buy more than 4.9 acres. Less than five months after the beginning of the land sale program, 85 percent of the former Japanese lands had been sold; the program was completed by American personnel shortly after the establishment of the Republic of Korea on August 15, 1948.

Upon completion, Dr. Mitchell said that "South Korean farmers were apparently well satisfied with their bargain."[11] But many Koreans were puzzled: why had the American military authorities insisted on *selling* the Japanese-owned lands against the overwhelming opinion of the Korean people to distribute the land to the tenants without charge. To this question, one American official answered: "We Americans do not approve of the idea of free distribution of somebody's property to someone else."[12]

Land Reform in the Republic of Korea. The Constitution of the Republic of Korea provided that "farmland shall be distributed to self-tilling farmers: the method of distribution, the extent of possession, and the nature and restrictions of ownership shall be determined by law" (Article 86).

The Land Reform Law was promulgated on June 22, 1949.[13] Features of the law were: (1) the government was to purchase all holdings not cultivated by the owners and all holdings of more than 7.5 acres; (2) compensation was to be made by negotiable government-guaranteed bonds issued by the Republic of Korea; (3) ownership of the land could be passed on to heirs, but sale, donation, or transfer of ownership was to be prohibited until farmers had fully paid for the land.

The Land Reform Law, then, was based on government purchase and government resale of the land with a government subsidy. Professor Yun Chi-o of Korea University said that the objective of the law was "equal promotion of the livelihood of the people" without "revenge against the traditional landlords."[14]

The Rhee administration opposed the land reform law on the ground that the subsidy provisions would impose a financial burden upon the government and would lead to further inflation. This argument carried little weight, coming from a government that seemingly did not intend "to abate the tide of deficit-spending elsewhere" and did not adopt adequate measures to check the inflation. The Rhee administration never made a genuine effort to implement the land reform law because Rhee's political support came from the ultra-conservative landlord class in the country, and he did not want to destroy it through the land reform law.

The government report did not say how many farm families and how much land were included in the land reform, nor did it report the average acreage per farm family, or the exact percentage of grain payment of the farmers to the government, or the rate of compensation to landlords. Therefore, it is difficult to make any conclusive evaluation of the land reform.

All evidence indicates that the reform did not solve the agrarian problems[15] of South Korea, and that it did not raise substantially the living standard of the peasants. Every year from late spring to harvest time a great number of the farming families continued to suffer from food shortages.

One of the basic agrarian problems in South Korea is the shortage of arable land. Fifteen million out of twenty-two million of South Korea's population (1962) are crowded into 5.5 million acres of land, and the average rural family farm has 2.5 acres; one-third of these families depend for their livelihood on 1 acre or even less. And there is little possibility of reclaiming land in South Korea. Moreover, the soil has suffered a depletion of plant nutrients after centuries of intensive use without planned rotation. Consequently, good yields are possible only with adequate supplies of commercial fertilizers, which are not available in South Korea today. Under these conditions "the permanent relief of South Korean agriculture can come only from increasing industrialization which will gradually reduce the pressure upon the land." This means that reunification of the agricultural South and the industrial North is the answer to the agrarian problem.

The land reform failed to completely destroy landlordism, although it did away with the traditional variety. Because of the lack of a farm credit system and because of the government's do-nothing attitude on the low price of agricultural products (sometimes the rice price was below the cost of production), there has been a considerable turnover of land. Many farmer-tenants who acquired farm land under the land reform law were not able to meet the annual payments and were forced to turn over their lands to money-lenders, although resale was not allowed by law. In some cases crop production has declined because farmers are not sure of the future tenure of the lands they cultivate, and in other cases they tend to neglect the land because of debts.

Even after the land reform became effective, South Korea's agriculture failed to provide sufficient amounts of food. The best harvest year after the liberation was 1957, but even then South Korea had to import more than 30,000 tons of rice from Formosa, paying $4.5 million; and another $50 million worth of barley, wheat, corn, and rice from the United States.

INDUSTRIALIZATION

Unbalanced Development. The transformation of Korea's agricultural economy to an industrial economy commenced with the exploitation of the mineral and power resources of the country. In the last part of the nineteenth century, with the opening of Korea to the Western powers, the Korean government gave a number of mineral concessions to Western corporations, especially concessions to work gold mines. However, the most rapid development of the mineral resources of the peninsula took place under the Japanese administration. The Japanese constructed railroads, highways, and port and shipping facilities to transfer raw material to the Japanese home islands. Korea became a principal source of industrial raw material for Japanese industry, and a processing center of such material by the establishment of textile mills and chemical and food-processing plants.

The Japanese also constructed a large hydroelectric power plant on the Yalu River. The development of mineral resources, the construction of modern transportation systems, and the construction of the electric power plant opened the way for an industrial economy. Korea's economy was gradually knit together to become one unit of Japanese industry. Korea's industry did not develop naturally but was imposed on the country by the Japanese in preparation for war.

After World War II South Korea's industry was crippled by the division of the country, since most of the heavy industrial plants and mineral resources were in North Korea. In 1948, when the Republic of Korea was established, the composition of South Korean industry was as follows: Textiles accounted for 37.8 percent of the industrial capacity, employing 51.3 percent of the total industrial labor force; foodstuffs and chemical industries accounted for 22 percent; the rest was divided between metal and machine tool industries.

The problems of industrialization in South Korea could be summarized as follows:

(1) Coexistence of old and new. Some industries are still the handicraft type of home industry, using medieval methods of production; other industries are modern, using highly advanced technology imported from abroad, mainly from the United States through ECA. The simultaneous presence of these two types of production creates many problems in operation and management, as well as in social relations and wage scales.

(2) Lack of essential elements for industrial development. Raw material, technological know-how, national capital, trained administrative personnel, and modern entrepreneurs are lacking in South Korea. Furthermore, the native business class lacks independence of spirit and self-confidence in long-term enterprise, mainly because of political uncertainty due to continued

division of the country. The essential industries have been constructed with foreign aid and government subsidies. To obtain such funds, businessmen fawn upon government officials. "Politically oriented" businessmen seek high profits through bribery rather than through efficient industrial management. As a result, corruption is widespread in business, and inefficiency and mismanagement prevail in business establishments.

(3) Continuation of imbalanced industrial growth. During the Japanese administration the mining industry, food-processing facilities, and power were well developed, but the metal industry and machine tool industry were not. Since the liberation in 1945, a tendency to overproduction has continued in textile, sugar-refining, brewery, and flour-mill industries.

(4) Lack of purchasing power. About two-thirds of the population are engaged in farming and fishing, and the overwhelming majority of them have not enough food for their families. Even the present industrial output produced by the handful of industrialists in the urban areas has been threatened by poor consumption by the rural population. Many industries have gone bankrupt.

Any future economy for South Korea must rest on a sound and expanding agricultural base to increase the farmers' purchasing power.

The First Five-year Economic Plan (1962–66). In October 1960 the Chang Myun government drew up a five-year plan of economic development which replaced the three-year plan of the Rhee administration prepared in 1958. The details of the plan were almost completed at the time of the military coup d'etat. The plan included a tax reform, price control of certain commodities, reduction of the armed forces, and a revision of the foreign exchange rate. The immediate objectives were the stabilization of South Korea's economy and the introduction of modern industry. The final objective was the attainment of a self-sufficient economy.

The military government announced its first five-year economic plan on July 22, 1961.[16] Its objectives were "the reform and abolishment of vicious social and economic circles, whether existing or potential," and "the laying of a foundation for the erection of a self-sustaining economy." To achieve these objectives, the average rate of economic growth during the period of the first five-year plan had to be 7.1 percent per year. The ultimate objective of the plan was the industrialization of South Korea's agrarian economy. During the five-year period (1962–67), major emphasis was to be placed "on the development of power, coal, and other energy sources," on an increase of agricultural production, and on the expansion of key industrial facilities. Thus unemployment and the national deficit were to be reduced.

The economic policy of the plan was "a form of guided capitalism," under the principle of free enterprise but guided by the government.

The total capital investment for the plan was estimated at $2.5 billion (3,184 billion *hwan*), and funds were allocated as follows: 41 percent for power, transportation, communication, and housing; 34 percent for mining and manufacturing; and 16 percent for agriculture, forestry, and fisheries. The government was to undertake 37 percent of the total investment, and 63 percent was to be met by private investment. About 28 percent of the total was to come from foreign sources and 72 percent from domestic sources.

As sectorial targets, the plan expected to increase grain production by an additional 210,000 tons, rice by 29 percent, coal by 120 percent, iron by 53 percent, and limestone by 240 percent. Particular emphasis was placed on manufacturing industries, such as fertilizer, steel, cement, and chemicals. Electric power was to be increased 97 percent to reach 908 megawatts in the target year as compared with 460 megawatts during the base year. Therefore, more than 50 percent of the thermoelectric power-plant projects, that is, four of the eight new power plants being constructed, should be completed by 1966. Nevertheless, South Korea will not produce enough electric power for domestic requirements at the end of the first five-year period.

Information on the results of the five-year plan is still incomplete at the time of this writing. Most European production has been rising 6 percent annually, and in the underdeveloped countries 5 percent has been the maximum. Therefore, in a country like poverty-stricken South Korea, an annual growth of 7.1 percent will be difficult to attain.

To meet the financial requirements of the plan, the government planned to do two things: seek foreign aid, mainly from the United States and possibly from Western Germany and Italy; and increase taxes from 12.6 percent in the base year to 16 percent in the target year.

It might be taken for granted that the United States will continue to contribute funds in order to compete with Communism in Asia, but it is doubtful whether any foreign private entrepreneurs will invest capital in a South Korea of inflation and political uncertainty. In 1962 a group of South Korean industrialists headed by Lee Byung-chul failed to get two billion dollars in capital from the United States and other countries for the expansion of Korea's industry. The U.S. Development Loan Fund, World Bank, and the International Monetary turned down the request on the ground that "a stable government was needed as an inducement for private foreign investment."

Since the liberation, the South Korean government, including the American military government and the Rhee and Chang administrations, has not been able to collect more than 75 percent of taxes every year, because many farmers are too poor to pay their taxes and too much tax evasion takes place among those in the high-income brackets. Without elimination of tax evasion and an increase of the farmers' income, the raising of taxes will not increase national revenues.

As pointed out previously, many South Korean businessmen have engaged in short-term projects and speculative business; many became excessively wealthy through the American aid program during the Rhee regime. After the military takeover many businessmen were arrested and charged with illicit practices, but most of them were released when they promised to work for the economic reconstruction of the country. Lee Byung-chul was one of this group.

FOREIGN AID

Reliable statistics are not available on the exact amount of foreign aid given to South Korea during the past 15 years (1945–60). However, it is certain that South Korea has received more than three billion dollars in aid from the United States and UNKRA (United Nations Korean Reconstruction Agency). The overwhelming proportion of this came from the United States. Until recently, aid was characterized by overemphasis on defense expenditures, consumption goods, and relief; and it had strong political overtones. But without foreign aid South Korea's economy would be in great danger, and perhaps collapse within a short period.

Summary of American Aid. The history of American aid to South Korea can be divided into four stages: the period of military occupation (1945–

48); the period before the Korean war (1949–50); the war period (1951–53); and the postwar period (after 1953).

American aid during the occupation is estimated at $300 million, 90 percent of which was in grants under the Government Appropriation for Relief in Occupation Areas, and the rest in loans. The annual interest rate of the loan was less than 3 percent. The aid was designed principally to eliminate hunger, disease, and social unrest. At the same time, part of the aid was intended for economic rehabilitation and for a land reform program, especially for the sale of former Japanese land.

The Korean-American Agreement on Aid was signed four months after the establishment of the Republic of Korea on August 15, 1948. The agreement provided for the establishment of the "counterpart fund," which was to be composed of Korean money and an equivalent amount of dollars; and, also, in it the Korean government agreed to encourage investment of foreign capital.

An Interim Foreign Aid Administration Bureau was set up in South Korea, while the U.S. government transferred the authority of Korean aid to the Economic Cooperation Administration. The amount of ECA aid from 1949 to 1951 was estimated at $200 million. A great proportion of this was spent for the military, governmental expenditures, and relief work, but none for rehabilitation.[17]

During the Korean war there were three types of aid.[18] (1) The Civil Relief in Korea (CRIK) program carried out by U.S. Army authorities under the U.N. Command. About $460 million was spent for importation of relief supplies and for rehabilitation facilities. (2) The UNKRA program launched in accordance with a U.N. General Assembly resolution adopted in December 1951. The aid fund totaled $141 million and was mostly used for relief purposes, reconstruction of schools, hospitals, and the like. This program was begun after the cease-fire agreement was signed in July 1953, and lasted until 1955, after which no new projects were undertaken by UNKRA because of a lack of funds. (3) The Armed Forces Assistance to Korea (AFAK) program launched by the U.S. Army in South Korea. Nearly $20 million worth of material was spent for the rehabilitation of schools, health centers, and orphanages.

Plans for long-term economic aid by the United States after the war were made public on August 7, 1953, through a joint communique signed by President Syngman Rhee and U.S. Secretary of State John F. Dulles. (On the same day the Mutual Defense Treaty between the two governments was also signed.) According to the communique, the United States would extend one billion dollars in aid for the reconstruction of South Korea in the next four years.[19]

In accordance with a U.S. presidential directive, the Office of Economic Coordinator was established in Seoul in 1954 to direct the aid program in South Korea. Mr. Tyler Wood was appointed to that position with the rank of minister. He was given authority not only to supervise the economic aid program but also to assume the duty of coordinating the economic and military activities of the United States government and UNKRA. In 1959 the Office of Economic Coordinator incorporated itself under the name of United States Operation Mission to Korea (USOMK), and at the same time terminated its relationship with the United Nations Command and UNKRA. USOMK became the only economic aid organization, with Dr. Raymond T. Moyer as its head. For the past few years the amount of American aid has constantly been decreasing.

The Political Implications of Economic Aid. The U.S. government attached various political conditions to its aid to the South Korean government. On February 9, 1950, the U.S. House of Representatives approved $60 million of ECA aid to South Korea with the proviso that the aid should be immediately terminated "in the event of the formation in the Republic of Korea of a coalition government which includes one or more members of the Communist party or of the party now in control of the government of North Korea."[20] Hereafter the South Korean government became a super anti-Communist regime, accusing anyone who did not support Rhee's administration of being a Communist.

In the spring of the same year, the U.S. government was greatly concerned about inflation in South Korea as well as about Rhee's plan to postpone the May election until November. Finally, Secretary of State Dean Acheson sent a virtual ultimatum to Rhee through the American ambassador in Seoul, stating that if measures were not immediately taken to halt mounting inflation, and if the election were postponed, the U.S. government would be forced to cut off economic aid. As a result Rhee declared that his government would hike taxes in an attempt to check inflation and that the election would be held in May. On May 3, 1950, the U.S. Congress passed a $110 million bill as additional economic aid to South Korea.

One reason for the delay in signing a truce agreement between the U.N. command and the North Korean command was the stubborn opposition of President Rhee. He wanted, even if it meant a unilateral march toward the North, to unify the country by the South Korean armed forces. Finally, Rhee "accepted" the truce when the United States government promised postwar economic aid for the reconstruction of South Korea's economy.[21]

Following the armistice of the Korean war, President Eisenhower proposed, and Congress approved, $200 million in aid to South Korea before the start of a program of long-term economic assistance. In the meantime, the United States government stressed the desirability of a private enterprise economy. In one instance, Congressman Charles B. Brownson, chairman of the International Operation Subcommittee, and Governor Dan Thornton, head of the presidential commission, urged Rhee to "increase efforts to stimulate private enterprise and private foreign investment."[22] In the end, the South Korean constitution was amended to change from a planned economic system to "free enterprise," and most government-owned enterprises were denationalized.

When the military junta established a dictatorial regime in South Korea after the 1962 coup d'etat, the U.S. government recognized the new regime, and then pressed it to transfer political power to the civilian administration as soon as possible if the junta wanted a continuation of American economic aid. General Park agreed, and the civilian government was formed in 1963.

Emphasis on Consumer Industry over Basic Industry. Generally American aid consisted of two branches: project (installation) assistance, and nonproject (salable consumer goods) assistance. The former supplied raw and processed materials to basic industry, the latter fertilizers, fuel, and electric machinery.

Korean and American authorities always disagreed on the rate between project and nonproject assistance. The Koreans wanted a large share of project assistance on the ground that since Korea cannot expect foreign aid indefinitely, emphasis should be placed on development of her own basic industry. The Americans argued that economic stabilization by control of inflation should come as the first step in developing basic industry, and a bigger share of aid should be spent on the import of consumer goods. This controversy was repeated every year, and the Koreans yielded each time. Total aid in 1956 was $277 million; the ratio of aid was typical. The Koreans proposed the following ratio: project, 52 percent; nonproject, 43 percent; and relief and technical assistance, 5 percent. The American side disagreed, and the final ratio was: project, 30 percent; nonproject, 68 percent; and technical assistance, 2 percent.

The overallocation of nonproject funds for the import of agricultural materials, especially U.S. farm surplus goods, affected the South Korean economy in general and the farmers in particular. The price of South Korean agricultural products declined, and the general market price was many times lower than that of the cost of production. As a result, thousands of farming families were forced to give up farming and migrated to the already overcrowded urban areas, thus creating an unemployment problem. The farm population, which still amounts to more than 60 percent of the total South Korean population, has virtually no purchasing power, and prospects for industrial progress are poor.

CHAPTER 17

SOVIET CONTROL OF NORTH KOREA

Working through the Koreans. No reliable data about the development of Soviet-controlled North Korea are available. Many sources are one-sided, in favor of, or opposed to, the Soviet administration.

On August 15, 1945, the Soviet Commanding General T. F. Shtikov issued a proclamation when Japan accepted the surrender terms of the Allied Powers, in which he said: "The Red Army enabled the Korean people to start for their new freedom by rendering all necessary conditions. Therefore, Korean happiness must be created by the Korean people themselves."[1]

A comprehensive Russian policy followed, announced by a directive issued by the political office of the Soviet general headquarters on September 14, in Pyongyang. The directive proposed:[2] (1) the early establishment of a national government representing the working people, peasants, industrial workers, and other Koreans opposed to the Japanese; (2) land distribution to the farming population based on the number of family members in each household; (3) placement of the Japanese-owned industry under the control of a worker's committee and temporary employment of Japanese technicians until the Korean technicians could replace them; (4) immediate purge of all pro-Japanese Koreans from every field of Korean society; and (5) public control of all educational and cultural institutions.

The Soviet military authorities openly recognized the People's Committee as the de facto ruling organ of the Korean people. All large industries, mines, and means of communications and transportation, as well as banks, were first taken under the control of the Soviets, but soon transferred to the People's Committee. Then the committee nationalized them as the property of the Korean people. The committee divided the former Japanese-owned land and the native landlord land among the landless tenants and ousted all pro-Japanese Koreans from economic and political life. Mass organizations were formed, such as farmers' unions, trade unions, women's associations, and youth organizations, and were placed under the control of the People's Committee.

The Soviets freed thousands of Korean political prisoners, who had been underground leaders before and during the Second World War. Many of the former political prisoners and overseas revolutionary leaders joined the People's Committee and became leaders of North Korea.

The Soviet authorities allowed Koreans to organize political parties. Four different parties were formed within a month: the North Korean Communist party (the name of which was later changed to the Labor party), the New People's party, Chungwoo-dang (Young Friend's party), and the Korean Democratic party. As described later, the first three were left-wing parties and the last was the rightist party. But all parties soon were under the complete control of the Communists by the creation of the Communist-dominated North Korean Democratic Front.

A simple voting technique was introduced by the People's Committee to select the leaders of the people: a black box for no and a white box for yes under a single-slate ticket. The Soviet authorities introduced 36-year-old Kim Il-sung[3] (a Russian-trained Communist known as an army commander in Manchuria) to the North Koreans as a patriot and national hero, who had been fighting for national liberation. Soon General Kim became the unchallenged ruler in the Soviet zone. The men around him had also been young and militant underground leaders. They included nationalists, liberals, Christian ministers, and Communists. But they were all radicals of sorts, advocating a "people's democracy" and supporting Soviet policy.

The Soviet military authorities followed the policy of placing trustworthy Korean protégés, most of them Communists, in key positions in important political institutions and allowing them to exercise authority in administration. The important policy decisions, however, were made by the Soviet political officer, who rarely appeared in public. He had the ranking members of the political parties support his decisions to give the impression that the policies were Korean in origin and implementation. Working through the Koreans, the Soviet authorities were able to give the appearance of encouraging self-government, while actually retaining policy-making power in their hands.

The People's Committee: A De Facto Regime (1945–48). The People's Committee was not a political organization imported from the outside but established by the Korean people themselves. The leaders of the committee were the freedom fighters against the Japanese, including nationalist patriots, moderates, and Communists. Most North Koreans (excluding the pro-Japanese) joined the committee soon after it became the de facto regime.

The exact day of the organization of the People's Committee is not known;[4] in some places, such as Hamhung in south Hamkyung province, a committee was formed even before the landing of the Soviet troops in North Korea,[5] and in other places, such as Pyongyang, one was established after the entry of the Soviet military command.[6] In the former case it was a secret organization, because the Japanese were still in full control of Korea, and in the latter case it was formed with the approval of the Soviet authorities.

During the initial stage of Soviet occupation, the main task of the committee was to carry out the directives of the Soviet command, to maintain law and order, and to distribute food to Koreans under the supervision of the occupation forces. Soon the Korean people's militia (*inmingun*) was organized as a security force to assist the Soviet occupation forces. The Central People's Committee was established in Pyongyang, and all local people's committees were placed under its jurisdiction.

Since the Central People's Committee was fitted into the Soviet way of control, no formal Soviet military government was necessary in North Korea. With Soviet recognition, the Central People's Committee became a "self-constituted Korean authority," a de facto regime representing the vast majority of North Koreans. Up to that time, the committees, local and central, were not completely dominated by the Communists but were a coalition of nationalists, liberals, and Communists. Because the Communists were the minority in the people's committees, they were not ready to take over political power even under Soviet protection. Furthermore, South Korea, not North Korea, had been the stronghold of the Korean Communist party ever since it was organized in 1925 in Seoul. Many nationalist leaders, like Cho Man-sik and Paik Young-rup (a Christian minister), served as chairmen of the Central People's Committee.

However, the Communists gradually began to control the committees at the local and central levels by purging the nationalist leaders, charging them with antirevolutionary activities against the interests of the people. Within a few months the people's committees were placed more or less under the complete domination of the North Korean Communist party, which in turn was under the guidance of the Soviet political officers of the Soviet occupation army. Therefore, the relationship between the Central People's Committee, the North Korean Communist party, and the Soviet commanding general could be described as a triangle; the ultimate power was in the hands of the Soviet commanding general.

The structure of the people's committees was based on the principle of centralization of power. Each committee had a chairman or head. The size of each committee varied: the village committee was composed of five members; the district committee had seven to nine; the county committee thirteen to fifteen; the city committee fifteen to seventeen; and the provincial committee nineteen. Members of the village committee were elected by the village people; members of the district committee by electors from the districts; members of the county committee by electors from the counties; members of the city committee by the city population; members of the provincial committee by electors from the provinces. Each committee chairman was elected by the members of the committee. The method of voting was simple: two boxes, one white and one black, were placed at the polls; the voter was given a card which he threw into the box he chose. Thus a multiple-stage election procedure was practiced: direct elections in the village and city, and indirect elections in district, county, and province.

At the county and city level each committee had several departments, such as trade and industry, education, and finance. The provisional committee had additional departments: justice, communications, transportation, and police. All these local committees were under the direct control of the next higher committee—the village committee under the district committee, the district committee under the county, the county under the province, and the province and city under the central committee in Pyongyang.

By the beginning of 1946, the Central People's Committee decided to carry out drastic reform measures in the political and economic fields. As a result, on February 9 the committee called a political conference to which various political parties and social groups sent their delegates. At the conference the Provisional People's Committee was created to replace the Central People's Committee. The reason for this change was not given, but it must be assumed that the word "provisional" was considered preferable to "central" in anticipation of eventual unification of the country.

The Provisional People's Committee (hereafter referred to as the Provisional Committee) was composed of twenty-three members, and General Kim Il-sung was elected its chairman. The Provisional Committee created a five-man presidium, which consisted of a chairman, a vice-chairman, a secretary, and two elected members of the presidium. As the executive branch of the Provisional Committee, there were established ten departments (industry, agricultural and forestry, finance, transportation, communication, trade, public health, education, justice, and security) and three bureaus (general affairs, planning, and propaganda). The People's Court was continued as the judicial branch of the Provisional Committee. Thus the actual form of government was completed under the name of the Provisional Committee, which acted as the de facto government with full authority. Under the Provisional Committee, as similarly under the Central People's Committee, the political power was concentrated in the hands of the chairman, Kim Il-sung.

The Provisional Committee adopted an eleven-point program:[7] (1) the purging of pro-Japanese and antidemocratic elements from the local government; (2) the introduction of land reform measures; (3) the revival of industrial enterprises and promotion of the general standard of living; (4) the reconstruction of communication and transportation facilities; (5) the increase of foreign trade; (6) the reform of the financial system; (7) the development of handicraft industry; (8) the promotion of the trade union movement; (9) the creation of measures to solve food shortages; (10) the development of popular cultural education; and (11) the introduction of "true democracy" by supporting all measures proposed by the Soviet military authorities.

About five weeks later, Chairman Kim Il-sung issued a statement entitled "Basic Policies for a Future Korean Government." The timing of the statement was significant, for the first full-dress U.S.-U.S.S.R. Joint Commission was under way in Seoul to discuss the establishment of a unified Korean government in conformity with the Moscow Agreement. The statement contained twenty articles,[8] covering political, economic, and social policies.

Politically, Kim promised a cleanup of reactionary antidemocratic elements in Korean society, and guaranteed basic human freedoms, including freedom of speech, press, assembly, religion, civil rights, and equality before the law. Economically, he called for nationalization of all heavy industries, communication and transportation facilities, banks, mines, and foreign trade. He also called for the encouragement of private business and land reform by distribution of land to the landless peasants and recognition of private land ownership. The program for social legislation covered the eight-hour working day, abolition of child labor, compulsory education at government expense, establishment of socialized medicine, and construction of public parks, public libraries, and public theaters. The purpose of Kim Il-sung's statement was to gain the support of the South Korean people by challenging South Korean political leaders and mobilizing all political forces of North Korea under the leadership of the Provisional Committee and in the name of "democratization."

In a few months economic programs and social reform programs were inaugurated over a wide area, including nationalization of large industry, land reform, financial and monetary changes, and social security. As will be discussed later, these changes laid the groundwork for the broadly conceived economic development plans announced in 1947.

The political reorganization programs were accelerated under the leadership of the North Korean Communist party, which at that time was called the Bureau of the Central Committee of the Communist party of North Korea since the Communist party headquarters was in Seoul. The Independence Alliance, headed by Kim Du-bong (a former member of the Korean provisional government in China and a liberal nationalist), was reorganized and named the New People's party. The North Korean Worker's Alliance changed its name to North Korean Occupational Alliance. Two new political groups were established: the North Korean Democratic Young Men's Alliance and the North Korean Women's Alliance. Then the North Korean National Democratic Front was created, with the participation of all existing political parties and social organizations. The front elected its four chairmen from the major political parties: Kim Il-sung (Communist party), Kim Dubong (New People's party), Choi Yong-kun (Korean Democratic party), and Kim Dal-hun (Chungwoo-dang, the native religious party). The membership of the front was estimated at about five million. All political parties and social organizations pledged themselves to support Kim Il-sung's program as containing the basic policies for a future Korean government.

One drastic reorganization was the union of two leftist parties: the North Korean Communist party and the New People's party combined into the North Korean Labor party. The name "Communist party" thus came to an end in North Korea (the South Korean Communist party soon followed suit). The Communists wanted to avoid the criticism that North Korea was being dominated by the Communist party; they considered it easier to mobilize the general public on their side under the name of the Labor party rather than under the Communist party. The membership of the North Korean Labor party was estimated at 360,000 in 1946.

After the political reorganization, the Provisional People's Committee issued the electoral decree of September 5, 1946;[9] the deputies for the province, county, and city people's committees were to be elected; the right to nominate candidates for deputies was given to all democratic parties, social organizations, and occupational groups that registered with the Provisional People's Committee; the elections were to be held on a territorial basis, and the number of deputies was to be based on population—one deputy for 30,000 people. The elections were to be direct, equal, and by secret ballot, with a minimum voting age of twenty for both sexes. Those deprived of civil rights by a court decision on pro-Japanese activities, however, were barred, from voting.

Elections were held November 3, with the results as follows:[10] 99.6 percent of the registered voters, or 4,501,813 out of 4,516,120 persons, went to the polls; the North Korean National Democratic Front swept the elections, receiving 97 percent of all ballots cast in the provincial people's committee; in those for county committee 96 percent; in those for municipal committee 95.4 percent. A total of 3,459 deputies, including 453 women, were elected for county, municipal, and provincial people's committees. The political affiliations of the deputies were: North Korean Labor party, 1,102 (31 percent); Korean Democratic party, 351 (10 percent); Chungwoo-dang, 253 (8.1 percent), and independents, 1,753 (50.1 percent).

Kim Il-sung, chairman of the Provisional People's Committee, issued a statement which said that "through the elections the Korean people have demonstrated that they are . . . united as one body . . . and . . . have confidence in their representatives as their leaders."[11]

The Provisional People's Committee took the next step in setting up a North Korean government soon after the November elections. The convention of the Congress of the People's Committee was held on February 17, 1947. The delegates of the congress were chosen by the provincial, municipal, and county committees, which elected one-fifth of their members to represent them. The delegates numbered 1,159; 149 from the provinces, 121 from the municipalities, and 889 from the counties; 149 delegates were women. The record of party affiliations was as follows: North Korean Labor party, 579; Democratic party, 137; Chungwoo-dang, 122; and independent, 321. The occupational distribution of the delegates was: farmers 318, industrial workers 329, businessmen 330, professional groups (including teachers, doctors, and scholars) 107, religious men 34, and others 41. Young people were comparatively well represented at the convention (those aged from twenty to forty numbered 865, those over forty-six numbered 294), and many of them had served in Japanese jails for independence activities.[12]

The Congress of the People's Committee approved unanimously all legislation enacted by the People's Provisional Committee since its inception a year before, including the laws on land reform, nationalization of heavy industry, and the election decree. The congress also adopted a national economic plan proposed by Kim Il-sung, as well as the National Democratic Front's proposal for the establishment of a people's assembly of North Korea as the supreme organ of the North Korean people until a national democratic government was established. The congress passed a resolution requesting from the government of the Soviet Union and the United States the immediate resumption of the joint conference in order to discuss the formation of a unified Korean government in accordance with the Moscow Agreement.

The congress created the People's Assembly, which was to meet every two years. It was composed of 237 members elected through a secret vote by the delegates of the Congress of the People's Committee. The size of the assembly was about one-third of that of the congress, but it had equal representation of provincial, municipal, and county committees. The party ratio of the assembly members were: Labor, 86 (36 percent); Democrats and

Chungwoo-dang, 30 (13 percent); and independents, 91 (36 percent). Of the 237 members, 34 (15 percent) were women. The average age of the members was less than forty; the majority of them had been freedom fighters during Japanese rule.[13] The occupational distribution of the members was: peasants, 62 (26 percent); laborers, 52 (22 percent); office workers, 56 (24 percent); intelligentsia, 38 (15 percent); merchants, 10 (4 percent); clergymen, 10 (4 percent); entrepreneurs, 7 (3 percent); and handicraft industrialists, 4 (2 percent).

The People's Assembly was only two days in session (February 21 and 23) but long enough to elect the members of the Supreme Court and a new eleven-man presidium headed by Kim Du-bong, chairman of the North Korean Labor party, and to form a new twenty-two-man People's Committee headed by Kim Il-sung. This time the word "provisional" was dropped from the title of the Provisional People's Committee.

Except for Kim Il-sung and Kim Du-bong, most members had received a Japanese-oriented education. The propaganda chief was Miss Huh Jung-sook, the only woman in the "cabinet"; one of the vice-chairmen of the People's Committee was the Christian minister, Rev. Hong Ki-ju; and a well-known novelist, Han Sul-ya, became head of the Department of Education. The average age of the cabinet members was forty-four; chairman Kim Il-sung was the youngest, 37 years old, and Kim Du-bong was the oldest, 66 years old.

The elections for the villages and districts were then held. The results were: 99.85 percent of the eligible voters cast their votes, electing 53,314 deputies, including 7,049 women; of this number, 86.6 percent voted for the candidates of the North Korean National Democratic Front.[14]

For the elections for the districts the voting percentage was higher than for any other local elections: 99.98 percent of the eligible electorate voted; 96.2 percent voted for the candidates of the Democratic Front. The total number of elected deputies was 13,444, of which 2,986 were women.[15]

The voting percentage of the village and district elections was high, more than 99 percent, and the average percentage in the county, municipal, and provincial elections was about 97 percent.

The occupational composition of the people's committees was: in the village committees 87 percent of the deputies were peasants, in the district committees 58 percent, in the county, city, and province committees 36 percent.[16] The peasant population was the backbone of the North Korean Labor party, but not the county, city, and provincial committees. The presidium and the People's Committee in the capital were under the absolute control of the Labor party.

Establishment of the Democratic People's Republic. Soon after the Soviet Union rejected the American proposal for U.N.-supervised elections in Korea, the Korean Communists took steps to establish a separate govenment in the North. In November 1947 a thirty-one-man committee was formed to draw up a constitution.[17] It was ratified by the People's Assembly, and in May 1948 the People's Committee announced a new constitution and a new flag for all Korea. In early July the People's Committee announced that nationwide general elections would be held on August 25 to select 572 deputies, of which 212 would represent the population of the North and 360 that of the South.

According to the North Korean report, the elections were held in the South despite the bitter opposition of South Korean authorities, and 77.5 percent of the electorate participated.[18] However, what actually happened was that a convention of 1,002 "delegates" representing the South Korean population was held in Haeju, north of the 38th parallel, on August 22–24, and the delegates selected 360 deputies to represent South Korea in the Supreme People's Assembly.[19] In North Korea 99.7 percent of the electorate voted in selecting 212 deputies. The occupational classification of the deputies of the Supreme People's Assembly was: professional politicians, 47.2 percent; peasants, 16 percent; factory workers, 8.2 percent; white-collar workers, 2.8 percent; others, 0.3 percent. The distribution according to political parties was: North Korean Labor party, 17.9 percent; North Korean Democratic party, 6.2 percent; Chungwoo-dang, 6.2 percent; Labor Union Alliance, 4.7 percent; Peasant's Alliance, 4.7 percent; South Korean Labor party, 9.6 percent; Laboring People's party (South), 3.5 percent; Social Democratic party (South), 3.5 percent; and Korean Independence party, 1.2 percent.[20]

From September 3 to 10, 1948, the Supreme People's Assembly in Pyongyang was attended by 572 deputies. The assembly first ratified the constitution which had already been announced by the People's Committee on May 1. Thus the "new" constitution was the same as the previous one. The constitution declared Korea to be a Democratic people's republic; the sovereignty of the country to be in the people and to be exercised by the Supreme People's Assembly through the People's Committee. It confirmed land reform and nationalization of all natural resources, guaranteed the people the right to engage in small and medium-sized industry and commerce, guaranteed equal rights to the people regardless of sex, race, education, and profession, and guaranteed freedom of speech, assembly, press, and religion. The constitution also included the provisions of the previous labor decree concerning the principles of equal remuneration for equal labor, the right to rest as well as the obligation to work, and retirement with pension at a certain age.

The constitution confirmed the Supreme People's Assembly as the highest legislative organ, and the presidium as the supreme legislative organ when the assembly was not in session. The cabinet ministers were designated as the supreme executive organs of the state; the cabinet was headed by the premier. The local units of the administration were the province, city, county, district, and village; each level of the people's committees was subordinated directly to the next higher level. Thus a pyramidal power structure was established.

Kim Il-sung was elected premier by the Supreme People's Assembly, and he formed a cabinet composed of three vice-premiers and twelve ministers.[21] On September 10 the Supreme People's Assembly unanimously approved the appointment of the cabinet ministers. Eight out of the twelve were South Koreans: the most prominent among them were Park Heun-yong, vice-premier and minister of foreign affairs; Hong Myung-hi (former leader of the middle-of-the-road group), vice-premier; and Kim Won-bong (former defense minister of the Korean provisional government in China), minister of inspection. The chairmanship of the Supreme People's Assembly went to Kim Du-bong (chairman of the Central Committee of the North Korean Labor party), and the head of the South Korean Labor party, Huh Heun, was elected chairman of the standing committee of the Supreme People's Assembly.

Although some leaders of minority parties were appointed to the cabinet, most ministers were members of the Labor party (Communists), as had been the case in the previous People's Committee regime. Furthermore, all key positions of the new government were occupied by the members of the Labor party. Therefore, the Democratic People's Republic of Korea was not the coalition the Communists claimed, but a regime established and dominated by Communists.

On September 11 the Supreme People's Assembly formally requested the Russian and American governments to simultaneously withdraw their troops from Korea. The Soviet Union responded to the request, stating that the Soviet occupation forces would be withdrawn at the end of December 1948.[22] On October 13 the Soviet Union formally recognized the Democratic People's Republic of Korea as the only government in Korea.[23] On March 17, 1949, a Russo-Korean agreement on economic and cultural cooperation was signed.[24]

Comparison of the Governments of North and South. The political ideologies as well as the structure of the two governments were different. The Southern Republic was based on the principles of Western democracy, the Northern People's Republic on Communist political philosophy, or as it was called, the philosophy of a people's democracy. The Southern government's structure was modeled after the American system of the separation and balance of power, with the president as the head of state. The Northern government was patterned after the governmental structure of the Soviet Union, that is, centralization of power under one-party control.

The social and economic backgrounds of the cabinet members of the two governments were also markedly different: most of the Southern cabinet members belonged to the upper social stratum of Western-educated Koreans; many of them had lived long periods abroad, most in the United States and a few in China. President Syngman Rhee had resided in the United States for more than thirty-five years; Prime Minister Lee Bum-suk had lived in China for more than twenty years. Some of the cabinet members had served prison terms under the Japanese for anti-Japanese activities; all of them were conservatives, and none of them had administrative experience.

Most Northern cabinet members came from middle-class families. Most of them had received their higher education in Korea, Japan, or China; none of them were educated in Western countries. Two cabinet members had received a Russian education: Premier Kim Il-sung had served in the Soviet army during the Second World War and had become a major; Vice-Premier Park Heun-yong had studied in Moscow and in later years visited the Soviet Union a few times as the delegate of the Korean Communist party. The Northern Korean regime contained a large number of militant revolutionaries and was headed by the Russian-trained Communist dictator, thirty-seven-year-old Kim Il-sung; the Southern regime was headed by the Machiavellian rightist dictator, seventy-three-year-old Syngman Rhee, and his henchmen.

Kim Il-sung formulated the concept of *juche* (principle of self-reliance) as the guideline of the Democratic People's Republic. He stated that all Korean problems, including unification, should be resolved on the basis of the self-reliance principle, without interference by foreign powers. Thus *juche* could be interpreted as Kim's version of the principle of self-determination. Recently Kim changed his unification tactics from peaceful means to direct military action, and the Northern Communist regime once again is attempting to overthrow the Southern republic by force.

Soon after General Park Chung-hee—who received his early military training in Japan, Korea, and the United States—overthrew the Second Republic in the 1961 military coup, he established himself as the unchallenged leader in South Korea. During the military junta period, he removed al rivals from the high power structure. Then he retired from the army and ran for the presidency twice, being elected both times. Now he is preparing for a third term by revising through undemocratic procedures in the assembly the two-term limitation set by the constitution.

President Park advocated the policy of "economics first and democracy second," arguing that the reconstruction of the economy was "a basic prerequisite for a genuine free democracy that guarantees man's freedom and dignity." He promised to build "a welfare state for the greatest benefit to the greatest number possible." Park's administration has made impressive economic progress during the past five years, although the realization of a self-supporting economy is still remote.

More recently President Park announced that he is ready to discuss the unification problem with North Korean leaders, if they will completely abandon guerrilla and other subversive activities in South Korea and accept peaceful and free competition in economic reconstruction and unification.

Government Structure during and after the War. Soon after the outbreak of the Korean war, a War Committee, similar to the State Defense Committee of the Soviet Union during the Second World War, was established as a temporary organ of the state. Kim Il-sung was given the title of marshal and assumed the chairmanship. The committee was composed of seven members, including Marshal Kim, and exercised absolute power. All citizens, organs of power, and political and social organizations were obliged to submit themselves without reservation to its decisions and directives.[25]

Some changes of the government structure took place as a result of decisions of the Supreme People's Assembly in March 1955, but the fundamental power structure of the state remained the same. In accordance with the newly adopted law, the cabinet of ministers was to have a plenum and a presidium. This system was based on the principle of collective leadership. The plenum was composed of the chairman, vice-chairman, chairman of the committee, and ministers; and the presidium consisted of the chairman and vice-chairman of the cabinet of ministers.

The law also provided that, depending upon the circumstances, groups of colleges of from seven to ten members were to be appointed by the minister. The group headed by the minister was to discuss the major issues, but their decisions were to be carried out only on the order of the minister, "who is not bound to execute it if it conflicts with his judgment."[26]

The local administrative units also were rearranged.[27] The provincial territorial units were redivided by the creation of three new provinces, so that now North Korea has nine provinces: South Pyongyang, Jagan (new), South Hwanghai, North Hwanghai (formerly combined as Hwanghai), Kangwan, South Hamkyung, North Hamkyung, and Ranggang (new). Meanwhile, from the existing 91 counties, 168 counties were created, whereas the number of village administrative units was reduced from 10,120 to 3,650. Within the village administrative units, there were people's groups, known as *imminban,* composed of from ten to twenty-five households. In each group a "people's elder," who was the leader of the group, was appointed by the village people's committee. This group was not designed as an administrative unit, but as a "social" group to aid the People's Committee.

The local organs, formerly called people's committees, now became known as people's assemblies; the executive body of each people's assembly, formerly called the presidium, was now named the people's committee. Before 1954, the term of the deputies to the local assemblies was not fixed, but now the deputies of the provincial assemblies were to hold office for four years and those to the county and village assemblies for two years. The people's assemblies on all levels were entitled to create commissions, according to need, to take care of such problems as crops, preparation for the new school year, and adult education.

The provincial, city, and county people's committees were allowed to establish departments under their jurisdiction, but these departments were in a subordinate position both to the people's committees and to the corresponding departments of higher people's committees and ministers. There were no departments in the village people's committees, because the work was divided among the deputies. Under the reorganization plan the district administrative units were completely eliminated, by transfering their work to higher organs.

It would seem that the purpose of the reorganization of the local administrative units was to enable the highest organs of power to more tightly control the lower organs.

After the reorganization of the local units was completed, local elections took place, in November 1956.[28] As usual, the overwhelming majority of the voters cast ballots: more than 99.7 percent of the electorate voted for some 53,000 deputies of the village people's assemblies. The only change in the village elections was the considerable decline of the peasant vote, whereas those of the office workers and intelligentsia showed a sharp increase. In the provincial, city, and county people's assemblies the number of deputies increased from 5,800 to 10,000. This was the result of the elimination of the district administration units; their work was to be carried out by either the county, city, or provincial people's assemblies. The proportion of office workers also increased, although not so much as in the village elections. The local elections had taken place almost eight years after the 1948 elections. During this period considerable industrial progress had been made and many peasants had become industrial and office workers.

In August 1957 the election for deputies to the Supreme People's Assembly was held. This was also the first election since 1948, although the constitution provided for one every three years. Kim Il-sung explained that "we have been compelled to put off until now the elections of the Supreme People's Assembly because of the three-year war forced upon us by the enemy . . . and because of the complicated and urgent work of rehabilitation of the national economy following the war."[29]

The election procedure was the same as before: the single-slate ticket and the white box for yes, the black box for no.[30] The results were reported as follows: 99.92 percent of the registered voters cast their votes; 215 deputies were elected, of which only 71 were reelected deputies, the rest newcomers. Among the latter, 61 had prison records for anti-Japanese activities, 5 were patriots who fought against the U.N. forces during the Korean war, 15 were labor leaders who distinguished themselves in the struggle for the reconstruction of the national economy, and 2 were artists. There were 180 deputies who had received medals of various kinds for outstanding services in the struggle for independence and economic reconstruction of North Korea.[31]

The first session of the newly elected Supreme People's Assembly opened in Pyongyang on September 18; the next day it entrusted the formation of a new cabinet to Kim Il-sung. Kim formed a new cabinet with 30 ministers, 23 of whom were members of the Central Committee of the Labor party. Thus the interlocking character of the state and party hierarchies was demonstrated.

The newly elected presidium and the newly appointed cabinet members were as follows:

Presidium—president, Choi Yong-kun; vice-presidents, Yi Kuk-no, Hyun Chil-chong, and Kim Won-bong. The vice-presidents were South Koreans who had gone North to attend the North-South Political Leaders Coalition Conference. They were not Communists at that time and were considered moderate leftists. Gen. Choi Yong-kun was considered a militant Communist leader; he had fought against the Japanese in northern China.

Cabinet—premier, Marshal Kim Il-sung; vice-premiers, Hong Myung-hi (a South Korean, formerly leader of the middle-of-the-road group), Nam Il (a Russian-trained Communist general and chief delegate of the Northern Korean regime to the truce conference, minister of foreign affairs), Chung Chen-taek, and Chung Il-yong. Most new cabinet members were not known to the public, except the minister of education, Han Sol-ya, a novelist.[32]

Political Groupings under Communist Control. In North Korea a multiparty system exists under Communist control. The Korean Communist party itself was reorganized several times after the war. In August 1945 the South Korean Communist party was reorganized in Seoul under the leadership of Park Heun-yong, one of the founders of the party in 1925, who became secretary general of the party. In North Korea, the Communist Committee of South Pyongang province was established in September 1945, and in October a North Korean Communist party conference was convened with representatives from the five northern provinces. At the conference, the Communist leaders split over the basic policy of the party into three groups[33] —left, right, and moderate. The leftist group, known as the Changan faction, insisted that a proletarian dictatorship should be established in Korea by the Communist party, because, they argued, the Second World War was a war of social revolution, as a result of the participation of Soviet Russia, and the bourgeois revolution had successfully taken place in Korea with the destruction of Japanese imperialist rule. The rightists said that the first task of the Communist party was to bring about the bourgeois revolution with the cooperation of the conservative nationalist forces, because the feudalistic socioeconomic structure was intact even after the termination of the Japanese rule; therefore, a proletarian dictatorship was out of the question at this time. The moderate group opposed both of them on the ground that they were deviationists, who did not understand the socioeconomic conditions of Korea. The moderates believed that Korea was not ready for a proletarian dictatorship, because the bourgeois revolution, which is one of the prerequisites for the socialist revolution, had not yet been completed, and, also, the bourgeois revolution could not and would not be achieved through cooperation with the right-wing political forces. The moderates advocated a "people's democratic revolution" based on the principles of socioeconomic reform and alliance with all progressive social forces under the leadership of the Communist party.

Another controversial issue was the location of the Bureau of the Central Committee of the Communist party. One group favored Pyongyang and the others Seoul. After much debate the moderate group prevailed, and Kim Il-sung succeeded himself as secretary of the Bureau of the Central Committee. The party immediately announced the programs for the people's democratic revolution: land reform, nationalization of heavy industry and natural resources, and elimination of the feudalistic social structure, pro-Japanese Koreans, and traitors. For the rapid realization of the people's democracy, the party emphasized cooperation with the peasants, the labor movement, patriotic nationalists, and liberal intellectuals. The Northern Communists penetrated the mass social movement, such as the Peasant's Alliance, Worker's Alliance, Democratic Young Men's Alliance, and Democratic Women's Alliance. Many Communist leaders also got into the new political movements and eventually became party leaders.

Three other political parties were formed in 1945. The New People's party was organized by the former members of the League of Independence, which was established in 1942 in Yenan, China, under the leadership of Kim Du-bong. Many members of the Independence League fought with the Chinese Communist Eighth People's Revolutionary Army against Japan during the Second World War, and returned to North Korea following the Soviet landings; most of the members of the New People's party were considered to be left-oriented nationalists. Kim Du-bong became head of the party. The New People's party soon merged with the Communist party to form the North Korean Labor party.

The Democratic party was established under the leadership of Cho Man-sik, a nationalist leader known as the Korean Gandhi. The party membership was composed of intellectuals, businessmen, and professional groups. Many leading Christian leaders and patriotic nationalists joined the Democratic party, which became an influential nationalistic political force in North Korea. When the party opposed the Moscow Agreement, Cho Man-sik was replaced by the Communist Choi Yong-kun as the new leader of the Democratic party.

The Chungwoo-dang (Young Friend's party) was formed by members of the native nationalistic religion, Chundokyo. Many leading members of the religion had participated in the independence movement since 1919. As in the Democratic party, the party leaders were gradually replaced by Communists or sympathizers. Kim Dal-hun, a pro-Communist, became head of the Chungwoo-dang.

In the summer of 1946, there were four political parties and twelve semi-social organizations. Then the Communist leaders created a North Korean National Democratic Front[34] to include all existing political parties and semi-social organizations. The purposes of the front were to unify political action under Communist leadership. The Communists insisted that this was absolutely necessary to meet the threat of the reactionary forces supported by the United States military government in South Korea.

The front established, the Communists next undertook the task of merging the North Korean Communist party with the New People's party by creating a new party, the North Korean Labor party (or Worker's party). In August 1946 a party unification conference was held: Kim Il-sung, representing the Communist party, and Kim Du-bong, representing the New People's party, issued a statement explaining that the merger of the two parties was natural under the existing social circumstances in North Korea.

The eight hundred delegates to the conference unanimously approved the unification. The Labor party announced the party platform, according to which the ultimate objective was "the building of a strong, independent, democratic state."[35] For the attainment of this objective it set forth the following tasks: (1) the strengthening of the land reform; (2) the nationalization of all Japanese industrial establishments, all land, all heavy industry, and all natural resources; (3) the introduction of the eight-hour working day and a system of social security; (4) the introduction of a new tax system; (5) universal suffrage, guarantying all citizens the freedom of speech, assembly, demonstration, and organization; (6) the placing of all power in the people's committees; (7) rapid raising of the living standard of the masses; (8) introduction of a free public education system; (9) introduction of a system of obligatory military service; and (10) the establishment of friendly relations with all "peace-loving" states.[36]

Kim Il-sung became the chief of the party, and Kim Du-bong became chairman of the Central Committee. It is interesting to note that the party's objective was stated as the "building of a strong independent democratic state," which was in complete harmony with the proclaimed objective of the provisional People's Committee, and it was silent on the building of a "socialistic state" as the Marxist party.

To sum up: All political parties and social and labor organizations were "united" in the North Korean National Democratic Front. Any member or leader of the party dissatisfied with government policies was either purged or forced to flee to South Korea. The Labor party became the government party, and the Communists, though in a minority, controlled the political scene, guided by Soviet authorities. The North Korean political system was under one-party control but presented itself as a multiparty system.

The Nature of the Labor Party. Until the Korean war the Labor party's goal was the building of an independent and unified democratic state through the cooperation of patriotic and progressive political and social organizations in the North and South. However, as soon as the war broke out, the Labor party professed its adherence to Marxism and its link with Moscow. Kim Il-sung declared that "the victory of the Great October Socialist Revolution in Russia and success of the world's first socialist country exerted an enormous influence on the development of the national liberation movement in Korea. . . . The theoretical basis of the Labor party is Marxism and Leninism."[37]

After the Korean war the Labor party revised its rules at the third party congress in 1956.[38] Article one stated that the Labor party was "a vanguard, an organized detachment of the working class and all the toiling masses of the country," and it was "guided in its activities by the theory of Marxism-Leninism." The immediate aim of the party was the actualization of a democratic-social revolution against imperialism and feudalism on a nation-wide scale, and the ultimate aim, the building of a Communist society." The Labor party pledged itself to achieve the unification of the country on a democratic basis.

The organization of the Labor party was similar to that of the Soviet Communist party. It was based on democratic centralization, stressing the subordination of members to the party and of lower bodies to higher bodies. The central party congress was the highest organ of the party; it convened once every four years. The party congress was given authority to select a central committee (71 members), which, in turn, formed the 11 member (5 alternative members) presidium to act and guide its work between the sessions. In place of the secretariat of the party, like the Soviet Communist party secretariat, the Labor party had the organizing committee carry out such work as controlling the implementation of the party decisions, and selecting and assigning of personnel.

The organization of the Labor party was based at the provincial, district, county, and city levels; the highest level was the party conference, because the party committee was chosen by this conference. The committee, in turn, organized an executive committee. Elections to the highest bodies were held indirectly, and the provincial party conference had the right to select delegates to the party congress, while the county, city, and district party conferences were given the right to elect delegates to the provincial party conference.

The basic unit of the party was the cell, formed by three or more members of industrial, cooperative farm, military, or governmental institutions. Each group had a leader, who acted in accordance with the directives received from the party committee.

All working people who were Korean citizens were eligible to become members of the party. Party membership increased rapidly because of this lenient admission policy: in 1948 the membership was estimated at 750,000, in 1956 at 1,164,000. This meant that the Labor party membership was about 11 percent of the total North Korean population, higher than that of the Soviet Union or China.

The power struggle within the party became acute after the Armistice Agreement in July 1953. There were two factions within the Labor party: the pro-Russian group and the Southern group. The former was headed by Kim Il-sung, the latter by Park Heun-yong. In this connection, it should be pointed out that the Communist party of South Korea (changed to the Labor party of South Korea) was completely destroyed as an organized force by U.S. occupation authorities and by the police of the South Korean government; finally, the South Korean Labor party was outlawed and many Communists fled to the North.

The most prominent Communist to flee North was Park Heun-yong, who escaped during the American military occupation period; he became vice-premier and minister of foreign affairs in the Democratic People's Republic; in addition, during the Korean war he served as one of the seven members of the War Committee.

Park Heun-yong was born in 1906, the son of a poor peasant family in

Yisan, South Chungchong province. He graduated from Lenin University in Moscow. In 1919 he and other Communists organized a Korean Communist Youth Club in Shanghai; in 1925 he was one of the founders of the Korean Communist party in Seoul. He was arrested twice by the Japanese and served many years in prison. He attended many international Communist meetings as the delegate of the Korean Communist party. During the Second World War he participated in the anti-Japanese resistance movement. After the Japanese defeat, Park reorganized the Korean Communist party and became general secretary of the party. The American military government issued a warrant for the arrest of Park, charging him with counterfeiting money. In 1946 he fled to the North. Park is considered a nationalistic Communist and has many followers.

The background of Kim Il-sung remains somewhat obscure. According to one source,[39] his real name was Kim Song-ju. He had been a Soviet army officer (a major), and as a celebrated guerrilla assumed the name of Kim Il-sung. According to this source, the present Kim cannot have been the same person, because he is much younger than the real Kim Il-sung, who would be more than seventy years old if he were alive today (1970). But the official biography[40] states that the present Kim Il-sung was born in 1921 near Pyongyang, capital of the Democratic People's Republic of Korea; at the age of fourteen he emigrated to Manchuria. He joined the Communist party in 1931 and became a leader of a partisan detachment against the Japanese army; in 1935 he organized the Society for the Rebirth of the Fatherland, in which a number of Korean revolutionary and patriotic groups were united. Since 1937 Kim (still according to the same official biography) commanded the People's Revolutionary Army of Korean Partisans against the Japanese in Manchuria; he and his army entered North Korea when the Soviet troops landed in August 1945. The Russian occupational authorities introduced Kim Il-sung to the North Korean people as a national hero, who had been fighting for the cause of national independence.

Soon after the armistice a purge was carried out: in August 1953 ten Communist leaders were sentenced to death, charged with espionage and terrorism during the Korean war. Lee Syung-eup, former secretary of the central committee of the Labor party, was charged with being the ringleader.[41] Park Heun-yong was removed from his posts as vice-premier and foreign minister and replaced by the Soviet-trained general Nam Il, the former chief truce-negotiator. No public announcement was made about the status of Park for two years. Finally, in December 1955, the government disclosed that Park had been sentenced to death, charged with "espionage and anti-state activities."[42]

The purge has been variously interpreted: some observers believe that it was connected with Beria; others think the purge meant the defeat of the Korean nationalistic Communists in favor of the Russian-trained and Chinese-trained Communists, for the victims of the purge were related to the leading Communists who had fled North. In the past, personal rivalry for leadership existed between Kim Il-sung and Park Heun-yong: the Kim group charged that Park and his followers concentrated on recruiting party members indiscriminately in order to strengthen their own group, while the Park group criticized the Kim group because the key positions of the government were filled by Russian and Chinese-trained Communists.

The official version of the purge was expressed by Kim Il-sung at the plenum of the Central Committee of the Labor party.[43] Kim blamed the so-called revisionists, who "advocated unprincipled democracy and freedom, opposing the party's centralism." To this day (1971) Kim Il-sung has been the predominant figure in North Korea, occupying the highest posts in party and state and acting as spokesman for both on important issues.

CHAPTER 18

NORTH KOREA'S ECONOMY

Geography. North Korea is mountainous and essentially continental rather than maritime. The cold winter and short growing season limit agriculture to one crop a year. This has been one of the reasons for the low population density compared to that of South Korea. Mineral deposits and hydroelectric power resources made North Korea the industrial zone of Korea, especially with respect to the development of heavy industry.

North Korea, composed of nine provinces, can be divided into three regions: the northern interior region, the northeastern coast region,[1] and the northwestern region. Each region has its own characteristics of geography, natural resources, and economic activities.

The northern interior section is comprised of fifteen thousand square miles, with a population of 100,000. It is a land of mountains and hills, and has relatively warm summers but bitterly cold winters. The region is rich in forests, hydroelectric power potential, and mineral deposits. For years it has been the frontier for land-hungry Korean farmers who clear the forest by fire. The main mineral products are iron ore, gold, copper, and ferroalloy metals; the main agricultural products are millet, rye, buckwheat, barley, potatoes, and oats. It is a self-sufficient rural economic region; farmers supplement their incomes by lumbering and by raising domestic animals.

The northeastern coast has an area of about eleven thousand square miles and 2,000,000 inhabitants. It is also mountainous, but the maritime influence (Sea of Japan) is strong in contrast to the other two regions. During Japanese rule, economic activities were intensified by the development of a transportation system—the construction of a railroad and of a harbor for coastal shipping. In the 1930's, after the beginning of military expansion in Manchuria by the Japanese, this region became the center of heavy industry in the peninsula. The basis of industrialization was the rapid development of hydroelectric power plants, such as those in Chungjin and Pujon, which produced nearly 600,000 kilowatts of electric power in 1944. Another power plant at the Hochon River could provide an additional 390,000 kilowatts. Hungnam became the most industrialized city in the peninsula. The industry and commerce of this region, however, depended largely upon outside resources for raw materials and on export markets for purchase of industrial products.

The northeastern region, which comprises more than sixteen thousand square miles with 4,800,000 people, is a well-balanced area. It has thick forests, rich soil, considerable mineral deposits, good ports, hydroelectric power potential, and heavy and light industries.

An important mineral resource in this region is gold. The deposits were first owned by Western companies, which obtained the concessions without compensation from the Korean king. Later the Japanese took them over and developed silver, copper, iron-ore, and coal mining industries. During the Second World War, the Supung hydroelectric power plant was constructed, and Pyongyang and Shinuiju became industrial centers for aluminum products, chemicals, textiles, electrical equipment, bicycles, and other consumer goods.

Agricultural products are rice, soy beans, cotton, tobacco, apples, and millet. This region has always been economically self-sufficient.

The northwestern region has been the political and cultural center of the peninsula; the legendary Chinese ruler Kija established his capital at Pyongyang in 1122 B.C.; the native Koguryo kingdom, the strongest among the three kingdoms in the peninsula, ruled this region until A.D. 668 after defeating a series of Chinese invasions; this area became the main route of the Sino-Korean tributary missions; it also was the battleground of the early Mongolian invasions, the Japanese invasion, the modern Sino-Japanese war, the Russo-Japanese war, and the Korean war. Pyongyang has been one of the cultural centers in Korea, as the capital of Kija, Koguryo, and the present Democratic People's Republic of Korea.

The northwestern region has been the center of economic activities in Korea because of its ties with the economic development of Manchuria. Under Japanese rule, the main railroad lines of the peninsula were connected with the Manchurian railroad system. Today the economic link between the Northern Korean regime and the Chinese Communist government has made northwestern Korea one of the most important economic areas in northeastern Asia.

Human Resources. During the Japanese administration the population of North Korea increased rapidly (to 8,233,000 in 1940), aided by industrial development. Nearly 70 percent of the population is still engaged in farming, and 12 percent in industry, mining, commerce, and transportation. The personnel shortage in industry was so acute in North Korea that the Soviet Command retained some Japanese technicians. Soon an intensive technical training program was launched; many Russian technicians were invited to teach Korean workers, and many Koreans were sent to Russia for advanced training. In 1947 alone, fifteen hundred experts and twenty thousand skilled workers finished their training. The labor shortage continued during and after the Korean war and is likely to plague North Korea for some time.

Economic Planning. As already noted, the Soviet occupation army first seized all Japanese property—land, industry, and means of transportation and communication—and then turned them over to the Soviet-sponsored People's Committee, which not only nationalized them but also the property of Koreans who were pro-Japanese. The nationalization of industry was simple, because more than 90 percent of all heavy industry was owned by the Japanese; and the nationalization of the means of transportation and communication was no problem at all, because they belonged to the government even under the Japanese administration.

The North Korean Communists did not carry out a forthright nationalization of enterprises owned by Korean citizens. The People's Committee even encouraged the development of private initiative by issuing Decision Number 91[2] on October 4, 1946. The essential points of the decision were: (1) The People's Court was given authority to decide what constituted personal property and personal business. (2) Industry owned by Koreans was not to be included in the nationalization. (3) Korean citizens were entitled to be compensated for their holdings in former Japanese concerns. (4) The People's Committee authorized the department of industry and of commerce to sell to Koreans general consumer-goods factories which were formerly owned by Japanese and employed less than fifteen laborers.

The decision clearly indicated the protection and encouragement of private ownership in industrial and commercial activities. It did not mention the nationalization of basic industries and public ownership of the means of transportation and communication, because these properties had already been nationalized under the committee's rule.

The decision also classified who was a traitor in terms of economic interest. Pro-Japanese Koreans were classified as traitors, and their properties were confiscated without compensation; they were excluded from the business world, and from the right to own property. Korean citizens who had not lost their citizenship for traitorous activities were entitled to own property.

In doing this, the authority of the People's Committee made itself felt in matters of economic policy-making. Subsequently economic reform programs were launched covering a wide area: land reform, financial and monetary reforms, social security, and labor legislation.

The objective of economic planning was the maximization of production in every field. In February 1947 Kim Il-sung outlined the objectives before the Assembly of the People's Committee: double the volume of production over that in the previous year, increase the productivity of labor by 48 percent, increase coal production in order to operate industry and transportation effectively, improve railroad facilities, increase grain production by expanding farm lands, and encourage production of consumer goods and household industry.[3]

Thus economic planning for the expansion of production was in operation in North Korea during the first two years after liberation.

Land Reform. The total cultivated acreage in North Korea was about six million acres, of which dry fields occupied five million acres. The ownership of 55 percent of the land was concentrated in the hands of about 4 percent of the farming population. Some 75 percent of the peasants were either without land or occupied at least part of their land as tenants: about 22 percent were owner-tenants and 53 percent landless tenants. The independent farmers or self-sufficient landowners accounted for 20 percent of the peasants.[4] The average holding of a poor farmer was half an acre. The average rent was between 50 to 70 percent of the crop, and more than half a million farming families could not feed themselves till the next harvest.

North Korea (like South Korea) was predominantly agricultural, 62 percent of the total population being engaged in farming. Northern farming has been characterized by a short growing season, little double-cropping, and little rice-growing as compared to that of the South. The important grains are barley, millet, buckwheat, oats, *kaoliang* (sorghum), and potatoes. North Korea has not produced sufficient food for its inhabitants, especially in the two northern provinces (North and South Hamkyong). But the fertilizer plant in South Hamkyong province was able to supply sufficient fertilizer for all Korea and increase rice production in South Korea before the division of the country. Large surpluses of rice produced in the South could offset the deficit in the North.

The first measure of agricultural policy to be enacted in North Korea was the reduction of rental payment to 30 percent of the crop; this came into effect in the fall of 1946. The land reform law[5] was promulgated in March 1946.

Article one of the law stated that the right to use the land should go to those who till it, and that the agricultural system in North Korea would be based on a farm economy which does not subject farmers to landlords, but recognizes the farmer's individual ownership of the land.

Article two provided for confiscation of land owned by Japanese, by traitors who collaborated with the Japanese, by Korean landlords in excess of 5 *chungbo* (1 *chungbo* equals 2.45 acres) per farming family; and land not personally tilled by the owner but rented out; and land owned by religious institutions in excess of 5 *chungbo*.

According to article four, land owned by schools, hospitals, and scientific institutions was not to be confiscated; and land owned by persons and their families who took an active part in the cause of independence against the Japanese or who made outstanding contributions for the development of national culture, science, and art would not be confiscated.

No compensation was to be made to those whose land was confiscated, and the land was to be distributed free to the farmers, who also were given title to "permanent ownership" of the land (article four). Thus "the right of private property" in land was recognized, as in the case of other property such as factories and industries.

Land given to peasants under the land reform law was exempt from debts and general liabilities (article eight). All lands distributed to peasants "shall not be bought, sold, or rented for tenancy, or mortgaged" (article ten).

The land reform was carried out by the village committees, which were composed of from five to nine members elected under the supervision of the county people's committees. However, the land distribution was ultimately subject to the approval of the provincial people's committee, because it issued a certificate of land ownership after screening each applicant.[6] The land distribution was completed in twenty-three days, by April 1, 1946.[7] The results were: total confiscated land, 2,450,796 acres; total distributed land, 2,395,209 acres; and land reserved by the people's committee, 45,590 acres. The number of households that received land was 724,522 or 72 percent of all farmers of North Korea; of those, 442,975, or more than half, had been farmers with no land; of the 6,933 landlords, 3,911 received land.[8] The average acreage of farming families was about 3 acres; the peasants were required to pay 25 percent of their crop to the government in tax.

The significance of the land reform was obvious: for centuries, the Korean peasants had lived as virtual serfs, if not slaves, under native landlords; during Japanese rule, their status changed to "tenant-slaves," because of the excessive rent and nonrecognition of tenant lease rights. Most peasants were in debt.

The land reform—the free distribution of land and recognition of permanent ownership—was heaven sent news. The North Korean peasants thought that at last they had liberated themselves from slavery.

Miss Anna Louise Strong, the only Western correspondent who visited North Korea during the Soviet occupation period, wrote: "By summer of 1947, the time of my visit, the land reform was well established, the cultivated area had been increased some 17.5 percent over that of 1945, and the fields were fertilized and better worked. So the big news in autumn of 1947 was that North Korea could feed itself properly on a harvest of two million metric tons, about a pound and a quarter of grain per person per day."[9]

The political impact of the land reform upon the peasants was even more significant: the age-old conservative political power supported by the landlords was completely broken, and a new progressive social force emerged from the peasants who comprised the bulk of the population of North Korea. The North Korean regime called the land reform "the people's democratization program" to create a "people's democracy."

Nevertheless, the reform program was criticized on the grounds that the right of permanent ownership of the land had no meaning, because the disposal right of the land was not given to the peasants and was reserved by the state. This meant, so it was said, that the government became the new landlord and that the peasants had merely become tenants of the new regime, the People's Committee; furthermore, that the farmers had to pay taxes and other levies, such as patriotic or special contributions, imposed by the government; and that they remained in essentially the same position as they had been after paying rent to landlords. Taxes and public levies ran between 50 to 70 percent of the farmer's crops.[10]

Collective Farms. The North Korean regime did not stop with the 1946 land reform, but in 1949 decreed a state-farm system. State farms were established on both provincial and national levels; the main task of the farms was to demonstrate to the farmers "the superiority of large farms with their ability to use mechanized equipment and modern methods." Labor was organized on the basis of so-called brigades, and wages were paid according to a man's ability, including quality and quantity of work performed.

The members of the Labor party (Communist party) became the leaders of the state-farm movement, and gradually the members of the peasant union also participated. During the Korean war the government used the state farms effectively to increase grain production. However, these farms could not be considered as cooperative in a real sense, because each unit on the state farm was composed of from three to five households.

The real cooperative movement[11] was launched by the government soon after the war, and was based on "voluntary participation." Three forms of agricultural cooperative were introduced:[12] (a) That in which the members retained ownership of the land, and shared their agricultural tools and draft animals; the income belonged to the individual members. This kind of cooperative system had been practiced for centuries among rural farming households. (b) That in which the land was in principle the private property of the farmer, but became a kind of shared land among the members of the cooperative, with the exception of private kitchen gardens; agricultural implements and draft animals became cooperative property; the labor was in common, and income, after payment of taxes and other expenses, was divided among the members, 80 percent for labor and 20 percent for land. (c) That in which the members put together all their land, agricultural tools, and draft animals with the exception of a small number of livestock—one head of cattle, two pigs, two sheep, and some poultry. The land belonged to each member as private property, at least in theory. The third form was predominant and was officially called an "agricultural cooperative."

On August 15, 1955, the tenth anniversary of the liberation, Premier Kim Il-sung reported that the number of agricultural cooperatives had reached more than ten thousand and that the number of farm families incorporated in these cooperatives was approximately 43 percent of the total number of farm families in the country.[13] He also said that the government gave great assistance for the development of cooperatives, providing capital funds, seeds, machines, and fertilizers. According to official statistics of 1958, over 95.6 percent of the farming families became members of the cooperatives. At the same time the first and second forms of cooperatives had more or less disappeared.[14]

Following the pattern of the Chinese Communist commune system, the North Korean regime, in October 1958, adopted the policy of "amalgamation of cooperatives."[15] The so-called right of private ownership of land was replaced by "joint ownership" of land under the ruling concerning agricultural cooperatives that went into effect in January 1959. In accordance with the directive for the amalgamation of cooperatives, 13,309 cooperatives merged into 3,880 within two weeks. The new rules of the cooperatives stated that the members should not only cultivate the land together but should also construct "socialist, cultural, rural villages" by constructing various kinds of educational, cultural, sports, and welfare facilities. Thus the community kitchens, day nurseries for children, rest homes for elders, clinics for free medical services, and schools were established as cooperative projects.

The collectivization program was guided by members of the Labor party. Under the new ruling, the chairman of the village people's committee became chairman of the amalgamation cooperative. He was supposed to be the sole administrative head of the cooperative, but most chairmen were also members of the Labor party. Therefore he had to follow the directives of the party: he also had to report on the cooperative's activities in party meetings.

The Labor party acted as watchdog in checking how well the chairmen of the cooperatives fulfilled the policy decisions of the party.

All evidence indicates that in North Korea the family-centered farming system has now been completely transformed into state-directed collective farming. It was thought that a rapid increase of agricultural production could be more easily achieved by large-scale collective farming rather than by the system of divided and scattered individual family plots; and, at the same time, the development of "prioritied heavy industry" would be more successful when the people had sufficient food. Heavy industry and agriculture are therefore the main objectives of the Northern Communists.

Industrial Structure: Nationalization. In 1945, at the time of liberation, the Japanese share of industrial enterprises and means of transportation and communication was 94 percent. More than 70 percent of Korea's heavy industrial output and 30 percent of consumer goods were produced in the North.

As pointed out, the Japanese-owned industry was first seized by the Russian army and then transferred to the North Korean Provisional People's Committee. In August 1946 the committee issued a decree by which all Japanese-owned industry and other properties, including personal property and cultural institutions, were nationalized.

During the first two years an attempt was made to encourage private enterprises to increase production: the government sold or rented small-scale Japanese industries to Korean private industrialists. However, the government controlled closely all business activities of these private enterprises, by requiring them to obtain government permission to operate or to enlarge. Jail sentences and fines were imposed on businessmen found guilty of hoarding or making illicit profits. Furthermore, price policy, direct credit, taxes, and trade unions were used to regulate the expansion of private enterprises. Private persons engaged in foreign trade were required to file detailed reports on the disposition of their merchandise.

Under the nationalization plan, more than one thousand industrial enterprises, which comprised 90 percent of all industry of North Korea, became state property. The Constitution of the Democratic People's Republic of Korea, adopted on September 3, 1948, confirmed the nationalization of all heavy industry and natural resources; it also provided for the protection of "private property rights," of income savings, and of the right to inherit property; it recognized cooperative ownership between state and private individual. The government adopted comprehensive social and labor legislation, such as an eight-hour working day, the right of work, equal pay for equal work regardless of age or sex, and social security in the form of old-age pensions, disability benefits, and medical care. At the same time, the government exercised tight control over labor: labor unions, trade associations, marine-product associations, consumer's cooperative societies, and all government-operated factories, mines, and business establishments were required to register the number of their employees with the government. The skilled workers and technicians were compelled to work at any industry that needed their services and were not allowed to leave or change their positions without permission from the authorities.

An economic administrative apparatus was established under a single ministry of industry: nine ministers, each directing a major branch of the economy, were appointed. Heavy industry was controlled by the central administration, light industry by local administration. The cooperative enterprises which produced most of the daily necessities were placed under the supervision of the central government.

Before the outbreak of the Korean war, the North Korean regime adopted a policy of economic recovery based on short-term yearly plans for 1947 and 1948 and a two-year plan for 1949–50. Emphasis was placed on raising local production and improving transportation and communication facilities. The government also called for the expansion of the state and cooperative sectors of the economy, and for further development of local industry through private enterprises.

During the three-year war the North Korean industrial facilities were almost completely destroyed. On May 28, 1954, the Pyongyang radio stated: North Korea suffered more than three billion dollars worth of damage; lost about eighty-seven hundred factory buildings, including chemical industries, electric power plants, fisheries, and forestry industries; means of communication and transportation were crippled; tens of thousands of human lives were lost.[16] The industrial section of northwestern Korea, especially the area around the capital city was in ruins. Industrial production dropped to 64 percent of that of 1949; the generation of electric power dropped to 26 percent; fuel production to 11 percent; metallurgical production to 10 percent; and chemical production to 22 percent.[17]

Postwar economic plans were outlined by Kim Il-sung at the Sixth Plenum of the Labor Party Central Committee. He stated that there would first be a six-months period for overall rehabilitation of the destroyed industries; then a three-year plan aimed at the attainment of prewar levels by all branches of the national economy; and then a five-year plan to lay the foundation for socialist industrialization.[18] The three-year plan covered the years 1954 to 1957, and resulted in substantial economic reconstruction. The government claimed that the objectives of the three-year plan were fulfilled in only two years and eight months.

The following increases in heavy industrial production were reported.[19] Coal production reached 3,900,000 tons, an increase of 5.5 times over 1953. The production capacity of steel increased 13 times over 1953: structural steel showed an increase of 44 percent, and electrolytic copper increased 31 percent. Electric power capacity reached 5.1 billion kilowatts annually, an increase of 5 times over 1953, the year of the truce agreement. Six new factories were constructed, including machine-tool, mining-machine, farm-machine, electric appliance, and textile-machine factories. In restoring the Hungnam fertilizer plant, the biggest in the Far East, 1.5 billion *hwan* were spent. New brick, cement, and glass factories were built. At the end of 1956, brick production increased 2.6 times and roof tiles 6.2 times over 1953; cement output increased 43 percent over 1953. One hundred twelve kilometers of forestry railways were laid and thirty-two lumbering centers were constructed in eighteen different places. In 1956 the volume of timber output exceeded that of 1949 by 60 percent. Over ten billion *hwan* was allocated for reconstruction work of the communication and transportation systems which were almost completely destroyed during the war; the number of locomotives increased by 26 percent compared with 1953; the Pyongyang-Moscow and Pyongyang-Peking through train lines were opened, which strengthened the ties between the three Communist states. In 1956 the total length of telephone lines increased by 123 percent and the number of post offices by 111 percent compared with 1953. International telephone lines were opened between Pyongyang and Moscow, Peking, Prague, Warsaw, Berlin, Budapest, Sofia, Bucharest, and Ulan Bator. A central broadcasting station was established with a 150 kilowatt capacity and modern facilities. Similar advances were reported for light industry and agriculture.

The North Korean regime announced the first five-year plan in 1956 and outlined the main objectives:[20] promotion of "socialist construction in the Northern part of the country by laying a solid foundation for socialist industrialization and by completing socialist collectivization of agriculture"; priority for development of heavy industry; technical reconstruction and increasing labor productivity; and increase in the output of agriculture and light industry.

The five-year plan meant that North Korea was being transferred from a "Democratic People's Republic" to a socialist state.

PART III

KOREA'S FUTURE

CHAPTER 19

THE SOLUTION FOR KOREA: PERMANENT NEUTRALITY

HISTORICAL BACKGROUND

The following historical sketch attempts to establish the background for the proposition that Korea, torn by war, rent by division, and the plaything of the great powers, can only find permanent peace through permanent neutrality[1] and nationwide free elections under the supervision of the United Nations.

Korea, surrounded[2] by Japan, China, and Russia, was many times a battleground in the struggle for power. Korea was the main cause of the Sino-Japanese war, 1894–95, the Russo-Japanese war, 1904–5, and the Korean war, 1950–53.

The gradual destruction of Korea's independence between 1905 and 1910 was the result of power politics. In 1905 a secret pact on Korea was signed by the representative of President Theodore Roosevelt, U.S. Secretary of War William Howard Taft, and Japanese Prime Minister Count Katsura, and contained the following memorandum of a conversation on July 29 of that year: "Count Katsura . . . positively states that Japan does not harbor any aggressive designs whatever on the Philippines. . . . In [Taft's] personal opinion, the establishment by Japanese troops of suzerainty over Korea to the extent of requiring that Korea enter into no foreign treaties without the consent of Japan was the logical result of the present war and would directly contribute to the permanent peace in the East."[3]

President Theodore Roosevelt held that "realistic politics demanded the sacrifice of Korean independence, and that a Korea controlled by Japan was preferable to a Korea controlled by Russia."[4] Later "Roosevelt, through his personal representative, gave the Tokyo Foreign Office an assurance that the reorganization of Korea by the Japanese would meet no opposition from the United States."[5]

On August 21, 1905, an alliance between Britain and Japan (renewing an earlier agreement signed in 1902) referred to Japan's interests in Korea:

> Japan possessing paramount political, military, and economic interests in Korea, Great Britain recognizes the right of Japan to take such measures of guidance, control, and protection in Korea, as she may deem proper and necessary to safeguard and advance these interests.[6]

On September 5, 1905, in Article II of the Treaty of Portsmouth, defeated Russia likewise acknowledged Japan's "paramount political, military, and economic interests in Korea."

With this international backing, Japan forced Korea first to sign the Japanese protectorate treaty[7] of November 17, 1905; and then to accept the Proclamation and Treaty of Annexation of Korea[8] on August 29, 1910. Thereafter Korea remained under Japanese colonial rule for thirty-five years.

In December 1943, President Franklin D. Roosevelt, Prime Minister Winston S. Churchill, and Generalissimo Chiang Kai-shek, at Cairo, in a joint declaration, stated: "The . . . three great powers, mindful of the enslavement of the people of Korea, are determined that in due course Korea shall become free and independent."[9] The Soviet government concurred in the Cairo Declaration when it declared war against Japan on August 8, 1945.

In accordance with General Order No. 1,[10] which was approved by the Allied Powers, Korea was divided, as a military expedient, into two occupation zones: the Soviet troops accepted the Japanese surrender north of the 38th parallel[11] and the American troops south of it. On December 27, 1945, at the Moscow Conference,[12] the powers agreed on steps toward the future political settlement of Korea. They decided to establish a joint American-Soviet commission which would assist in the formation of a unified provisional government. Two sessions of the joint commission were held at Seoul and Pyongyang in 1946 and 1947, but they failed to agree on which Korean political parties and which social organizations should be consulted in forming a unified national government. The late George McCune stated:

> The underlying reason for the failure of negotiation was the clash of opposing powers: the United States was determined to create a Korean government favorable to its interests; the Soviet Union was equally determined to provide for a Soviet-oriented Korean nation.[13]

In November 1947 the United States government submitted the Korean problem to the United Nations General Assembly for further action, rejecting a Soviet proposal of "withdrawal of foreign troops from Korea, leaving the Korean affairs in the hands of the Korean people."[14]

The First Unity Conference. In addition to the efforts by the Allied Powers, the Koreans themselves have attempted, since 1948, to unify their divided country. Thus, on April 22, 1948, the North-South Political Leaders' Coalition Conference was held in Pyongyang, capital of North Korea. The conference was attended by delegates from all political and social groups from the North and South, except for two South Korean rightist parties: the National Society for the Rapid Realization of Korean Independence, which was headed by Syngman Rhee, and the Korean Democratic party, which was headed by Kim Sung-soo.

The delegates from South Korea included the scholar-statesman Dr. Kim Kiusic, a middle-of-the-road party leader and chairman of the South Korean interim assembly; and Kim Koo, a rightist party leader and former president of the Korean provisional government which had been formed in 1919 at the time of the Korean independence movement. And from North Korea, there were Kim Il-sung, head of the People's Committee, and Kim Du-bong, head of the Labor party.

After two days, the conference issued a joint communique[15] demanding withdrawal of foreign troops from the territory of Korea, peaceful unification without interference of foreign powers, and the organization of a democratic government by a national political conference representing all sections of the Korean people. This communique, which opposed separate elections in South Korea, was signed by the leaders of fifteen political parties and social organizations of South Korea.[16]

The unification efforts of the North and South Korean leaders, however, were abortive, because of the two opposing approaches on the unification issue of the two power blocs. As already mentioned, the Soviet Union proposed withdrawal of all foreign troops from Korea, a proposal which paralleled one of the demands of the declaration of the coalition conference. However, the United States took the position that the Korean unification problem should be solved through general elections supervised by the U.N.; this position was supported by Syngman Rhee, Kim Sung-soo, and their political groups who opposed the coalition conference.

Lt. Gen. John R. Hodge, the commander of the U.S. Army in South Korea, said about the leaders of South Korea who attended the conference: "They [Kim Kiusic, Kim Koo, and others] were blind men who had been baited by the Communists."[17] Dr. Rhee issued a statement saying that the conference served the cause of Soviet political objectives.[18]

U.N. Elections in South Korea. On May 10, 1948, U.N.-supervised elections were held in South Korea,[19] but many political parties, such as the middle-of-the-road Democratic Independence party, the rightist Korea Independence party, and all leftist parties, boycotted the elections. Only two rightist parties, the National Society for Rapid Realization of Korean Independence and the Korean Democratic party and their affiliates participated in the elections. Some of the candidates ran for the South Korean national assembly without party affiliation. As the result of the U.N.-supervised elections in South Korea the Republic of Korea was established on August 15, 1948. The United States and many other states recognized the Republic of Korea as the legal government of Korea. No U.N.-supervised elections were held in North Korea because of Soviet objections.

The Second Unity Conference. Since the coalition conference of April had not only failed to unify the country, but also had not prevented elections in the South, the North Korean leaders convened a second conference in late June 1948 to establish the People's Republic of Korea as a counterpart to the Republic of Korea in the South. This plan was carried out two months later. Many South Korean leaders, including Kim Kiusic and Kim Koo, who had attended the first conference in April, did not participate in the second conference, insisting that it was contrary to the principles of the joint communique of April. They also warned that separate elections and the establishment of two governments in Korea would result in permanent division.[20]

Elections and Establishment of the Northern Republic. On August 25, 1948, general elections were held in North and South Korea; according to North Korean reports, 77.5 percent of the qualified voters in South Korea cast their ballots despite suppression by the South Korean government,[21] but actually this reflected the voting of South Korean delegates. Representatives of the population of South Korea were to occupy 360 seats from a total of 572 in the Supreme People's Assembly. On September 9, 1948, the Democratic People's Republic of Korea was inaugurated in Pyongyang. The Soviet Union and its allied states recognized the North Korean government as the legal government of Korea. Thus an American-backed Republic of Korea in the South and a Soviet-backed Democratic People's Republic of Korea in the North came into being in an area of eighty-five thousand square miles, and each claimed to be the legitimate government of Korea.

The Korean War. On June 25, 1950, United States armed forces, which became the main contingent of the U.N. forces during the Korean war, were sent to aid the U.N.-sponsored Republic of Korea.[22] During the war Chinese Communist "volunteer" forces entered the fight, supporting North Korea.

The reasons for Communist China's intervention in the Korean war were stated by the Chinese historian Dr. Kuo Pin-Chia as follows:

> Following Chinese entry into the Korean war, in November 1950, certain students of history advanced the thesis that Peking's action represented a reassertion of China's traditional interests in her "border dependencies." This view is not entirely accurate. From the T'ang to our own time, every major intervention in Korea by either China or Russia was caused by rivalry with Japan rather than by a mere desire to regain a "border dependency."
>
> The latest Korean war was . . . inspired by the ambition of Soviet Russia and Communist China to eliminate the influence of Japan and together with that the domination of the United States.[23]

The immediate reason for the entry of Communist Chinese armed forces in the Korean war was the crossing of the 38th parallel by U.N. forces. The boundary between North Korea and Manchuria is the Yalu and Tuman rivers. On October 1, 1950, with MacArthur's troops already rolling across the 38th parallel Chou En-lai, premier of the Peoples' Republic of China, in an address on the first anniversary of the Chinese Communist state, warned that "his country would not . . . tolerate an invasion of North Korea."[24] As for Russia, the Associated Press reported from Moscow that "the Soviet Union, which like Communist China, borders on North Korea, would unquestionably take a grave view of any effort by the United States or Allied forces to push up beyond the 38th parallel."[25] Korea's strategic position was not changed by the atomic age: the big neighboring powers would not tolerate each other's control of the Korean peninsula.

The Korean war ended, without military victory for either side, by the signing of the Armistice Agreement in July 1953.[26] In April 1954 a political conference in Geneva discussed unification of Korea. Participants of the conference were the sixteen member states of the U.N. which had aided the Republic of Korea during the war, and the representatives of South Korea, North Korea, Communist China, and the Soviet Union.

All delegates agreed on the necessity of establishing a united democratic government of Korea, but they disagreed on how to achieve it. South Korean Foreign Minister Pyun Yung-tae proposed fourteen points,[27] whose main proposals were: (1) free elections in North Korea under U.N. supervision and in South Korea in accordance with the constitutional processes of the Republic of Korea; (2) withdrawal of the Chinese Communist troops from Korea one month before the election date; (3) withdrawal of the United Nations forces to start before the elections, but not to be completed before effective control over entire Korea would be achieved by the unified government of Korea and certified by the United Nations; and (4) the independence of unified Korea to be guaranteed by the United Nations.

In contrast to these proposals, North Korean Foreign Minister Nam Il and the Communist Chinese delegate Chou En-lai stated their position:[28] nationwide free elections to be held under the supervision of neutral countries, who did not participate in the Korean war; and withdrawal of all foreign troops from Korea as a prerequisite for the Korean people to express their will in the elections.

The differences of position could not be bridged. The Korean unification issue remained stalemated.

No prospect of unification has been in sight since 1948; neither of the two regimes has been willing to compromise in bringing about national unity. On many occasions, Syngman Rhee advocated a renewal of the fighting as a means of uniting the country, risking atomic war.[29] But after the April

Student Revolution which brought down Rhee, the new South Korean government (the Second Republic of Korea), controlled by the Democratic party, was in favor of peaceful unification and, in principle, of a nationwide free election under U.N. supervision.

The North Korean regime, more recently, suggested the formation of a confederation by an alliance of the two regimes. Under this system each regime would retain control of its own internal affairs. The South Korean government opposed the confederation on the ground that it resembled the Soviet type of federation and might lead to the Sovietization of Korea. The North Korean regime still rejects U.N.-supervised elections, arguing that they would create an American-oriented Korean government.

PERMANENT NEUTRALITY AND U.N.-SUPERVISED ELECTIONS

At this writing, neither the official policies of the big powers nor the resolutions of the U.N. offer a realistic formula for a settlement of the Korean problem in the true interests of all. The only solution, it is submitted, is *permanent neutrality of Korea brought about by an international agreement of the big powers* including Communist China and Japan, *and the holding of U.N.-supervised nationwide free elections*. The formula of permanent neutrality, of course, is not new; the neutral state of the Swiss Confederation has existed since the Congress of Vienna, 1815, after an agreement between France, Great Britain, Austria, Prussia, and Russia. As an axiom of Swiss foreign policy, neutrality goes back to 1674. More recently, in May 1955, permanent neutrality for Austria was recognized by the United States, the Soviet Union, Great Britain, and France.

The formula of U.N.-supervised elections as a solution of Korean unification was proposed by the United States government to the United Nations General Assembly in 1947 and was passed by a majority vote of the U.N. This formula was reaffirmed in the General Assembly on many occasions in the past, rejecting the Soviet proposal of withdrawal of foreign troops and leaving the unification in the hands of the Korean people. The U.N. resolution became a rigid official policy of the United States after 1947; today the majority of the Korean people support the idea of U.N.-supervised elections.

Many Koreans have been advocating neutrality of Korea since the liberation in 1945.[30] In February 1955 the Korean Committee for the Neutralization of Korea (KCNK) was organized in Tokyo. It proposed the following points to the three heads of government at a Summit Conference at Geneva in July 1955: a unified Korea, neutralized by a general agreement of all powers; the two present regimes in Korea to be dissolved and replaced by a single government of a united Korea; a commission of neutral powers to be formed for the preparation of nationwide general elections.[31] This committee was equally composed of rightists, moderates, and leftists, yet the Republic of Korea (Syngman Rhee's government) denounced it as a traitorous group, and the North Korean regime remained silent.

Many political leaders, including former U.S. Senator William F. Knowland, British Labor party leader Hugh Gaitskell, Burmese Prime Minister U Nu, and U.S. Senate Majority Leader Mike Mansfield, support the neutrality of Korea guaranteed by the great powers. In July 1953 Senator Knowland said on the American Broadcasting Company's "Crossfire" program:

> You could get a unified Korea whose neutrality is guaranteed by all the great powers, not as United Nations trusteeship, but as a free nation. Russia and China would be reasonably assured that Korea would not be used as a jumping-off place for war against them. At the same time we and Japan would have the same assurance that Korea would not be used as a jumping-off place for aggression against us.[32]

Prime Minister U Nu, who made a good-will tour in the United States in 1955, was guarded in his opinion on the unification of Korea and permanent neutralization when I interviewed him at the Mark Hopkins Hotel on July 15. He wanted to know Syngman Rhee's reaction to the idea. When I answered that the eighty-year-old South Korean ruler would not be in power forever and that there was no need to worry about his attitude, U Nu merely said he would study the Korean issue.[33]

Mr. Gaitskell, who visited the United States in January 1957 to deliver three lectures at the University of California, Berkeley, said in answer to my question on the unification and neutrality of Korea:

> I favor peaceful unification: unification by force is an unthinkable and barbarous method. However, the unification problem of Korea must come as the result of the overall settlement of Far Eastern problems. In the past I have opposed neutralization of Germany because it might be

> used by one big country as a means of dominating Germany; but if the big powers agree on definite safeguards that Korea is not to be dominated by any of the big powers, then, I favor neutrality of Korea.[34]

Senator Mansfield, after a trip to the Far East in the summer of 1960, in his report to the Committee Chairman, said that the "United States should consider most carefully the possibilities of a solution to the problem of Korean unification in terms of neutralization on the Austrian pattern."[35]

Prof. Robert A. Scalapino believes that, although the Austrian type of neutralization seems remote for Korea at the present time, it would be worthwhile to explore the possibilities in the following manner:

1. Foreign troops would be withdrawn and the peninsula would be neutralized with proper inspection procedures established. The armies of North and South would be reduced to forces sufficient for police functions only. The present boundaries applying on the Korean peninsula would be guaranteed by the United Nations until unification could be achieved by mutual agreement, and any violation would automatically bring U.N. action.

2. Using the "strategic balance" principle (the principle that disarmament shall be so conceived and conducted as to maintain the approximate balance of strength among potential opponents), Chinese Communist, Nationalist, Russian, and American forces would be reduced in the Northeast area. If agreement could be achieved, military alliances would be canceled, with economic and political agreements substituted; and once again, U.N. responsibility for the maintenance of any demilitarization agreement would be obtained.[36]

Some Korean politicians oppose permanent neutrality, arguing that there can be no neutrality of philosophy and political conviction, that neutrality might be used by one power bloc to dominate Korea, and that a status of permanent neutrality would reduce Korea's sovereignty.

As for the first point, it is true, of course, that there is no neutrality of conviction. But neutrality has nothing to do with ideologies. The Swiss historian Edgar Bonjour has said that neutrality in no way prevents a Swiss citizen "from having a judgment of his own on world politics and from examining foreign ideologies and forming his own opinion on them.[37] Julius

Raab, federal chancellor of Austria, said: "The intellectual and political freedom of the individual, in particular freedom of press and of opinion, is not touched by the permanent neutrality of a state."[38] As the examples of Switzerland and Austria have shown, permanent neutrality would in no way prevent or restrict a Korean citizen from studying political ideologies and institutions, as well as economic theories and their practices, and forming his own opinion on them. Neutrality does not hamper domestic political, economic, or social progress.

The second argument of the opponents to neutrality is based on a wrong assumption, for the agreement on neutrality would provide that Korea is not to be dominated by any of the big powers and that they will respect the permanent neutrality of Korea. The pertinent clause in the text for Switzerland reads: "The neutrality and inviolability of Switzerland, and its independence from all foreign influences, are in the true interests of the policy of the whole of Europe."[39]

When the four powers signed the State Treaty of Austria in 1955, Soviet Foreign Minister Molotov said:

> The signing of the Austrian state treaty is an event of great international importance. The successful conclusion of the negotiations proves that possibilities exist for settling other current international problems. . . . The government of the Soviet Union, the United States of America, the United Kingdom, and France have expressed their willingness to observe the neutrality of Austria.[40]

The third argument—that neutrality means loss of sovereignty—carries no weight either. Permanent neutrality was never meant to reduce sovereignty. Both Switzerland and Austria remain as sovereign as the United States or the Soviet Union; the only obligation assumed by neutral states is to remain neutral in all wars[41] unless they are attacked, not to join military alliance with foreign powers, and not allow foreign states to establish military bases on their territories. Domestically, the neutral states can set up any form of government or economic system based on self-determination and majority decision.

The text for Austria defines the meaning and purpose of permanent neutrality as follows:

> Article 1. For the purpose of maintaining her continuous independence and for the purpose of establishing the inviolability of her territory, Austria, out of her own free will, declares her permanent neutrality. Austria will maintain and defend this neutrality with all means at her disposal.
>
> In order to protect these purposes for all the future, Austria will not join military alliances, and will not tolerate that foreign countries establish military bases on her territory.[42]

In the conduct of external affairs, neutral states exercise their own independent judgment based on their national interests: for example, Switzerland was a member of the League of Nations but has chosen not to become a member of the U.N.,[43] yet she has joined many U.N. agencies. Permanently neutral Austria, however, became a member of the United Nations on December 15, 1955.[44]

South Korean authorities, including the prime minister and the foreign minister, have rejected the idea of an Austrian-type neutrality of Korea for three reasons: The geographical position of Korea is not the same as that of Austria or Switzerland because Korea is surrounded by two powerful Communist states; in Austria one government existed even during the four-power occupation, but in Korea two regimes, based on entirely opposite political ideologies, are in power; and Korea would be dominated by Communists if it were unified through neutralization.[45]

The first two of these arguments are quite hazy, and none of them carry much weight. If Korea is surrounded by Communist states, so is Austria, a country which borders on Hungary, Czechoslovakia, and Yugoslavia; invasion of Austria is certainly not a military problem for the Soviet Union. Secondly, "two Koreas" could be neutralized just as well as one; besides, external unification by joint neutralization might be a powerful incentive for internal unification as well. Thirdly, that a neutralized South Korea might turn Communist is possible; but it is equally possible that a neutralized North Korea, freed of the tension of outside invasion, might "relax into a democracy." In a neutralized Korea the contest of ideas would continue just as it is now, and one could argue that in a neutral atmosphere democracy would have a better chance of winning than in the present rigid, hostile atmosphere which encourages a militant authoritative North.

The North Korean authorities have been silent on the idea of permanent neutralization of Korea. They still demand withdrawal of the U.N. troops from the South and insist on a general election under the supervision of neutral countries who did not participate in the Korean war.

The solution of the Korean problem is permanent neutrality plus U.N.-supervised nationwide free elections. This conforms with the national interests of the Korean people and would pave the way for peaceful unification of the country, for the establishment of a single democratic national government based on self-determination, and for the future protection of national independence and territorial integrity. It would reduce tension in East Asia generally and would be a significant step toward a durable peace in that part of the world.

CHAPTER 20

THE PROSPECTS OF THE KOREAN PEOPLE

A REVIEW

Independence is a nation's birthright, and life, liberty, and the pursuit of happiness are the inalienable rights of the people: Koreans are entitled to have these. Up to now, however, the Korean people have either been totally denied or have not fully enjoyed these rights and freedoms. There are two reasons for this: the threat and domination of foreign powers, and the rule of native authoritarian regimes in the name of Buddhism, Confucianism, democracy, and Communism.

Korean history is a record of human suffering and misery. More than a hundred wars, including civil wars, have been fought in the Korean peninsula, and more than fifty times the peninsula was invaded by foreign powers. The most serious periods were the four-hundred-year occupation of the southern peninsula by the Chinese Han dynasty (200 B.C.–A.D. 200), the Mongol conquest of the Koryo kingdom in the thirteenth century, the Japanese invasion of the sixteenth century, the Sino-Japanese war of 1894–95, the Russo-Japanese war of 1904–5, the thirty-five-year Japanese domination of Korea, the division and three-year military occupation of Korea by the United States and the Soviet Union (1945–48), and the three-year Korean war (1950–53).

Most of the Korean ruling classes and intellectuals accepted the foreign political ideologies, cultures, and religions without serious examination or evaluation of the native social and historical background, and they superimposed foreign ideals on the Korean people as a means of retaining their power. The imported ideologies lost their real meaning and vitality as soon as they became the political tools of the privileged ruling classes. As a consequence, factionalism developed among the ruling circles as they contended for power among themselves. The constant presence of foreign ideologies hampered the rise of a native political ideology, culture, and religion.

Buddhism became the political ideology of the ruling classes during the Silla and Koryo period, and the civilization of Buddhism influenced the way of life of the intellectuals. The Mahayana branch of Buddhism was popular in Korea because it preached the doctrine of "blessing and happiness" of the aristocratic ruling classes and the "protection of the state." The capital cities, especially Kyongju, capital of the Silla kingdom, became the center of Buddhist intellectual activity and a model of Buddhist civilization in the Korean peninsula. Hundreds of temples, monasteries, and pagodas throughout the country were built by slaves under the supervision of government officials. The king bestowed land on the temples together with the slaves who cultivated it. Members of royal families and aristocrats also contributed land and slaves to the Buddhist temples to obtain Buddha's blessings. Priests gradually emerged as big landlords and became the intellectuals of the ruling class.

The moral and intellectual leadership of the priests began to deteriorate as their life became luxurious and their power increased. Buddhism never became an active living philosophy of the Korean people, because it preached a retired or passive philosophy of life: Buddhists sought blessings and happiness from Buddha by just praying and contributing money and land to the temples. The Buddhists were not interested in the vital social or national issues, such as slave labor, economic hardship of the common people, and the threat to independence by foreign powers. The millions of Korean Buddhists were only spectators of events in their own society.

Confucian ethical principles, based on the five virtues and the five fundamental human relationships, were the expression of an authoritarian feudal social order established between superior (the rulers) and inferior (the ruled). Responsibility and absolute authority were in the hands of the superior virtuous man, whereas filial devotion and unconditional obedience were the duties of the inferior commoners. The concepts of individual rights, freedom, and equality were alien to Confucian thought. According to Confucian theory, inequality among nations, like inequality among individuals, was the natural order of the world, because "equality in relations between two equal nations may produce disorder and war." Naturally the Chinese rulers believed that China was the superior virtuous state and non-Chinese states were uncivilized inferior states which needed guidance from the Chinese.

Confucianism became the new creed of the Yi dynasty, and the Confucian scholars acted as advisers to the king in place of the priests. The Confucian gentry class emerged as the landlord class. In Korea, the doctrine of Chu Za (one of the sects of Confucianism) was introduced: it emphasized "formalism," such as ancestor worship, marriage, and funeral services; it also preached the concept of asceticism, which advocated purity of scholarship based on the idea of fidelity and avoidance of material gain. The followers of Chu Za considered manual labor low and, at the same time, discouraged commercial and industrial enterprises on the ground that they were profit-seeking occupations.

Toward the end of the nineteenth century, Western civilization along with Christianity was introduced into Korea. The ideas of democratic principles, individual freedom, civil rights, and equality were spread among Korean Christians, especially among the youths who received their education in missionary schools. About the beginning of the twentieth century, many young Koreans rose for freedom by opposing the oppressive and corrupt age-old feudal political and social institutions. Such struggles continued until Japan's annexation of Korea in 1910; hereafter, the national independence movement was launched under the leadership of nationalists, including many Christian leaders and leftists. Today there are more than one million Christians in South Korea alone, and many Christian educational and social (humanitarian) institutions, such as universities, hospitals, orphanages, which were established with the aid of missionaries, especially those from the United States.

Nevertheless, the Korean people do not trust Christian leadership and Western civilization, because during the Japanese domination many Christian leaders cooperated with the Japanese expansion policy; they also participated in the American military government under the guise of being "democrats"; most Christians, including the American missionaries, supported Syngman Rhee's regime, and the Korean churches became powerful political machines of the Liberal party. Thousands of Christians and their ministers alike were opportunists.

Korean politicians have been attempting to superimpose American political democracy upon the people, contending that democracy would solve all Korean problems. The American way of life has greatly influenced the privileged upper classes, which obtained wealth through American aid after the liberation of the country from the Japanese in 1945. They read American newspapers, magazines, and books; they attend cocktail parties, dance to American music, live in Western-style residences, and drive American cars. After 1945, the pro-American groups, both civilians and militarists, succeeded in establishing themselves as the ruling class in South Korea.

On the other hand, the Korean Communists believe that communization of Korea will be a cure-all and, since the liberation, have concentrated on the establishment of a political, economic, and social structure that is socialist and Soviet-oriented. Northern Koreans have been forced to live in a state-controlled, regimented totalitarian society: the Communists introduced communal life in rural areas and the people work together, eat together, and live together as one economic unit. The teaching of Marxism-Leninism and the Russian language and history along with socialist culture in general occupy a large percentage of the school curriculum. No ideological dissent about Communism is allowed in North Korea; the members of the Korean Communist party have succeeded in establishing themselves as the unchallenged ruling class.

THE DUTY AND FUTURE OF THE KOREAN PEOPLE

Aristocrats ruled Korea in the past; opportunistic politicians rule it today. But the future Korea will be the people's Korea, and the Korean peninsula will become the real home of the Korean people. With this confident expectation, the following proposals are submitted to the Korean people.

The Duty of Revolution. Many political "revolutions" have occurred in Korea: the most notable ones were the Hong Kyong-nai insurrection in 1811, the Kapshin Chungbun uprising in 1884, the Tonghak uprising in 1894, the March First Independence Movement in 1919, the Student Revolution in 1960, and the military coup d'etat in 1961. The Independence uprising was the only nationwide revolution; the others were either local uprisings or uprisings centered in the capital; the Hong Kyong-nai insurrection took place only in North Korea; the Tonghak and student uprisings spread in South Korea alone; the Kapshin uprising and military coup were uprisings in the capital. The four uprisings (Hong Kyong-nai, Tonghak, Independence, and Student) were initiated and directed by the people; the Kapshin Chung-bun was a Japanese-inspired political coup by Korean intellectuals; and the military coup d'etat was initiated and directed by young officials. The Independence and Student uprisings followed the nonviolent method; all others used force. The uprisings aimed at the overthrow of the existing governments, but only three out of the six uprisings were able to achieve that objective. Nevertheless, the life of the "revolutionary governments" was short; three days (Kapshin Chung-bun); nine months (Chang's government or second republic); and about two years (military government). None of the uprisings was directed by trained professional revolutionary leaders or groups with definite socioeconomic-political principles. In most cases they rose against corrupt incompetent administrations; no socioeconomic revolution took place in the Korean peninsula.

Although Korea has had six revolutions within the past 150 years, all indications in Korea today lead to the conclusion that revolution has not ended but has just begun, because age-old social injustice and evils have not been removed and the people have not obtained their basic rights, freedom, and equality. The main social injustices and evils have been the wide gap between the privileged few and the underprivileged majority in economic and social status, the constant official corruption and moral degradation of the intellectuals, and the rise of factional fights and *sadae-sasang* (reliance upon a big power) among the ruling classes. The Korean people have lost the spirit of self-confidence and are overburdened with fear; the intellectuals have lost the capacity to say no in time of national crisis; the ruling classes have lost the spirit of independence and, instead, have developed a slave mentality of dependence on a big power. Today Korea appears like a drowning man in the deep sea. The first duty of the Korean people, therefore, is to rescue themselves.

The Duty of Unifying the Country. Unification of the country is one of the main duties of the Korean people. Many attempts have been made to bring about unification: the U.S.-U.S.S.R. Joint Commission in 1946 and 1947, the U.N.-supervised elections in South Korea in 1948, the three-year war (1950–53), and the Geneva Conference in 1953. Some Korean political leaders attempted to unify the country by holding the North-South Political Leaders Coalition Conference in 1948. All these attempts have failed because of the conflict of interest of the two power blocs: the "free world" bloc wanted to establish a United States–oriented Korean government, and the Communist bloc was determined to install a socialist satellite.

The native postwar ruling circles of the North and South, which came to power by the support of the two power blocs, have sided with these blocs. They appear more as faithful servants to their Moscow-Peking masters and to Washington than to the Korean people. There is little hope that the divided country will be unified by the efforts of the two power blocs; nor can it be accomplished by the two native ruling classes. This means that the Korean people themselves will have to solve the unification problem.

It would seem that there is one way to do this; namely, a revival of the March First Independence Movement, which used nonviolent methods against Japanese domination. The Student Revolution in 1960, which ousted the South Korean dictator Syngman Rhee, was an example of a successful peaceful revolution. Through it the Korean people have learned valuable lessons: they, the people, are the masters of the revolution; the most powerful weapon is to treat the enemy as a moral human being and appeal to his conscience. When the people rose in the past and united as one body for the cause of justice, world opinion always sided with them.

If the Korean people both in North and South rise up and cross the 38th parallel, as the Israelites crossed the Red Sea, or Gandhi and his followers launched their famous March to the Sea, a new era will have dawned. The task of unifying Korea is the duty of the Korean people.

NOTES

CHAPTER 1. THE THREE KINGDOMS

1. During the Han dynasty, the peninsula was divided into four sections as administrative units, and this system was called *sa-gun-jedo*. Because of the strong opposition of the natives against the Chinese, the Han dynasty was forced to give up its administration in three sections within 26 years. But the fourth, Nakrang-gun, was under the Han's domination for about 400 years. Hahm Suk-heun, *Tusuro bon Hanguk Yoksa* (Meaning of Korean History), Seoul, 1962, pp. 142–45.
2. The rise and fall of the Koguryo kingdom is important in Korea's histroy. The Koguryo people and their rulers established a powerful kingdom extending its jurisdiction over Manchuria and the southern sections of the Korean peninsula. *Ibid.*, pp. 149–66.
3. Kotetsu Hayashi (Lim Kwang-chull), *Chosen Rekishi Tokuhon* (A Textbook of Korean History), Tokyo, 1949, p. 30.
4. Takashi Hatada, *Chosen-shi* (A Korean History), Tokyo, 1956, pp. 32–34.
5. Hayashi, *op. cit.*, p. 46. See also Hatada, *op. cit.*, p. 37, and Nan-wun Hyaku (Paek Nam-woon), *Chosen Shakai Keizai-shi* (Korean Socioeconomic History), Tokyo, 1928, pp. 389–414.
6. Hayashi, *op. cit.*, pp. 76–78. See also Hatada, *op. cit.*, pp. 38–39.
7. See also Hayashi, *op. cit.*, pp. 53–56.
8. Hyaku, *op. cit.*, pp. 355–62 and Hayashi, *op. cit.*, pp. 58–61.
9. Hyaku, *op. cit.*, pp. 207–15, 258–62, and 340–43. For the general character of the agrarian economy, see Hayashi, *op. cit.*, pp. 61–70.

CHAPTER 2. SILLA UNIFIES THE PENINSULA

1. Balhai-wang-guk unsuccessfully attempted to reestablish the Koguryo kingdom.
2. Some historians, like Hahm Suk-heun, say that the unification of the peninsula under the Silla kingdom was achieved at the expense of the

Koguryo kingdom, the kingdom that truly represented the Korean national character. Reliance on a strong power (the T'ang dynasty of China) increased among the Silla ruling classes; from the T'ang they adopted a political ideology based on Buddhism, a centralized administrative system, and general social customs. Thus the Korean people more or less lost their original national character due to T'ang influence. Hahm Suk-heun, *Tusuro bon Hanguk Yoksa* (The Meaning of Korean History), Seoul, 1962, pp. 164–67.

3. Kotetsu Hayashi, *Chosen Rekishi Tokuhon* (A Textbook of Korean History), Tokyo, 1949, pp. 73–74.
4. Takashi Hatada, *Chosen-shi* (A Korean History), Tokyo, 1956, pp. 51–52. For further detailed discussions of the military reorganization program see Nan-wun Hyaku, *Chosen Shakai Keizai-shi* (Korean Socioeconomic History), Tokyo, 1928, pp. 335–38.
5. Hyaku, *op. cit.*, pp. 350–55.
6. *Ibid.*, pp. 344–49.
7. Hayashi, *op. cit.*, pp. 86–91.
8. Hyaku, *op. cit.*, pp. 372–78.
9. The king said, "In recent years the subjects have been living in extreme poverty, so that many incidents of thievery and robbery occurred throughout the kingdom: these incidents demonstrate how bad the administration of the kingdom has been: hence I, the king, have no choice but to resign from the throne." Hayashi, *op. cit.*, p. 98.

CHAPTER 3. THE KORYO KINGDOM (935–1392)

1. One of the best books on the Koryo kingdom from the socioeconomic point of view is Nan-won Hyaku, *Chosen Hoken Keizai-shi, Korai no bu, Chosen Shakai Keizai-shi, Dai-ni-kan* (Korean Feudal Economic History of Koryo Period: Korean Socioeconomic History, Vol. II), Tokyo, 1931.
2. For further information see Lee In-yung, *Guksa Kam* (Outline of Korean History), Seoul, 1949, pp. 85–87 and 231–42.
3. Nan-won Hyaku comments that a pro-Japanese historian like Choi Nam-sun belongs to the conceptional school of thought, because his argument was not based on facts and scientific analysis. Hyaku, *op. cit.*, pp. 1–6.
4. See summary review "Feudalism and Asian Society" by James T. C. Liu in *Pacific Affairs*, June 1956, pp. 181–86.
5. Lee, *op. cit.*, pp. 85–87 and 231–42.

6. A detailed discussion on the land system will be found in Hyaku, *op. cit.*, pp. 51–115, 145–201, and 224–46. See also Hayashi, *Chosen Rekishi Tokuhon* (A Textbook of Korean History), Tokyo, 1949, pp. 122–31.
7. Hyaku, *op. cit.*, pp. 271–97.
8. Hayashi, *op. cit.*, pp. 152–57; also Hyaku, *op. cit.*, pp. 298–334 and 727–91.

CHAPTER 4. THE YI DYNASTY (1392–1910): CENTRALIZED FEUDAL SOCIETY

1. See full text in D. G. Tewksbury, *Source Materials on Korean Politics and Ideologies,* Institute of Pacific Relations, New York, 1950, pp. 21–23 (From *Current History Magazine,* Oct., 1924, pp. 15 and 18, with photostatic reproduction of the original document).
2. Tewksbury, *op. cit.*, p. 22.
3. A. J. Grajdanzev, *Modern Korea,* Institute of Pacific Relations, New York, 1944, p. 33.
4. J. K. Fairbank, *The United States and China,* "The Great Learning" in the Chinese Classics, English translation, Harvard University Press, Cambridge, Mass., 1948, p. 74.
5. Fairbank, *op. cit.*, p. 75.
6. M. F. Nelson, *Korea and the Old Order in Eastern Asia,* Louisiana State University Press, 1946, p. 7.
7. James Legge, *The Chinese Classics,* Clarendon Press, Oxford, 1895, p. 23.
8. For characteristics of the Yi dynasty's state system, see Kang Ji-woon, *Kundai Chosun Jungchi-sa* (Recent Korean Political History), Seoul, 1950, pp. 20–24.
9. For detailed discussions on relations of China with non-Chinese states in general and with Korea in particular, see Nelson, *op. cit.*, pp. 86–106.
10. Hatada Takashi, *Chosen-shi* (A Korean History), Tokyo, 1956, pp. 111–14. See also Lee In-yung, *Guksa Kam* (Outline of Korean History), Seoul, 1949, pp. 133–51.
11. Hyaku Nan-wun and others, *Chosen Minzoku Kaiho Tosho-shi* (History of the Liberation Struggle of the Korean People), Tokyo, 1954, pp. 11–14 and 65–67. See also Lim Kwang-chull, *Yicho Bongkun Sahai-sa* (Feudal Social History of the Yi Dynasty), Tokyo, 1954, pp. 29–36.
12. Kang, *op. cit.*, pp. 175–76.
13. For detailed discussion, see Hyaku and others, *op. cit.*, pp. 16–18 and 67–69.

14. The total number of the handicraft industrial workers is estimated at 6,300. See Hyaku and others, *op. cit.,* p. 18.
15. Kang, *op. cit.,* p. 137.
16. Perhaps the only reference book on commerce, business, and money-lending during the Yi dynasty is by Sai Ko-chin (Choi Ho-chin), *Kindai Chosen Keizai-shi* (Recent Economic History of Korea), Tokyo, 1942.
17. Sai, *op. cit.,* pp. 97–130.
18. H. B. Hulbert, *The Passing of Korea,* Young People's Missionary of the U.S. and Canada, New York and London, 1906, p. 283.
19. *Ibid.,* p. 50.
20. Sai, *op. cit.,* p. 226.
21. Sai, *op. cit.,* pp. 175–91.
22. *Ibid.,* p. 244.
23. For detailed discussion, see Lee In-yung, *Guksa Kam* (Outline of Korean History), pp. 135–51.
24. Hahm Suk-heun, *Tusuro bon Hanguk Yoksa* (Meaning of Korean History), Seoul, 1962, pp. 266–71.
25. Lim, *op. cit.,* pp. 68–69.
26. Kang, *op. cit.,* pp. 53–64.
27. For different views on the failure of Yi's arbitration, see Hahm, *op. cit.,* pp. 271–78.
28. Kang, *op. cit.,* p. 60.
29. Daewon-gun reform measures were based on the principle of *sasaik-pongdung inchai-dongyong,* equality in politics regardless of party affiliations and equal opportunity of talented men to public position. See Lim, *op. cit.,* pp. 148–49.
30. Nelson, *op. cit.,* p. 74.
31. *Ibid.*
32. *Ibid.,* p. 94.
33. See Korean language text of the treaty, Kang, *op. cit.,* pp. 190–93.
34. Nelson, *op. cit.,* p. 170. According to another report, the Japanese government gave 17,000,000 yen to the Korean Reform party. See also Hyaku and others, *op. cit.,* p. 92.
35. Nelson, *op. cit.,* pp. 170–71.
36. For the Japanese text of the program, see Hyaku and others, *op. cit.,* p. 95.
37. For Korean language text of the recommendations, see Kang, *op. cit.,* p. 247.

38. Tewksbury, *op. cit.*, pp. 35–37.
39. Hyaku and others, *op. cit.*, p. 124.
40. Nelson, *op. cit.*, pp. 232–40.
41. *Ibid.*, p. 243.
42. *Ibid.*, p. 238.
43. For further information on Iljin-hai and its activities, see Hyaku and others, *op. cit.*, pp. 153–56.
44. Grajdanzev, *op. cit.*, p. 33. See also a letter from the emperor of Korea to President Roosevelt, October 1905, in Tewksbury, *op. cit.*, pp. 23–25.
45. Tewksbury, *op. cit.*, p. 22.
46. *Ibid.*, pp. 28–29.
47. Nelson, *op. cit.*, p. 279.
48. *Ibid.*, p. 280.
49. For detailed analysis of annexation, see Kang, *op. cit.*, pp. 336–55.

CHAPTER 5. THE YI DYNASTY: PAWN OF THE BIG POWERS

1. Although Korea was known as the "hermit kingdom," it still maintained a close relationship with China.
2. The Okubo group was called *shimpo-ha* (progressive faction) and Soejima group *hoshu-ha* (conservative faction). See R. A. Scalapino, *Democracy and the Party Movement in Prewar Japan,* University of California Press, Berkeley and Los Angeles, 1953, pp. 43–45.
3. M. F. Nelson, *Korea and the Old Order in Eastern Asia,* Louisiana State University Press, 1946, p. 128.
4. *Ibid.*, p. 130.
5. For text of treaty, see *British and Foreign State Papers,* LXVII, pp. 530–33.
6. Nelson, *op. cit.*, p. 131.
7. *Ibid.*, p. 133.
8. Kang Ji-woon, *Kundai Chosun Jungchi-sa* (Recent Korean Political History), Seoul, 1950, pp. 190–91.
9. Hyaku Nan-wun and others, *Chosen Minzoku Kaiho Tosho-shi* (History of the Liberation Struggle of the Korean People), Tokyo, 1954, pp. 89–90.
10. Kang, *op. cit.*, p. 196.
11. G. N. Steiger, *A History of the Far East,* New York, Ginn and Co., 1944, p. 623.

12. Hyaku and others, *op. cit.,* p. 98.
13. Kotetsu Hayashi, *Chosen Rekishi Tokuhon* (A Textbook of Korean History), Tokyo, 1949, pp. 198–99.
14. See pp. 127–32, of this book.
15. Nelson, *op. cit.,* p. 207.
16. Steiger, *op. cit.,* p. 625.
17. Nelson, *op. cit.,* p. 211.
18. *Ibid.,* pp. 25–26 and 209.
19. Hyaku and others, *op. cit.,* p. 113.
20. *Ibid.*
21. Nelson, *op. cit.,* p. 227. Quoted from *Korea: Treaties and Agreements with and concerning China,* ed. by J. V. A. MacMurrary, New York, 1921, pp. 18–22.
22. Nelson, *op. cit.,* p. 233.
23. For Japanese text of memorandum, see Hyaku and others, *op. cit.,* pp. 171–72.
24. Nelson, *op. cit.,* p. 236.
25. For detailed discussion of the military importance of Masan, see Kang, *op. cit.,* pp. 229–30.
26. Nelson, *op. cit.,* p. 238.
27. F. A. McKenzie, *The Tragedy of Korea,* London, 1908, p. 302.
28. Hayashi, *op. cit.,* p. 224.
29. Nelson, *op. cit.,* p. 245.
30. *Ibid.,* p. 248.
31. *Ibid.,* pp. 249–50. Quoted form *Archives Diplomatiques,* Paris, 1861, Vols. XCI–XCII, p. 844.
32. Grajdanzev, *Modern Korea,* Institute of Pacific Relations, New York, 1944, p. 30. Quoted from R. H. Akagi, *Japan's Foreign Relations,* Tokyo, 1936, p. 240.
33. Nelson, *op. cit.,* p. 258.
34. Article 2 of the Portsmouth Treaty.
35. Nelson, *op. cit.,* pp. 257–58.
36. D. G. Tewksbury, *Source Materials on Korean Politics and Ideologies,* Institute of Pacific Relations, New York, 1950, p. 22.
37. Grajdanzev, *op. cit.,* p. 30. Quoted from Akagi, *op. cit.,* pp. 266–67.
38. Stevens was killed by a Korean, Chang In-hwan, in San Francisco on his way to Washington, D.C. in 1908. Stevens had been advocating Japanese domination over Korea.

39. Tewksbury, *op. cit.*, p. 27. See also Henry Chung, *The Case of Korea*, New York, 1921, pp. 52–53.
40. Kang, *op. cit.*, pp. 343–48.
41. Tewksbury, *op. cit.*, pp. 28–29.
42. A secret message to the President of the United States was sent because of the following clause in the treaty between Korea and the United States: "If other powers deal unjustly or oppressively with either government, the other will exert their good offices, on being informed of the case, to bring about an amicable arrangement, thus showing their friendly feelings." Chung, *op. cit.*, p. 329. "But President Theodore Roosevelt, as the Japanese put it, completely ignored the appeal." Grajdanzev, *op. cit.*, p. 33.
43. Nelson, *op. cit.*, p. 277. Quoted from a photograph copy of the imperial credentials in Prince Yi We Chong's "A Plea for Korea," *Independent*, Vol. LXIII, 1907, p. 425.
44. For text of the six points, see Nelson, *op. cit.*, p. 280.
45. *Ibid.*, p. 283. Quoted from F. A. MacKenzie, *op. cit.*, p. 175.
46. Tewksbury, *op. cit.*, p. 37.
47. For text of the treaty, see *ibid.*, pp. 38–39.
48. Hayashi, *op. cit.*, p. 174.
49. Hong called himself "Jongsai Daewonsa," which corresponds to the title of commander in chief.
50. The doctrine is known as Chunji-kaibuk-sul.
51. Lim Kwang-chull, *Yicho Bonggun Sahai-sa* (Feudal Social History of the Yi Dynasty), Tokyo, 1954, pp. 170–71.
52. Hyaku and others, *op. cit.*, pp. 105–6.
53. The government branded the army as rebels.
54. Hyaku and others, *op. cit.*, p. 109.
55. For text of the 12 points, see *ibid.*, p. 110.
56. Later the Tonghak sect took the name of Chondokyo (Heavenly Way Teaching), and their leaders participated in the March First Independence Movement of 1919. For further information, see C. Osgood, *The Koreans and Their Culture*, The Ronald Press Co., New York, 1951, pp. 204, 208–9, 252, and 288.
57. The Independence Arch still stands in Seoul.
58. Tewksbury, *op. cit.*, pp. 12–14.
59. The editorial was drafted by Confucian scholar Chang Ji-youn. An English translation appeared in *Korean Review*, vol. I, March 1906, pp. 41–42.

60. Tewksbury, *op. cit.,* p. 31. Quoted from *ibid.,* vol. 6, July 1906, pp. 6–7.
61. For an English translation of the Korean protest against the Japanese protectorate, see *ibid.,* p. 32. Quoted from MacKenzie, *op. cit.,* pp. 136–37.
62. The activities of the Righteous Army spread throughout the country spontaneously for the next five years.
63. Hyaku and others, *op. cit.,* pp. 167–68.
64. This author recalls the independence army commonly known as *doknip-dang;* usually three to five persons visited his house on various occasions during the winter demanding money for independence activities.
65. In Korean it is called *aeguk munhwa gemong-undong.*
66. See pp. 168–73, of this text.

CHAPTER 6. KOREA UNDER JAPANESE DOMINATION (1910–45)

1. During the more than thirty years of its existence the council had been consulted only nine times, on subjects which dealt with native customs and religious ceremonies. See A. J. Grajdanzev, *Modern Korea,* Institute of Pacific Relations, New York, 1944, pp. 46–47.
2. *Ibid.,* pp. 47–48. Quoted from the *Annual Report on the Administration of Chosen 1911–1912,* p. 54.
3. The Christian leaders were nationalists; they formed a secret society called Shinmin-hai (New People's Society). The Japanese police arrested the members of the society and charged them with plotting to assassinate the governor-general.
4. Hyaku and others, *Chosen Minzoku Kaiho Tosho-shi* (History of the Liberation Struggle of the Korean People), Tokyo, 1954, p. 214. According to the Japanese official report, 553 Koreans were killed, 1,409 wounded, and 19,054 (of whom 471 were women) imprisoned. See also *Annual Report on the Administration of Chosen 1918–1919,* pp. 158–59.
5. Grajdanzev, *op. cit.,* p. 57.
6. The author, on many occasions, was rejected by Japanese house owners when he wanted to rent a room as a student in Tokyo.
7. Grajdanzev, *op. cit.,* p. 61.
8. *Ibid.,* p. 63.
9. *Ibid.*
10. *Ibid.,* pp. 68–69.
11. *Ibid.,* pp. 108–9.

12. Hyaku and others, *op. cit.,* p. 296. Quoted from *Chosen Sotokufu Tokei Nempo* (Statistics of the Government-General of Korea), n.d.
13. Christians had to recite the oath before the worship services.
14. G. M. McCune, *Korea Today,* Harvard University Press, Cambridge, Mass., 1950, p. 26.
15. Hyaku and others, *op. cit.,* p. 298.
16. Kotetsu Hayashi, *Chosen Rekishi Tokuhon* (A Textbook of Korean History), Tokyo, 1949, p. 261.
17. Grajdanzev, *op. cit.,* p. 54.
18. Hayashi, *op. cit.,* p. 263.
19. *Ibid.,* p. 264.
20. *Ibid.*
21. *Ibid.*
22. Grajdanzev, *op. cit.,* pp. 45–46.
23. Hyaku and others, *op. cit.,* 181.
24. *Ibid.,* p. 184. According to Grajdanzev's calculation the per capita consumption of rice in Korea decreased from 0.707 *suk* in 1919 to 0.396 *suk* in 1939. Grajdanzev, *op. cit.,* p. 118.
25. For details of the plan, see Grajdanzev, *op. cit.,* p. 92.
26. "Extraordinarily high rice price produced a series of riots all over Japan in August, 1918, with property damage and casualties running very high. This climaxed the ministry's unpopularity, which has been growing because of its general fiscal policies and its severe suppression of the popular movement. On September 28, 1918, the cabinet resigned." R. A. Scalapino, *Democracy and the Party Movement in Prewar Japan,* Berkeley and Los Angeles, University of California Press, 1953, p. 210.
27. Hyaku and others, *op. cit.,* p. 236.
28. *Ibid.,* p. 237.
29. Grajdanzev, *op. cit.,* p. 119.
30. *Ibid.,* p. 108.
31. *Ibid.,* p. 93.
32. *Ibid.* See also Hyaku and others, *op. cit.,* p. 290.
33. *Ibid.,* p. 94. Quoted from *Chosen Keizai Nempo (Korean Economic Report),* 1940, p. 160.
34. The law was issued in December 1910. For discussion of the nature of the law, see Hyaku and others, *op. cit.,* pp. 185–86.
35. Grajdanzev, *op. cit.,* p. 52. Quoted from *Annual Report, 1915–1916,* p. 113.

36. Hyaku and others, *op. cit.,* p. 186.
37. K. Takahashi, *Gendai Chosen Keizairon* (Modern Korean Economy), Tokyo, 1935, p. 350.
38. Hyaku and others, *op. cit.,* p. 239.
39. Ibid., p. 239.
40. For detailed statistics, see Grajdanzev, *op. cit.,* pp. 171–77.
41. Takahashi, *op. cit.,* p. 67.

CHAPTER 7. THE ANTI-JAPANESE STRUGGLE

1. *New Korea* is being published by the Korean National Association in Los Angeles.
2. For full coverage of a conversation between Ahn Chang-ho and Ito, see Yi Kwang-su, *Tosan: Ahn Chang-ho* (Biography of Ahn Chang-ho), Seoul, 1947, pp. 41–43.
3. *Ibid.,* pp. 79–80.
4. *The Constitution of the Hung Sa Dahn,* Article 2.
5. Yi, *op. cit.,* pp. 4–5.
6. *Ibid.,* pp. 349–67.
7. R. T. Oliver, *Syngman Rhee: The Man Behind the Myth,* New York, Dodd, Mead and Co., 1954, p. 140.
8. Kim, Warren Y., *Chaimi Hanin Oship-nun-sa* (Fifty-Year History of the Korean People in the United States), Reedley, California, 1959, p. 360. See also Yi Man-kyu, *Lyugh Woonhyung Sunsang Tuzang-sa* (The History of Lyugh Woonhyung's Fight), Seoul, 1946, p. 31.
9. Hyaku and others, *Chosen Minzoku Kaiho Tosho-shi* (History of the Liberation Struggle of the Korean People), Tokyo, 1954, p. 203.
10. For an authentic source on the plan and organization of the Independence Movement, see Park Un-sik, *Hanguk Doknip Undong-ji Hul-sa* (Bloody History of the Korean Independence Movement), Seoul, 1946, pp. 59–134.
11. Text of declaration in Korean, *ibid.,* pp. 69–71. English translation, Chung Kyung-cho, *Korea Tomorrow,* The Macmillan Co., New York, 1956, pp. 301–3.
12. C. Osgood, *The Koreans and Their Culture,* The Ronald Press Co., New York, 1951, p. 286.
13. Oliver, *op. cit.,* p. 141.
14. F. A. McKenzie, *The Tragedy of Korea,* London, 1908, pp. 223–24.
15. Kim, *op. cit.,* pp. 451–63.

16. *Ibid.*, pp. 465–68.
17. *Ibid.*, pp. 498–501.
18. Hyaku and others, *op. cit.*, p. 224.
19. Hahm Suk-heun said: "The March First Independence Movement was a spiritual movement, which was led by the Korean people themselves as the master of the movement. Therefore, Korean democracy began from this people's independence movement." Hahm Suk-heun, *Inkan Hukmyung* (Human Revolution), Seoul, 1962, pp. 158–59.
20. Hyaku and others, *op. cit.*, pp. 267–72.
21. A. J. Grajdanzev, *Modern Korea,* Institute of Pacific Relations, New York, 1944, p. 68.
22. Hyaku and others, *op. cit.*, p. 279. According to this source 54,000 students were arrested, but this seems in error, because the number of participants in the demonstration was estimated at 54,000. See Kin Shyo-mei (Kim Chong-ho), *Chosen Shin-minshu-shugi Kakumei-shi* (New Democratic Revolutionary History of Korea), Tokyo, 1953, p. 57.
23. Stevens was an American who worked for the Japanese government as adviser to the Korean foreign affairs department and supported Japanese control of Korea.
24. Article 2 of the constitution. For the Korean text, see Kim, *op. cit.*, pp. 113–14.
25. *Ibid.*, pp. 203–4.
26. *Ibid.*, p. 203. For political activities of the Dongji-hai, see *ibid.*, pp. 203–14.
27. *Chosun Haibang Ilnun-sa* (One-year History of Korea's Liberation), ed. by the Committee of the Korean National Democratic Front, Seoul, 1946, p. 217.
28. The party platform was composed of 17 articles. *Ibid.*, pp. 155–56.
29. G. M. McCune, *Korea Today,* Harvard University Press, Cambridge Mass., 1950, p. 41. McCune, who took charge of Korean affairs in the State Department, said that "as for the recognition of the Provisional Government, there was complete agreement that action would be premature and unwise." Acting Secretary of State Grew on July 8, 1945, stated that "it is the policy of this government in dealing with groups such as the 'Korean Provisional Government' to avoid taking action which might, when the victory of the United Nations is achieved, tend to compromise the right of the Korean People to choose the ultimate form and personnel which they may wish to establish." *Ibid.*, p. 42.

30. Grajdanzev, *op. cit.*, p. 114. Quoted from S. Shirushi, *Chosen no Nogyo Chitai* (Korea's Agricultural Regions), Tokyo, 1940, pp. 14–15.
31. See table and discussion on the formation of a proletarian class, Hyaku and others, *op. cit.*, pp. 248–56.
32. *Ibid.*, p. 262.
33. For a detailed discussion on the formation of the Communist party in Korea as well as the factional fights, see *ibid.*, pp. 263–76. See also J. N. Washburn, "Soviet Russia and the Korean Communist Party," *Pacific Affairs*, XXIII, March 1950, pp. 59–65.
34. Washburn, *op. cit.*, p. 60.
35. Hyaku and others, *op. cit.*, p. 264.
36. For activities of Kim's partisan movement, see *ibid.*, pp. 316–25.
37. *Ibid.*, p. 319.

CHAPTER 8. POSTWAR KOREA (1945–48)

1. The action program was composed of 27 articles. For Korean text, see *Chosun Haibang Ilnun-sa* (One-year History of Korea's Liberation), ed. by the Committee of the Korean National Democratic Front, Seoul, 1946, pp. 88–89.
2. G. M. McCune, *Korea Today*, Harvard University Press, Cambridge Mass., 1950, p. 49.
3. For the full text of General Hodge's statement, see *ibid.*, p. 49.
4. *Ibid.*, p. 50.
5. *Crisis of the Colonial System: The National Liberation Struggle of the Peoples of East Asia*, report presented in 1949 to the Pacific Institute of Academy of Science, U.S.S.R., Bombay, 1951, p. 160.
6. McCune, *op. cit.*, p. 52.
7. Truman said: "Neither in Stalin's message to me nor in Antonov's to MacArthur nor in any other communication from the Russians was there any comment or question regarding the line of demarcation for the occupation of Korea. The 38th parallel, which was designed to loom so large in later years, was not debated over nor bargained for by either side. When General Order No. 1 was submitted to me for approval, it provided that south of latitude 38° north the surrender should be accepted by our forces and north of that line by the Russians. I was told that Secretary Byrnes had suggested that American forces receive the surrender as far north as practicable. The Army authorities, however, were faced with the

insurmountable obstacles of both distance and lack of manpower. Even the 38th parallel was too far for any American troops to reach if the Russians had chosen to disagree." H. S. Truman, *Memoirs by Harry S. Truman: Year of Decisions,* Doubleday and Co., Garden City, N.Y., 1955, Vol. 1, pp. 444–45. See also L. M. Goodrich, *Korea: A Study of U.S. Policy in the United Nations,* Council on Foreign Relations, New York, 1956, p. 12, and Shannon McCune, *Korea's Heritage: A Regional and Social Geography,* Charles E. Tuttle Co., Rutland, Vermont, and Tokyo, 1956, p. 47.

8. G. M. McCune, *op. cit.,* p. 44.
9. Goodrich, *op. cit.,* p. 13.
10. For the United States' point of view, see *ibid.,* pp. 13–14.
11. Chung Kyung-cho, *Korea Tomorrow,* The Macmillan Co., 1956, p. 303.
12. Goodrich, *op. cit.,* pp. 10–11.
13. G. M. McCune, *op. cit.,* pp. 275–76.
14. Goodrich, *op. cit.,* p. 18.
15. *Crisis of the Colonial System,* p. 161.
16. General MacArthur suggested to General Hodge to greet Rhee "as a home-coming national hero." R. T. Oliver, *Syngman Rhee: The Man Behind the Myth,* Dodd, Mead and Co., New York, 1954, p. 213.
17. *Chosun Haibang Ilnun-sa,* p. 110.
18. Oliver, *op. cit.,* p. 219.
19. For full text, see *The Voice of Korea,* November 16, 1946.
20. *Summation of USAMGIK* [United States Army Military Government in Korea], No. 14, November 1946, p. 18.
21. For a complete list of names and party affiliations of the assemblymen, see *South Korean Interim Government Activities,* March 1, 1947, p. 28.
22. G. M. McCune, *op. cit.,* p. 80.
23. The election law was composed of 62 articles. The Korean text of the law will be found in *Chosun Nunkam 1948* (Year Book of Korea in 1948), ed. by the Korean Press, Seoul, 1948, pp. 155–57.
24. Kim Jun-youn, *Doknip Nosun* (Road of Independence), Seoul, 1951, p. 53.
25. G. M. McCune, *op. cit.,* p. 75.
26. For a detailed discussion of the rightists' political activities, see *Chosun Haibang Ilnun-sa,* pp. 105–16 and 213–18. Also *Chosun Nunkam 1948,* pp. 100–13.
27. *Chosun Haibang Ilnun-sa,* pp. 79–105 and 136–47.
28. *Ibid.,* p. 80.
29. *Ibid.,* pp. 93–105.

30. G. M. McCune, *op. cit.*, p. 88.

CHAPTER 9. THE FOUR NATIONAL ISSUES

1. R. T. Oliver, *Syngman Rhee: The Man Behind the Myth,* Dodd Mead and Co., New York, 1954, p. 217.
2. *Ibid.*
3. For the text of the agreement, see *Summation of USAMGIK,* May 1947, p. 18. For the communication between the two foreign ministers, see G. M. McCune, *Korea Today,* Harvard University Press, Cambridge Mass., 1950, pp. 284–89.
4. The fifth joint communique stated that "the Joint Commission will consult with Korean democratic parties and social organizations which are truly democratic in their aims and methods and which will subscribe to the following declaration: 'We . . . declare that we will uphold the aims of the Moscow decision on Korea as stated in paragraph I of this decision.'" *Summation of USAMGIK,* May 1946, p. 17.
5. For the text of the declaration of the chief commissioner of the Soviet delegation, see *Summation of USAMGIK,* July 1947, pp. 23–25.
6. This writer attended General Brown's press conference, and the information is based on personal observation. See also *Summation of USAMGIK,* July 1947, pp. 28–31. The lists and numbers of the parties and social organizations were different from my own information.
7. *Chosun Nunkam 1948,* p. 103.
8. Oliver, *op. cit.*, p. 219.
9. *Ibid.*, pp. 228–29.
10. For details of Rhee's speech, see *Chosun Nunkam 1948,* p. 102.
11. Oliver, *op. cit.*, p. 231.
12. *Ibid.*, p. 232.
13. *Ibid.*, p. 233.
14. *Ibid.*, p. 234.
15. Kim Jun-youn, *Doknip Nosun* (Road of Independence), Seoul, 1951, pp. 53–54. This is the only source for the antitrusteeship movement.
16. *Ibid.*, pp. 65–68.
17. *Ibid.*, pp. 76–77.
18. *Ibid.*, p. 78.
19. Oliver, *op. cit.*, p. 239.

20. McCune, *op. cit.*, p. 91.
21. *Summation of USAMGIK,* May 1947, p. 16.
22. For a summary of the statements, see *Chosun Nunkam 1948,* pp. 108–9.
23. *Ibid.*
24. *New Cycle in Asia: Selected Documents on Major International Development in the Far East, 1943–1947,* The Macmillan Co., New York, 1947, pp. 93 and 299.
25. For the text of the appeal, see *ibid.*, pp. 91–94.
26. For the text of resolution, see McCune, *op. cit.*, Appendix A, pp. 299–301.
27. Hans Kelsen, *The Law of the United Nations: A Critical Analysis of Its Fundamental Problems,* The London Institute of World Affairs, London, 1951, pp. 199 and 807. "In the decisions of the First Committee some delegates denied the competence of the United Nations to deal with the problem of the independence of Korea."
28. For the text of the resolution, see McCune, *op. cit.*, pp. 301–2.
29. For a full statement of the report, see *United Nations Temporary Commission on Korea,* Press Release No. 30, February 19, 1948.
30. *Ibid.*, p. 14.
31. *Ibid.*, p. 15.
32. *Ibid.*, p. 16.
33. Leon Grodenker, "The United Nations, the United States Occupation, and the 1949 Election in Korea." *Political Science Quarterly,* LXXIII, September 1958, p. 442.
34. For the attitude of the United Nations Temporary Commission on Korea, see U.N. Document A/AC. 19/Sc. 4/SR., 13, June 21, 1948. Choi was arrested on charges of "plotting" to assassinate Rhee, and died in prison.
35. Kim Kiusic made a speech before the mass meeting for the formation of the Independence Movement Conference for Unification, stating, "I advocated first the idea of the North-South Leaders' Coalition Conference." *The Sai Han Times,* 2, No. 9, Seoul, April 1948, p. 9.
36. For text of the letter in Korean, see *ibid.*, p. 10.
37. *Ibid.*
38. For a complete list of individual names and organizations, see *ibid.*, 2, No. 10, Seoul, May 1948, p. 10.
39. See the supporting declaration signed by more than one hundred prom-

inent political, social, and religious leaders entitled "Support the North-South Coalition Conference." *The Sai Han Times,* 2, No. 9, Seoul, April 1948, p. 14.

40. *Ibid.,* 2, No. 10, Seoul, May 1948, p. 8.
41. For the full text and speeches, resolutions, and statements of the delegates of the conference, see *Chun Chosun Chungdang Sahai Danchai Daipyoza Yunsuk Haii Bokoso* (The Resolutions and Reports of the Delegates of the Unity Conference of All Korean Political and Social Organizations), Pyongyang, 1948, 55 pp.
42. *Soviet News,* London, May 5, 1948, pp. 95–97.
43. McCune, *op. cit.,* p. 264.
44. *The Sai Han Times,* 2, No. 9, Seoul, April 1948, p. 8.

CHAPTER 10. THE FIRST REPUBLIC UNDER SYNGMAN RHEE

1. Rhee was familiar with Eastern and Western culture and politics. He was born in 1874 into an upper-class Korean family and received a classical Confucian education. As a young man he participated in the political reform movement against the decadent Yi dynasty and was a member of the Independence Club, formed by Dr. Shu Chai-phil, a Korean who later became a naturalized American citizen. In 1904, Rhee came to the United States where he studied political science. For more than forty years he was a politician in the Korean community in Hawaii and in the continental United States. He became the first president of the Korean provisional government in 1919 and chairman of the Foreign Commission of the Korean Overseas Associations in Washington, D.C., during the Second World War.

   Until 1945, he was a frustrated nationalist leader similar to Nehru of India. His political fortune began in October 1945, when he left Washington for Seoul as top political adviser to Lt. Gen. John R. Hodge, then the commanding general of the U.S. occupation forces in South Korea. This was his first return to Korea after more than 30 years. For a detailed biography of Rhee, see R. T. Oliver, *Syngman Rhee: The Man Behind the Myth,* Dodd, Mead and Co., New York, 1954, 372 pp.
2. Oliver, *op. cit.,* pp. 323 and 324.
3. *Ibid.,* p. 310.
4. *Dong A Ilbo* (Dong A Daily News), Jan. 24, 1955, p. 1.
5. Oliver, *op. cit.,* p. 323.

6. *Ibid.*, p. 322.
7. C. C. Mitchell, *Korea: Second Failure in Asia,* The Public Affairs Institute, Washington, D.C., 1951, p. 25.
8. Oliver, *op. cit.*, p. 323.
9. The story of Rhee's return to Seoul is controversial. According to the late Dr. George M. McCune, head of the Korean section in the State Department, Rhee, because of his unreasonable stubbornness and ultraconservatism, was not the State Department's first choice, but the influence of the War Department, especially of General Douglas MacArthur, supreme commander of SCAP, and General John Hilldring, Assistant Secretary of State for Occupied Countries, who was close to MacArthur and "admired and respected Rhee," determined Rhee's return to Korea. He was the first political repatriate in Seoul.

   Rhee never made it known to the Korean public whether he became a citizen of the United States. According to Oliver, one of Rhee's closest friends, Rhee requested a passport from Mrs. Ruth Shipley, head of the passport division, and she secured authority from Secretary of State Byrnes to issue it just before his departure for London on September 5. Oliver, *op. cit.*, p. 210. If Oliver's statement is correct, Rhee must have been a naturalized citizen of the United States.
10. *Facts on the Korean Crisis,* Committee for a Democratic Far Eastern Policy, New York, n.d., p. 4.
11. *Ibid.*, pp. 4–5.
12. *San Francisco Chronicle,* May 29, 1952.
13. *Seoul Shinmun* (Seoul Daily News), Nov. 20, 1954.
14. Syngman Rhee wrote the article under the title "I advocate *ilmin-jui*" in *Minzok Kongron* (National Opinion), November 1948, p. 1.
15. See Niccolo Machiavelli, *The Prince and the Discourse,* with introduction by Max Lerner, The Modern Library, New York, 1940, 540 pp.
16. G. M. McCune, *Korea Today,* Harvard University Press, Cambridge, Mass., 1950, p. 254.
17. *Far Eastern Spotlight,* Committee for a Democratic Far Eastern Policy, New York, n.d., p. 7.
18. For details of Rhee's idea of winning of the war against Soviet Russia, see *U. S. News and World Report,* August 13, 1954, pp. 46–53.
19. *Department of State Bulletin,* March 7, 1948, pp. 297–98.
20. McCune, *op. cit.,* p. 306.
21. For text of the constitution, see *The Voice of Korea,* August 14, 1948.

22. Mitchell, *op. cit.*, p. 30.
23. U.N. General Assembly, *Official Record,* Fourth Session, Supplment No. 9 (A/336), pp. 28–29, paragraph 95.
24. *United States Policy in the Korean Crisis,* Department of State, 1950, p. 9.
25. *The Soviet Press in the Current Digest,* July 29, 1950, pp. 37–38.
26. *Ibid.*, August 5, 1950, pp. 35–36.
27. See Keyes Beech's report to the *San Francisco Chronicle,* May 29, 1952, under the title "Rhee Sets Himself up as a Military Dictator."
28. *Year Book of 1953,* pp. 282–83.
29. *Time,* May 17, 1954, pp. 38–39.
30. *Dong A Ilbo* carried the full text of Ham's statement on Oct. 7, 22, 23, and 31, 1954. See also Shin Do-sung's comments on Ham's statement, *ibid.*, Oct. 31, 1954.
31. For the text of the testimony of the three witnesses, see *Dong A Ilbo,* Nov. 6 and 7, 1954.
32. *Time,* December 13, 1954. p. 24.
33. *San Francisco Chronicle,* Nov. 29, 1954, p. 13.
34. *Dong A Ilbo.*, Feb. 5, 1955.
35. *Ibid.*, March 4, 1955.
36. *Ibid.*, March 16, 1955. See also editorial comment, *ibid.*
37. *Han Guk Ilbo,* March 24, 1955. Rhee awarded the highest national medal to General Won Yong-duk on June 20, 1955, because of his success in obtaining release of anti-Communist war prisoners during the truce negotiations between the U.N. commander and the representative of the North Korean regime. See *Seoul Shinmun,* June 21, 1955.
38. *The Voice of Korea,* April 1955.
39. *Dong A Ilbo,* critical of Rhee's administration, was suspended for one month, from March 17 to April 18, 1955.
40. *Dong A Ilbo.*, July, 29, 1955.

CHAPTER II. RHEE SETS UP A POLICE STATE

1. *The Korean Times,* March 6, 1956.
2. *The Voice of Korea,* May 3, 1956.
3. *Ibid.*
4. *Ibid.*
5. *Ibid.*
6. *Reuters,* May 20, 1956.

7. *Dong A Ilbo,* May 23, 1956.
8. *The Voice of Korea,* June 12, 1956.
9. For detailed discussions on the election platforms of the two parties, see *ibid.,* July 26 and August 29, 1956.
10. *Ibid.*
11. *Dong A Ilbo,* May 3, 1956.
12. Election Law, Article 73.
13. *Ibid.,* Article 155.
14. *The Korean Times,* July 1958.
15. *Sasanggye,* August 1958.
16. *Dong A Ilbo,* August 11, 1958.
17. *The Voice of Korea,* July 23, 1958.
18. *Ibid.*
19. The bill took less than three minutes to pass the Judicial Committee. *Yunhap Shinmun,* December 12, 1958.
20. See Rhee's interview with a CBS correspondent about the National Security Law on December 12, 1958.

CHAPTER 12. THE KOREAN WAR

1. I. F. Stone, *The Hidden History of the Korean War,* Monthly Review Press, New York, 1952, p. 12.
2. *Ibid.,* p. 17.
3. *Ibid.,* p. 7.
4. *Ibid.*
5. *Ibid.,* p. 4.
6. The head of the field observer team of the U.N. commission was a Nationalist Chinese representative. *Ibid.,* pp. 9–10.
7. See General Dean's personal experiences as a prisoner of war in North Korea. William F. Dean, *General Dean's Story,* Viking Press, New York, 1954.
8. Stone, *op. cit.,* p. 47.
9. *Ibid.*
10. For an interpretation of the Security Council's resolution of June 25, see Hans Kelsen, *The Law of the United Nations,* London, The London Institute of World Affairs, 1951, pp. 927–35.
11. Leland Goodrich, *Korea: A Study of U.S. Policy in the United Nations,* Council on Foreign Relations, New York, 1956, p. 107.

12. Stone, *op. cit.,* p. 70.
13. Goodrich, *op. cit.,* p. 108.
14. Stone, *op. cit.,* p. 70.
15. Goodrich, *op. cit.,* pp. 108–9.
16. See text, *ibid.,* p. 222.
17. Kelsen, *op. cit.,* p. 931.
18. Stone, *op. cit.,* p. 75.
19. Goodrich, *op. cit.,* p. 109.
20. Stone, *op. cit.,* p. 87. According to Premier Kim Il-sung of the North Korean regime, Syngman Rhee's troops invaded the North along the whole line of the 38th parallel. The Soviet Union representative supported this.
21. Article 32 says: "Any member of the United Nations which is not a member of the Security Council or any state which is not a member of the United Nations, if it is a party to a dispute under consideration by the Security Council, shall be invited to participate, without vote, in the discussion relating to the dispute. The Security Council shall lay down such conditions as it deems just for the participation of a state which is not a Member of the United Nations." The Yugoslav representative proposed "to invite the Government of North Korea to state its case before the Council," but this proposal was defeated, and the South Korean government representative alone was invited before the council. See Goodrich, *op. cit.,* p. 106.
22. See comments on the Security Council's resolution of July 7. Kelsen, *op. cit.,* pp. 935–36.
23. For an eyewitness report of the U.N. offensive, see Marguerite Higgins, *War in Korea,* New York, Doubleday, 1951.
24. Goodrich, *op. cit.,* p. 127.
25. For the text of the surrender terms see *Seattle Times,* September 31, pp. 1 and 12.
26. Stone, *op. cit.,* p. 113.
27. *Ibid.,* p. 124.
28. *Ibid.,* pp. 124–25.
29. *Ibid.,* p. 126.
30. *Ibid.,* p. 160.
31. For the text of the speech by Wu Hsiu-chuan, see *People's China Stands for Peace,* published by Committee for a Democratic Far Eastern Policy, San Francisco, 1950.

32. Goodrich, *op. cit.*, p. 179.
33. *Ibid.* Quoted from the *New York Times,* March 24, 1951.
34. *Ibid.*, p. 170.
35. Goodrich, *op. cit.*, p. 183.
36. *Ibid.*
37. For the text of the broadcast, see *ibid.*, p. 184, from *U.S. Department of State Bulletin,* XXV, July 9, 1951, p. 43.
38. For details on the armistice negotiations see Mark Clark, *From the Danube to the Yalu,* New York, Harper and Brothers, 1954.
39. Goodrich, *op. cit.*, pp. 187–88.
40. *Ibid.*, p. 190.
41. *Ibid.*, p. 191.
42. See *New York Times,* June 5, 1953.
43. Goodrich, *op. cit.*, p. 195.
44. The Mutual Defense Treaty between the United States and the Republic of Korea was signed on October 1, 1953: For the text, see Goodrich, *op. cit.*, pp. 234–35.

CHAPTER 13. THE STUDENT REVOLUTION AND THE SECOND REPUBLIC

1. See Royce Brice's comment: "Rhee Follows a Familiar Road," *San Francisco Chronicle,* April 22, 1960, p. 28.
2. *Time,* March 21, 1960, p. 30.
3. Lee Kang-hun, *Minju Hukmyung ui Baljachwi* (Footsteps of Democratic Revolution), Seoul, 1960, 282pp. This book is one of the best available sources concerning the student revolution. See also the collection of photographs about the student revolution published by *Dong A Ilbo,* Seoul, 1960.
4. *Time,* April 25, 1960, p. 33. Lee Kang-hwak, chief of the South Korean police, admitted during his trial that he authorized a subsidy of $120,000 to print the fake Communist leaflets. Lee, *op, cit.,* May 16, 1960, p. 31.
5. The three resolutions are: complete academic freedom, complete retirement of the older generation from politics, and immediate release of all students arrested during the demonstrations. *Yunhap Shinmun,* April 19, 1960.
6. *San Francisco Chronicle,* April 20, 1960.
7. *Yunhap Shinmun,* April 23, 1960.

8. Lee, *op. cit.*, p. 213. For the text of the protest statement, see *Dong A Ilbo,* April 26, 1960.
9. Lee, *op. cit.*, pp. 219–20.
10. *Time,* May 9, 1960, p. 24. For U.S. pressure on Rhee for resignation, see *Yunhap Shinmun,* May 6, 1960.
11. *Dong A Ilbo,* April 27, 1960.
12. *Time,* May 9, 1960, p. 24.
13. *Yunhap Shinmun,* April 1, 1960.
14. *San Francisco Chronicle,* April 27, 1960.
15. *Yunhap Shinmun,* April 26, 1960.
16. *Ibid.,* April 23; *The Voice of Korea,* May 1960.
17. For the text of the party principles declared by the preparatory committee, see *Dong A Ilbo,* July 18, 1955, and Sept. 2, 1955.
18. See *The Voice of Korea,* June–July 1960.
19. U.N. *General Assembly Record:* 15th Sess., Supp. No. 13 (A/4466 and Add. 1), 1960; also *The Voice of Korea,* Dec. 1960.
20. For a complete list and a brief personal history of the new cabinet members, see *Dong A Ilbo,* August 23, 1960.
21. Prime Minister Chang Myun outlined an eight-point program as the Democratic administration policy; see *Dong A Ilbo,* August 28, 1960.

CHAPTER 14. THE MILITARY COUP D'ETAT

1. For General Park Chung-hee's view on economic, political, and social conditions before the military coup, see "What Has Made the Military Revolution Successful," *Korean Quarterly,* Summer, 1961, pp. 20–24.
2. *Dong A Ilbo,* May 5, 1960.
3. *Korean Report,* Oct. 1961, pp. 6–7: also May 1962, pp. 10–12.
4. *Ibid.,* p. 10. See also *New York Times,* May 19, 1961.
5. *The Voice of Korea,* April–May 1961.
6. *Ibid.*
7. *Ibid.*
8. *Ibid.*
9. *Ibid.*
10. *Ibid.*
11. *Ibid.*
12. The Korean text of the law published by the Department of Public Information of the military government under the title *Chungbu Jungyo*

Sichaik Mit Yupjuk (Government Policies and Their Results), Seoul, 1961, p. 119. For English translation of the law, see *The Voice of Korea,* April–July 1961.

13. *Korean Quarterly,* Summer, 1961, pp. 19–21.
14. *Ibid.,* p. 19.
15. *Korean Report,* Oct. 1961, pp. 19–21.
16. *Ibid.*
17. *Ibid.*
18. *Ibid.*
19. *Two Months Achievement of the Revolution,* published by the Office of Public Information of the Supreme Council for National Reconstruction of the Republic of Korea, Seoul, August 15, 1961, p. 10.
20. *Ibid.*
21. *Korean Quarterly,* Summer, 1961, p. 7.
22. Kim Yong-jeung, publisher of *The Voice of Korea,* condemned the military coup as a "military tyranny." See *The Voice of Korea,* April–July 1961. But Yun Chin-o, president of Korea University, and Hong I-sup, dean of the graduate school of Sukmyung Women's University, defended the military take-over as "historically inevitable." For their argument, see *Korean Quarterly,* Summer, 1961, pp. 7–17.
23. *Ibid.,* p. 25.

CHAPTER 15. SOUTH KOREA'S ECONOMY

1. Hyaku and others, *Chosen Minzoku Kaiho Tosho-shi* (History of the Liberation Struggle of the Korean People), Tokyo, 1954, pp. 178–80.
2. Japanese economic policy in Korea will be found in G. M. McCune, *Korea Today* (Harvard University Press, Cambridge, Mass., 1950, pp. 29–37; A. J. Grajdanzev, *Modern Korea,* Institute of Pacific Relations, New York, 1944, pp. 84–237; and Hyaku and others, *op. cit.,* pp. 177–98, 233–48, and 281–301.
3. McCune, *op. cit.,* pp. 52–60.
4. A. W. Zanzi, "Economic Reconstruction Problems in South Korea." This paper was submitted to the Institute of Pacific Relations at the Twelfth Conference held at Kyoto, Japan, in September 1954. Institute of Pacific Relations, New York, secretariat paper No. 2., p. 7.
5. Ordinance No. 33, December 6, 1945, Office of Military Government, Seoul.

6. *Ibid.*, p. 8.
7. C. C. Mitchell, *Korea: Second Failure in Asia,* Public Affairs Institute, Washington, D.C., 1951, p. 16.
8. *SKIG [South Korean Interim Government] Activities,* December 1947, p. 13.
9. *Ibid.*
10. Mitchell, *op. cit.*, p. 28.
11. Choi Moon-hwan, "The Path to Democracy: A Historical Review of the Korean Economy," *Korean Quarterly,* Summer, 1961, pp. 64–70.
12. Zanzi, *op. cit.*, pp. 8–9.
13. McCune, *op. cit.*, p. 254.
14. Choi Ho-chin, *Hanguk Kungchai-wa Kungchai-hwak* (Korea's Economy and Economics), Seoul, 1959, p. 153.
15. Choi, *op. cit.*, pp. 199–201.
16. Pu Wan-hyoke, "The History of American Aid to Korea," *Korean Quarterly,* Summer, 1961, pp. 80–82.
17. Zanzi, *op. cit.*, pp. 11–12.
18. *The Voice of Korea* printed the text of the report in July, August, and September 1954.
19. *Ibid.*, July 1954.
20. Yu Chin-o, *Heunbup Hai-i* (Interpretation of the Korean Constitution), Seoul, 1960, pp. 258–59.
21. Pu, *op. cit.*, p. 93.
22. *The Voice of Korea,* July 1954.
23. *Ibid.*, Jan. 1961.

CHAPTER 16. PROBLEMS OF SOUTH KOREA'S ECONOMY

1. A. J. Grajdanzev, *Modern Korea,* Institute of Pacific Relations, New York, 1944, p. 112.
2. One *chungbo* (Japanese: *chō*) equals 2.45 acres.
3. See distribution of population by occupation, G. M. McCune, *Korea Today,* Harvard University Press, Cambridge, Mass., 1950, p. 32 (table).
4. The ratio of yen to dollars before the Second World War was 3 to 1.
5. The Korean measure for rice weight is the *suk* (Japanese: *koku*); one *suk* is about five bushels.
6. A. W. Zanzi, *Economic Reconstruction Problems in South Korea,* Institute of Pacific Relations, New York, 1954, p. 11.
7. McCune, *op. cit.*, p. 29.

8. For each party's land reform policy, see *Chosun Nunkam 1948* (Yearbook of Korea 1948), Seoul, 1948, p. 180, and *Haibang Ilnun-sa* (One Year History of Liberation), Seoul, 1948, pp. 88, 101, 148, 155–56, 210, 213, and 217.
9. McCune, *op. cit.*, p. 130.
10. *Ibid.*, pp. 129–33.
11. C. C. Mitchell, *Korea: Second Failure in Asia,* Public Affairs Institute, Washington, D.C., 1951, p. 28.
12. *Ibid.*, p. 29.
13. *Seoul Times,* Feb. 9 and May 19, 1949.
14. Yu Chin-o, *Heunbup Hai-i* (Interpretation of Korean Constitution), Seoul, 1960, pp. 261–62.
15. For reasons of the failure of land reform in South Korea, see Pu, "The History of American Aid to Korea," *Korean Quarterly,* Summer, 1961, pp. 62–64; also Zanzi, *op. cit.*, pp. 13–14.
16. See *Summary Draft of the Five-year Economic Plan (1962–1966)* published by the Economic Planning Board, Republic of Korea, Seoul, 1961, p.24.
17. Pu, *op. cit.*, p. 73.
18. *Ibid.*, p. 80.
19. *Ibid.*, p. 92.
20. McCune, *op. cit.*, p. 255.
21. Pu, *op. cit.*, p. 85.
22. *The Voice of Korea,* July 1954.

CHAPTER 17. SOVIET CONTROL OF NORTH KOREA

1. Kin Shyo-mei (Korean: Kim Chong-ho), *Chosen Shin-minshu-shugi Kakumei-shi* (New Democratic Revolutionary History of Korea), Tokyo, 1953, pp. 163–64.
2. For the Korean text, see *Chosun Haibang Ilnun-sa* (One-year History of Liberation), Seoul, 1948, pp. 118–19.
3. For Kim's biography, see p. 385 of this book.
4. Kin, *op. cit.*, p. 163.
5. Philip Rudolph, "North Korea's Political and Economic Structure" (mimeographed), Institute of Pacific Relations, New York, 1959, p. 1.
6. The Pyongyang People's Committee was established in September 8, 1945. Kin, *op. cit.*, p. 181.
7. *Ibid.*, p. 183.

8. *Ibid.*, pp. 184–85.
9. Rudolph, *op. cit.*, p. 13.
10. Kin, *op. cit.*, p. 201.
11. *Ibid.*, pp. 202–3.
12. *Ibid.*
13. Rudolph, *op. cit.*, p. 15.
14. *Ibid.*, p. 14.
15. *Ibid.*
16. *Ibid.*, p. 15.
17. For text of the constitution, see D. G. Tewksbury, "Source Materials on Korean Politics and Ideologies," Institute of Pacific Relations, New York, 1950, pp. 119–21.
18. Hyaku and others, *Chosen Minzoku Kaiho Tosho-shi* (History of the Liberation Struggle of the Korean People), Tokyo, 1954, p. 396.
19. G. M. McCune, *Korea Today,* Harvard University Press, Cambridge, Mass., 1950, p. 247.
20. Kin, *op. cit.*, pp. 246–48. Quoted from the Supreme People's Assembly, first session record.
21. For a complete list of the cabinet members, see Kin, *op. cit.*, pp. 249–50.
22. Tewksbury, *op. cit.*, pp. 121–22.
23. See the correspondence between North Korea and the Soviet Union on recognition, Tewksbury, *op. cit.*, pp. 123–24.
24. The agreement was composed of six articles. Tewksbury, *op. cit.*, pp. 127–28.
25. Rudolph, *op. cit.*, p. 19.
26. *Ibid.*, p. 20.
27. *Ibid.*, pp. 20–21.
28. *Ibid.*, p. 21.
29. *The Voice of Korea,* November 27, 1957.
30. *Ibid.*
31. *Ibid.*
32. *Ibid.*
33. Kin, *op. cit.*, pp. 175–77.
34. The North Korean Democratic Front was formed on July 22, 1946, and issued a policy statement consisting of twenty articles. *Ibid.*, pp. 186–87.
35. Rudolph, *op. cit.*, p. 27.
36. *Ibid.*
37. *Ibid.*, pp. 28–29.

38. For the complete text, see *The Third Party Congress Record,* Pyongyang, 1956, pp. 385–405.
39. *The Selected Biography of Kim Il-sung,* published by San-ichi Shobo, Tokyo, 1952.
40. Hyaku and others, *op. cit.,* p. 278.
41. Rudolph, *op. cit.,* p. 32.
42. *The New York Times,* December 19, 1955, p. 6.
43. *New Korea,* December 1957 (supplement), pp. 12–13.

CHAPTER 18. NORTH KOREA'S ECONOMY

1. Shannon McCune discussed the regions of North Korea in his book *Korea's Heritage: A Regional and Social Geography,* Charles E. Tuttle Company, Tokyo, 1956, pp. 116–47.
2. George M. McCune, *Korea Today,* Harvard University Press, Cambridge, Mass., 1950, pp. 186–87.
3. *Ibid.,* p. 183.
4. *Chosun Haibang Ilnun-sa* (One-year History of Liberation), Seoul, 1948, pp. 411–12.
5. *Ibid.,* pp. 412–14.
6. Rudolph, "North Korea's Political and Economic Structure," Institute of Pacific Relations, New York, 1959, p. 48.
7. Anna L. Strong, *In North Korea: First Eye-witness Report,* Soviet Russia Today, New York, 1949, p. 29.
8. Rudolph, *op. cit.,* p. 48. Most authors use *chungbo,* but this author uses acres.
9. Strong, *op. cit.,* p. 26.
10. Rudolph, *op. cit.,* pp. 50–51.
11. For the cooperative movement and agricultural progress, see *Choguk Tongil-i Sukkwang* (Bright Side of the Fatherland's Unification). This report was made by Vice-premier Lee Chong-ok to the Supreme People's Assembly on November 19, 1960, pp. 174–90.
12. Rudolph, *op. cit.,* p. 52.
13. *The Voice of Korea,* March 1, 1956.
14. *Ibid.,* March 30, 1956.
15. Rudolph, *op. cit.,* p. 53.
16. Shannon McCune, *op. cit.,* p. 127.
17. *The Voice of Korea,* April 14, 1958.

18. Rudolph, *op. cit.*, p. 43.
19. *The Voice of Korea,* April 14 & 30, 1958.
20. For the official report on the plan, see *Choguk Tongil-i Sukkwang,* pp. 141–74.

CHAPTER 19. THE SOLUTION FOR KOREA: PERMANENT NEUTRALITY

1. The meaning and character of neutrality vary. The Swiss political scientist Walter Hofer said: "Neutrality cannot of its very nature become a philosophy, a political ideology, still less a way of life; it is simply an instrument, the specifically Swiss instrument, of foreign policy, of protecting the Swiss outlook on life and way of life against attack, an outlook and a way of life which are in spirit identical with the spirit of freedom and democracy." Hofer, *Neutrality as the Principle of Swiss Foreign Policy,* Zurich, 1957, p. 39. For general differences between ordinary neutrality and perpetual neutrality, see *ibid.,* pp. 5–6. Jawaharlal Nehru said: "We proclaimed during the past year that we will not attach ourselves to any particular group. If there is a big war there is no particular reason why we should jump into it. Nevertheless, it is a little difficult nowadays in world wars to be neutral. We are not going to join a war if we can help it: and we are going to join the side which is to our interest when time comes to make the choice. There the matter ends." Nehru, *Independence and After,* The John Day Co., New York, 1950, p. 200. For general characteristics of postwar neutralism in Asia, see R. A. Scalapino, "Neutralism in Asia," *The American Political Science Review,* XLVII, 1 March 1954, pp. 49–62.
2. For a general background on Korea's strategic position, see Shannon McCune, *Korea's Heritage: Regional and Social Geography,* Tokyo, Tuttle, 1956, pp. 3–10.
3. Full text: D. G. Tewksbury, "Source Materials on Korean Politics and Ideologies," Institute of Pacific Relations, New York, 1950, pp. 21–23.
4. Paul H. Clyde, *The Far East: A History of the Impact of the West on East Asia,* Prentice-Hall, New York, 1949, p. 355.
5. G. N. Steiger, *A History of the Far East,* Ginn and Co., New York and London, 1946, p. 730.
6. M. F. Nelson, *Korea and the Old Order in East Asia,* Louisiana State University Press, Louisiana, 1947, p. 257.

7. For Korean text, see Kang Ji-woon, *Kundai Chosun Jungchi-sa* (Recent Korean Political History), Seoul, 1951, pp. 350–51.
8. Korean text: Kang, *op. cit.*, pp. 382–84.
9. G. M. McCune, *Korea Today,* Harvard University Press, Cambridge, Mass., 1950, p. 42.
10. For full text, see Harry S. Truman, *Memoirs by Harry S. Truman: Year of Decisions,* Doubleday and Co., New York, 1955, p. 439.
11. L. M. Goodrich, *Korea: A Study of U.S. Policy in the United Nations,* Council of Foreign Relations, New York, 1956, pp. 12–16.
12. Many Korean political and social organizations opposed the trusteeship provision (Article 3), insisting that the people were ready for self-determination.
13. G. M. McCune, *op. cit.*, p. 62.
14. For further discussion on the competence of the U.N. to deal with the problem of the independence of Korea, see U.N. Doc. A/C. 1/S.R. pp. 87–94.
15. For text and speeches, resolutions, and statements of the delegates of the Unity Conference, see Tewksbury, *op. cit.*, pp. 97–98.
16. The conference was attended by 545 delegates from both North and South Korea. G. M. McCune, *op. cit.*, pp. 262–64.
17. G. M. McCune, *op. cit.*, p. 264.
18. *Saihan Minbo,* Seoul, April 1958, p. 8.
19. For an analysis of the May elections, see Benjamin Weems, "Behind the Korean Election," *Far Eastern Survey,* June 23, 1948, pp. 142–46.
20. Dr. Kim Kiusic expressed his views before the U.N. Temporary Commission in these terms: "Any Korean who talks about a South Korean unilateral government will go down in history as a 'bad egg' because once that term is used, the Communists in the North under the direction of the Soviet Union will establish what is called 'The People's Republic,' or the 'People's Committee.' Then you will have two unilateral governments in this little space of something over 85,000 square miles. Not only that, but once such a thing occurs in history, it will go down forever, and it will be perpetuated; then you are responsible, and we are responsible for perpetuating the division of Korea into a northern half and a southern half." U.N. Temporary Committee of Korea, on Feb. 19, 1945, Seoul, Press Release No. 30, p. 16.
21. "Election Result for the People's Committee of North Korea," Tass

dispatch, *Izvestia,* November 16, 1948, translations from the *Soviet Press,* December 14, 1948, p. 21.

22. For a legal interpretation of the United Nations action in Korea, see Hans Kelsen, *The Law of the United Nations,* The London Institute of World Affairs, London, 1951, pp. 927–49.
23. Kuo Ping-chia, *China: New Age and New Outlook,* Alfred A. Knopf, New York, 1956, pp. 144–46.
24. Quoted from I. F. Stone, *The Hidden History of the Korean War,* Monthly Review Press, New York, 1952, p. 126.
25. *Ibid.,* pp. 125–26.
26. For full text of the truce agreement, see Chung Kyung-cho, *Korea Tomorrow,* The Macmillan Co., New York, 1956, pp. 314–29; and for an intrepretation of the armistice, see Goodrich, *op. cit.,* pp. 176–213.
27. For text, as well as the statements of John Foster Dulles, Vyacheslav M. Molotov, and Chou En-lai, see *The Voice of Korea,* May 27, 1954.
28. *Ibid.*
29. *U.S. News and World Report,* August 13, 1954, pp. 46–53.
30. Kim Yong-jeung, editor and publisher of *The Voice of Korea,* has been advocating the idea of neutralization of Korea. The present author also supported permanent neutrality of Korea in his article "The Organization of the Switzerland Government," *Bupchung* (Law and Administration), Seoul, April 1948, pp. 8–11. See also "Problems of Korea," *American Friends Service Committee,* Seattle, August 1, 1950, p. 7; and "A Proposal for Solution of the Korean Problem: Permanent Neutralization of Korea," *Progressive,* October 1953, p. 31. S. K. Kim and C. H. Shin issued a joint statement about neutralization of Korea in Tokyo in February 1955; see text in *The Voice of Korea,* Feb. 21, 1955. In November 1960 the Unification Committee for Rapid Realization of Permanent Neutralization of Korea was formed, headed by Kim Kap-moon, South Kyongsang province.
31. *The Voice of Korea,* Feb. 21, 1955.
32. *San Francisco Chronicle,* June 2, 1953, p. 4.
33. Quoted from the present author's personal memo on July 15, 1955.
34. *Ibid.,* January 4, 1957.
35. In November 1960 the *Dong A Ilbo,* one of the leading conservative newspapers in South Korea, submitted written questions to Senator Mansfield regarding his views on neutralization of Korea. The first question was: "Do you believe Korea could be neutralized along Austrian

lines?" The paper added: "We Koreans think such a method is not realistic; it would mean an advantage for the Communist bloc." Mansfield reafirmed his views saying that it was necessary to start preparing for the neutralization of Korea based on the Austrian pattern in order "somewhere, sometime, and somehow to abolish the present two zones of Korea." He also was asked: "Do you believe the Soviet Union, Communist China, and the Northern Communists will allow the Korean people to have a democratic way of unification?" He replied that "without trying we will never know." *Dong A Ilbo,* November 6, 1960.

36. "The Tasks Ahead," *The Korean Reporter,* March 15, 1961, p. 4.
37. Quoted from Hofer, *op. cit.,* p. 37.
38. *Austria: Facts and Figures,* Vienna, 1956, p. 24.
39. George Soloveytchik, *Switzerland in Prospective,* London and New York, 1954, p. 184.
40. *The Voice of Korea,* May 28, 1955.
41. Kelsen, *op. cit.,* p. 85.
42. *Austria: Facts and Figures,* p. 23.
43. The reason for not becoming a member of the U.N. was that the voting provision (veto right of the big powers) of the Security Council "does not even hold out the promise of collective security against great-power aggression. At the same time, however, it deliberately subordinates the rights and liberties of small states to the will of the great powers without offering them any protection." Soloveytchik, *op. cit.,* p. 268.
44. "The republic, as a member of the United Nations, will not only be enabled to pursue a policy of honest and genuine neutrality, she will also feel herself secure in the community of nations." *Austria: Facts and Figures,* p. 26.
45. *Dong A Ilbo,* October 1960.

BIBLIOGRAPHY

I. BIBLIOGRAPHIES

A. In English

Kerner, Robert J.: "Korea," *Northeastern Asia: A Selected Bibliography,* vol. 2, University of California Press, Berkeley, 1939.

Marcus, Richard, ed.: *Korean Studies Guide,* University of California Press, Berkeley, 1954.

McCune, Shannon: *Bibliography of Western Languages Materials on Korea,* Institute of Pacific Relations, New York, 1950.

Underwood, Horace H.: "A Partial Bibliography of Occidental Literature on Korea from Early Times to 1930," *Translations of the Korean Branch of the Royal Asiatic Society,* vol. 20, Shanghai, 1931.

United Nations Documents Index, vol. 1, January, Document Index United Nations Library, New York, 1950.

United States Library of Congress: *Korea: An Annotated Bibliography of Publications in Western Languages,* Library of Congress, Washington, D.C., 1950.

———: *Korea: An Annotated Bibliography of Publications in Far Eastern Languages,* Washington, D.C., 1950.

B. In Japanese and Korean

Chosen Sotokufu (Government-General of Chosen): *Chosen Tosho Kaidai* (Bibliography of the Korean Publications), in Japanese, Seoul, 1919, 2nd ed., 1931.

Chosun Chulpan Munhwa Hyophai (Korean Cultural Publication Association), in Korean, Seoul, 1949.

2. BOOKS

A. In English

Bishop, Isabella L.: *Korea and Her Neighbors,* 2 vols., Murray, London, 1898.

Bonjour, Edgar: *Swiss Neutrality: Its History and Meaning.* George Allen and Unwin Ltd., London, 1948.

Caldwell, John C.: *The Korea Story,* Henry Regnery Company, Chicago, 1952.

Carles, W. R.: *Life in Korea,* Macmillan, London-New York, 1888.

Clark, Mark W.: *From the Danube to the Yalu,* Harper, New York, 1954.

Gale, James S.: *A History of the Korean People,* The Christian Literature Society of Korea, Seoul, 1924.

Goodrich, Leland M.: *Korea: A Study of U.S. Policy in the United Nations,* Council on Foreign Relations, New York, 1956.

Grajdanzev, Andrew J.: *Modern Korea,* Institute of Pacific Relations, New York, 1944.

Griffic, William E.: *Corea: The Hermit Nation,* 8th ed., Scribner's, New York, 1907.

Higgins, M.: *War in Korea,* Doubleday, New York, 1951.

Hulbert, Homer B.: *The History of Korea,* 2 vols., Methodist Publishing House, Seoul, 1905.

———: *The Passing of Korea,* Young People's Missionary of the United States and Canada, New York, 1906.

Joy, C. Turner: *How Communists Negotiate,* Macmillan, New York, 1955.

Kang, Younghill: *The Grass Roof,* Scribner's, New York, 1931.

———: *The Happy Grove,* Scribner's, New York, 1933.

Kelsen, Hans: *The Law of the United Nations,* The London Institute of World Affairs, London, 1951.

Kim, Agnes D.: *I Married a Korean,* John Daily, New York, 1953.

Kim, Changsoon, ed.: *The Culture of Korea,* Korean American Cultural Association, Honolulu, 1946.

Kim, Helen: "Rural Education for Regeneration of Korea," Columbia University Doctoral Dissertation, New York, 1931.

Kim, San, and Nym, Wales, eds.: *Song of Ariran,* John Daily, New York, 1941.

Kundra, J. C.: *India Foreign Policy 1947–1954,* Wolters & Co., Bombay, 1955.

Kuo, Ping-chia, *China: New Age and New Outlook,* Knopf, New York, 1956.

Latourette, K. S.: *A Short History of the Far East,* Macmillan, New York, 1951.

Lee, Hoon-koo: *Land Utilization and Rural Economy in Korea,* University of Chicago Press, Chicago, 1936.

McCune, George M., and Grey, Arthur L.: *Korea Today,* Harvard University Press, Cambridge, Mass., 1950.

McCune, Shannon: *Korea's Heritage: A Regional and Social Geography,* Charles Tuttle, Rutland, Vermont, and Tokyo, 1956.

Meade, E. Grant: *American Military Government in Korea,* King's Crown Press, New York, 1951.

Mitchell, Clyde, C.: *Korea: Second Failure in Asia,* Public Affairs Institute, Washington, D.C., 1951.

Nelson, M. Frederick: *Korea and the Old Order in Eastern Asia,* Louisiana State University Press, Baton Rouge, Louisiana, 1946.

Oliver, Robert T.: *Korea: Forgotten Nation,* Public Affairs Press, Washington, D.C., 1950.

———: *Syngman Rhee: The Man Behind the Myth,* Dodd Mead, New York, 1954.

Osgood, Cornelius: *The Koreans and Their Culture,* The Ronald Press, New York, 1951.

Paik, L. George: *The History of Protestant Missions in Korea, 1832–1910,* Union Christian College Press, Pyongyang, Korea, 1924.

Pyun, Y. T.: *Korea My Country,* The International Cultural Association, Seoul, 1959.

Rudolph, Philip: "North Korea's Political and Economic Structure," mimeographed, Institution of Pacific Relations, New York, 1959.

Shoemaker, James H.: *Notes on Korea's Postwar Economic Position,* Institute of Pacific Relations, New York, 1947.

Steiger, G. N.: *A History of the Far East,* Ginn and Co., Boston, New York, and San Francisco, 1944.

Stone, I. F.: *The Hidden History of the Korean War.* Monthly Review Press, New York, 1952.

Tewksbury, D. G.: "Source Materials on Korean Politics and Ideologies," mimeographed, Institute of Pacific Relations, New York, 1950.

Thompson, Reginald: *Cry Korea,* MacDonald, London, 1952.

Truman, Harry S.: *Memoirs by Harry S. Truman: Year of Decision,* vol. 1, Doubleday, New York, 1946.

Underwood, Horace G.: *The Call of Korea,* new ed., Fleming H. Revell Co., New York, 1908.

Vinacke H. M.: *History of the Far East in Modern Times,* Appleton-Century-Crofts, New York, 1941.

Wagner, Ellause: *Korea: The Old and New,* Fleming H. Revell Co., New York, 1931.

Zanzi, A. W.: "Economic Reconstruction Problems in South Korea," mimeographed, Institute of Pacific Relations, New York, 1954.

B. In Japanese

Chosen-shi Gakkai (Korean History Association): *Chosen-shi Taikei* (Outline History of Korea), 5 vols., Seoul, 1937.

Chosen Sotokufu (Government-General of Chosen), *Chosen-shi* (History of Korea), 35 vols., Seoul, 1931–38.

Kida, Sadakichi: *Kankoku no Heigo to Kokushi* (The Annexation of Korea and Its History), Sansho-do, Tokyo, 1910.

Kasei, Yoshihisa: *Nikkan Gappo Hishi* (The Secret History of the Annexation of Korea), Kokuryo-kai, Tokyo, 1931.

Kin, Shyo-mei [Korean: Kim Chong-ho]: *Chosen Shin-minshu-shugi Kakumei-shi* (New Democratic Revolutionary History of Korea), Gogetsu-sho, Tokyo, 1953.

Hayashi, Kotetsu [Korean: Lim Kwang-chull]: *Chosen Rekishi Tokuhon* (A Textbook of Korean History), Hyakuyo-sha, Tokyo, 1949.

Hyaku, Nan-wun [Korean: Paek Nam-woon]: *Chosen Shakai Keizai-shi* (Korean Socioeconomic History), Kaizo-sha, Tokyo, 1928.

———: *Chosen Hoken Keizai-shi* (Korean Feudal Economic History), Kaizo-sha, Tokyo, 1931.

——— and others: *Chosen Minzoku Kaiho Tosho-shi* (History of the Liberation Struggle of the Korean People), Sanichi-sho, Tokyo, 1954.

Hatada, Takashi: *Chosen-shi* (A Korean History), Iwanami Shoten, Tokyo, 1956.

Sai Ho-chin [Korean: Choi Ho-chin]: *Kindai Chosen Keizai-shi* (Recent Economic History of Korea), Keiyo-sho, Tokyo, 1942.

C. In Korean

Ahn Chai-hong: *Chosun Sangko Sakam* (Outline of Ancient Korean History), 2 vols., Minyu-sa, Seoul, 1947.

Chaimi Hanzok Wiwon-hai [Korean Association in America]: *Haiban*

Chosun (Liberated Korea), Korean Association in America, Los Angeles and Hawaii, 1948.

Choi Ho-chin: *Hanguk Kungchai-wa Kungchai-hwak* (Korea's Economy and Economics), Ilhan Dosu, Seoul, 1959.

———: *Kundai Chosun Kungchai-sa Yunku* (Study of Modern Korean Economic History), Minjung Sukwan, Seoul, 1956.

Chosun Tongshin-sa [Korean Press]: *Chosun Nunkam 1948* (Year Book of Korea 1948), Seoul, 1948.

Chosun Haibang Ilnun-sa (One-Year History of Korea's Liberation), edited by the Committee of the Korean National Democratic Front, Munyu-insu-kwan, Seoul, 1946.

Chung Chang-sun, ed.: *Tongmun Hwigo* (Documents of Foreign Relations), 60 vols., compiled at the request of King Chongjo (1777–1800), 1779.

Chung, In-po: *Chosun-sa Yunku* (Research in Korean History), Seoul Shinmun-sa, Seoul, 1947.

Gukcho Bokam (National History of Korea), 28 vols., Seoul, 1909.

Hahm Suk-heun: *Tusuro Bon Hanguk Yoksa* (Meaning of Korean History), Ilyu-sa, Seoul, 1962.

———: *Inkan Hukmyung* (Human Revolution), Ilyu-sa, Seoul, 1961.

Kang, Ji-woon: *Kundai Chosun Junchi-sa* (Recent Korean Political History), Daihwak Sanghwal-sa, Seoul, 1951.

Kim, Jun-yun: *Doknip Nosun* (Road of Independence), Hunghan Chaidan, Seoul, 1948.

Kim, Puki: *Samguk Saki* (History of the Three Kingdoms), 14 vols., Kiza Chosun Yunku-sa, Seoul, 1914.

Kim, Warren: *Chaimi Hanin Oship-nun-sa* (Fifty-year History of the Korean People in the United States), Charles Kim, Reedley, California, 1959.

Lee, Chong-ok: *Choguk Tongil-i Sukkwang* (Bright Side of the Father Land's Unification), Pyonghwa Chull-pan, Pyongyang, 1960.

Lee In-yung: *Guksa Kam* (Outline of Korean History), Minyu-sa, Seoul, 1949.

Lee, Kang-hun: *Minju Kukmyung Ui Baljachwi* (Foot Steps of Democratic Revolution), Dong A Ilbo Press, Seoul, 1960.

Lee, Kwang-su: *Tosan: Ahn Chang-ho* (Biography of Ahn Chang-ho), Ahn Chang-ho Memorial Press, Seoul, 1947.

Lee, Pyong-to: *Koryo Sidai Yunku* (A Study of the Koryo Period), Tongji-sa, Seoul, 1948.

———: *Guksa Taikwan* (General Survey of National History), Munyu-sa, Seoul, 1949.

Park, Un-sik: *Hanguk Doknip Undong-ji Hulsa*(Bloody History of the Korean Independence Movement), Seoul Shinmun-sa, Seoul, 1946.

Son, Chin-tai: *Chosun Minzok Munhwa Yunku* (Study of Korean Culture), Ulyu Munhwa-sa, Seoul, 1948.

Yijo Sil-lok 1392–1864 (Annals of the Yi Dynasty), reproduced by photo-offset by the government-general of Chosen and Keijo [Seoul] Imperial Univeristy, 1930–1934.

Yu Chin-o: *Heunbup Haii* (Interpretation of Constitution), Ilcho-kak, Seoul, 1956.

3. ARTICLES

"Appeal of the Korean Supreme People's Assembly to the Government of the U.S.A. and Soviet Union," *Pravda,* September 14, 1948. Translation in *Soviet Press Translations,* November 1, 1948, pp. 581–82.

Bertsch, Leonard M: "Korean Partition Prevents Economic Recovery," *Foreign Policy Bulletin,* January 28, 1949.

Choi Moon-hwan: "The Path to Democracy: A Historical Review of the Korean Economy," *Korean Quarterly,* Summer, 1961, pp. 52–70.

Choy, Bong-youn: "Proposal for the Solution of the Korean Problem: Permanent Neutralization," *Progress,* Oct. 1953, p. 31.

Deane, Hugh: "Economic Deterioration in South Korea," *China Weekly Review,* Oct. 30, 1948, p. 233.

Dull, Paul S: "The South Korean Constitution," *Far Eastern Survey,* Sept. 8, 1948, pp. 205–7.

"Election Results for the People's Committee of Northern Korea," *Tass* Dispatch, *Izvestia,* November 14, 1946; translation in *Soviet Press Translations,* December 14, 1946.

Gayn, Mark: "Cold War: Two Police States in Korea," *New Republic,* September 15, 1948, pp. 15–16.

Guins, George C.: "Korean Plans of Russian Imperialism," *The American Journal of Economics and Sociology,* Oct. 1946, pp. 71–86.

Kang, Younghill: "How It Feels to Be a Korean in Korea," *United Nations World,* May 1948, pp. 18–21.

Kim, Du-yong: "Labor Legislation in North Korea," *Amerasia,* May 1947, pp. 156–60, translation from the Japanese periodical *Zenei,* May 1946.

Kim, Yongjeung: "The Cold War: The Korean Election," *Far Eastern Survey,* May 5, 1948, pp. 101–2.

Lee, Seyoul: "A Picture of North Korea's Industry," *Amerasia,* February 1947, pp. 61–62.

Lerch, Maj. Gen. Archer L.: "Expediency Decision to Divide Korea Created 90 percent of Troubles," *Commonwealth* [club], San Francisco, August 18, 1947, p. 162.

McCune, George M.: "Korea: The First Year of Liberation," *Pacific Affairs,* March 1947, pp. 3–17.

———: "The Korean Situation," *Far Eastern Survey,* Sept. 1948, pp. 197–202.

———: "Postwar Government and Politics of Korea," *Journal of Politics,* Nov. 1947, pp. 605–23.

McCune, Shannon: "Land Reform in Korea," *Far Eastern Survey,* Jan. 1948, pp. 13–18.

Mitchell, Clyde: "The Korean Tenant Purchase Program," *Land Economics,* Nov. 1948, p. 105.

———: "Land Reform in South Korea," *Pacific Affairs,* Ju. 1949, pp. 144–54.

Noble, Harold J.: "North Korean Democracy, Russian Style," *The New Leader,* May 1947, sec. 2, pp. 2–12.

Oliver, Robert T.: "Korea's President," *Eastern World,* June–July 1948, pp. 131–32.

———: "The Tragedy of Korea," *World Affairs,* Spring 1947, pp. 27–34.

Park, Chung-hee: "What Has Made the Military Revolution Successful," *Korean Quarterly,* Summer 1961, pp. 18–27.

Pu, Wan-hyok: "The History of American Aid to Korea," *Korean Quarterly,* Summer, 1961, pp. 71–96.

Rudolph, Philip: "North Korea at the Path to Socialism," *Pacific Affairs,* June 1959, pp. 131–43.

Scalapino, Robert: "Neutralism in Asia," *The American Political Science Review,* March 1954, pp. 49–62.

———: "The Tasks Ahead," *Korean Reporter,* March 15, 1961, pp. 1–5.

Snow, Edgar: "We Meet Russia in Korea," *Saturday Evening Post,* May 1948, p. 18.

Strong, Anna L.: "North Korea," *The Statesman and Nation,* London, January 17, 1948, p. 47.

Van Fleet, Gen. James A.: "Van Fleet Tells Story of Korea," *U.S. News and World Report,* March 23, 1952.

———: "The Truth about Korea," *Life,* May 11 & 18, 1953.

Washburn, John N.: "Russia Looks at North Korea," *Pacific Affairs,* June 1947, pp. 152–60.

———: "Soviet Russia and the Korean Communist Party," *Pacific Affairs,* March 1950, pp. 59–65.

Yu, Chin-o: "Korean Democracy Under Overlapping Attack," *Korean Quarterly,* Summer 1961, pp. 7–10.

4. OFFICIAL PUBLICATIONS

A. North Korea

Chosun Chungang Nunkam (Central Yearbook of Korea), home edition, 1949. Reprinted in Tokyo without name of publisher or date; a later edition (1951–1952) of the same work, compiled by the Chosun Chungang Tongshin-sa, Pyongyang, 1952, was reprinted and published with a slightly different title on the cover, and with the date changed to 1953, by Toko Shon, Tokyo, 1953.

Chun Chosun Chungdang Sahai Danchai Daipyoza Yunsuk Haii Bokoso Kup Kulchungso (The Resolutions and Reports of the Delegates of the Unity Conference of all Korean Political and Social Organizations), Pyongyang, 1948.

Dyakov, A. M, ed.: *Crisis of the Colonial System: National Liberation Struggle of the Peoples of East Asia,* Peoples Publishing House, Bombay, 1951.

Kim, Il-sung: *All for the Postwar Rehabilitation and Development of the National Economy,* New Korea Press, Pyongyang, 1954.

———: *The Great Liberation War of the Korean People for Freedom and Independence,* Pyongyang, 1951.

Postwar Rehabilitation and Development of the National Economy in the Democratic People's Republic of Korea, Foreign Language Publishing House, Pyongyang, 1957.

Third Congress of the Worker's [Labor] Party of Korea: *Documents and Materials,* April 23–29, 1956, Foreign Language Publishing House, Pyongyang, 1956.

B. United Nations

Department of Information: "Assembly Endorses Korean Government," *United Nations Bulletin,* January 1, 1949, pp. 46–48.

———: "Committee Approves Korean Commission," Nov. 11, pp. 635–38.

———: "Divided Korea: A Grim Reality," Nov. 15, 1948, pp. 921–22.

———: "The Mission to Korea," Aug. 1, 1948, pp. 615–31.

General Assembly Official Record, 3rd Session, Supplement No. 9: *First Report of the United Nations Temporary Commission on Korea,* Lake Success, 1948, vol. 1, Document A/576.

———: *Second Part of the Report,* Paris, 1948, vol. 1, Document A/575, Add. 3.

———: 4th Session, Supplement No. 9, *Report of the United Nations Commission on Korea,* Lake Success, 1949, vol. I, Document A/936.

———: 5th Session, Supplement No. 16, *Report of the United Nations Commission on Korea,* New York, 1950, A/1350.

———: 6th Session, Supplement No. 2, *Report of the United Nations Commission for the Unification and Rehabilitation of Korea,* New York, 1951, A/1881.

———: 9th Session, Supplement No. 15, *Report of Agent-General of the United Nations Korean Reconstruction Agency,* New York, 1952, A2222.

C. United States, South Korea, and Others

Austria: Facts and Figures, The Federal Press Service, Vienna, 1956.

Bank of Chosen: *Economic History of Chosen,* Seoul, 1920.

Bank of Korea: *Republic of Korea Economic Summation,* 1948.

Government-General of Chosen: *Annual Reports of the Administration of Chosen,* Seoul, 1923–36.

Republic of Korea [ROK] Army: *Republic of Korea Army,* vol. 1, Office of Public Information, Seoul, 1954.

———: *Bank of Korea; Annual Economic Review of Korea, 1948–1954,* Seoul.

United States Armed Forces in Korea: *Summation of United States Army Military Government Activities in Korea,* Nov. 1945 through March 1946, General Headquaters, Commander-In-Chief Far East, Seoul.

———: *South Korean Interim Government Activities,* August 1947 to September 1948, prepared by the National Economic Board and Statistical Research Division, Office of Administration, Seoul.

———: *The Present Agricultural Position of South Korea,* 1947.

United States Army: *Korea, 1950.* Washington, D.C., 1952, 281 pp.

United States Congress: *The United States and South Korean Problems,* documents 1945–1953, Senate Document No. 74, July 1953, 83rd Congress, First Session.

———: *Relief and Rehabilitation in Korea,* 23rd Intermediate Report of the Committee on Government Operations, H. R. No. 2574, July 1954, 83rd Congress, Second Session.

United States Department of State: *Mutual Defense Assistance Agreement Between the United States and Korea,* Jan. 1950.

———: *Action in Korea under Unified Command,* 1950.

———: *Background Summary: Korea,* Aug. 1947.

———: *Korea, 1945 to 1948,* Publication No. 3305, Oct. 1947.

———: *Korean Economic Mission: Land Reform in Korea,* Seoul, Sept. 1947.

———: *Economic Cooperation with Korea,* Publication No. 5322, agreement between the United States and Republic of Korea, Dec. 1948.

———: *The Korean Problem at the Geneva Conference, April–June 1954,* Publication No. 5609, Washington, D.C., 1954.

———: *United States Policy in the Korean Crisis,* Publication No. 3922, July 1950.

———: *Economic Survey of South Korea,* May 1949.

U.S.S.R. Ministry of Foreign Affairs: *The Soviet Union and Korean Question,* Moscow, 1948.

5. PERIODICALS

Bupchung (Law and Administration), monthly, Bupchung-sa, Seoul.

Department of State Bulletin, weekly, U.S. Department of State, Washington, D.C.

Korean Quarterly, quarterly, International Research Center, Seoul.

Korean Report, monthly, Korean Information Office, Washington, D.C.

Korean Review, semi-annual, The Korean American Cultural Association, Washington, D.C.

Pacific Affairs, quarterly, The Institute of Pacific Relations, Richmond, Va.

Political Science Quarterly, quarterly, Columbia University, New York.

Sai-Byuk, monthly, Sai-Byuk-sa, Seoul.

Sai Han Minbo, weekly, Sai Han Minbo-sa, Seoul.

Sasanggye, monthly, Sasanggye-sa, Seoul.

The American Political Science Review, quarterly, The American Political Science Association, Mensha, Wisconsin.

The Voice of Korea, monthly, The Korean Affairs Institute, Washington, D.C.
Time, weekly, Time Inc., Chicago, Ill.
United Nations Bulletin, United Nations, New York.
U.S. News and World Report, weekly, Washington, D.C.

6. NEWSPAPERS

Chosun Ilbo, Seoul.
Dong A Ilbo, Seoul.
Han Guk Ilbo, Seoul.
Korean Independence, Los Angeles.
Korean Republic, Seoul.
Kyung Hyang Shinmun, Seoul.
New Korea (Shinhan Minbo), Los Angeles.
New York Times, New York.
San Francisco Chronicle, San Francisco.
Seoul Shinmun, Seoul.
Yunhap Shinmun, Seoul.

INDEX